# United States Christian Commission.

## THIRD REPORT

OF THE

# Committee of Maryland.

"When he saw him, he had compassion on him, and went to him and bound up his wounds, pouring in oil and wine, set him on his own beast, and brought him to an inn and took care of him."—*Luke x:* 33, 34.

"I was a hungered and ye gave me meat: I was thirsty and ye gave me drink:
I was a stranger and ye took me in: I was naked and ye clothed me:
I was sick and ye visited me: I was in prison and ye came unto me."
—*Matt. xxv:* 35, 36.

"Inasmuch as ye have done it unto one of the least of these my brethren ye have done it unto me."—*Matt. xxv:* 40.

BALTIMORE:
PRINTED BY JAMES YOUNG,
114 WEST BALTIMORE STREET.
1864.

# UNITED STATES
# CHRISTIAN COMMISSION.

COMMITTEE OF MARYLAND.

G. S. GRIFFITH, Chairman. GEO. P. HAYS, Treasurer.

J. N. M'JILTON, Secretary.

THE OFFICE OF THE COMMITTEE IS

89 & 91 West Baltimore street,

BALTIMORE.

# To the Friends of Suffering Humanity.

As a kind of preface to their report the Maryland Committee of the United States Christian Commission present an appeal to the friends of their cause, all of whom are the friends of humanity, to lend a helping hand to the great work which engages and engrosses their attention and their services. There was a time when there was less demand upon their labor and means, then less supplies were sufficient. But now the field has largely increased in the progress of war by the terrific results of which hundreds of thousands of men have been killed and disabled, and hundreds of thousands of families afflicted, many of them impoverished and thrown upon the charities, not of a cold and inconsiderate world, but of a Christian public for assistance in their support.

Still the demand comes in upon us from the battle-fields and the hospitals which they have caused to be erected. Fresh arrivals of the wounded and the sick are announced every day, and more extended hospital area and provision are rendered an absolute necessity.

To afford relief to all the sufferers is an impossibility. To perform the service as far as we have ability is a duty. Such is our design. Not a thrill of pain, nor a sigh of sorrow that we have the opportunity and the means of relieving, or of mitigating, must be allowed to remain uncared for, or without the effort to assuage. In proportion to the opportunities and means afforded us, will this work be accomplished? In order to accomplish it, the services of delegates, money and stores must be furnished. No delegate should be prevented from visiting the field and the hospital who is willing to devote his time and labors to the duty. To enable us to send the delegates to the scenes of their service, the money and the stores must be supplied, and it is the duty of every man and woman and child who has the money, or who can provide the stores, to contribute to the supplies however large or however small may be the opportunities and abilities of the contributor.

Let not the contribution be withheld because it is small. The man or the woman who has the large means, may appropriate of the abundance into this treasury of humanity and religion. The man or the woman who has the small means may appropriate the same according to the ability, not withholding it on account of any supposed insignificance in the estimate of its worth. The widow or the child may cast the mite into this treasury, in the certainty that it will perform the full measure of its service. The treasury of humanity and religion thus opened is God's treasury and the mite of the widow or the child may receive God's blessing, and thus blessed it may accomplish more than the larger and apparently more important gifts of the wealthy and the distinguished.

It is hardly necessary for the Committee to direct attention to its locality near the field of service. The slaughter that supplies us with the suffering subjects of our ministration, is accomplished in our vicinity. The annihilation of but little of the space between us and the battle-fields, would render the thunder of battle terrific in our hearing. The groans of the sufferers reach us. They may be heard in the hospitals of the district. We have heard them. We have witnessed the writhings, and we have heard the moanings of the sufferers. We would have closed our eyes and ears, and we would have retreated from the scene. But we dared not. We could not. Religion, conscience, humanity, morality, all forbad it. We were obliged by the moral necessity that bound us to hold our position by the mangled body of our unfortunate fellow-being and to assist in relieving him from the peril in which his misfortune had placed him. Nor did we wait to inquire whether the afflicted one was a friend or a foe, a Union soldier or a rebel. He was hurt. He was in pain. He was in peril. He was a sufferer; that was sufficient. We lifted him from the place of his suffering and bore him to a place of safety and comfort. We administered the oil and the wine, and did all that was possible to relieve him, and to save him.

Such is the Christian labor that we are called upon to perform. Such is the christian labor in behalf of which we ask your assistance in performing. Shall we lack the agencies and the means while our fellow-citizens possess them in abundance? Shall we lack those agencies and means because they are not possessed in abundance, but in small measure? We trust not. We believe not. We have faith sufficient to cause us to enunciate the belief that we shall be sustained, and that the good work will prosper in our hands.

Fellow-citizens, listen to our appeal. It is not for ourselves, nor for any personal advantage that we plead. It is for the disabled, the crippled, the bleeding sufferer of the battle-field and the hospital that we ask assistance. Shall he be relieved, or shall he be left to bear in the bitterness of neglect the severity of his affliction. Reader! these are questions for you to answer. Reader! these are questions which you will answer. You will answer them by your action, you will answer them by your contribution, or by withholding it! You will answer them by your prayers or by withholding them! Look at the field! It is red with blood from Harper's Ferry to Petersburg and Atlanta. Consider the appeal. It comes from the places of carnage in the valley of the Shenandoah and all along the front to the trenches near Richmond. It comes in the mangled form of the sufferer. It comes in the name of bleeding humanity. It comes in the wail of the widow. It comes in the cries of starving orphans. Look at the field!! Consider the appeal! Consider the scenes of suffering and blood, and starvation and death, in their contrast with your own comfortable and pleasant and elegant and happy home. Contrast the scenes of suffering and horror with the once comfortable and happy homes of the sufferers! Where are those homes now, and what is their condition? The home of the widow. The home of the orphan. The home of the bleeding victim of the battle-field. The home of desolation. The home of wretchedness. And all this for what? Was it for the safety of your country and your property? Was it for the safety of your home? It was the call of the Government that made the citizen a soldier and caused him to hasten to the defence of his country, his home and his rights—of *your* country, of *your* home of *your* rights. He went to the place of peril on your account as well as his. He went to insure you prosperity and protection as well as to secure them for himself. He fell to prevent you from falling. Will you reach forth a hand to help the sufferer, or will you withhold it and let him suffer on? Christian men, Christian women, Christian children, answer this inquiry. Christian father, mother, teach your children to answer it.

We want, most of all, money, because money will buy everything. We want clothing, shirts, undershirts, drawers, socks, shoes, canned fruits, dried fruits, pickles, oranges, lemons, onions, condensed milk, condensed beef, corn starch, tapioca, coffee, tea, sugar, wine, brandy, whiskey, essence of ginger, all cooking essences, paper, envelopes, pens, needles, reading matter of every proper kind.

The office of the United States Christian Commission is at 89 and 91 Baltimore street. The Flag of the United States Christian Commission designates the place. WE HAVE USE TO-DAY FOR FIFTY THOUSAND DOLLARS, and during the year will want one hundred and fifty thousand more. We shall have use in months to come for ten times that amount. Send us money. Send us stores. Send as you have ability. Send as God has prospered you. Send as conscience demands of you. Send, and the sufferers, the widows' prayers are yours. Send, and God will bless you.

## To Clergymen.

Our cause would be greatly assisted if our brethren of the clergy would remember the labors we are performing in behalf of the suffering, and make collections in their congregations in aid of our funds. There is no charity at the present time more pressing, and none more worthy of consideration. A word in season may serve our cause essentially by securing friends and funds in its support. A collection occasionally, if but a trifle, were secured by each, when the amounts are gathered may be of importance. We hope we may be assisted by our brethren in this way. Send the amounts to the office of the United States Christian Commission, 89 and 91 Baltimore street.

# United States Christian Commission,

## CENTRAL OFFICE, PHILADELPHIA, No. 11 BANK STREET.

### Officers.

GEORGE H. STUART, Esq., *Chairman.*
JOSEPH PATTERSON, *Treasurer.*
Rev. W. E. BOARDMAN, *Secretary.*
Rev. LEMUEL MOSS, *Sec'y of Home Organization.*
Rev. BERNICE D. ARNES, *Sec'y of Field Organization.*

### Members.

Charles Demond, Esq., Boston.
Rev. Rollin H. Neale, D. D., Boston.
Rev. Bishop E. S. Janes, D. D., N. Y.
Rev. James Eells, D. D., Brooklyn.
Mitchell H. Miller, Esq., Washington.
John P. Crozier, Esq., Philadelphia.
Jay Cook, Esq., "
Rev. M. L. R. P. Thompson, D. D., Cin.
Brig. Gen. Fiske, St. Louis.
John R. Farevell, Esq., Chicago.
John D. Hill, M. D., Buffalo.
Sam'l B. Caldwell, New York.
Rt. Rev. Bishop Lee, Delaware.
A. E. Chamberlain, Esq., Ohio.
Rt. Rev. C. P. McIlvaine, Esq., Ohio.
Rev. J. Mulhauser, Wisconsin.
Hon. Hiram Price, Iowa.
G. B. Roberts, California.
Hon. Gov. Nye, Nevado.
Rev. R. Breckenridge, Kentucky.
W. S. Carter, Esq., Milwaukie.
Walter S. Griffith, Esq., Brooklyn, N. Y.
Rev. Bishop M. Simpson, D. D .Phila'd.
R. G. Jones, Esq., Philadelphia.
G. S. Griffith, Baltimore.
Hon. Mr. Patton, Maine.
Rev. Col. James Pike, New Hampshire.
Hon. E. Fairbanks, Vermont.
Edward S. Toby, Boston.
Rev. S. Wayland, D. D., Rhode Island.
Hon. Gov. Buckingham, Conn.
Nathan Bishop, L. L. D., New York.
Morris K. Jessop, New York.
Rev. Charles Hodge, D. D., N. Jersey.
William Frew, Esq., Pennsylvania.
Hon. Gov. Pierpont, Virginia.
Hon. W. S. Willey, West Virginia.
Hon. S. Colfax, Indiana.
Hon. John Owen, Michigan.
Hon. John Evans, Colorado.
Rev. E. Lihman, Minnesota.
Rev. F. Pennington, Kansas.
Rev. S. Cornelius, Oregon.
Prof. L. M. Stoaver, Gettysburg.
Wm. E. Dodge, Esq., New York.
Rev. H. Dyer, D. D., New York.
Stephen Colwell, Esq., Pennsylvania.

### Executive Committee.

George H. Stuart, Esq., Phila'd.
Rev. Bishop E. S. Janes, D. D., N. Y
Charles Demond, Esq., Boston.
John P. Crozier, Esq., Philadelphia.
Joseph Patterson, Esq., Philadelphia.
Rev. Bishop M. Simpson, D. D., Philad.
Jay Cook, Esq., Philadelphia.
G. S. Griffith, Esq., Baltimore.
Stephen Colwell, Esq., Penn.
William Dodge, Esq., New York.
Rev. Herman Dyer, D. D., New York.
Walter S. Griffith, Esq., Brooklyn.
H. G. Jones, Esq., Philadelphia.
Rev. W. E. Boardman, Ex. off., Philad.

### Committee of Maryland as now Organized.

G. S. Griffith, Esq., Chairman Baltimore.
Rev. Geo. P. Hays, Treasurer, Baltimore.
Rev. J. N. M'Jilton, D. D., Secretary, Baltimore.
Rev. T. Stork, D. D., Baltimore.
Chas. W. Ridgley, Baltimore.
Rev. Isaac P. Cook, Baltimore.
Rev. R. C. Galbraith, Govanstown, Baltimore county.
Gideon Bantz, Frederick city.
Rev. J. D. Curtis, Elkton, Cecil county.
Rev. J. Evans, Hagerstown, Washington county.

THE CHARACTER AND WORK OF

# THE CHRISTIAN COMMISSION.

The Christian Commission is a voluntary association. It was organized in New York on the 16th November, 1861. The persons by whom it was organized were delegates from several societies existing in as many cities and other places known as the Young Men's Christian Associations. The delegates were sent to New York for the purpose of organizing a body to be known as the Christian Commission. The purpose of this body at the first and at the present, is the performance of such service to the disabled of the Army and Navy as Christian sympathy suggests. In bodies consisting of large numbers of men it is well known that their must be many sick, and in the sad work of the battle-fields it is as well known that there must be large numbers of the wounded. It is to minister to the temporal and spiritual wants of these sick and wounded men that the Christian Commission performs its voluntary offices.

The character of the Commission was fixed at the meeting of the delegates at the instance of George H. Stuart, Esq., by whose happy forethought and succeeding labors the body was brought into existence. The philanthropic features of the Commission have not been changed. The work as suggested by Mr. Stuart of performing the service of the good Samaritan to the sick of the army and the disabled of the battle-fields is still continued. The area of the work has been greatly extended and the number of the workmen have been greatly increased. Following, as the Commission has done, in the footsteps of the Army and in the wake of the vessels of the Navy, in the expansion of its labors the obligation has been forced upon it of increasing its laborers and means. Wonderful has been its success in meeting this emergency. An all-wise and over-ruling Providence has raised up friends as they were needed and means as they were demanded. Although at the first it was difficult to accomplish the smaller amount of necessary service, it has not been much more so to perform the same over the greatly extended field that is now whitened for the harvest and demands the laborers and the material necessary for the performance of their work. It is is not pretended that the service contemplated has been fully performed in the relief of all the suffering and privation that have appeared in the view of the Commission's agents and delegates. Our means have never been adequate to this demand; but as far as the men and the means could be provided they have been appropriated, and although all the needed service could not be rendered, a very great proportion of the suffering necessarily occasioned by the war, has been relieved. Had there been more men and more money, the greater had been the service and the more nearly perfect had been its performance.

As a voluntary association, the Christian Commission has no official relation either to the Government or to the Army and Navy. There is no detriment to the service, however, on this account. The work of the Commission is approved and sanctioned by the Government, and directions have been given that its delegates should be respected and protection and every possible facility afforded them in the pursuit of their labors. The name of the President of the United States and the of names of a number of the gentlemen of the Cabinet and Generals and other officials of the Army and Navy, have been associated with the Commission, and thereby the connection of the Commission with the Army and Navy service has been rendered as nearly official as is desirable. No surgeon or Chaplain of the Army and Navy who understands the relationship of the Commission with the service ever thinks of impeding the progress of the work or of doing any thing in its connection that does not facilitate its purpose. But few difficulties have arisen on account of misunderstandings in this relation, and the few that have occurred have been readily adjusted, when the proper relationship of the parties were understood.

An association known as the Baltimore Christian Association for the relief of the disabled of the camps and hospitals, was in the service before the organization of the Christian Commission. It was fairly at its work in May, 1861, preceding the date of the order establishing the United States Christian Commission. As soon as the Committee of Maryland of the Commission was appointed, the Baltimore Association became auxiliary to the United States Christian Commission, and has ever rendered efficient service in the connection.

Previous to the date at which the Christian Commission was organized, the Secretary of the Maryland Committee was in treaty with clergymen of Baltimore for the purpose of making application to the Government for the provision of a chaplain service for the hospitals. A correspondence was entered into with persons connected with the hospitals for that purpose. On one occasion, that of a hospital at which four clergymen were in the habit of visiting, an application was made for assistance in obtaining from the Government the appointment of a chaplain for the hospital and one for each of the hospitals then established. The reply to the application was unfavorable. The number of unofficial visitors was said to be, and doubtless were, so great that they were in one anothers way. What was wanted was a proper head and a system by which the work should be regulated. The suggestion was not appreciated that the appointment of a single chaplain with official relations and authority would regulate the attendance of others and render their assistance of much greater use by being more systematic and regular. Letters were written by the Secretary to members of Congress, but without effect. To President Lincoln is due the honor of having the chaplaincy service established, and from him the Christian Commission has received every necessary evidence of favor, and by his encouraging efforts its service has been rendered much more effective than it could possibly have been without it. By a late act of Congress the rank of the Chaplain is that of Major, which gives them higher authority and greater influence than they have heretofore had.

The voluntary service of the United States Christian Commission in the relief of the sick and wounded of the Army and Navy, is rendered almost official by the approval and protection of the Government. It is now making up the deficiences in the religious service, and in the administration of delicacies to the sick and wounded that probably could not be otherwise supplied. It is not at all probable that Army and Navy officials, however well remunerated, and however well supplied with means, would answer the demands made upon the Christian Commission. The character of the service indicates the voluntary supply, and in such relation only can the labor be properly performed.

It is not to be inferred from our remarks in relation to the necessity of the service of the Christian Commission that the Government does not make ample provision for the pursuit of its purpose in the management of the war, nor that the agencies provided are not sufficiently humane for the purpose. Never was there such provision made by any Government for the relief of the sufferings necessarily occasioned in the conduct of a war as there has been by the Government of the United States, in the present sad emergency. Surgeons and Chaplains have been supplied for regiments and hospitals; and these are sufficient for ordinary purposes. But all the surgeons in the country would be insufficient for the demand upon the service after such battles as have been fought in the present contest. Nor in such emergency could all the religious service that could be secured be sufficient for the supply of the battle-fields and camps and hospitals. It were well therefore that there should be an agency that could wait on the outside and in calmness and with due consideration, measure the field demanding the relief, and make provision for its supply.

Such is the work of the United States Christian Commission. It is waiting in its place outside of the Army, and of any of the official relations of the Government. It has its delegates composed of Christian ministers and laymen of every religious denomination. The supply is always at hand, and with such means as we have, we send them forth where-ever their services are needed. The good pleasure of the Lord has hitherto prospered in their hands, and there can be no doubt of the immense service they are now rendering, and may continue to render in the cause of suffering, bleeding humanity.

The following letter from Secretary Stanton expresses his approval of our Commission and its purpose:

WAR DEPARTMENT, WASHINGTON CITY,
April 16th, 1864.

DEAR SIR:—Among the benevolent associations organized by patriotic and charitable men during the present war, none has surpassed, and few, if any, have equalled the Christian Commission in zeal, energy and disinterested devotion to the humane objects of their institution. Their efficient labors in the field, in the hospital, and in the camp have been felt by soldiers and officers, and have frequently been brought to the notice of this Department. It is not only a pleasure, but I regard it as an official duty to commend the Christian Commission to public confidence and respect, as an institution whose labors cannot fail to contribute greatly to the welfare of our armies.

Yours truly,
EDWIN M. STANTON,
Secretary of War.

The following is an extract from a letter received by the Secretary of the Maryland Committee:

"No one more heartily sympathises with the objects, or more highly appreciates the labors of the Christian Commission than your very humble servant,
WILLIAM H. SEWARD."

Letters of the same nature have been received from President Lincoln and from other members of the Cabinet, as well as from a number of the most distinguished officers of the Army and Navy.

# REPORT.

OFFICE OF THE UNITED STATES CHRISTIAN COMMISSION,
*Committee of Maryland,* 89 *and* 91 *Baltimore Street.*
BALTIMORE, September 1, 1864.

TO GEO. H. STUART, ESQ.,
*President United States Christian Commission:*

DEAR SIR:

It is now a year since we presented you a general report of the labors of our Committee. In accordance with the arrangement agreed upon that we should report annually, we proceed to lay before you a third detail of such portions of our work as may be of sufficient interest and importance to embody in an official record and place among the archives of the Commission.

### First Duty—to God.

Our first duty in this detail, is to express our thankfulness to God for His many favors, and for the signal blessings that have succeeded our efforts to serve Him in the relief afforded our suffering fellow-men amid the strifes of the battle-field, and in the amelioration of their sanguinary and fearful results.

The difficulties that have appeared in the way of this labor of love and mercy could not have been foreseen, nor could they have been overcome, except through the divine aid with which He has been pleased to favor us. We gratefully acknowledge the leading of His Providence over every step of the path we have pursued, and desire to lay the tribute of our service, feeble and imperfect though it be, in humble acknowledgements at His feet.

### Hospitals of the District.

The following is a list of the Hospitals of the District of Maryland with their locations. A notice of each will be given in its proper place in this report. They are all designated by the common title of "United States General Hospital:"

Jarvis—W. Baltimore street, Baltimore, Maryland.
Patterson Park—E. Lombard street, Baltimore, Maryland.
West's Building—Union Dock, Baltimore, Maryland.
National—Camden street, Baltimore, Maryland.
McKim's—McKim street, Baltimore, Maryland.
Newton—Lexington street, Baltimore, Maryland.
Officers Hospital—Navy Yard, Annapolis, Maryland.
Division Hospital, No. 1—Navy Yard, Annapolis, Maryland.
Division Hospital, No. 2—St. John's College, Annapolis, Maryland.
Annapolis Junction—Annapolis Junction, Maryland.
Camp Parole—near Annapolis, Maryland.
Tilton—Wilmington, Delaware.
Point Lookout—St. Mary's Co., Maryland.
Fort Delaware—Delaware Bay, Delaware.
Frederick City—Frederick City, Maryland.
York—York, Pennsylvania.

### Points of Labor other than Hospitals.

Points of labor other than Hospitals, have been occupied by Delegates sent by Committee, with Stores, Books, Tracts, &c. A number of these are outside of the District; notwithstanding which, they have received the attention of the Committee, and in some instances, have been favored with very important and necessary services:

Fort Marshall—Baltimore, Maryland.
Fort Federal Hill—Baltimore, Maryland.
Fort McHenry—Baltimore, Maryland.
Camp Bradford—Baltimore, Maryland.
Camp Carroll—Baltimore, Maryland.
Camp Bourney—Baltimore, Maryland.

Invalid's Camp Hospital—Northern avenue, Baltimore, Maryland.
Fortifications around Baltimore—Maryland.
Magnolia—Harford Co., Maryland.
Harper's Ferry—Virginia.
Sandy Hook—Maryland.
Point of Rocks—Frederick Co., Maryland.
Monocacy Junction—Frederick Co., Maryland.
Martinsburg—Virginia.
Winchester—Virginia.
Shenandoah Valley—Virginia.
Near Petersburg—Virginia.
Bermuda Hundred—Virginia.
Fortress Monroe—Virginia.
City Point—Virginia.
Mount Savage, Maryland.
Cumberland, Maryland.
Clareyville, Maryland.

### Hand of God Mysteriously Interposed.

The lot of our labor has been one of anxious and earnest solicitude. It has been wrought amid varying circumstances and conditions. We have been obliged to work, on the one hand, against the diversified views of army officials, and on the other, through the conflicting sentiments occasioned by denominational divisions. It was not, therefore, to be supposed that we would be able to steer our bark over waters ruffled by these antagonizing agencies without interruption. But the hand that led us has been mysteriously interposed. The opposing elements have been harmonized. The antagonizing agencies have been reconciled. The troubled waters have been calmed. We have been enabled to work the devious passage with comparatively but little hindrance. The warring elements of political and sectional dissention have appeared upon the horizon. They were stormily portentous, but they failed to do us harm. The threatening instrumentalities that foreshadowed evil in the prospect have been reduced as we approached them, and instead of arresting us in our course, or resulting in serious damage, they have been converted by an unseen power into potent auxiliaries, and greatly assisted us in facilitating our progress. It is true that a momentary pause has sometimes been occasioned by the impending providence, and we have waited to consider the consequences of our action, and to determine upon the propriety of our procedure, but the arrest has been temporary, and the discouragement slight. The difficulties have been removed, we have hardly known how, and our progress has been rendered the more certain, and our labor the more effective by the interruption. When the storms of nature pass over, the sky seems brighter and more beautiful than it was before they appeared. The removal of the dark clouds reveals a brilliancy unenjoyed before their gloomy forms came lowering over the heavens. So with our transient troubles; they were momentarily fearful and discouraging. But when they were passed, the path in the prospective has seemed to be the more pleasant and inviting.

### Friendly Association with Army Officials.

When it is considered that our service is voluntary and admissible only on sufferance, while that of the army and navy is compulsory, and regulated by stringent laws, the dissimilar natures of the departments indicate the probability that misunderstandings may occur, and suggest the propriety of every precautionary measure that may be used in order to prevent them. That such precautionary measures have been used we have abundant evidence in the correspondence of the Committee. In the few cases of interruptions that have occurred through the misunderstandings and misapprehensions of army officers and agents in relation to supposed interferences with established regulations, after proper explanations, the parties have expressed, not only their satisfaction in the adjustment of the difficulty, but their gratification that an auxiliary of relief as effective as the Christian Commission had been instituted. The temporary opponents of the Commission have thus been changed into fast friends and co-laborers, so that we have lost but little and gained considerably in the issue.

### Kindness and Courtesy of Officers.

The officers generally of the Army and Navy with whom we have had to hold intercourse have been kind and courteous to us, and they have afforded us every needed facility for the prosecution of our work. Through their co-operation and assistance many opportunities of doing good have been opened before us and much efficient help afforded in occupying them. It is but justice to those gentlemen that we should acknowledge with thankfulness their uniform kindness, and the courteous and gentlemanly manner in which they have wrought with us in the performance of our labors. To many of the Surgeons in charge of hospitals and Chaplains we are greatly indebted for the assistance they have given us, for the kind approval of our plans, and their generous acknowledgement of the services rendered their respective departments in the labors performed in behalf of our Commission. In making this acknowledgment it is gratifying to state that we include officers of the Army and Navy from the highest in command, through all the departments with which we have been in association. By the orders of commanding Generals our delegates and agents have been protected and assisted in the discharge of their duties. In obedience to their instructions, officers of every grade have willingly and cheerfully co-operated with us in the performance of our Christian work.

### Respect of all the Generals of the Army of the Potomac.

It is with a high degree of satisfaction that we refer to the fact that all the Generals that have been at the head of the Army of the Potomac have treated our Commission with the most marked respect and kindest consideration. As the actual witnesses of our work, they have been convinced of its necessity, and it has seemed to afford them pleasure to act as co-laborers with us in its performance. Passes and letters have been received from them whenever they were desired, and it was proper to give them, by means of which our delegates and agents have been afforded facilities which could not otherwise be obtained. Their efficiency has been greatly enhanced by this assistance.

### Faithfulness of Delegates.

It is proper in this connection to add that in no case have we heard that an accredited delegate or agent has, in the least degree, abused the confidence reposed in him, either by the Commanding General or any other official of the Army or Navy. But very few have, in any way, given cause for regret in their appointment. Faithfully and efficiently, and in accordance with general and special orders, with but two or three exceptions, all have wrought under the badge of the Commission. Testimonials of this fact have reached us from officers of various grades, who have strongly commended our work and urged the importance and necessity of its continuance. Mention has been made, both officially and otherwise, of the unobtrusive manner, as well as of the faithfulness and self-devotion in which the badge of our Commission has been used. Several instances are upon record in which the workmen of the Commission have received especial commendation for the timely interposed and important service they have rendered.

### Emergencies from Various Causes.

Emergencies have arisen from partial invasions and raids and more extended battles when it has become necessary that we should hasten with all possible dispatch in the furnishment of the men and means by which the disabled were to be relieved, and proper ministrations afforded to the dying and the dead. With stores on hand, and delegates in waiting, we have always been prompt in the application of the needed aid. In no instance have we been taken by surprise, but with our facilities immediately at hand we have entered at once upon the work of relief. Our means, though abundant, have not always been sufficient for the demand. In the needed supply, after heavy battles, we have sometimes fallen short, both in delegates and stores, but to the extent of our ability our resources have been used. We have employed them to the very best advantage, in the discharge of the obligations we have assumed, under our Christian title to our disabled defenders, and in the relief of the sufferings, even of those of our enemies, who have fallen wounded into our hands.

### Always Prepared for the Emergency.

In the case of each emergency as it arose, whether from the raid, the skirmish, or the sanguinary battle, we have had numbers of excellent delegates and agents in attendance, who, at a moment's warning, have obeyed the call of the roll, and equipping themselves at our office, they have started in eager haste, impelled by earnest hearts to the scenes of their labor. While there engaged in the performance of their painfully oppressive duties, frequent telegrams and letters have informed us of the faithful manner in which they have discharged their obligations, self-imposed and eagerly sought, to their suffering fellow-men. Assistance has been rendered by them to Surgeons and Chaplains. In many instances, after the battle, but for the aid thus afforded, hundreds and thousands of the sufferers of the battle-fields must have perished from the effects of their wounds. The relief extended in this way has been very considerable.

### Various Services of Delegates.

Not only have our delegates assisted Surgeons and other officers and agents of the army in bearing the wounded from the field of battle and placing them as comfortably as possible in hospitals, and attending them while there, but they have rendered a large amount of aid in the burial of the dead, and relieving the fresh battle-field from the frightful aspect presented in the indiscriminate mass of mangled forms that were stretched upon it. It is a work worthy of humanity, but severely oppressive in its execution, to hunt out the living among the dead of the battle-field in order to bear them to places of security and comfort. The first impulse of a badly wounded man is to crawl away from the dead bodies that surround him, and find, if possible, a place of relief; a spot perhaps where he may die in loneliness, and away from the scenes of horror that he has witnessed and experienced in the shrieks and groans of the mortally wounded and dying. Such have been found in frequent instances. Some have died, leaving evidences of great agony upon their persons; others were dying and craving but a drop of water to moisten a swollen and fevered tongue.

Others have but needed the ministrations of the good Samaritan to relieve immediately the intensity of their sufferings, and to strengthen them for removal to the gathering place of the field, or the hospital. The appearance of humanity thus presented in its multiplied forms of suffering and death, is truly shocking, and it requires a degree of nerve not possessed, even by every strong man, to endure its horrors and to perform the labor required in its removal. Our delegates have proved themselves competent for the duty. They have not hesitated to approach the field from which the thinned ranks of the contestants have just departed; they have selected the living from among the mangled and far outstretched masses of the dead, the wounds of many yet pouring forth the blood that becomes chilled and clotted as it comes in contact with the atmosphere. The yet living bleeding form has been removed from its place beneath a pile of the dead to another, where the little life that was left the sufferer might have the opportunity of expansion, and the system, that of the recovery of its lost powers.—Many are now living who were taken from the bloody resting places upon which they had fallen; dragged out perhaps from amid the dead and restored to consciousness before removal. Others have been almost dug out of the complicated mass that covered them, composed of implements of war, blood-matted clothing, human limbs and earth. They are now in the enjoyment of health, and tell over with heartiest interest, the tales of their deliverance and of their indebtedness for their lives to the Christian Commission.

### Vivid Glance at the Field of Labor.

A friend of the Commission, of active and energetic habits, whose power of thought was rapid and vivid during the process of his absorbing and trying labors, has remembered the events that transpired around him with an interest that has never yet failed to produce an involuntary thrill through his system whenever the recollection of them has occurred. Like the ever-changing visions of a terrific dream the ranks of the fallen have appeared. The living who were badly wounded, were seen, struggling under bodies of the dead, others crawling over them, apparently for the purpose of reaching places of relief and security, or spots upon which to die. Among the living and the dead were the men of both armies, the enemies that had fought in the sanguinary conflict. The scene was terrific in its ever-varying variety. There were mangled masses of animal matter composed of the bodies and parts of bodies of dead horses, human forms, limbs and heads, with features yet horrible in the contorted lineaments of the death agony; the web-work of iron, wood, leather, and matted clothing, all, the shattered implements of war and war-like equipments, and shred-worn habiliments of the soldier. The area of horror thus presented, was rendered yet more horrible by the activity everywhere in motion of hundreds of laborers with picks and spades, digging trenches, and dragging into them the bodies of the dead, and covering them with earth. Great was the relief afforded the view in the appearance of the delegates of the Christian Commission with their towels and cloths and pails and basins of water. They were quenching the thirst of the suffering, bathing their foreheads and faces, and washing their wounds, and applying the necessary restoratives to the fainting and exhausted system. They were removing gently, and with the most anxious concern, the bodies of such as would bear it. They were whispering the words of comfort and heavenly consolation to the dying. They were receiving the last messages of love to friends and relatives at home. They were receiving pledges of affection for loved ones and giving assurances of remembrance, and that their dying testimonials and requests should be faithfully and promptly delivered. The same attention and services were rendered the fallen of the enemy that were given to the soldiers of the Union army. Upon the arm of the delegate the head of the dying rebel has reclined, and while assurances of remembrance to friends, were it possible, and words of consolation were spoken, the spirit has passed to its place among the departed.

**Duty in the Varying Forms of Trial.**

Such, in varying forms and results, is the issue of every battle, and it is with great thankfulness to God that the opportunities afforded are used by the members of the Christian Commission in the performance of the labor they have taken upon themselves. It is in the Providence of God that these scenes of conflict and affliction have been permitted to come near to us, and it becomes us to employ every agency within our reach for the relief of sufferings we cannot prevent, and for the amelioration, as far as may be possible, of the horrors of one of the fiercest, bloodiest, and most disastrous contests that ever took place upon earth.

### Visits and Assistance of Committee.

Members of our Committee and delegates have assisted in the erection of temporary hospitals near the battle-fields and in the relief immediately desired by the badly injured. From these hospitals they have assisted in bearing the dead for burial and the partially convalescent to places of more permanent attention. Closely and intimately, their labors have been associated with those of the officers and agents of the Government, and in nearly all cases the harmony of labor has been undisturbed, and the parties have wrought together as friends and brethren in the great cause of affording the desired and needed relief to suffering humanity.

### The Delegates have Followed Armies after Invasions.

On the several occasions, when bodies of the enemy, in various numerical force, have invaded the territory held by our troops along the line of the Potomac, in Virginia, Pennsylvania, and Maryland, we have visited in person or sent delegates for service amid the scenes of disaster and bloodshed. On occasions of anticipated invasion, our delegates have been in readiness with stores prepared for the purpose, and they have followed swiftly upon the movements of the armies and performed extended service to the needy they have left upon the fields behind them. In some instances they have barely escaped capture, sometimes with loss. In several ins'ances, their clothing and other property, have fallen in the hands of the enemy. One of our chaplains, the Rev. Mr. Pormer, on one occasion, escaped with his life, but lost all the clothes and property he had with him; his loss was nearly two hundred dollars.

### Religious Services Wherever Practicable.

Religious services have been established, through the agency of the Commission, in many places where they have been needed. At every possible point at which our delegates are laboring, meetings for preaching, experience and prayer have been held. The benefits of this service have been repeatedly acknowledge by Government officials and others, who have witnessed their effects not only upon the sick and dying, but upon the soldier in health and in the active service of the camp. Testimonials of the dying of a most gratifying character are upon the record, and many who are living, bear continuous testimony of their effect in the witness of faithfully devoted religious lives.

### Sunday Schools in Hospitals and Camps.

Sunday Schools have been established in camps and for the convalescing of the hospitals. The operations of some of these schools have been continued through rapidly successive changes of the camps. The "boys" have been taught, and are ready enough to believe that they can occupy themselves in the duties of the Sunday services and lessons, as well as do any thing else, or do nothing amid the changes and interruptions of camp life. The Sunday School is now a permanent arrangement in some of the hospitals. The enjoyments of the members of these schools are very considerable. The engagements allotted the members are much the same as those pursued ordinarily in such institutions. They consist of religious worship in reading, exhortation, and prayer; the study of the geography and history of the Holy Land; study and recital of hymns, and such other exercises as are considered proper, and may be rendered profitable to the adult pupils. The experience of those engaged in this department, is satisfactory and encouraging.

### Chapels and Chapel Tents for Worship and Prayer.

Chapels for religious worship are erected at the more permanent hospitals. Tents are used in camps as chapels for the same purpose. In some of the camps the tent is appropriated for prayer, and is open at all times for the use of the devout soldier. In groups or singly those who are disposed, visit the tent and engage in the services of religion. Periods of varying length are thus spent in the devotional exercises. Copies of the Scriptures are placed in the tent with devotional books and tracts, in the use of which many of the hours of the camp life may be occupied with profit both to body and soul. Hours that might be otherwise wasted, or worse than wasted in the immoral pursuits of idle association may be redeemed and rendered highly serviceable by these engagements.

### Witness of the Use of the Tent for Prayer.

We have stood by the tent of prayer and watched for a time in the hope of witnessing the ingress and egress of its worshippers. It was gratifying to learn, as we did, that even a few of the men were disposed, occasionally, to spend a few moments in religious meditation. Such was our experience. We could hear the laugh and the exulting ejaculation from many who were engaged in sport, but the appearance of but a small number, one at a time, tested the value of the tent of prayer. The result shows that there is a great work in the view of the Christian Commission. The current must be changed if labor and prayers and the expenditure of money can effect it. The fearful truth is apparent now as it was in apostolic days, that there are few that be saved. We cannot render the camp and the hospital the substitute for the home in every particular, but as far as the work can be performed, it ought to be done, and the effort should not be slighted nor neglected, to render the home what it ought to be in its education of its inmates for the pursuits of the religious life. Partially may this be accomplished by sending back to their homes reformed and prepared for the pursuit of amended life, those who have left it in ignorance of God and religion, and utterly regardless of all religious responsibility. This is a great work. But it is not too great a work for Christianity to accomplish. Christianity fails of its duty if it does not accomplish it. Its schemes, and divisions, and systems of theology should be set aside and its votaries and servants should resolve that the morality of the Bible, which is the religion of the Bible, should be the great theme of their instructions, and the grand purpose of their labors.

**Experience in the Work of the Commission.**

A number of terrific battles have been fought since our last report was prepared. Through all these the Commission has followed the army rendering needed service to the dead and wounded of both the contending armies. The cases are but few in which the sufferer of either army has been overlooked; never do we believe has he been wilfully neglected. In the wake of these battles we have had experienced delegates. The experience was attained on former occasions of services, and it has rendered the labors of delegates much more ready as well as much more efficient. Our own experience in arranging for the prosecution of our labors has been valuable to us. It has forced upon us the knowledge of the sort of work we have to perform, and enables us to accomplish it with much greater readiness and ease than were possible when we started in the enterprise. Our field is now much more systematically arranged and much better worked than formerly. Its points of duty generally are distributed with a degree of regularity throughout the departments of the army in the occupancy of our district. The movements of delegates are ordered in such manner as best enables them to communicate with field, local, and traveling agents, with army officials and with each other. In this order the work of the Commission is rendered comparatively convenient, and is accomplished with a good degree of satisfaction.

It is a sad reflection that the cost of our continued experience and attainment of proficiency should be the blood of hundreds of thousands of our countrymen, and of thousands of millions of treasure that might be expended in the building up rather than in the destruction of cities, and in the beautifying rather than the devastation of the valuable territory occupied and trodden down by the hostile armies. But our misguided fellow-citizens will have it so. The terrible issue is forced upon us. Painful as is the process we must educate ourselves for the afflictive service, or leave unaccomplished one of our most important and necessary duties to humanity, to our country, and to our God.

### Relief of the Prisoners at Richmond.

To the suffering prisoners of the Union Army at Richmond, we have been able to send relief on various occasions. Our own supplies, without an exception that we have heard of, have reached their destination. The benefits experienced by the starving men, in the receipt of sufficient provisions to relieve their necessities may well be imagined. Letters have been received from the prisoners, acknowledging the receipt of boxes of first quality hams, beef, bread, coffee, tea, sugar, with the best of wines that could be found, &c. These letters have contained expressions of gratitude, and desires for remembrance of friends and families, which are of most touching and interesting character. The like has hardly been recorded in history of such abundance of provisions being sent into the heart of an enemy's home for the relief of the needy captives taken in the pursuit of an imbittered and terrific and dreadfully afflictive war. It is admitted that no such fighting has ever occurred as that which has been recorded of the armies of the Anglo Saxon descent now in the field. It must also be admitted that no such concern has been experienced for the suffering, and no such relief afforded them as that which appears on the records of the Christian Commission. Our history will be a tale of mercy unknown among the archives of the nations of either ancient or modern times. The fallen and afflicted enemy of the battle-field finds a friend and protector in the people against whom his hand has been raised amid the fearful strife of rebellion and war, and the captive in the distant prison of the enemy finds relief and support in the abundance provided and transmitted by the friends from whom he has been separated in his capture.

### Assisted by Families of Prisoners.

In the labor of affection we have been frequently relieved by the families and friends of the prisoners who have sent us large amounts of stores with the request that we should forward them to Richmond. In all cases the desire has been complied with, and we have become the willing and thankful agents of friends who, although more personally interested than ourselves, have only assisted us in our labor of relief.

### Receipt of Stores by Prisoners.

We have the gratification of being able to state in this connection, that we have reason to believe that very nearly all the stores sent by us to the South were received by those to whom they were addressed. We know with certainty of no failure, and in most cases have had acknowledgements, either directly at the office, or through the families and friends of the prisoners.

### Flag of Truce Boat.

In this agency of relief we have found the Flag of Truce Boat plying between City Point and near Richmond to be of very great service. The officers of the boat have carefully executed the orders committed to them, and, as far as we have heard, they have performed their part of the service with commendable fidelity.

### Large Team for Transportation.

To supply an emergency which pressed upon us, we purchased a team consisting of six horses, with a large wagon, which has been kept in constant use running between Bermuda Hundred, City Point and the Front. By this means of transportation, nearly all the stores we have sent by the way of Fortress Monroe have been conveyed.

### Charter of Steamboats and other Vessels.

Several vessels and steamboats have been hired by our Committee for stated periods for the conveyance of stores and Delegates to their places of destination. This has been an expensive means of transportation, but the emergency required the outlay and we have been obliged to submit to it, or leave important fields of necessary labor unoccupied.

### Steam Fire Engine.

In the process of our work at City Point the novel feature of the use of a steam engine has been introduced, and is performing as much really needed service as any other agency of the Commission. The General Hospital of the army at City Point which is situated at the mouth of the Appomatox river is the most extensive agency of its kind ever constructed. It covers forty acres of ground. The tents of the Christian Commission connected with the hospital are fifteen in number. In the use of the Fire Engine, with more than two thousand feet of hose, the eastern hospital is supplied with water. The lives of thousands of our men have been saved through this instrumentality, and the health of thousands more preserved. At the suggestion of the Rev. Andrew B. Cross, one of our most experienced, active and efficient co-laborers, Mayor Chapman, of Baltimore, was requested to loan one of the city engines for the purpose here stated. It was a novel request, and the Mayor smiled as he most cheerfully complied with it, as though he imagined the enterprise to be one of somewhat utopian character. "Any thing, gentlemen," said he, "any thing, cost what it may, to relieve and support the army if within my power shall be contributed."

The engine was procured and conveyed to its position of usefulness, and there it has been in daily use, sending its abundant supply of excellent water through the avenues of the camp, and among the tents, affording the refreshing waters of life and health to the suffering multitudes of, perhaps, the largest hospital, or hospital camp ever constructed.

### Relief of Needy Families.

Frequent appeals are made upon us in behalf of the needy and suffering families of soldiers who are in the field risking their lives for the small wages they receive, and leaving their wives and children to the care of their fellow-citizens whom they hope and believe will not allow them to suffer during their absence, and engaged in their defence. The result has proved that the trust to charity for support, to say the least of it, is a doubtful dependence. Humanity is selfish and unwillingly parts from even what it can conveniently spare when the demand is made for the exercise of its sensibilities. The relief we have been able to afford in cases of appeal from this source bears no comparison with the necessities that have appeared, and we have frequently been pained when administering the merest pittance in the partial relief of the applicants.

### State Fair by Loyal Ladies.

A number of the loyal ladies, representing nearly all the counties of Maryland, united for the purpose of assisting the Christian and Sanitary Commissions by holding a general Fair. Preparations were made upon quite an extensive scale, and the Fair was held in the Maryland Institute. It was the most brilliant and attractive effort of the kind ever made in Maryland, and seldom equalled any where else. All the rooms of the large building of the Maryland Institute were filled, and crowded to overflowing day and night for two weeks. It was at first contemplated that the Fair should be continued but a single week, but so great was the pressure, and so universal the desire of the citizens of Baltimore for its continuance that the rooms were continued open during the second week. The scenes of mingled beauty, brilliancy, taste and fashion, that were witnessed at the Institute during the two weeks of the continuance of the Fair were perhaps never surpassed in this country. A distinguished visitor, a member of the Cabinet, remarked, that Baltimore had sustained its reputation most thoroughly in its display of beautiful women. "Such a galaxy of beauty," said he, "was never before witnessed. It is worth a million to stand at a given point for an hour and gaze upon the stream of beauty that appears to be upon its continual passage."

A novel feature of this Fair appeared in a volume prepared expressly on its account by Mrs. Almira Lincoln Phelps, Corresponding Secretary of the Ladies' Fair Association. The volume is entiled "Our Country," and is composed of articles written by American authors, several of our lady writers are represented among its pages. As a literary effort, this book is worthy of its authorship, and of its distinguished editorship. It will remain as a standing evidence of the enterprise of Maryland in the association of literature with the benevolent purpose, and of the ability and taste of American authorship. A description of the Fair and a further notice of the book will appear in their places in this report.

### Statistics of Receipts and Disbursements.

In our supply statement we have given an account of our receipts, expenditures, and disbursements. We make a distinction between expenditures and disbursements, because we have disbursed a large amount of stores which were not received by purchase and for which money was not actually expended by us. From the account it may seem that a large amount of means have been appropriated to the uses of the various needs that have claimed our notice. But so much larger than our resources has been the demand for relief, which has come to us from every part of the immense field occupied, that we have been obliged to distribute our money and stores, after mature consideration, to the best possible advantage, leaving but partially supplied many interesting cases of appeal which it would have been most pleasant and gratifying to have entirely relieved. The money and stores sent us have been duly acknowledged through the newspapers. Supplies are always in demand, and must be while the soldiers are in the field exposed to the casualties of war, and their families are left at home to struggle with the oppression of poverty which is inevitable when the family is large, and the pay of the soldier per month not much more than sufficient to support one or two persons.

### Trust for Success.

Our trust for success is in the great Author and Giver of all our blessings. It is of His will that we are disposed to labor in the cause of His afflicted servants, and that supplies are granted to us to be applied to the purpose. As it is known to Him to be for the best, so will the means be provided. And as He affords the ability and the agencies, so may we be the instruments in His hands of doing good to our suffering fellow-men. From Him comes the powers by which the service is performed. His be the praise for its performance.

### The Army's Progress and its Battles.

Close upon the marches of the army and fast upon its battle-fields have been the movements of the Christian Commission. We had scarcely narrated the services of our delegates and ourselves in the battles of the summer of 1863, when the enemy appeared in different places along the line of the Potomac, and not only threatened the States of Maryland and Pennsylvania with invasion, but in several instances actually crossed the river and appeared on the Maryland and Pennsylvania shores in pursuit of whatever plunder they could find.

Our last report closed September 1, 1863, and on the 22d of that month the Rebels crossed the Potomac and entered Maryland at Rockville, Montgomery county. They scoured the country for several miles, and secured a considerable amount of plunder in cattle and different kinds of store goods, when they were attacked by the Union troops and forced to return to their own camping grounds in Virginia. It was not without several skirmishes in which many lives were sacrificed, and many of both armies disabled, that they were allowed to escape. As early after this raid as September 25, Mosby's men attacked and destroyed a portion of the Orange and Alexandria Railroad. While at their work they were fallen upon by the Union troops and driven back with some slaughter on both sides. Again, October 5, Winchester and Harper's Ferry were attacked and captured by the enemy, who as usual held them but a few days, when the Federal army drove them out and re-took the captured towns and vicinities. October 7, skirmishes took place near Martinsburg with various results in the capture of Union troops by the Rebels and the capture of Rebels by the Union troops. On all these occasions men were killed and wounded, and work provided for the delegates of the Christian

Commission. Delegates were sent from our office to the scenes of conflict, where there accustomed services were performed with their accustomed success.

At different periods during the year these raids were repeated. The invasion of the 6th of July, is, perhaps, the most formidable of the efforts of the kind that transpired in the vicinity during the year. It commenced in the plunder of Frederick city, and was continued in various depredations until after the burning of Chambersburg, which took place on the 6th of August. The result of these raids left by far the most of the dead and wounded of the enemy on our hands. In hurried retreats it was not possible for them to bury their dead, or to take their wounded from the field. Our hospitals were occupied by large numbers of Rebels on account of whose sufferings the sympathies of our people were excited, and a vast deal of labor and money were expended in their relief. The hospitals at Frederick city were sometimes filled with the wounded of the two armies, while many of the disabled were sent to Baltimore and Washington cities.

While the raids were in progress along the upper Potomac the most severe and sanguinary battles of the campaign were fought during the passage of General Grant's army towards Petersburg and Richmond. The contest for Fredericksburg had been severe and bloody, and while the power of possession seemed to be alternately in the Union and Rebel forces, a number of very hardly contested skirmishes took place, in which many were killed and wounded on both sides. At length when the scale was permanently inclined in favor of the Union army, nearly all the wounded of the enemy fell into our hands. The provisions of the hospitals which were sufficient in all cases for our own wounded, were insufficient for the accommodation of the crippled of both armies. Shelter tents, and such temporary accommodations as could be hastily provided were brought into use until the men could be conveyed to distant places of security and comfort. On all occasions the delegates of the Commission were near and ready with their stores for their work of Christian liberality, providing for the sufferer with whatever means they had on hand, laboring with ceaseless and untiring industry until the objects of their greatly excited interest were as comfortable as they could render them.

Afterwards came on the battles of the Wilderness, Chancellorsville, Spottsylvania, North Anna, Cold Harbor, Bermuda Hundred, Weldon, then the siege of Petersburg and Richmond. The slaughter in these battles was immense. The numbers of the wounded were counted by tens of thousands. They were to be hunted out from among the dead. They were to be taken to the ambulance, or if too badly hurt for the jolting of the ambulance, to the shelter tent of the field. In these shelter tents, rapidly constructed to screen the sufferer from the scorching rays of the summer sun, the Surgeons were in waiting with their instruments for amputation, and for searching the wounds. In the changes of the armies here from Fredericksburg to the North Anna, thence to the White House, thence to City Point, there were perils to be encountered unknown in human warfare. At every point the enemy was stationed in force, and it was only through the most extreme perseverance and at the most fearful risk and expense of life and suffering that these necessary objects were accomplished. Sure as the battle and the bloodshed was the appearance of the delegates of the Commission.

In large numbers from Maryland, and in larger numbers from the central office in Philadelphia, they crowded into our apartments. We were well provided with haversacks and blankets and stores. Haversacks and blankets were delivered to each delegate; the haversack was filled with articles for immediate use, and the boxes were packed and sent by the steamboat, or the railroad, or by the wagon team, as became necessary. In some instances the stores were sent in advance of the delegate, and were in waiting when he arrived. It was indeed cheering, amid the harrowing reflections occasioned by the terrific slaughter of human life, and the fearful mangling of the human form in such multitudes, to witness the eagerness and earnestness with which our men buckled on their armor of peace and humanity, the haverersack and the blanket and hurried out of the office to the depot of conveyance for the field of their labor. It was a sacrifice to them of time and money and strength, and a risk of sickness and accident. But these drawbacks were not in their consideration. The cost was counted in the duty to which they were committed in the relief of their suffering fellow-men. The duty was imperative. It was counted in humanity's covenant with God. It was God's own work in His care over His creatures, and the trust was in God that He would bless His own work and lead His own self-sacrificing servants through it. The hour for the meditation and the formal prayer with them had passed when they appeared for their equipments for the service, and like men engaged in business transactions, or in pursuit of journeys in business relations, they entered their names and received their supplies and left for the conveyance. We say formal prayer, because Christian men have their hours and their postures for prayer, but they do not always wait for the hours and for the opportunity of placing themselves in the posture. They pray while in the pursuit of their purpose in God's service. They do not always want the books nor even the immediate thoughts of prayer. The very act is prayer, the business is prayer without a word, and apparently without a conscious thought. There is its conscious thought in the act, there is faith in the act, there is trust in the act; the unconscious thought, the faith, the trust, each is prayer, all is prayer. The prayer is in the act. It is the prayer of faith. It is heard on high. It will be answered.

As we have looked upon these men in the pursuit of their purpose, as anxious as if the large estate were in their view and the extensive business profit to be realized, we have inwardly rejoiced in the view of the better type in which humanity presented itself, and we have prayed that there might be guardian spirits with their unseen protection to shield these messengers of mercy from danger, and conduct them safely through their work. We prayed that there might be such guardian spirits, and we believed there would be. We doubted not that God's invisible leaders and protectors would be with His servants, and that they would be conducted in safety through the period wrested from other necessary life pursuits and devoted to this humane, this Christian-like, this noble service.

There they were, and there they are, at the front, in the battle's wake waiting for it to subside, and rushing as soon as it is over as if to make amends by Christian services for the sad havoc that selfish humanity would make of itself. In fierce conflict the deed of blood was wrought. In the quiet composure of the peaceful tent the flow of blood was stayed. In maddened frenzy the unfortunate were thrown violently down. In the labor of meekness the fallen was raised up. In the terrific onslaught the bullet and the sword were the agents that brought the ruin. In the merciful intervention the prayer and the word of counsel were the ministers that would have produced the restoration. The intended victim was seized by the hand of Mercy's minister and drawn forth from the place of his peril to be restored to life, to himself, and to the friendships that were as dear as life. The deeds have followed each other in rapid succession. The sword and the bullet have scarcely strewn the soil with their victims when the hand of the delegate has been stretched forth for the relief. The blood was stanched as it flowed from the wound freshly made, and the life of the fallen one has been prevented from passing with the current as it reddened the soil. The living principle still left in the system has been nourished and nursed, and encouraged and strengthened, and from the very dust of death the form has been brought forth and restored, and the strong man has once more appeared upon his feet and asked readmission into the ranks of his country's defenders. It is thus that Heaven's mercy follows fast in the personnel of the Christian Commission in the footsteps of war, and effects the relief of the afflicted, and the restoration amid the ruin.

It is a strange history that our nationality is now writing. It is the record of the field that tells of the friendly intervention. The tale is written in blood and tears. The mourner stands by the bleeding form, and in the rage and roar and devastation of the battle, all is terrible, all is afflicting, all is heart-harrowing, and working wretchedness.

But silently, stealthily, and imperceptibly the relief agent appears. He comes like Mercy's angel with the means of comfort, and with words of consolation. He tells of the trials of earth and of the triumphs of heaven; he points to the brief pilgrimage of sorrow that man passes below, and to the enduring bliss that he is to possess in the world above. The pilgrimage is soon over with its woes and pains and wretchedness, but the bliss is to remain forever. The passing spirit realizes the relation. It looks from its suffering tenement to the joys that await its release. It springs from the clay that holds it in its earthly thrall and flies away to its heavenly rest. So dies the soldier on the field. So passes the human spirit from the wards of the hospital to its home in heaven.

The history of the hospital must pass along with that of the battle-field. The history of the hospital not only tells of the triumph of the redeemed spirit. It tells also of the restoration of the sufferer; of the reformed life; of the righteousness that superseded the wickedness; of the usefulness that came after the penitence on account of the waste of years; of the earnest labors for God that the willing hands performed when the heart was filled with the love of Christ.

Such is the strange history our nationality is now writing. In this history the Christian Commission must have its part. In the generations of the future its tale of love and mercy must be told. It were well that the hand that binds up the wounds of the sufferer on the battle-field should be painted on the picture that represents the hand with the dagger in its grasp. It were well that the bearer of religious counsels and consolations should be represented on the canvass that exhibits the bearer of the sword. War may devastate and destroy, but the Christian Commission will ever appear in its wake, with the relief and the religious counsel. The field may tell its tale of wo, but the hospital that of the relief.

## HOSPITALS, LOCATIONS, &c.

The hospitals of the district are variously located. Some of their sites are high and healthy, others are not so well located. All of them are favored with an abundant supply of good water. Each hospital is under the direction of a Surgeon, and has a regularly appointed Chaplain. It appears to be the purpose of the Government that the Religious service shall follow closely upon the Medical. In the absence of such an officer as a Chaplain General, to whose management might be committed the religious department of the army, the department is in the control of the Surgeon General, who supervises the work of the chaplaincy in connection with that of the Surgical or Medical Staff. Each hospital is designated by the title "General" to distinguish them from Division Hospitals.

The number of regular hospitals now in the district is sixteen; six of these are in Baltimore; four are in and near Annapolis; one at Annapolis Junction, on the Washington Branch of the Baltimore and Ohio Railroad; one at Wilmington, Delaware; one at Point Lookout, at the extreme end of St. Mary's county, Maryland; one at Fort Delaware, in the Delaware bay, some fifteen miles below Wilmington, Delaware; one at Frederick city, in Frederick county, Maryland; and one at York, in Pennsylvania.

It will be observed by the location of these hospitals, that they are distributed over different parts of Maryland and its adjoining States of the North and East. This distribution was designed for convenience in relation to those points near the territory occupied by the battle-fields of Virginia and the States near her northern and eastern border. To hospitals thus located the badly wounded of the battle-fields may be readily conveyed. They are convenient to railroads and water communications, by means of which the wounde men and all necessary supplies may be transported.

The wisdom of this general distribution of the hospitals of the district is apparent in the propriety of diffusing, as much as possible, the evil effects that must necessarily arise from the putrid atmosphere occasioned by masses of decaying flesh and the exhalations of infectious effluvia always given off from the bodies of diseased persons. The concentration at any given point of atmosphere thus affected would not only aggravate the diseased condition of the patients of the hospitals, but produce malarious effects in the localities in which the hospitals are situated. Were all the hospitals located in Baltimore, or in any other city, the health of the citizens would be endangered by the concentration of the malaria arising from them. This evil would be accomplished by the aggravation of local diseases, peculiar in every district, and in the inducement of contagion, a condition always to be dreaded.

In this distribution of the hospitals, the Government, under the best medical advisement, has had in view the comfort of the patients and the inducement of every opportunity and facility for their restoration to health, and the preservation of the inhabitants of the city from the ill effects of concentrating malarious atmosphere in their vicinity.

In visiting the hospitals of the district, the committee have been frequently impressed with the importance of the sanitary facilities apparent in almost every location selected for their occupancy. High and commanding sites have generally been chosen, and in some instances the hospital is surrounded with spacious grounds on which grass plats and shrubbery are in cultivation, affording pleasant and healthful employment to the convalescing, and grateful views and wholesome air to the more seriously afflicted.

It is not possible that all the localities of the hospitals should possess equal facilities in their sanitary relations. The hospital is sometimes situated in the midst of the city's population, and on the closely occupied street and thoroughfare. In such cases the supply of pure air is not so abundant as it is in the suburban district. Nor are the opportunities for exercise and recreation for the convalescing so frequent. It would be well if this deficiency could be obviated by the removal of such hospitals to suburban localities. In the summer months especially, the concentrated temperature of the atmosphere from heated walls and pavements, and the lack of a sufficient supply of pure air, render the situation of the patients oppressively uncomfortable. The cleanliness and comparative purity of the atmosphere in all the hospitals are remarkable. It is but seldom that any impurity is detected in the clean and well ventilated wards. This remark applies as well to the city as well as the surburban hospitals. The advantages of the surburban locality is altogether in its better supply of wholesome air and facilities for exercise among the productions of nature.

We regret to say that all the hospitals of our district are not equally provided with facilities for religious services. Connected with some of them are very appropriate and convenient chapels, in which the convalescing patients are frequently assembled for religious engagements. That these provisions are as profitable as any others, and much more so, is proved by the results which appear among the records of the Chaplains. That they are as necessary as any others, and more so, is apparent in the improved morals and orderly habits of the patients wherever their influence has opportunity of being exercised. It were a cruel wrong to both the body and soul of the patient to deprive him of the ministrations of religion. The Government is fully aware of this, and provides the Chaplain to supply the admitted necessity. Why not then with the Chaplain provide the means and agencies of his official relationship? We have remarked the difference, and it has been admitted by Chaplains and others, between the employments and enjoyments of the men of the hospitals where chapel facilities are afforded and those where they are not. In the wards of the bed-ridden, the convalescing may sometimes be assembled for profitable religious engagements, but this is not the only means of assembling for worship that should be afforded them. The chapel is the place where they desire generally to meet one another and engage together in devotional exercises. They would lose sight, for the time, of their beds and the weary days and nights they have passed upon them and worship God with each other in the freedom of thought and purpose which such association implies and needs. Some of the Surgeons do not concern themselves in relation to the Chaplain's labors. They neglect the chapel services and refuse to co-operate in facilitating them. It is earnestly hoped that the hospitals that have no chapels for religious worship and instruction may be supplied with them, and that every possible facility may be afforded to this department of the service. We are satisfied that the order for the provision for religious worship should be peremptory, and that no local officer should be allowed to prevent it.

Connected with every hospital is an association of ladies who are engaged in the praiseworthy enterprise of preparing delicacies for the sick and wounded and of ministering to the relief of their sufferings. In the ministration of all such services as they can render, the work of the ladies is performed under the direction of the Surgeon with whom they co-operate in the labor of relief to the patients. We have received by letter and otherwise the warmest approvals and commendations by Surgeons and Chaplains of the invaluable services they are rendering.

It is with pleasure that we have observed on every occasion of our visits the marked influence produced by the efforts of the Medical Director, Dr. James Simpson. The blank forms of reports which are filled by the Surgeons of the hospitals daily and sent to his office with such other information as always accompanies them, enables him to judge of the condition and character of each hospital. Should there appear any irregularity, it is promptly corrected. All cases of mismanagement on the part of subordinate officers are investigated and the proper remedy applied. In this labor the Doctor is assisted by the Surgeons in charge of the hospitals who co-operate with him in the most courteous and friendly manner in the discharge of the duties in which their associated labors are required. In occasional visits, the view of the hospital is presented to his personal inspection, and in counsel with the Surgeons of his department a mutual understanding is experienced and a high degree of satisfaction enjoyed in the performance of the arduous and responsible labor of hospital direction.

In the pursuit of our work among the hospitals we were put in possession of the following circular, which we read with much pleasure and were rendered most happy in witnessing its effects. In a number, perhaps in all the hospitals the order is read to the subordinate officers and their co-operation is desired in its enforcement. If proper attention be given, such as the circular requires, there must pass through the wards and other departments, such a reforming influence as must be felt throughout the district:

MEDICAL DIRECTOR'S OFFICE, MIDDLE DEPT. 8TH A. C.
*Baltimore, Md., August 16th,* 1864.

Circular No. 37.

From the reports of the several Hospital Chaplains, forwarded through this office, to the Secretary of War, there is good reason to believe that their labor for the religious, and moral instruction of the soldiers, does not meet with proper support from the subordinate Medical Officers connected with the several hospitals in this Department.

Chaplains having been appointed by the President, for the purpose of affording moral and religious instruction to officers and soldiers in the General Hospitals, it is expected that all Medical Officers connected with these institutions will, by precept and example, sustain them in their arduous and responsible duties.

It is earnestly urged upon all the Medical Officers in this Department, by their presence to encourage attendance upon divine service, and to use their utmost efforts to suppress profanity and other vices that tend so greatly to degrade the soldier.

"The discipline and character of the National forces should not suffer, nor the cause they defend be imperiled, by the profanation of the day, or name of the Most High."

J. SIMPSON, Surgeon U. S. A.
Medical Director.

*Acknowledge receipt.*

The quotation with which the circular closes, is extracted, we believe, from one of the proclamations of the President of the United States. Whether or not it is original in the proclamation, it discloses the views of that high functionary on the subject, and is sufficient authority for its use throughout the Medical and Religious departments of the army.

We have been favored with another order which was issued by Dr. Simpson a few days after the date of our last report. The humanity of the order is apparent, and its effect has been most salutary upon the attendants at the funerals of the deceased. The direction in relation to post-mortem examination is well timed and appropriate. We have had repeated evidences of the good effects of the circular of the Medical Director on the orders of Surgeons and the manner in which they have been carried out in several of the Hospitals.

MEDICAL DIRECTOR'S OFFICE, MIDDLE DEPT. 8TH A. C.
*Baltimore, Md., Sept. 3d,* 1863.

Circular No. 42.

It is eminently proper those dying in General Hospitals in the service of our country should receive that respect due patriot soldiers. Surgeons in charge of hospitals are hereby instructed, that prompt and full notice of the decease of each patient, and the time of burial be given to the Hospital Chaplain, and that the medical officer of the day be present at the funeral exercises, that they may be conducted with proper decorum. When post-mortem examinations become necessary, Surgeons in charge are to be held responsible, that no needless mutilation occur, and that proper care and neatness be observed.

J. SIMPSON, Surgeon U. S. A.
Medical Director.

---

We now proceed to notice each Hospital in the several relations in which the Commission is laboring in them.

### Jarvis Hospital.

Dr. De Witt Peters, Surgeon in charge.

Rev. F. W. Brauns of the Presbyterian Church, Chaplain.

Capacity, 1,400. Patients, Sept. 1st, 1864, 1,203. Admitted from Jan. 1st to Sept. 1st, 1864, 3,240. Deaths, same period, 105. Discharged on account of disability, 58.

This hospital is situated on the Western extreme of Baltimore street, Baltimore. The place it occupies was formerly the residence of Gen. Geo. H. Stewart. The hospital was sometimes designated by the title of "Stewart's Hospital." The site of the hospital is high and the location one of the healthiest about the city. The barracks, which are wooden houses and tents, are regularly arranged in rows with grass plats and flower beds between. The flowers are cultivated by the convalescing inmates, who appear to enjoy much pleasure in being able to occupy their time in so interesting and instructive an employment. We have visited the grounds a number of times, and have always found the best posssible order prevailing, and all the work of the hospital in performance in the best manner. Pleasant countenances greeted us wherever we went, and there was not apparent to us a single person in the service that was not laboring with cheerfulness and with a seeming desire to afford every possible means of relief to the suffering inmates.

The chapel is a wooden structure that was erected for the exclusive use of the Chaplain. It is only used for other collateral purposes on occasions of emergency. Religious services are regularly held by the Chaplain, the Rev. F. W. Brauns, who is one of the most attentive and faithful of the Chaplains of the army hospitals. Large supplies of books, tracts, religious newspapers, &c., are provided for him at our office, and on the several occasions of our visits we have found them in extensive use by the men. "At the book," said we to a middle aged man as we stopped for a word in passing near the place where he was sitting engaged in reading. "O yes," he returned, "our Chaplain brings us very nice books and papers from the Christian Commission." "And do you like to read them?" we inquired. "We do indeed," was the reply. "We cannot do without them." "Do all the boys read?" we asked. "Not all, some of them don't care much about reading, but the number is very small. Most of us like to read, and we should be very unhappy if we had no books and papers. I have read several books through, and I always read the newspapers all over."

The further conversation held with the man convinced us that he had been greatly benefitted by the chapel services and the opportunities afforded for improvement by reading. A double agency of good was wrought by the chapel services and the supply of reading matter. The chapel services encouraged him to read, and the reading rendered the chapel services more attractive and profitable. We spoke with a number of the patients on our round, and all bore the same testimony to the labors of the Chaplain and the benefits they received from them.

Doubtless the readers of this report will enjoy the same satisfaction that we have received in reading the Chaplain's account of his funeral services. The benefit of such engagements, so systematically and solemnly performed, must be very great. The sight of a departed comrade, an associate perhaps in the loose habits of the camp life or in danger, or a companion in suffering in the hospital must always be more or less impressive, and it must be gratifying to the survivors to assist, as they may be able, in performing the last rites of religion and humanity to the dead. Impressions made on such occasions are beneficial. They *must* produce temporary and they *may* occasion lasting interest. Respect for the dead is one of the most grateful, as well as one of the most universal feelings of humanity. It may be abused, however, by neglect, irregularity and carelessness. Such should never be allowed. The dead should always be treated with respect. When the spirit even of the vicious has passed from its earthly tenement, it leaves the form cold in its inanimation and utterly helpless for such ministrations as survivors may be able to perform. The heart of an enemy is sometimes touched and softened by the view of the helpless remains of the once despised object of his hostility. Death is the great canceller of all worldly obligations, and his invasion of the homes of the living ever brings with it the suggestions of the condition to which all must in time be reduced, and of the equality of all in their quiet resting place in the cemetery. But not only towards the dead are the survivors more feelingly disposed. There are heart searchings impelled on such occasions that induce a more tender regard for the living and a desire for the pursuit among them of a less reprehensible and more approved course of life. Altogether the well managed funeral must have a subduing and moralizing effect, while quite the contrary may be the result of the indifferent consignment of the dead to the dust. It would be well if the system pursued by

Chaplain Brauns, or something of similar character, were universally observed. And should there be no Chaplain present, a Bible may be always on hand, and some friend may read a passage appropriately selected rather than allow the burial of the corpse without a word to indicate that while the body is committed to the earth, the spirit has gone to God who gave it, and that for the award of its condition as earned by the deeds of a faithful or faithless life. It is happily the order of the Surgeon in charge that the officer of the day shall attend the funerals that occur during his charge.

The dead house of this hospital is one of the most admirable of its features. It is neat and clean and altogether unlike the departments generally appropriated to such purposes. It is the especial order of Dr. Peters that the bodies of the dead shall be treated with due respect. The order means that they shall not only be handled with care, but that the surrounding circumstances shall indicate the solemnity worthy of the presence of the mortal remains of a human being. The moral effect of this arrangement is beneficial to the living.

Another feature which we most highly approve and commend in this relation is found in a circular addressed by Dr. Peters to the Surgeons of his charge. It requires that there shall be no post-mortem examination unless in cases of peculiar disease, and then with the consent of the relations or friends of the deceased.

From the arrangements alluded to above the character of Dr. Peters, as Hospital Manager and a humane man, may be readily estimated. He is a gentleman of first quality business habits, and has an eye to every department of his labor. It is to his continuous supervision that the regularity and order of his hospital are so well preserved. He has expressed himself warmly in our presence in relation to his approval of the work of the Christian Commission under its proper regulations, and in its ministrations temporally and spiritually to the wants of the suffering. Efforts have been made by him on several occasions to induce the convalescent of his charge to attend religious services both inside and outside of the hospital. In this relation he has the counsel and support of his excellent lady, whose sympathies are with the suffering, and her efforts to relieve them have extended beyond the boundaries of her husband's highly responsible field of labor.

The department of the Christian Commission is eligibly and conveniently located at the eastern end of the hospital enclosure. It is composed of wooden buildings, most of which have been in use since the first organization of the Ladies' Association under Mrs. Alph Hyatt. The department is now under the management of a number of excellent ladies, at the head of whom is Mrs. S. S. Spear. This lady is the President of the West End Ladies' Union Aid Association. The ladies of the association are in daily attendance, and perform their work of ministering to the comfort of the patients with the approval, and under the supervision of Dr. Peters, who highly commends their activity and the benefits they are conferring upon disabled subjects of his extensivs charge.

Jarvis Hospital has been fortunate in the labors of a number of influential Christian ladies, who have consecrated a portion of their time and means to the relief of disabled and suffering humanity. They are now working harmoniously and pleasantly with the Surgeon in charge, and Chaplain, and performing a large amount of service to the suffering subjects of their anxious and laborious solicitude.

There is a committee of the Christian Association of Baltimore in attendance upon this hospital for the purpose of holding meetings for prayer and other social religious engagements. They assist the Chaplain in his meetings during the week. The Christian Association is, in its organization, composed of gentlemen of the various Christian denominations of the city. Their labors are extensive among the hospitals and camps in and around the city, and they are effective, as faithful men in all such associations must be, in the accomplishment of good. We regret that we have no report of their labors at Jarvis Hospital.

The following statement is from Rev. F. W. Brauns, Chaplain of Jarvis General Hospital, Baltimore, Maryland:

"During the past summer our hospital has been much

enlarged. Our capacity is now about 1,400 beds. Many improvements have been made in our internal arrangements, and it is not venturing too much to say that, for beauty and healthfulness of situation, cleanliness, good order, kind nursing, and medical skill, this hospital is rarely surpassed. The rate of mortality is very low, and the recovery of patients in most cases has been remarkably sure and rapid.

One of the most interesting classes of patients during the year were the released prisoners from Richmond, of whom some 250 arrived at this hospital in April last. Many of them were in the lowest stage of vitality, slowly but surely sinking to the grave under the exposure and starvation to which they had been subject in their captivity. Not only were their bodies thus reduced, but in some cases the mental faculties were weakened, and the moral sense blunted. It was difficult to influence their minds by moral argument, and they were not fit subjects for military discipline. Their habits in some cases were almost beastly, and it was only by gentle treatment and patient endurance that they were gradually brought to resume the soldierly habits to which they had been previously trained. So weakened were their mental faculties that they did not seem capable of receiving religious instruction, and some of them sank away in death apparently not able to realize their condition, or to appreciate the importance of the truths of the gospel which were presented for their consideration. Of course all were not in this lamentable condition, and quite a number, having entirely recovered, are now doing good service for their country. The evidences, however, of deliberate cruelty on the part of the enemy were too strong for even the most incredulous charity to resist the conclusion that the barbarity of their treatment, if not a part of a well laid scheme to render them unfit for service in the Union cause, could, at the least, have been prevented by a little care and attention, if the Rebel authorities had been so disposed.

Our chapel services have been well attended, and the moral and religious tone of the institution has been good, althouhg there are always and will be many among the patients who are indifferent to their religious interests, and much depraved in their morals. Our proximity to the temptations and vices of a great city is often a great obstacle to the cultivation of good morals. On the other hand, our nearness to the churches of the city induces many to attend religious services by ministers of the various denominations, and in this way they have received much spiritual benefit.

We have been much indebted to the Christian Commission for their weekly supplies of religious papers, which are gladly received, and usually, thoroughly read. The gifts of the Commission in clothing and diet departments have likewise been very acceptable and useful.

The agent of the Maryland Bible Society has been very attentive in supplying the men with Bibles and Testaments, and never in the history of the hospital has there been so much Bible reading as at present.

One of the noticeable features of this hospital is the attendance upon our funerals. Great care is taken by all concerned to have the highest respect shown to the soldier who has lost his life in his country's cause. The deportment of the men and the interest they manifest on these occasions present a very gratifying feature. The church call is sounded and the convalescents gather in the chapel. The coffin is carried in covered with the United States Flag, and bearing flowers gathered by the soldiers, or presented by some lady friends. A military escort, composed of disabled soldiers of the Veteran Reserve Corps, stands at the door to receive the corpse with presented arms. A choir composed of ladies and soldiers sings an appropriate hymn. The Scriptures are read and commented on, and an account given of the religious views of the deceased. Prayer is offered, another hymn sung, and the benediction pronounced. The escort then resumes its place at the door, and the unarmed soldiers stand outside, in line, facing the chapel. The corpse is then brought out and placed in the hearse, whilst the escort presenting arms, and the drum beats a muffled roll, the attending soldiers standing with heads uncovered till the procession slowly moves away. I have no doubt that these funeral services are among the most important means that can be employed for producing a good religious impression, and the moral effect upon the men of witnessing and joining in the respect shown their departed comrades cannot be otherwise than highly beneficial.

The recent passage by Congress of a law defining the status of Chaplains and giving them certain privileges not heretofore enjoyed has been instrumental in increasing their influence and enlaying their prospects of usefulness. The provisions of the act are carefully observed by the Medical Director of this department, whose recent circular on the duty of all medical officers in hospitals to sustain the Chaplains and aid them in suppressing vice and encouraging religion, promises to have an excellent effect.

I append a few statements of individual cases for which you possibly may have room in your report.

F. W. Brauns,
Hospital Chaplain, U. S. A.

## Hospital Notes by Rev. F. W. Brauns, Chaplain.

Chaplain Brauns has copied the following notes of especial cases from his diary. They are of a highly interesting character, and afford a view of the work he is engaged in, and the manner in which he is performing it.

### CASE OF W. L. HART.

Sometime in March, 1864, I went one morning into the ward set apart for the reception of patients, suspected of having small-pox. I found there a young man of strong and stalwart frame, completely covered with the disease. I expressed my sympathy and regret at finding him in such a condition. His reply showed me at once that he was in a remarkably peaceful and happy state of mind. He stated that he was not afraid to die, that he was perfectly ready to go at any time, that he had no fears in regard to the future. His confidence was so strong as to excite some apprehension that he was based upon wrong views of christian truth, or that he was trusting in his own righteousness. I therefore questioned him as to the ground of his hope, endeavoring to detect the false foundation if such it were. Here however he was already with a satisfactory answer. His hope and trust were entirely in Christ his Saviour. He had not lived a christian life until recently. He had been converted some weeks since in camp, and had united with the church organization in his regiment, which was the First Connecticut Cavalry, encamped in the surburbs of the city. My conversation with him was not protracted, but was still of sufficient duration to develope a very unusual peace and comfort in view of the danger of his present illness.

As I was about to leave he stated that he wished to ask me a favor, which of course I readily promised to grant. He said that he was here under an assumed name. He had formerly been in our navy, where a majority of the men enlist under false names. He gave me his real name and told me that his father was a minister of the Congregational Church, if I remember aright, living on Margee River, County of Victoria, Island of Cape Breton. He had likewise a wife living on the same island, whose exact residence he was unable to give. He gave me his father's address, requesting me in case of his death to inform him and his wife of the circumstances. He was then removed to the small-pox hospital, some eight miles distant, whence in a week or two we were informed of his death. I wrote to his father, according to promise, and it was with peculiar satisfaction that I could state to him, a minister of Christ's Gospel, the extraordinary calmness and confidence with which his long absent and erring son looked forward to eternity. I regret that I received no reply to this letter, as I had hoped to learn further particulars that would increase the interest attaching to the case.

### CASE OF ALBERT DREW.

This man was one of the paroled prisoners who arrived from Richmond on the eighteenth of April, 1864. He was one of the most emaciated men we have ever had in this institution. Starvation and exposure had rendered him miserable to behold. I was informed by his nurse soon after his arrival that he would not recover, and embraced the earliest opportunity of ascertaining his views on the subject of religion. I was glad to find that although he had not been a member of the church he was very much interested, and expressed a hope that all was well within. One of our pious soldiers, who had held a long conversation with him, gave me a very hopeful account of him. On the Sabbath after his arrival he appeared to be worse, and as the day advanced we thought he was rapidly approaching his end. The chapel in which our afternoon services was held, is near his ward, and the weather being warm and the windows open, he had heard with much enjoyment the songs of Zion. After services I visited him, but finding him asleep, did not disturb him and left the ward. He soon awoke and inquired for me. Whilst the messenger was gone, he sang the well-known chorus, "I'm going home to die no more." As I entered his face lighted up and with a fervent grasp and great earnestness of manner, he exclaimed, "*Chaplain I'm all prepared.*" He then expressed a great desire to see the soldier who had conversed with him so fully a few days before, but as he had left on a furlough, his wish could not be gratified. Seeing a young soldier at the foot of his bed, he inquired whether he was a professor of religion, and spoke of the danger of putting off repentance till sickness and suffering have seized upon the body. He did not die that day, but lingered on till the next Saturday. All through the week his cheerfulness continued. He would always greet his friends with a pleasant smile, and when questioned as to his hope for eternity, would invariably declare his faith in the Lord Jesus Christ as his Saviour. On the ensuing Sabbath at our usual afternoon worship, his burial services were performed, just one week after he had listened with so much pleasure to our singing.

Four or five days afterwards his aged father arrived from Ohio. Having heard of his son's illness he had hastened to his bed side, but was too late. He was informed of all the particulars of his son's dying hours, and seemed greatly comforted by the evidences of his fitness for the change. The officers and attendants were kind and sympathizing, and everything was done to soften the stroke, but it was doubtless with a heavy heart that he started the same evening on his homeward journey, for he grieved in anticipation at the effect the sad news would have upon the departed boy's aged mother.

CASE OF FREDERICK SCHULTZ.

Wounded in the leg at Spottsylvania Court House, May 10, 1864. Supposed to be a flesh wound. Came to this hospital a few days after. Appeared to be doing well until the fifth day after his arrival, when he complained of stiffness in his jaws. He attributed it to a cold, but the circumstance immediately attracted the notice and alarmed the fears of the attending Surgeon. A consultation was held, and it was decided that there was great reason to apprehend lockjaw. Next day the symptoms were so decided as to leave no doubt that the patient was a victim to that terrible disease. His case was at once reported to me by the physician of his ward, and I conversed with him in regard to his religious views. I found that he was a native of Germany, but had lived in this country since he was two years of age, and was a member of German Lutheran Church in Buffalo, New York. As far as I could ascertain he seemed to be trusting in Jesus as his Saviour, and felt that he could safely commit all things into his hands. As yet nothing was said to him about the approach of death ; but on the succeeding day when the disease was in its full development, and his departure might be near at hand, I asked him if he were willing to leave this world in case it should please God to take him away. His teeth was tightly grasping the little twig that was placed between them to prevent his biting his tongue during his spasms, and it was difficult for him to speak. He immediately answered, however, in a decided tone, "*Any time the Lord wants me he can have me. He has given me my life, and—,*" the rest of the sentence was so so indistinctly uttered as to be unintelligible. All this time he was very cheerful, and would sometimes smile when addressed. Towards evening I again asked him if his hopes were fixed on the Lord, and if he felt ready to go? and his answer was a simple "yes." He continued in the same quiet and comfortable frame of mind unto the end.

During the night, on awaking from a short sleep, he told his nurse that he had seen a beautiful vision, and with the pleasant recollections of that vision on his mind he soon after passed away.

### CASE OF SAMUEL CRAMER.

Wounded in the arm June 2, at Cold Harbor. Amputation June 30. He had not been a professor of religion, and frequently used profane language. The day before his death he asked for me, and on going in I fonnd him looking forward to death with great fears in regard to his soul. After conversing with him a while, I prayed with him. He immediately commenced praying himself in an audible tone, which increased in loudness and earnestness, so as to attract the attention of many outside the ward. His anxiety was most intense, and his prayer was full of humble confession and pleading for Christ's sake. I remained with him about three quarters of an hour, during the most of which time he continued to pray in the same excited manner, and refused to be comforted. He insisted that he must pray on until he died. I endeavored to show him that he would not be saved by virtue of his prayers, and that he must endeavor to believe that Christ would save him, and that God would answer his prayer. He became more quiet whilst I read and commented on a few verses of the 14th chapter of John. He continued, however, to pray in a lower tone nearly two hours longer. Afterwards on visiting him I found him quiet, and hoping, though faintly, that he would be saved. In answer to my question as to how he felt in view of death, he said "If I should drop off at any time I think I shall make the connection so as to save myself." That night he uttered in a calm tone a beautiful and impressive prayer, pleading for God's blessing upon his family and friends, upon his nurses, and all in the hospital. The next day he was still quiet and somewhat hopeful, though not confident, but his strength was nearly gone, and he soon relapsed into a stupor, from which he never recovered. It was the most remarkable case of conviction and prayer that we have ever had in this hospital, and although his views were not without error the evidences of his conversion and acceptance were very strong.

### Letter of Dr. Peters, Surgeon in Charge,

The approval and commendation of the labor of the ladies of the West End Aid Association contained in the letter of

Dr. Peters are highly gratifying to the committee. May the good work be thus performed and thus commended as long as it may be needed.

JARVIS U. S. A. GENERAL HOSPITAL.

*Baltimore, Sept. 13th,* 1864.

MY DEAR MADAM :—The Christian Commission have been, during the past year, very liberal to the inmates of this hospital in furnishing religious books, tracts and newspapers. Also in other matters they have afforded much aid and comfort to our sick and wounded patients. Most of their contributions have been expended through the society of ladies over which you preside, and therefore it is not necessary for me here to recapitulate them. This commission is a self-supporting institution, and has undoubtedly performed much meritorious work for our wounded on the fields. Their aim is to assist the Medical Department in alleviating the sufferings of our soldiers and in supplying whatever may be required to that end, and as such true friends, they are highly appreciated by our unfortunate soldiers, who often take pleasure in speaking in terms of praise of the Commission, and hence nothing new can be added by one of the colaborers in our humane mission which is not over and over again expressed by the invalid soldiers who receive.

I am very respectfully

Your obedient servant,

DR. M. W. C. PETERS,

Assistant Engineer U. S. A., in charge.

MRS. SPEAR, President of the Ladies West End Union Relief Association, Baltimore.

---

Briefly but sufficiently to the point is the following letter of Mrs. S. S. Spear, President of the West End Ladies Union Aid Association. It tells its tale of relief to suffering humanity in the detail of supplies, furnished from our office and their distribution. But this is not all. The ladies of the association are constantly engaged in procuring means from other sources, which, with our own supplies, are prepared and delivered by their own hands to the sufferers in behalf of whom their sympathies are enlisted.

*Baltimore, Md., Sept.*, 1864.

G. S. GRIFFITH, *Chairman:*

DEAR SIR:—Please accept the thanks of the West End Ladies Union Aid Association, for the many favors received at your hands during the year just closed. Donations of clothing, lint, bandages, fruits, jellies, wines, and in fact every article that we could need for distribution in the performance of our daily duties, have been frequently and liberally supplied from your office. How important that the nation's liberality shall enable you to continue these good deeds.

With many kind wishes for yourself and gentlemanly assistants, I remain very respectfully, &c.,

MRS. S. S. SPEAR,

President West End Ladies Union Aid Association.

---

The following commendatory note was received by Mrs. Spear from Chaplain Brauns:

JARVIS U. S. A. GENERAL HOSPITAL.

*Baltimore, Aug.* 30, 1864.

MRS. SPEAR, *President Ladies Union Aid Society:*

DEAR MADAM:—I have been in the habit of making daily visits to the rooms of your association at this hospital, and have been a constant witness of your operations. The industry, perseverance and self-denying benevolence of the various committees command the highest admiration of the true friends of the soldiers, and any contraction of the sphere of your labors or diminution of your resources would be sadly felt by all connected with the hospital. Not only are the general operations of the extra diet department, which is under your care, of great service, but the personal visits of the ladies to the bed-sides of the patients render them intimately acquainted with their particular wants and afford them an opportunity of cheering and comforting the sick and wounded with their kind acts and gentle words. In addition to administering to their physical wants they have rendered incalculable service in promoting their religious welfare, and their assistance both in private visitation and in conducting the singing of God's praises in the congregation, has been highly effectual in helping the cause of truth and righteousness among our men.

I trust that your means may be ever ample, and your zeal and efficiency in the future, equal to what they have been in the past.

Yours sincerely,

F. W. Brauns,

Hospital Chaplain, U. S. A.

---

**Patterson Park Hospital.**

Dr. Thomas Sim, Surgeon in charge.

Rev. R. Spencer Vinton, of the Methodist Episcopal Church, Chaplain.

Capacity, 1,200. Patients, Sept. 1st, 1864, 927. Admitted during the year, 5897. Whole number in the hospital during the year, 6459. Discharged during the year, 53. Died, 45.

Patterson Park Hospital occupies the City Park, known by the name. It is situated at the eastern extremity of Lombard street, Baltimore. The position is high and commanding. It overlooks an extensive portion of the Patapsco river and Chesapeake Bay on the southeast, and a considerable proportion of the city on the west. The site of the Park and Hospital is very near to the fortifications that were erected for the defence of Baltimore against the British army in 1812. Portions of the fortifications are within the Park enclosure.

The barracks erected for hospital use form a hollow square, in which there are grass plats with intervening walks leading to every portion of the hospital. On occasions of our visits we have been conducted through the dining room, officers quarters, and wards, and we have always been attracted by the neatness and cleanliness apparent throughout every department. The Chaplain is one of the best of men and well adapted to the service he is called upon to perform. He is closely engaged at his work either in the meeting or in the wards or in his office. During the entire period that we were present in his office, there were calls by convalescents with papers and books they were returning and which they desired should be exchanged for others. The visitors were received by the Chaplain with kindness, and a word of counsel given to every one as he passed in and out. In a number of cases he described the visitor and had some story to tell of the manner in which he was brought to consider his religious estate, or of some especiality in relation to his character and actions as a believer in Christ. "That man," said he in one case, "when he came here could not be prevailed upon to take a book or a paper into his hand. I thought sometimes that he was almost sorry that he had learned to read. I talked to him frequently without effect, and suddenly, when I was about to give him up, he came for a paper, and now if I was to try I could not keep a paper or book out of his hand. He uses up every thing he can lay his hand on, and you gentlemen of the committee must not be too sparing of your reading matter or I will not be able to keep him busy."

We assured the Chaplain of the satisfaction with which we heard the story, and that he should not lack the desired supply of reading for his men, while we could secure it for him.

This is but one of the number of little sketches given while we were present and which delighted us very much. The same sort of entertainment was afforded us in passing through the wards and over the grounds. With the histories of many of his charge, he appeared to be quite familiar, and was quite as ready in communicating his knowledge, and that in the most interesting manner. The Chaplain is known, and well known by the subjects of his ministrations, and they apply to him in the certainty of being relieved on every occasion of necessity.

We have supplied our Rev. brother on several occasions with Bibles and Testaments and books and religious newspapers. He remarked as the stream of applicants for reading matter continued to pour in. "The Christian Commission will have to open its stores liberally to the old Chaplain, or his boys will complain. He don't like to stint them."

We hope the old Chaplain will not stint his boys in their reading while the supply can be furnished sufficiently to keep them busy in the engagement. An hour in his office will be sufficient to convince any one of the large amount of good he is accomplishing in the continuous circulation of his books and tracts and papers. The tracts and newspapers are returned and exchanged in the same manner as the books of the library. In this way they are caused to perform almost a perpetual service. There is no chapel building connected with this hospital. As in other cases the religious services are held in the dining room, which is large and accommodates an extensive congregation. The convalescing appear to be highly gratified at the opportunity thus afforded them of religious engagements. This is doubtless owing to the freedom of communication between their Chaplain and themselves.

It is due to the Surgeon in charge of this hospital that we should say that his influence is very considerable over the men under his care. The evidences of his attention are apparent in the respect they entertain for him. His presence in the chapel on all occasions of worship has an excellent effect upon the men, and induces many of them to be punctual in their attendance upon the exercises of religion.

The burial service is performed over the dead by the Chaplain, with great solemnity. The effect of the perfomance is apparent on frequent occasions in the attentive countenance and moistened eye. Impressions for good are made on the survivors, who sometimes express their gratification in witnessing the respect shown the remains of their departed associates.

The dining room of the hospital is commodious and well arranged for its purpose, and we have had the pleasure on thanksgiving days and other festive occasions of witnessing the large number that were accommodated within its walls. They have been entertained on these occasions with speeches and music, which they seemed very much to enjoy.

The ladies of the association in attendance upon the hospital are very constant in their ministrations. They have comfortable accommodations, which they use to the best advantage in preparing delicacies for the disabled of the wards and stronger food for the diet table of a designated portion of the convalescing. We are disappointed in not receiving a communication from the ladies which would have given us a better view than we have had of their proceedings. There are doubtless many interesting incidents connected with the department of the Commission that might be recited in their connection with this hospital. We would be pleased to embody some of them in this report. Patients from this hospital attend the meetings of the Christian Association. On one occasion a patient in attendance stated that with a number of his associates he felt it to be his duty to visit places of prayer whenever the opportunity was afforded. He took pleasure in associating with his companions in the distribution of tracts and papers furnished by the Christian Commission, among the wards of the hospital. "I recollect," said he, "the case of a soldier who was converted by reading Baxter's call to the Unconverted, loaned him by a delegate of the Commission." Our meetings at "Patterson Park," he continued, are conducted on a local principle and are very satisfactory to us all. We talk over our religious experience and tell one another how we overcome the trials that beset us and the difficulties in our way. We do good to one another in this way. He expressed great satisfaction in the knowledge that he had received much benefit from his connection with the members of the Christian Association and from reading the books and tracts delivered to him through the agency of the Christian Commission.

The following letter from the Chaplain, affords a glance at his work, with which every one that witnesses, as we have done, must he highly pleased. We most earnestly pray for the success of his labors among the men of his interesting charge:

U. S. Army General Hospital, Patterson Park.

*Baltimore, September 7th,* 1864.

G. S. Griffith, Esq., *President of the Christian Commission :*

Very Dear Brother :—It gives me much pleasure to express my indebtedness to the Christian Commission through you, for the reading matter and other things you have furnished me for the benefit of the patients in this hospital. I can truthfully say, that I have never been denied, when I have asked a donation for the benefit of our soldiers. I have been compelled to make frequent applications and draw heavily on the Christian Commission for writing paper, ink, pens, reading matter, &c. The size of our hospital is really as great as that of any other in the city. It is capable of accommodating 1,200 patients at least, and hence the necessity of extra efforts on my part, to make our soldiers comfortable while they remain with us. On the first day of last month, we had remaining in the hospital 787 patients; we admitted during the month 1659, making 2,446. Returned to duty, 317. Furloughed, 72. Deserted or absented themselves, 20. Deaths, 18, snd transferred, 1093. Remaining in this hospital on the first day of September, 926, since which time, we have received considerably over an hundred.

It gives me pleasure to say, I have not been absent a day, since my appointment. Although my duties are arduous, I delight in attending to them, and especially so, when I *know* my efforts have been crowned with success. In the death of several, the power of christianity has been made manifest, and the truth of religion acknowledged by such as witnessed their dying exercises. We have preaching every Sabbath and two prayer meetings through the week. Our congregations are large and attentive, and the best order prevails. The Surgeon in charge is seldom absent from our religious services, and this may account in part for the size and good order of our congregations.

We are doing all we can to increase our Library. Besides your donation of books, &c., Messrs. Cushing and Baily presented us with some very valuable books, also writing paper, envelopes, pens, pen-holders, pencils, &c.

We have loaned out of our library for reading purposes, 900 volumes, besides the distribution of news papers and tracts to a large amount. I devote all my time in attending to my hospital duties, such as preaching and praying for the sick and wounded. And in all our religious services we pray for the president of the United States and his Cabinet, the officers of our army and navy and the suppression of this rebellion.

At my request our chief clerk has answered your several questions, which you will find enclosed within.

Very respectfully your obedient servant,

R. Spencer Vinton,

Chaplain U. S. A.

---

The committee of the Christian Association appointed to labor at this hospital have performed a faithful duty in their attendance upon it. In a brief communication from the Chairman of the Committee we learn something of their work, enough to create the desire for more.

On the occasion of a monthly meeting of the Association a soldier from Patterson Park hospital was present. The members were giving in a detail of their labors, and the Committee in charge of the hospital presented a brief abstract of their proceedings. At the conclusion of the statement, the soldier arose and asked if he might be permitted to say something in relation to the operations of the Committee. He was of course encouraged to proceed with his remarks. He expressed great pleasure in being able to speak a word for his hospital, and on behalf of the Committee of the Association. He had been a constant attendant for several months upon their meetings, and could testify of their benificent effects upon himself as well as upon a large number of those who attend their meetings. It was with continually necessary interest as well as an increasing desire to be benefitted that the men engaged in those religious exercises. He expressed the belief that the distribution of books, and tracts, and religious newspapers, together with the meetings for God's worship was working a revolution in the minds of hundreds of the inmates of the hospital who otherwise might never feel any concern for their spiritual welfare. Many of the men were his daily associates. He knew their habits and dispositions, and was very sure that engagements of wickedness would be their daily pursuit unless attracted from them by those other and better engagements suggested by the Chaplain or the delegates of the Christian Association and Christian Commission, who were assisting him in the good work. He stated that he remembered the instance to which we have alluded, in which the habits of a wicked soldier were entirely changed, and he became a devotedly religious man from the reading of a book presented him by a delegate of the Christian Commission.

The meetings held at Patterson Park were of exceeding interest to him. Many of them were of social character in which the men engaged in conversation with each other and gave in their experience, which was generally an encouraging feature.

The testimony thus given by the visitor from Patterson Park Hospital was received with expressions of thankfulness by the members of the Association and they were encouraged to greater diligence and perseverance in the prosecution of their work.

The following communication is from the Committee of the Christian Association in attendance upon the Patterson Park Hospital. The Committee has been actively engaged in visiting the hospital and assisting the Chaplain in his services. They hold two prayer meetings each week, and rejoice in witnessing the success of their labors. Their statement tells a good story of faithful, efficient and successful labors:

*Baltimore, September* 2, 1864.

G. S. Griffith, Esq.

Dear Sir:—In compliance with your request, I submit herewith my Report in regard to the Patterson Park Hospital.

The Religious status of this hospital, we presume, will compare favorably with any in this department. Dr. Sim, who has charge, manifests a lively interest in the spiritual welfare of the men under his charge, and most willingly accords every privilege your Committee has asked of him. The Chaplain, Rev. R. Spencer Vinton, is very diligent in the work assigned him, and is greatly beloved by the men. There are now, and have been through the entire year past two prayer meetings each week, and preaching by the Chaplain on Sabbath. These services, in the general are well attended, and especially for some months past, an unusual interest has been prevalent among the soldiers in regard to their eternal interests. The Prayer Meetings are not wholly dependent for leadership upon your Committee (as they were a long time,) but there are men among the soldiers who are both able and willing to direct them. Men in whom their fellows have the utmost confidence. Men who visit the sick and tell of the Saviour of sinners, and exhort them to give their hearts to Him. There have been several triumphant deaths in this hospital, proving the power of Grace to be sufficient under the most trying circumstances to sustain the child of God in life's last struggle. The relation of Christian experience by the soldiers during the hour of prayer is often most encouraging. Many testify to the power of grace to comfort and sustain them amidst the shock of battle, and while wounded on the field of carnage and death, they rejoice, that although much of wickedness prevails in the army, yet, thank God, there are men even there, who stand up for Jesus, and by their Christian integrity, and corresponding faithfulness to God, not to be deterred by the wickedness of their fellows. There are many such in the army. Would to God there were more, and that all our patriot soldiers were good and faithful Christians.

Respectfully submitted,

J. SANNER,
Ch'n Com. Vis. P. P. Hospital.

---

### West's Buildings Hospital.

Dr. A. Chapel, Surgeon in Charge.

Rev. J. T. Van Burkalow, of the Methodist church, Chaplain.

Capacity, 425. Number of patients 407, of whom 181 are Union soldiers, and 226 are prisoners of war. Number in the hospital during the year 1,041 Union, and 402 Rebel soldiers. In all, 1,443. Discharged, 5. Died, Union, 62; Rebel 7. Total died, 69.

West's Buildings consist of a row of six large warehouses, erected some years ago, by William West, Esq., a well-known wealthy citizen of Baltimore. They are situated on Union Dock, which is in the south-eastern part of the city, and is approached by Concord street. The location of this hospital has advantages over others in being in proximity with the Patapsco river, and there being no obstructions by other buildings to the free circulation of the air. The buildings are well ventilated by rows of large windows through which during the warmest part of the summer there are almost always passing cool and refreshing breezes. The buildings occupy an extensive wharf at which steamboats and other vessels are moored, and by means of which conveniences of transportation of both men and stores are afforded.

The facilities of transportation induced the use of these buildings as a hospital of distribution, and thousands of wounded men from the battle-fields of Maryland, Pennsylvania and Virginia, a large proportion of whom were Rebels were passed through the buildings. We have been present while large numbers were in transit and witnessed the dressing of their wounds, and their refreshment in the appropriation of an abundance of wholesome food.

After the battles of Antietam and Gettysburg, large numbers of both armies were shipped from Union Dock, for transportation to Northern cities. There are no grass plats nor spots of green with shrubbery to enliven the view ; but there is an expanse of water near, to which affords many attractions, and the waves of which produce no unpleasant sound in dashing against the wharf.

The several stories of the buildings are erected into wards. Doors have been opened through the walls affording a continuous passage from one department to another through the entire extent of the buildings. Each of the stories is rendered alike in this respect. Part of the lower story is occupied by Surgeons and other officers, and by the Ladies' Relief Association.

It is a decided misfortune that in the establishment of this hospital no provision has been made of a room for religious services. It had been better to reduce the capacity of the hospital by appropriating one of the wards for purposes of religious worship and for the use of the Chaplain as the quarters from which Bibles, Testaments, Tracts, &c., might be distributed. It is frequently said that the Government has no soul to be saved. But those in the leadership of the Government have. And they know that the people of the country, and the officers, and the soldiers of the army have souls. And they have heard often enough of the declarations of the Book which they receive as the Word of God in relation to the concern that every man ought to experience in relation to the safety of his soul. The least that God can demand, or man ought to desire in this consideration is, the appropriation of one of the many rooms of the hospital for religious worship, and to whatever religious labor the Chaplain may have to perform besides that of attending upon the bed-ridden in the wards and on their beds.

It is true that the convalescing can hear the word of God expounded, and receive instruction as well in the dining room or in the wards and seated upon the beds of the sick, as any where else. But it is just as true that the presence of the assembly of men in the sick room is an annoyance to the sufferers. It is no proper association for the very sick and the dying who are to be kept from all excitement, and as quiet as possible. We have been present while the services of religion were in pursuit in the ward and we have been called immediately after to the bedside of the dying man whose feelings were greatly excited, and his sufferings aggravated in consequence of the excitement.

There is no excuse for the omission of the proper provision for the Chaplain's labors. This work is as necessary as that of the Surgeon who has control of the hospital, and generally commands the use of several apartments. If the Chaplain's quarters should be in demand in cases of emergency, then let them be used for ward purposes, and let the Surgeon's quarters be used in the same way. We have no idea of this obscuring of the needs of the soul, while all the provision is expended upon the body. The officials of the Government may accommodate each other in the performance of their several duties, and by arrangement always, or generally afford opportunities for the services of religion. The gentlemen in control are answerable to their conscience and their God for the manner in which this great duty is overslaughed and obscured. The officials in the orders and in the administration of the orders of Government are those who will be held responsible for the issue. The officials who are involved in this responsibility are those who have control, from the highest in the authority, the President of the United States and his immediate officers, to the Hospital Surgeon and the lowest official engaged in his employment.

We most earnestly hope that this omission, the inconveniences and ill effects of which are forcibly represented in the report of the Chaplain, will no longer be allowed. One of the wards may be appropriated to his use without inconvenience. The hospital is not full, and a ward may readily be spared for the purpose. The removal of a few beds which are most generally unoccupied, and the preparation of a few shelves and a table are all that are necessary for the accomplishment of the desirable, and we think, very necessary object.

The apartments of Ladies' Relief Association are convenient in the provision for the storage and delivery of their goods. They are not as convenient, however, as is desirable for the preparation of the delicacies they administer. They are actively engaged in the service of the sufferers on whose account they are laboring. In common with the Chaplain, they are obliged to endure many privations in the absence of facilities needed in the performance of several of the departments of their service. Their shelves are generally filled with stores of various kinds necessary for the comfort of the sick and suffering, and they are daily and hourly engaged in administering them as they are called for by the patients of the several wards. Mrs. S. A. C. Norris has rendered very acceptable and profitable service to the inmates of this hospital. She is in attendance nearly every day and keeps in active progress the labors of her department.

We have no communication from the Committee of the Christian Association appointed for labor at West's Buildings. We presume, however, that they have performed their duty of visiting the wards, and conversing and praying with the patients. The absence of the provision for religious worship prevents the assembling of the convalescing patients for prayer and religious conversation. It is not improbable that the Committee has not been able on account of the causes to which we have alluded, to hold any religious meetings, and that they have not deemed their labors of sufficient importance to embody in a report. This is one of the evils, and not the least, that is occasioned by the want of a chapel, or Chaplain's room, to which all the appliances on account of religious worship may be concentrated, and from which all the resources of the same may be distributed. In visiting the hospital we have been very kindly treated by Dr. Wm. G. Knowles and Dr. A. Kessler, with whom we have spent some very pleasant moments.

The following report of Chaplain Van Burkelow embodies the difficulties he is obliged to encounter in the performance of his duties:

West's Buildings General Hospital,
*Baltimore, Maryland, August* 24, 1864.

G. S. Griffith, Esq., *Chairman U. S. Christian Commission*:

Sir:—In compliance with your request, I take pleasure in giving you an account of my work for your forth-coming Annual Report.

This Hospital was established on the 19th of September, 1862, and I reported for duty in it on the 20th of the following October. It was then filled with patients, who were wounded at the battle of Antietam. An extensive field of usefulness was open before me, but there was very few conveniences for my work. There was no chapel, nor Chaplain's office; and for lack of room none have been given me yet. I commenced to hold Divine Services in the *Dining room*, but, as it was not heated, I was soon driven by approaching winter to the wards, where, without any seats save the beds, and a few chairs, I have had to hold all our meetings ever since during cold weather. Until very recently funeral services were not allowed in the dining room, and, saving the use of a small tent a short time, they had to be held in the open air, without shelter, shade, or seats. From these unfavorable facts, together with many embarrassing circumstances, I have found it difficult to keep up a religious interest and an elevated moral tone. But, while I have often been mortified at the meagre fruits of my labors, I have the pleasant conscienciousness of having endeavored to do my duty, and am rejoiced to know that all has not been "altogether vain in the Lord." The greatest harvest of spiritual good has been reaped at the sick bed; and I expect to meet many a one in heaven who was born again in "West's Buildings" under my pastoral care.

After the battle of Gettysburg, ours was made a distributing hospital; and for a month the wounded poured through its portals by thousands, sometimes, only staying long enough to have their wounds dressed, and to be refreshed by something to eat, and—"tired nature's sweet restorer, balmy sleep." The Union soldiers came first, and then the Rebels. When this stream of bleeding humanity subsided, we retained enough to fill the hospital. The most of those remaining were Rebels. Many were professors of religion, and they generally attended Divine services well. Indeed, they urged me to hold extra meetings, and to gratify them, and at the same time keep up separate prayer meetings for Union men, I had to establish a system of double duty in this respect, and for nearly four months I held two meetings for each party of evenings, and one for both together on Sabbath afternoon every week.

On the 1st of January last, a Reading Room was opened in one end of an empty ward. We fitted it up with carpet and flags, maps and engravings, and furnished it with about thirty papers, daily and weekly. The most of the weeklies and the two German dailies of Baltimore were sent gratis, by the publishers. We already had a small library, collected by ladies of the Union Relief Association. This was considerably increased by a number of liberal contributions from booksellers in Baltimore, Philadelphia, and Boston. With all these attractions, it had many daily visitors and proved a great blessing to the hospital. But, alas! it was a short-lived institution. The room had to be taken for a ward again in the spring, and we have no other appropriate place for the books, and papers.

On the 18th of April, we received one hundred and five released prisoners of war from Richmond. They were mere living skeletons, the most emaciated and cadaverous set of human beings I ever saw, and they were literally covered with vermin and filth, while some had no shirts, and what clothes they wore were in shreds. Nearly all, when captured, were well, but when released they were almost dead. Their condition were striking contrast with that of the Rebels remaining here, who were brought from the battle-field severely wounded, but who were then well, fat, and fit for the field again, while our men, who were in robust health when they fell into Rebel hands, were then, from slow starvation, ready to tottle into the grave. Nearly half died in less than a month after their arrival, and others went home to die ere long. Oh! shame where is thy blush? But, thank God! there was some relief to the dark picture. A large majority of those who died, were lead by their sufferings to seek the Saviour, and were renewed in righteousness, while passing through the fires of affliction, kindled by Rebel cruelty and crime. Some had been Christians for years and had "kept the faith;" but the most "laid hold on the hope set before them in the Gospel," after reaching our hospital. One of the most triumphant deaths was that of John S. White, an Ohio soldier. His fatal disease was consumption. He was so weak when he arrived that he could not walk, and he gradually wasted away and went down to the grave. But he could say with one of yore, "when I am weak, then I am strong." He was "strong in the Lord," and happy in the hope of Heaven. His faith was unwavering, and his "peace flowed as a river." He often expressed to me a lively hope of a blessed immortality, and when the hour of his dissolution came, his joy was truly ecstatic, and after I had prayed with him, he exclaimed, while gasping for breath, "Blessed Jesus! Precious Saviour! Oh! that I had strength to praise Him! How I long to be with Him above!" Thus he passed away in holy, signal triumph.

We now have over three hundred rebel patients in hospital, who were wounded in the battle of Monocacy. Many of them are professors of religion, and the convalescents are generally regular in attendance upon Divine services. They even attended preaching on the day recently set apart by the President for *public humiliation and prayer*, and listened respectfully to a thoroughly anti-slavery sermon. True, some left the room instanter upon my pronouncing slavery a great national sin, and the chief cause of the war, but the most kept their seats until I closed. At their request, I am holding two special meetings a week in their wards, besides the two regular services. A few take part in the exercises, with humble manner and modest fervor; and, however paradoxical it may seem, I am sure that some of them are truly pious, notwithstanding the unparalleled political wickedness of the cause in which they are engaged. It is charitable to suppose that the power of prejudice and social influence produces moral disability on some subjects, in some sections, and that, in such a case, sin is not imputed. However, the most of those who are unmistakably walking in the narrow way of life, have, with more or less explicitness, assured me that they were opposed to the rebellion, and that but for compulsion, they would never have taken up arms. One of evident piety, told me so a few days ago upon a dying bed. He died yesterday in the triumphs of grace, and his disembodied spirit is doubtless to-day in the paradise of God. I met quite a number of Union men among the prisoners of war last year, and I have long since learned to pity a large proportion of the privates in the rebel army as poor sheep led to the slaughter, and unwilling agents of treason and death, under the iron despotism of the South.

Our hospital is greatly indebted to the *Christian Commission* for various stores, from time to time. The papers, pamphlets and tracts, which I often receive, are generally read by the men, and do much good. Your recent loan of books is highly prized, and will be the means of moral elevation and enlightenment to many a young man, I trust, through the grace of God.

Hoping that the *Christian Commission* may still prosper in its labor of love, and asking pardon for my prolixity, I will now come to a close.

Yours truly,
J. T. VAN BURKALOW,
Chaplain, U. S. A.

---

**National Hospital.**

Dr. Z. E. Bliss, Surgeon in charge.

Rev. T. J. Bowen, of the Unitarian Church, Chaplain.

Capacity, 400. Patients, 392.

The National Hospital occupies the building formerly known as the National Hotel, on Camden street near Howard street. Except the Newton Hospital, it is the least eligibly and advantageously situated of all the hospitals of Baltimore. It is on one of the streets of the city with but a small yard attached, which is entirely insufficient to afford any active recreation for convalescing patients. The wards are small and inconveniently situated and exhibit but few attractions. Notwithstanding these objectionable features, the National Hospital is one of the best managed in the city. The influence of Surgeon Bliss is realized in every department. The Medical officers, which are in the front part of the building, are open to the view of visitors, and present a well arranged and attractive appearance. The wards although small and irregularly situated, are clean and comfortable, and the patients seem to enjoy themselves as if hardly aware of the unfavorable contrast which their quarters bear to those of the hospitals on the suburbs of the city with extensive grounds and possessing much greater advantages in the more free circulation of air and the beautiful prospects presented in the woods and fields of the country.

The Chaplain of the National is in attendance upon his duties daily. He is most highly esteemed by the patients to whom he ministers, and is every way worthy of their regard. Like others he labors with inconvenience in the absence of a suitable room for chapel services. The dining room and the larger wards are the best substitutes provided, but they are insufficient for the purpose, and with a number of his brethren in the same relationship, the Chaplain has to regret that the men of his charge have not better accommodations and more encouragement in the pursuit and performance of their religious obligations. The number of patients in the hospital reaches so nearly its capacity as to require all the rooms for their accommodation. Were the spiritual interests of the men properly considered, the capacity of the building would without doubt be reduced and an apartment appropriated for chapel uses.

Our report in relation to the National is necessarily short, and of course unsatisfactory. This is occasioned by the want of information, although repeated efforts were made to obtain it. The capacity of the hospital and number of patients was received from the office of the Medical Director. We have no communication from the hospital but that of the committee of the Christian Association which we subjoin. Some of the convalescing patients of the National are praying men. This we know from their attendance upon the meetings of the Christian Association. At one of those meetings a patient of the hospital related an incident which is of sufficient interest to record among the pages of this report. He stated that he, together with a number of his fellow patients were in the habit of holding a prayer meeting some distance from the city in a country village. A liquor seller of the village, fearing damage to his occupation from the effect of the meetings, hired a number of rough characters to break up the meeting with the view of preventing their continuance. The leader of the hired party entered the room with his gang while the worshipers were at prayer, struck with amazement at the scene before him, he stood motionless until the prayer was ended. The appearance of the intruders was sufficient to indicate their purpose. The narrator approached the man and asked him his business, then turning to his companions he said let us all unite in prayer in behalf of this man and his company. The deed was at once performed. The man trembled and requested that he might be prayed for. "I am a member," said he, "of the Plug Ugly party, and have done much mischief in their association. I have had a praying mother and now feel that I desire to have her prayers answered. Pray my friends that they may be answered and that I may be saved." "I came," he continued, "to break up this meeting, but go on my friends I shall not disturb you." After remaining awhile with his party he peaceably retired.

In our visits to this hospital we had opportunities of conversing with Dr. Edward G. Waters, who is one of the most intelligent, active and faithful physicians engaged in the hospital service. We admire his precision and promptness in the management of his department of the service.

U. S. Christian Commission, 77 West Baltimore street.
*Baltimore August 28th,* 1864.

National Hospital, Camden street.

The prayer meetings at the Camden street Hospital on Sunday and Thursday nights have been kept up during the year with the usual interest. Some of them, even in the warmest part of the season, have been exceedingly interesting and very fully attended. At nearly all of them soldiers have spoken and prayed. Several letters have been received from men who have gone to their homes, showing their interest in these meetings, and making inquiries as to their continuance. Precious seasons some of them have been, and truly refreshing has it been to hear men, who have been in the heart and heat of the battle's commotion, telling how their firm trust in Jesus sustained them. Others again we have heard deploring the demoralizing influences of camp life; but all expressing their hope that God had not forsaken them, and their purpose still to continue in his service. Some in a lukewarm state have been aroused to greater zeal and efficiency in the service of Christ. Several ladies have encouraged us by their presence, rendering valuable aid in the singing. Occasionally, though rarely, ministers or Chaplains have also assisted us.

D. Maxwell,
G. W. Horner,
G. N. Cressy,
J. M. Grant.

**McKim's Hospital.**

Dr. L. Quick, Surgeon in charge.

Rev. George A. Leakin, of the Protestant Episcopal Church, Chaplain.

Capacity, 300. Patients, 318.

McKim Mansion, which is now occupied by the hospital, appropriated to the disabled of the colored troops, together with white patients, is situated on the northeastern suburbs of Baltimore city. It was once quite an elegant residence. It occupies an eminence that overlooks a large proportion of the city. Within the partial enclosure, formed by the barracks, there are patches of grass, and beyond are groves and fields, with Greenmount Cemetery close by, which afford a picturesque and attractive view. The hospital has a sufficient supply of water from the city works. The barracks are built of wood, and are two stories in height. The old mansion house affords convenient offices for the Surgeons and their assistants. The quarters of the Chaplain are in the second story of one of the buildings. The situation is eligible and accessible to the convalescents, and would be comfortable but for the burning rays of the sun which heat the roof to an insupportable degree in the summer months. The thin scale of plank and paper, saturated with pitch, that screens the Chaplain's head from the sun's rays is insufficient to protect him from the scorching heat. The relief of the fall and winter will doubtless be gratefully acknowledged.

The Surgeon in charge, Dr. Quick, is one of the first appointed of the Surgeons. His long service eminently qualifies him for the position he occupies. His natural business facilities are considerable. His name is but an indication of the rapidity with which his business engagements are performed. He is one of the most active, energetic, and efficient Surgeons of the army.

The Chaplain's services are conducted with great regularity and efficiency. Notwithstanding the uncomfortable quarters in which we found him on occasions of our visits, he is actively engaged in serving the "boys" who follow him about and look up to him for counsel as though they were children desiring the aid and direction of their parents. There appears to be more desire for religious service among the patients of this hospital than is apparent in any of the others. Singing and prayer are daily pursuits. In singing the "boys" greatly excel, and at times during the day and evening, they make up assemblies for the purpose, and in the engagement, possess a high degree of enjoyment. Public religious services are conducted in a small chapel, in which, with the white and colored population of the hospital, meet and worship God together. From the Chaplain's statement it will be seen that some of the white patients are men of wealth and standing. Others are ministers of the Gospel. The good examples of such, may produce impressions upon the more worldly, who, from a motive lower than that induced by the interest and feelings of a true patriotism, may have entered the army. The statement of the Chaplain, received while we are writing, is herewith presented. It affords evidence of a quiet and unobtrusive, yet efficient service among the inmates of the hospital.

We have but little knowledge of the department of this hospital in which the ladies usually labor. We believe it is in charge of a matron who is performing her duties acceptably and satisfactorily. A corps of excellent ladies at one time occupied the premises. They took charge of the department when the hospital was established and labored some time with great industry and energy in the performance of their duties. Large supplies were sent them from our warehouse, and we have often had assurances of the benefits they were rendering to the patients. The matron who now performs her part of the service, is a resident of the hospital, and is daily engaged in her ministrations upon the sick and disabled of the wards.

A report of services at McKim's has been received of the committee of the Christian Association. They have visited the premises every week during the year. At each visit they have ministered to the sick and wounded of the wards who are confined to their beds. They have held meetings regularly for prayer and religious counsel at which it is believed they have done much good. There is an encampment on the opposite side of the street from the hospital which is located in an open field. This encampment has been visited regularly by the committee of the Christian Association and religious services performed among the men composing it. We have supplied the committee with considerable reading matter, which they have assured us is received and read with interest and profit by the invalid as well as the convalescent. From one of the committee's communication, as well as from the frequent conversations we have had with them on the subject, we have reason to believe they are laboring successfully in this field of their service.

The letter from the Chaplain, expresses very favorable sentiments in relation to the circular of the Medical Director, counselling Surgeons and Chaplains to give all necessary attention to the exercises and ceremonies of religion. He believes it will have a good effect upon both officers and men, and induce greater attention and respect for religion. In this sentiment we heartily concur with the worthy Chaplain.

McKim's Mansion Hospital.

*Baltimore, August 27th,* 1864.

G. S. Griffith, Esq., *President of the Baltimore Christian Commission:*

Sir:—I respectfully report that the work of the Chaplaincy has been regularly carried on since your last annual issue. From the change of patients, it is difficult to state results, but we know from God's word, and from the constitution of the human mind, that "His word will not return void."

The hospital presents a better field for religious impressions than the camp, and in the hours of pain, seeds of truth are sown, which brings forth the fruits of good living. The ploughshare of war furrows society that sin may be extirpated and spiritual harvests ensue.

During the last six months, the hospital has contained both white and colored patients. They meet together in the little chapel, unite in the same hymns and prayers.

The hospital is a miniature world. Here are men of property who left their homes for their country's defence. Here are others of intelligent piety—preachers, who left their congregations for the same object, while many others have either no motive or a very low one; but even they, come under impressions unfelt at home.

The devotion of the colored patients is generally commendable. They rarely violate the rules of discipline. They spend much time in trying to improve by means of books, furnished by your Commission. Then hymns are sung with a ferver refreshing to the auditor.

I am indebted to you for much reading and stationery, which have cheered the routine of the hospital and brought the comforts of home to many sick beds.

My room is daily visited by numbers for a sheet of paper and an envelope, and through this small gift, my influence has increased. I am happy to have found an undeviating respect from the soldiers and pleasant relations with the officers.

I am yours truly,
GEO. A. LEAKIN,
Chaplain, U. S. A.

The following is the report of the committee of the Christian Association laboring at McKim's:

*Baltimore, August 30th,* 1864.

McKim's hospital has been our principal field of labor. We have regularly visited the premises once in each week, and also the encampment on the opposite field. Mr. Wm. H. Cary, Mr. Garrity, and Mr. Harrigan, have been faithful laborers in visiting and praying with the sick and wounded, and in distributing books, and tracts and religious papers among the convalescing. The hospital is composed of both white and colored soldiers, nearly all of whom I am happy to say have received our ministrations and the reading matter we have conveyed to them with thankfulness. We have good reason to think that much good has been done by our exertions.

About four months ago, with the Doctor's and Chaplain's permission, we established a Tuesday night prayer meeting, which has been well attended ever since. It is carried on with great interest by the persons in attendance. We generally open the meeting by singing and prayer, after which we read a lesson from the Scriptures, which is followed by a short exhortation. The soldiers are then called upon to assist, which they do with much interest, and to a good purpose. Many of them both white and colored, take an active part in the exercises. So interesting have been the exercises that I have frequently regretted when the hour arrived which admonished us of the propriety of closing the meeting. Much good has been done in the name of God at the McKim's Hospital.

Respectfully yours,
THOS. COGGINS.

**Newton Hospital.**

Dr. R. W. Pease, Surgeon in charge.

Rev. T. W. Simpson, of the Methodist Episcopal Church, Chaplain.

Capacity, 200. Patients, 150. Number in hospital during the year, 788. Discharged, 16. Died, 9.

Newton Hospital is located in the buildings on Lexington street near Calvert street, formerly occupied by the Newton University. Several private dwellings, reaching to the corner of North street, have been added to the hospital. It was known for some time as the Newton University Hospital. The name on the office documents has been changed to that of Newton Hospital. The situation of this hospital is similar to that of the others that are located on the streets of the city. The facilities for exercise and recreation are very inconsiderable, the yards connected with the buildings being small and necessarily occupied in part by a portion of the material required for hospital management. The active movements of convalescing patients are generally pursued in walks over the street on which the hospital is located and the adjacent streets of the city. We have had our attention frequently directed to this hospital since its establishment, and we have reason to believe that it has performed its full proportion of service in the cause of disabled humanity. An association of excellent ladies has been in attendance from a brief period after the establishment of the hospital, and they have been most actively engaged every day in preparing delicacies for the suffering objects of their care. The association is divided into small detachments, one of which is in attendance each day. The President, Miss E. E. Rice, is one of the most industrious and active of the ladies laboring in the hospitals. But few, if any, of the days of the week pass, in which she is not present at the hospital, either laboring herself or overlooking the labors of others. At times when such stores of the Commission as were desired were not on hand, the President, assisted by other ladies of the Association, has operated successfully in the solicitation of assistance from friends. In several instances appeals have been made by means of printed circulars, which have had the desired effect. One of these circulars having fallen into our hands, we herewith present it as a specimen of the manner in which the ladies work themselves out of their troubles, and as encouragement to others to pursue the same method when necessity requires:

LADIES' ASSOCIATION OF NEWTON UNIVERSITY HOSPITAL,
No. 11 Lexington Street.
*Baltimore, Aug. 30th*, 1863.

The Ladies of the Association of Newton University Hospital, find it necessary to appeal to their friends and the public for aid in the performance of their interesting and necessary duties, in the cause of suffering inmates of the Institution in their charge. There are in the hospital some three hundred sick and wounded soldiers, most of whom need constant attention. They require such food and nourishment as are necessary for persons in their condition.

In this very important and necessary mission in the cause of afflicted humanity, the ladies believe that they have only to call upon their friends in order to secure their co-operation and assistance.

Any articles of food and nourishment, such as are grateful to the sick and suffering, will be thankfully received. Under-clothing, shoes, slippers and socks are very much needed. Cast-off clothing can be used to advantage.

Boxes of stores and clothing may be sent by express from any part of the country.

Please direct to Newton University Hospital, No. 11 Lexington street, between Calvert and North streets. Donations may be addressed to either of the following names: Miss E. E. Rice, President; Mrs. John S. Price, Mrs. Thos. Wilson, Mrs. John Holliday, Mrs. A. M. Browne, Vice-Presidents; Mrs. James Glasgow, Treasurer; Miss N. Van Bibber, Corresponding Secretary; Miss C. Dorsey, Recording Secretary.

We have at various times supplied the ladies with stores from our warehouse and have sometimes been present while they were in preparation for the sufferers of the wards. In fact we have passed through the wards while they have been in the course of administration to the patients, and have been much pleased in witnessing the gratitude with which they have been received.

The wards of this hospital are kept as clean and as tidy as those of any of the hospitals of the districts. The same must be said of the culinary department, notwithstanding the contracted space in which the labors of those in charge of it are obliged to be conducted.

The labors of the Chaplain have been performed without any interruption during the year. He is daily at his post visiting the wards and conversing with the patients. We have supplied him with books and tracts and religious newspapers for circulation among them, and have been assured that they are received with expressions of interest and pleasure, and profitably used by the patients. As stated in his report, every thing about the hospital seems to move on in a noiseless manner, while the service it is designed to render is efficiently and effectively accomplished. There is no room of the hospital especially appropriated to chapel uses. Religious services are performed in the dining room and in the several wards, as the occasion offers or requires.

Members of the Christian Association visit the hospital and assist the Chaplain in the management of his prayer meetings. They report that good has been done to the patients through their labors, and express a high degree of satisfaction at the courteous manner in which they have always been treated by the Chaplain. Their thankfulness has frequently been verbally expressed in relation to the kind and Christian greeting with which they are always received.

It is always gratifying to the Committee to receive reports of a pleasant character from the hospitals exhibiting the harmonious working of the several departments of which the service is composed. The Surgeon and the Chaplain have their respective positions and duties appointed by the army regulations, and the Christian Commission assists both in the agencies of voluntary labor which it supplies. The ladies of the Relief Associations assists the Surgeons, and the members of the Christian Association render service to the Chaplain. In all cases when every thing is right, and the labors of the department properly rendered, due acknowledgments are made by all the parties approving and commending the services of the others, and expressing thankfulness on their account. Such, in almost all instances, has been the experience of the past. Disa greements and complaints and oppositions have been by no means frequent, and we rejoice to say, that we have reason to believe that in the mutual services of the respective agencies of the hospital work, a very great amount of good has been done to the patients. This assurance has not only come to us through the several agencies of the labor, but the patients themselves, who are the beneficiaries of the service, have warmly and gratefully expressed their acknowledgments of favors most kindly and feelingly bestowed. We are satisfied from personal observation that Surgeons cannot by any other agency supply the places of the ladies of the Associations. We must say the same of the services of the members of the Christian Association rendered to the Chaplain. It cannot be possible that the Surgeon can have his servants always at hand, and in as prompt and efficient attendance as are the ladies to wait upon the sick and prepare the delicacy for their use. The nurses of course perform their part of the duty in the wards, but in cases of extreme illness other labors than their's are necessary, and without them the patient must be exposed to suffering, that with them might be relieved. Neither is it possible that the Chaplains can hold the number of meetings that it is desirable they should hold among the sick upon their beds, and the convalescing of the wards. The "word in season," may not always be spoken in the official visit, and the occasional service when required, is generally to the extremely ill and dying. The meeting for prayer and religious counsel is refreshing to the minds and spirits of the men, and they engage in its exercises with an interest which shows that they are experiencing profit and are thankful for the opportunity of receiving it.

We make these observations on account of expressions given out and that have sometimes reached us, that the contracted accommodations of the hospital do not admit of the outside services, as they are sometimes called, of the Christian Commission. It is with deference to Surgeons and Chaplains, and others of a different sentiment that we say, that without detriment to the cause of humanity and religion, those services cannot be dispensed with. Humanity and

Christianity are the same, or nearly the same in all the cases and localities of their necessities; and these localities are wherever human sufferings are realized. It is true they are voluntary services, but they are no less important and no less necessary on that account. Suffering and dying men need them and it were cruelty to withhold them. An irreligious and profane Surgeon may do his patients more damage eventually, than his professional service may overrule; and an indifferent or negligent Chaplain may hinder the progress of a service that were better performed without him. This latter remark we have taken from the lips of the Rev. Mr. Simpson himself, whose earnest labors and the willingness with which he receives the services of his brethren are sufficient evidences of the depth of interest entertained by him on account of the spiritual necessities of his charge. In conversation with him we have learned how deeply he is interested on account of the sufferers that look to him for spiritual instruction and counsel, and from those to whom he has ministered we have been informed of the efficiency of his labors. So great is our interest on behalf of this hospital that we most earnestly hope the services of the various departments may continue to be harmoniously conducted and that the benefits of former periods and of the present time may be continued as long as the necessity exists for the perpetuation of its labors.

The subjoined letter of Rev. Mr. Simpson, Chaplain, affords a satisfactory view of his services, and of the pleasant manner in which he receives the assistance of his brethren of the Christian Association.

---

United Seates General Hospital, Newton University,
*Baltimore, Maryland, August* 19, 1864.

G. S. Griffith, Esq., *Chairman of U. S. Christian Commission :*

Dear Sir:—Yours of the 10th instant, requesting me to give you a letter containing an account of my work as Chaplain of the United States General Hospital, Newton University, reached me on the 16th instant. I have been daily in the discharge of the duties appertaining to a Chaplain since my assignment to duty in this hospital by the Medical Director of the 8th Army Corps, the 18th of July, 1862, to the present date, save a leave of absence of fifteen days, during which time my place was supplied by an efficient ministerial brother of your Commission, for whose services I feel very thankful. Since my report to you of September 1863, I can add little but what will be a repetition of what was reported you then. Every thing seems to move on in the same noiseless manner in the internal management of the affairs of this hospital as heretofore. Discipline, as far as I can ascertain, is well maintained. The Surgeon in charge is untiring in his efforts to promote the comfort of of the inmates of the hospital. The sick and wounded are well cared for temporally and spiritually. The mortality since my last report to you, has been less in proportion to the number that has been in the hospital than heretofore.

Your Commission furnished me weekly with suitable reading matter in the form of religious newspapers and tracts for distribution. Letter paper, envelopes and pens, have also been given me by your Commission for distribution to the inmates of the hospital, not having money in hand to purchase them. I take great pleasure in acknowledging a donation of several valuable books, numbering forty-seven, to our soldiers library, from the Chairman of your Commission. This library is every day accessible to the inmates of the hospital desiring to receive books from it. Religious services are held every Sabbath afternoon, and the attendance upon the same good. Our weekly prayer meetings are quite interesting, and kept up with much spirit, and I trust conduce not a little towards maintaining the good order that now prevails among the soldiers in the hospital, and also to their spiritual improvement and growth in grace. I feel very grateful to some of the members of the Christian Association in aiding me in conducting our weekly prayer meetings.

In visiting from time time the sick and wounded in the hospital and performing the duties incumbent upon me as a Chaplain, I am encouraged in my labors by the hearty welcome I receive from all with whom I converse and pray as regards their preparation for death and a coming judgment. My heart's desire and prayer to God for all over whom I am placed by the Government as a spiritual guide is, they may be saved from sin and eternal death, and be made monuments of God's saving grace, and that I may not prove a stumbling block over which any may stumble and fall into the gulf of perdition.

Very truly yours,
F. W. SIMPSON,
Chaplain, U. S. A.

---

In the following note, Miss Rice, President of the Ladies' Association of the hospital expresses her thanks and those of the ladies in relation to their connection with the Christian Commission in the labors of the Newton University Hospital:

*Baltimore, August* 30, 1864.

TO THE CHRISTIAN COMMISSION:

GENTLEMEN:—The Ladies' Association of Newton University Hospital in acknowledging the donations of money and other articles sent them at various times by the Christian Commission, desire to return their especial thanks for them, as by their timely and liberal aid their Association has been often helped in their utmost need, and when without such aid they would have been obliged to cease their efforts in behalf of the sick and wounded under their care.

Very respectfully,
E. E. RICE,
President Ladies' Association,
Newton University Hospital.

---

The report of the Committee of the Christian Association is brief but expresses the interest and the satisfaction of the Committee in the performance of their Christian labors:

*Baltimore, August* 30, 1864.

TO THE COMMITTEE OF THE CHRISTIAN COMMISSION:

GENTLEMEN:—In making our annual report of the Committee of the Christian Association in attendance upon Newton University Hospital, I beg leave to say that we have attended the prayer meetings regularly. They have been held on Thursday nights. We have often had the most interesting meetings with the patients, which have resulted in profit to ourselves, and we have reason to hope, no less so to the patients. Brothers W. F. Cary and Brown, Drs. Peck and Burlingame have been associated in assisting the Chaplain in the management of these meetings. The patients are always requested to take part in the exercises, which some do doubtless to their own individual benefit as well as to the benefit of others. I have myself been greatly profited by the exercises as conducted by the soldiers, and have heard some of my brethren express the same sentiment.

Yours respectfully,
On behalf of the Committee,
THOS. COGGINS.

---

**Officers' Hospital.**

Dr. B. A. Vanderkeift, Surgeon in Charge.

Rev. H. C. Henries, of the Methodist Episcopal church, Chaplain.

Capacity 409. Patients 297.

The Officers' Hospital occupies one of the buildings of the Naval School at Annapolis. It is fitted up with excellent accommodations appropriated exclusively to sick and wounded officers of the army service. A number of very worthy gentlemen, who have proved themselves to be brave and competent officers, are quartered in the wards of this properly ordered institution. In many instances wounded officers obtain permission to be removed to their homes where they receive the attention they desire from their families. There are cases, however, in which such removal is attended with inconvenience, and others in which it is impossible. Wounds of a dangerous character often render it necessary that the patient shall be conveyed to the nearest place provided for the purpose, and that immediate and constant attention shall be afforded him.

The institution, known formerly as the "Naval School at Annapolis" is easy of access both by land and water, and patients can be conveyed to it perhaps more readily than to any other place where the conveniences are as considerable and the situation as eligible in regard to both attractiveness and purity of air. The site of the hospital is on the Severn river, within a few miles of the Chesapeake Bay, into which the view opens upon an expanse of water stretching much farther than the sight can reach. The inequalities of land on either side, as the beholder looks out into the Bay, are picturesque, and beautiful; farm houses and farm lands in various stages of progress in cultivation present themselves to the view. At the season of their appearance, the wild swan are seen in large numbers, along the shores, and game fowl in abundance, such as geese and ducks, are ever upon the wing, or feeding in the inlets of the river and bay. Ducking grounds are dotted over the shores, and the hunter is frequently seen in pursuit of his amusing, and sometimes profitable employment. The surrounding waters are rich in their provision of the finest oysters, and salt water fish of almost every kind are swarming in their depths.

A more pleasant situation could hardly be found for the quartering of the army officers when disabled by sickness, or the casualties of the battle-field. The convalescing enjoy without stint the attractive view the landscape presents, and when allowed by their physicians, the luxuries in which both land and water abound.

One of our Chaplains, the Rev. Isaac O. Sloan, who has been serving several months in Annapolis in Division Hospital Nos. 1 and 2, and the Officers' Hospital, has given us cheering accounts of his services. Among the wounded officers who received his ministrations there have been gentlemen of wealth and distinction, some of them brother clergymen, all of whom have expressed their thankfulness for his kind and Christian labors among them. Repeated evidences of his Christian effort and their appreciation by those he served are upon the records. He speaks of his association with the Officers' Hospital and of the friendships contracted there with interest and pleasure, and will doubtless long remember the expressions of gratitude and blessings that have followed him while in pursuit of his noble work. Surely it were not for time to tell over all that has been done by the Chaplains and delegates and agents of the Christian Commission in this God-like service. It must be left for the revealments of eternity to disclose the thousands of cases in which temporary friendships—friendships of affliction—have been realized, and then passed away. Not forever is the passage of those fleeting realities. They were but momentary in the hospital and in the field, but they will be as durable as eternity in the world that is yet to be. These are thoughts that cheer the heart of God's servant as he imitates the example of his Divine Master and follows in the footprints He left upon the earth when He went about doing good From the correspondence of Mr. Sloan with the subjects of his interest, we select the following:

OFFICERS' HOSPITAL, ANNAPOLIS, MARYLAND,
*August* 27, 1864.

REV. I. O. SLOAN:

DEAR BROTHER:—Permit me to express to you and through you to the United States Christian Commission, my heartfelt gratitude for your personal kindness to me and the needed and timely aid afforded me by the Commission here and at Washington, in a time of sickness and destitution.

On my way South to join my regiment last spring, I lost all my clothing, and everything I took with me, excepting what I had on my person. I had not the funds to purchase things necessary to my comfort, and in a short time after joining the regiment, by reason of exposure, fatigue, &c., became sick, and was sent to the hospital, where I have been since the fifteenth of June.

Through somebody's neglect or mistake, I have not been able, as yet, to get any pay, and what I should have done, but for this and kindred agencies, the Lord knows, but I know not. At any rate, through these, God has supplied me with many comforts, for which I am truly and deeply thankful. Most heartily do I say what is said by thousands—"God bless the Christian Commission."

I have been at the hospital here and in Washington for between two and three months, and in both places have seen, day after day and week after week, the working of this benevolent agency, and *I know* it is doing a great, good, and *necessary* work. It is managed with wisdom and fidelity, *and in the best manner.* Its agents and delegates, Christian men, visit the needy personally, learn their wants, and administer to their wants, temporal and spiritual, according to their *personal* knowledge and judgment. No tongue can tell or pen describe the amount of good they are doing. God only knows, and eternity alone can reveal the suffering relieved, lives saved, and souls converted through this truly Christian agency.

The Christian community may well have perfect confidence in the Christian Commission. Funds and stores committed to its charge will be sure to reach the objects for which they are intended, and through it Christians are following the example of the Master, who, when on earth, went about doing good; especially to the sick, the suffering, and the sorrowing.

Again, with thousands of others who have witnessed and felt its blessed Christian influence, I say, "God bless the Christian Commission."

Fraternally yours,

N. RICHARDSON,

Chaplain 36th Mass. Vols.

---

U. S. OFFICERS HOSPITAL, ANNAPOLIS, MD.

*August* 30*th*, 1864.

DEAR BROTHER SLOAN:—Permit me, through you, to bear my testimony for the U. S. Christian Commission.

This is truly a Christian Institution; it is doing a great and important Christian work, and *in a Christian manner.* Its agents and delegates are good and faithful men; imitating their Master in going about doing good. I know of no other institution which is doing as much work, and doing the work so well for the sick, wounded and needy soldiers. The spiritual as well as the temporal wants of the sufferers are considered and relieved. Time can never tell the good which, in both these directions, the Commission is accomplishing. Thousands of soldiers are exclaiming "God bless the Christian Commission," and with all my heart, I say "God bless the Christian Commission." You, sir, as the agent for the Commission at this hospital, are *emphatically* "*the right man in the right place.*" This is saying much, but none too much. God bless the agent and his work. Indeed the prayer is answered, for *God is blessing him and his work.* This testimony is from experience and observation.

Let the Christian public place full confidence in this truly Christian agency, and keep its treasury full, with all the other means necessary for its continued and increasing usefulness. Above all, and more important than all, let unceasing and fervent prayer be offered for God's continued blessing on it and all the subjects of its benevolent work.

Fraternally yours,

N. RICHARDSON,

Chaplain 36th Mass. Vol's.

We desire thankfully to add our names to the above.

CHAS. B. KEYES,

Chaplain 9th N. Y. Cav'y.

JOHN H. ALLEY,

Captain and C. S. V.

U. S. A. OFFICERS HOSPITAL, ANNAPOLIS, MD.
*August* 30, 1864.

REV. I. O. SLOAN:

In duty to myself and the many interested ones, I feel like expressing to you as one of its noble agents here, my high appreciation of the good work of the "U S. Christian Commission" in behalf of the soldier. My observation of its workings both in field and hospital have led me to regard its agents as "angels of mercy" on visits of love to the weak, sick, wounded, and dying; and while seeking to smooth over his hardships and deprivations, and allay temporal sufferings, they would not forget the eternal and spiritual welfare of those they succor, and as they bind up their wounds and cool their fevered brow, pour into their hearts the "oil of joy and gladness," by their words of cheer and comfort, leading the suffering ones to bless God that there is such an institution in the land as the "U. S. Christian Commission," with its faithful votaries. Could the people at home realize the beauties of its workings by experience as I have, then I am sure its coffers never would become depleted or its supplies run short as long as there was one suffering defender of our nation's honor remaining for them to bestow their charities upon.

The friends at home need have no fear of its agents proving unfaithful to the trust reposed in them, as they are not actuated to engage in the work by the love of money, most of them being volunteers, coming among us with hearts fired with a love for the work of salvation, temporally and spiritually, of the soldier.

With a hearty God speed the "U. S. Christian Commission," and further on its noble efforts,

I am most respectfully,
A. H. HOLLISTER,
1st Lieutenant U. S. A.

---

### Division No. 1, General Hospital.

Dr. B. A. Vonderkeift, Surgeon in charge.

Rev. H. C. Henries, of the Methodist Episcopal Church, Hospital Chaplain.

Capacity, 1117. Patients, 1089.

All the buildings of the Naval School, except that occupied by the Officers Hospital, are appropriated to the service under the title of Division No. 1, General Hospital. The grounds covered by the buildings with the extensive areas around them, extend over several acres. The lawns and lanes between and around the buildings, are green and beautiful, interspersed with trees and shrubbery, and presenting a very pleasant and attractive appearance. Most of the buildings were elegant residences, erected by the Government for the use of the Officers and Professors of the Naval School. At the commencement of the war, by order of the President of the United States, the Naval School was removed to Newport, Rhode Island, and the quarters of the various agents and employees of the institution were dedicated to hospital uses. To such uses they have been applied ever since.

From our correspondence we learn of Surgeon Vonderkeift, that he is "a strict disciplinarian and a great worker; rises early, is a great organizer and possesses a large share of executive ability." Says one of our correspondents "I will venture to say that no General Hospital in this country is better managed either for the Government or for the soldiers who enjoy its benefits."

It is truly gratifying to receive such testimonial in behalf of an officer occupying a place of such responsibility as that of Surgeon of so large and important a hospital. We have no personal acquaintance with Surgeon Vonderkeift, but we have noticed on our visits to his premises, sufficient to convince us that the report made of him is true. Frequently on our passage through the wards and over the grounds have we remarked that the whole premises were managed with consummate ability. Nor did we on all our rounds hear a single expression that was indicative of anything but kindness and humanity on the part of the Surgeon.

Division No. 1 is one of the most extensive and important of the hospitals of our district. It accommodates a large number of patients and is generally well occupied and by the most disabled of the wounded soldiers. In its proximity to the passages, both of land and water, leading from the battlefields, it is readily accessible, and its situation of salubrity and extent of territory, renders it a desirable depot for the war worn and wounded soldier. It is well that it is in the hands of one who is both able and willing to distinguish himself in its management.

The same correspondence from which we obtain our information in regard to Surgeon Vonderkeift, informs us of the ability and faithfulness of his assistants. The acting assistants when our correspondent wrote, were fourteen in number, among whom Surgeon Wm. S. Ely is represented as being distinguished for his Christian-like behaviour and gentlemanly deportment.

Twenty hospital attendants in the persons of ladies, who are ministering in the wards, are spoken of in terms of high commendation. At the head of these at the time at our correspondent wrote was Mrs. Tyler, known familiarly in this State as Sister Tyler. We knew Sister Tyler formerly as the Principal of the Church Home of this city, which was commenced under her superintendence, and was so continued for several years. The Church Home is one of the most extensive and useful of the benevolent institutions of our city. We visited it frequently while it was under the superintendence of Sister Tyler, and what we were surprised at more than anything else, in the working of the institution, was the small amount of means appropriated to its use. The services of such a co-laborer are invaluable in a situation requiring the exercise of so many of the qualities that make up a great and noble woman. Sister Tyler is not now connected with the hospital. She has sought another sphere for the exercise of her extended abilities. We hope she may be spared for a long life of labor in the cause. Of the band of ladies in the service, our correspondent says "they are truly noble women and too much cannot be said in their praise." Mrs. Maria M. C. Hall, supplies the place of Mrs. Tyler as the Directress of the Ladies Relief Association.

The Chaplain, by whom almost every portion of the hospital and its grounds were shown to us, possesses a large share of executive ability, and is one of the most active and industrious of the officers of his grade in the army. In a communication which we have received from him, he represents his position as being between the living and the dead; one moment attending the bedside of the dying patient, the next on his way to deposit the remains of one departed in the grave. After severe battles this condition has doubtless been feelingly realized on several occasions.

Especial notice is taken by Chaplain Henries, of order No. 42, of Dr. Simpson, Medical Director, in relation to the proper respect that should be shown to soldiers that had perilled and lost their lives in the service of their country. Writing upon the subject he says, "I have frequently two funeral occasions in a day, and not unfrequently bury from three to four at a time. I am happy to state that the burial services of our dead are now conducted in a manner which must prove highly satisfactory to the friends of those who fall in our midst. The services are performed in the chapel in the presence of the Medical Officer of the day, the escort, and frequently of a large number of soldiers. Thanks to the Medical Director of the Eighth Army Corps for his circular regulating this matter."

The experience of Chaplain Henries is the same as that of a number of his brother Chaplains on the subject. The circular has had its effect in suggesting the means by which a decided reformation has been effected in one of the most delicate and important relations the chaplaincy holds to both the living and the dead. Upon this subject Chaplain Henries writes as follows:

"It may not be improper here to speak of the form of our burial service. The bodies of the deceased, under escort, are brought to the chapel; the coffins are placed upon a table in front of the altar, and the American flag is thrown over them; lady nurses, in whose wards they had died, put upon the coffin wreathes of flowers gathered and made by their own hands. The service commences by the singing of an appropriate piece by the choir, accompanied by the organ; then prayer is offered, reading selected portions of Scripture, remarks, singing and benediction. All occupy from twenty to thirty minutes. We then repair to the cemetery, already thickly strewn with the noble dead, some two miles distant, accompanied by the escort. This is the form of our burial service in sixty-three. Let us compare this to the number of buried in sixty-one. Then in one-half hour after the soldier's decease he was placed in his coffin and almost immediately borne to the grave, without religious services. In attending the first funeral after entering upon duty at this hospital. I had no escort, and frequently only a colored man and the driver of the ambulance in attendance, and was obliged myself to assist in the burial; then to perform the religious services in the presence of only the above persons. Thus it was in sixty-one, and I felt it my imperative duty to take some step that would assure the soldier more respect and better meet the desire of his friends. I accordingly presented the facts to Brigadier General Hatch, then commandant of the post. He very promptly furnished me with escort and bearers, and the authorities have continued to furnish the same, and thus have paid that tribute of respect to the dead, that the Union soldier is so justly entitled to. The religious interest in the hospital is good, and our meetings, public and social, are well attended. Many are inquiring what they shall do to be saved, and never were there a class of men more readily approached on the subject of personal religion than are the inmates of this hospital. We have many earnest and faithful laborers in the vineyard of the Lord; and although we have had several hundred leave the hospital, and among them many of our best and most intelligent Christian young men, yet God has not left Himself without a witness, but is raising up others to take their places and to carry on the work. Many have found peace with God through our Lord Jesus Christ upon their sick beds, some just before their departure from this life; others as they have slowly recovered have given good evidence of the real change God has wrought in them, many realizing the great goodness of God in his preserving mercy, and on their restoration to health have dedicated themselves to him and his service, by an open confession of faith in Christ, and a consistent character. This war, notwithstanding its terrible results, has been, in many instances, the means of developing Christian character, and, in my opinion, many a soldier will go to Heaven from the battle-field and hospital, who, under other circumstances, might not have given themselves to prayer and preparation for eternity."

In closing his interesting communication, the Chaplain writes as follows:

"I wish now to say a word in regard to the "Christian Commission." It gives me great pleasure to acknowledge valuable assistance rendered by its delegates. Their labors have been most acceptable, and have had a very salutary influence. Let me state that we have received at this hospital, from time to time, valuable reading matter for distribution, consisting of tracts, papers and books, and I wish to suggest that we should be most happy to receive them, as they come from the publishers weekly and monthly, for nothing is more acceptable to the men than papers—*new* papers. We need about two thousand monthlies, and as many weeklies as you can send us. I wish also to state that we need the services of at least one man constantly, which I hope the Commission will find it in their power to send me. We desire most earnestly to return our thanks to the Commission for hospital stores, clothing, &c., received at various periods. After the battle of Gettysburg your donation to this hospital was bountiful and timely. In fact, I hardly know what we could have done without stores, bandages, &c., sent from your Commission. Let me call your attention to the fact that our wants at this hospital are more pressing and numerous than at any other hospital in the country, from the fact that all the paroled prisoners arrive here from Richmond, and they come to us in the most destitute condition imaginable. Their tattered garments are so filthy that we are obliged to throw them away. Those men who have suffered almost everything but death, are coming to us by every flag of truce. You will therefore see that not only after battles do we need supplies, but constantly, especially for the above class of patients. The means being furnished by a grateful people, we hope it may be in your power to meet these demands. There is one thing more, perhaps, I should speak of. We have upon an average some fifty commissioned officers, who, by reason of wounds, and sickness, report here for examination before a board constantly in session, when they are admitted into the hospital for medical treatment. But I will no longer trespass upon your patience with these details, and will close by bidding you and all associated in this grand and glorious work of relieving the sufferings of our soldiers and sailors, God speed! And may I exhort you to continue your efforts with vigor as long as a sufferer remains in our noble army or navy! These brave defenders are worthy your best efforts and the people's greatest gifts.''

H. C. HENRIES, Chaplain.

The Chaplain's meetings for preaching and prayer are held on Sundays and during the week. They are of a most interesting and profitable character. The prayer meetings are well attended and highly estimated by the soldiers. Many express their thankfulness in their use, and frequently hold conversations in relation to the spiritual benefits they receive through their agency.

There is a Sunday School in operation in this hospital.

Of this Sunday School, soldiers are teachers and soldiers are pupils, and they work together harmoniously and earnestly in the mutual benefits they are conferring upon each other. The teachers, no less than the pupils, acknowledge the spiritual advantages they possess in their Sunday School engagements. The supervision of the School is under Chaplain Henries, who gives it as much attention as his other numerous labors admit of. There is great good done to the soldiers through the agency of the Sunday School. The religious exercises in which they engage in the school, prepare them for the reception of greater benefits from the services of the Chapel than they could otherwise secure. Many who have attended the school and the public worship, have declared the richness of the spiritual enjoyment they have experienced and felt in their hearts to bless God that He had wrought upon His servants as to induce them to institute such means of religious instruction for their benefit. We hope this feature of the Sunday service may be continued and extended, and that very great spiritual benefits may be realized in its use.

The importance of the station, and the great labor necessary in the performance of its duties, seemed to demand of the Christian Commission all the help it could render to the chaplaincy. Accordingly, the Rev. I. O. Sloan, who had been some time in our service and had attained a high degree of experience in the duties required, was sent to the Division where he has been laboring several months and is still laboring. If the bodies of a thousand men who are disabled by the damages of war require the attendance of fourteen or fifteen Surgeons, surely the souls of the same number require the services of more than one Chaplain. It is yet surprising, notwithstanding the many improvements that have been made in the religious department of the army, that so little provision is apparent for the performance of its all-important and necessary services. The Government allows a single Chaplain to a hospital, whether the number of patients be counted by hundreds or thousands. The present provision exhibits almost the lowest possible degree of respect for the service. Less might be regarded as a mockery and evince more of the desire to escape the charge of infidelity than of the design of rendering spiritual benefits to the defenders of our homes and laws.

The services of Mr. Sloan have been highly appreciated, both by Chaplain Henries and the suffering men under his charge. The work of the Christian Commission has been especially committed to his hands, and from him we have received at different periods, detailed accounts of his work. A statement of his labors will be found in another part of this report. The work of the Baltimore Christian Association is well represented at the Hospital in the person of Rev. Thos. Coggins.

The following communications indicate in part the value of the labors of the Commission's Chaplain at Annapolis:

U. S. General Hospital, Division No. 1.
*Annapolis, Md., Aug. 30th,* 1864.

Rev. I. O. Sloan:

Dear Sir:—Permit me through you to acknowledge my sense of the services the Christian Commission are rendering us in our work for the soldier at this hospital. Your ever ready supplies are among the most valuable aids we have. Your manifold chests, barrels and boxes, apparently containing all manner of necessities and comforts that even *whimsical* sick men can imagine needful.

Your recent supplies of wine and brandy have proved invaluable in many cases of extreme prostration, both from amputation and sickness.

Your own ready sympathy and help, personally, in the physical and spiritual needs of our patients, especially commands my gratitude and respect.

May you long be spared, and may God prosper and bless the noble Commission you represent.

Yours truly,
Maria M. C. Hall,
Directress of Ladies attending on the sick and wounded.

The letter of Mrs. Baldwin here presented, exhibits a single case of relief among many that might be noticed in a delicate and trying emergency. Far from home and among strangers, with a wounded husband, she had her hands and her heart full of the most exciting concern. The gratification was mutual in the relief afforded.

U. S. General Hospital,

*Annapolis, Md., Aug. 30th*, 1864.

Rev. I. O. Sloan:

My Dear Sir:—Allow me to express my gratitude to you for furnishing me with the means to reach my home in Illinois, 1,700 miles away. After my husband was wounded and brought here I came to attend him during his suffering. I expected he would receive his pay from the Government, but he did not receive a cent, so I have been left entirely destitute, and if it were not for your aid I don't know what I should do. The Lord reward you and bless the Christian Commission, the noble organization which you represent. My husband, if God spares him, will undoubtedly return you the $20 you loaned me for the purpose of returning to my home. Very respectfully,

Mrs. Mary M. Baldwin.

---

### Division No. 2, General Hospital.

Dr. G. S. Palmer, Surgeon in charge.

Rev. J. P. Hammond, of the Protestant Episcopal Church, Chaplain.

Capacity, 671. Patients, 326.

This hospital occupies the buildings of St. John's College. These buildings are situated in one of the most beautiful as well as one of the most healthy parts of Annapolis. They are about half a mile distant from the grounds formally occupid by the Naval School and now by the Officers' Hospital and Division No. 1, of the General Hospital. The convalescing patients amuse themselves on the College grounds on the green lawn and in Summer beneath the shade of the trees. Their quarters are as beautiful as they are comfortable, affording every facility for exercise and enjoyment.

We have received no word from any one connected with this hospital, except the excellent Chaplain, we can therefore say nothing of its surgical department or that of the ladies association. We know the Chaplain personally, and are well enough acquainted with his character to believe that his work is performed well and faithfully. His intelligence and industry are warrants for his capability and activity, and we are satisfied that he is not behind the most faithful and efficient of his brethren in the discharge of his duties.

The appearance of the wards and other apartments indicate great care and attention. Neatness and cleanliness and comfort are every where apparent. It sometimes happens that the hospital is overcrowded with patients, when it becomes necessary to erect tents in the lawn and in the yard in which to accommodate them.

The worthy Chaplain of Division No. 2, gives the following statement of his labors, exhibiting in brief an extended service. His activity and industry are indicated in the number of his official acts. The good effect of the circular of the Medical Director of the District was experienced in his presence, and highly esteemed. In conversation with him, we have learned how highly he valued the encouragement of a humane and moral service by this officer.

St. John's College Hospital,
*Annapolis, August* 30, 1864.

Rev. and Dear Brother:—In answer to your request that I would give you some account of the Chaplain's work in this hospital, I herewith send you a brief statement of my labors for the year ending October 1st, 1864. During this period I have held four hundred and five (405) public services and prayer meetings; have preached twice on every Sunday, and delivered an address at each prayer meeting. I have attended one hundred and twenty-seven (127) funerals, of which fifty-two were in the month of April last, and thirty-two in September last. The great mortality of these two periods were owing to the fact of large arrivals of sick and wounded prisoners from Richmond at these particular times.

I have also been engaged in the constant distribution of religious reading matter throughout the entire hospital. That I have been able to do so has been owing entirely to the fact that the Christian Commission has kept me well supplied with tracts, papers, &c. For this and every other good work in which this noble organization is engaged, I would return my heart felt thanks to it, and to God who put it into the hearts of His people to enter upon so glorious an undertaking.

During the month of August last, a circular was sent from the Medical Director of this department to every medical officer in the respective hospitals of the same, enjoining upon them the duty of co-operating with Chaplains in the work which they have been commissioned by the President to perform, and earnestly urging upon them the importance of attending Divine service, and using "their utmost efforts to suppress profanity and other vices that tend so greatly to degrade the soldier."

This circular has been a great encouragement to all hospital Chaplains in this department, for it assures them that their work is not looked upon with indifference by our worthy Medical Director.

Did my time permit I should be glad to furnish you a more extended account of my work. But it is without doubt the same as that of other Chaplains, and consists of temporal and spiritual ministration to the convalescent, the sick and wounded, and the dying. May God give us all grace and ability to perform it faithfully.

Yours truly in Christ,

J. P. HAMMOND,

Hospital Chaplain, U. S. A.

Rev. J. N. M'JILTON, D.D.

---

### Annapolis Junction.

Dr. C. Bacon, Assistant Surgeon, in charge.

Capacity 290. Patients 240.

Annapolis Junction is about midway between Baltimore and Washington cities, on the Washington Branch of the Baltimore and Ohio Railroad. It is about equi-distant, say nineteen miles from each of the cities of Baltimore, Washington and Annapolis. The site occupied by the hospital is passed on the north side by the Annapolis Branch, and on the west side by the Washington Branch of the Railroad. It is very nearly a continuous level, broken only by a slight elevation towards the east. The barracks, which are composed of wood, are arranged in rows with a space around which is used as a drill ground for convalescent patients, who are preparing to return to their regiments. The passages between the buildings, being generally flat, are rendered inconvenient in rainy weather by the thin mud which is peculiar to the soil, of whitish appearance and quite tenacious in its character. We happened to experience the inconvenience of passing the aisles of the camp on the occasion of a visit.

The spiritual services rendered to this hospital are but occasional. It has no Chaplain of its own, and is dependent for Chaplain's services upon the incumbents of hospitals at and near Annapolis. A number of our delegates have visited the premises, but no very favorable accounts have been given of their services. We had sent books, tracts, and religious newspapers for distribution among the patients, but we have no record to show how they were received, or what benefit was likely to result from their use. We may hope, however, that good seed has been sown, and that by the blessing of God it will bring forth its fruit.

The Acting Quartermaster of the hospital, Geo. McNeal, Esq., operates as a kind of local agent of the Commission in the administration of a portion of our department of the service. He assists us in the distribution of reading matter, and affording necessary facilities to visiting delegates.

The location of the hospital has but little to recommend it. There is a decided disadvantage in its proximity to the Railroad. It affords facilities for the convenience of loungers about the Junction, while delegates and visitors, who might render service in the premises are indisposed to stop while on their way to the camps and hospitals of the adjacent cities.

### Camp Parole and Hospital.

Dr. T. R. Gross, Surgeon in charge.

Rev. G. H. Townsend, of the Methodist Episcopal Church, Acting Chaplain.

Rev. Erastus Colton, of the Methodist Episcopal Church, Assistant Acting Chaplain.

Capacity of Hospital 2,000. Patients 1,831.

The following statistics of the camp have been furnished by the Acting Chaplains, who are in the service of the Christian Commission:

*Statistics of Officers, Surgeons and Soldiers, in Camp Parole, from September* 1, 1863, *to September* 1, 1864.

| | | |
|---|---|---|
| The Camp at present will accomodate, men | 7,000 | |
| " " " officers | 200 | |
| Aggregate capacity of accommodations | —— | 7,200 |
| Number of paroled prisoners who have been in camp during the year | 6,395 | |
| Number of convalescents, since June 1, 1864 | 3,550 | |
| Number of Surgeons, since June 1, 1864 | 15 | |
| Number of officers now in camp | 40 | |
| Aggregate from data, for the year | | 10,000 |
| Paroled prisoners now in Camp Parole | 360 | |
| Convalescents now in Camp Parole | 1,662 | |
| Officers now in Camp Parole | 40 | |
| Surgeons now in Camp Parole | 9 | |
| Number men on guard | 500 | |
| Aggregate number officers and men now in Camp | —— | 2,571 |
| Paroled Prisoners discharged from service | 163 | |
| Paroled Prisoners died | 13 | |
| Convalescents discharged from service | 16 | |
| Convalescents died | 10 | |
| Aggregate discharged and died | —— | 202 |
| Gone | | 7,200 |

The 7,227, denoted as *gone*, from this camp, consist of those who have been sent to their regiments; to Camp Chase, Ohio; to Benton Barracks, Missouri, and to Camp Distribution, Alexandria, Va.

All the foregoing facts were furnished by the Clerk at Head Quarters; but some of the items were defective in the record, or some of the actual events, as deaths, were not *reported*, perhaps, for record. There are no Rebel prisoners of war in this camp.

G. H. TOWNSEND,
Ag't U. S. C. C., and Act'g Chaplain,
Per ERASTUS COLTON,
Assis't & D. U. S. C. C.

Camp Parole, September 22, 1864.

About two miles from Annapolis and a short walk from the Railroad is the location of Camp Parole. It is on flat ground and surrounded on nearly all sides by shrubbery and trees. The situation is retired, and enjoys advantages of good supplies of water and pure air. The buildings are of wood and regularly arranged. Although working under the title of Camp Parole, and used as the place of temporary residence of the paroled men of the Federal Army, there is in connection with the camp one of the largest of the hospitals of the district. We have learned that over two thousand of the sick and disabled have been crowded into the hospital department. Until the present period we have not been able to secure the appointment of a Chaplain for the camp, although as many as thirty-two thousand men have been located there at one time. The Committee used every possible means for several months to secure a permanent supply of religious services for the camp without being able to accomplish it. At length a few Christian ladies, of years of experience, undertook the work. At the risk of neglect and ill treatment, they provided themselves shelter by the erection of wooden buildings, and made their residence among the large number, not less than seven to eight, reaching to over thirty thousand men, some of them among the most vicious and abandoned characters in the army. Through the perseverance of these noble spirited ladies, the work of reformation was commenced, and it was carried on until a change for the better was perceptible in every portion of the camp. For two years and a half all the religious services rendered the camp and hospital have been supplied by the Christian Commission.

The officers and Surgeons of the Camp during the first months of its existence were greatly troubled and perplexed by the conduct of the men. It was with great satisfaction that they beheld the work of reformation in its progress. They are represented as kind and gentlemanly in their treatment of those under their authority and care. Much of their kindness and gentlemanly treatment was lost upon characters, who appeared as though they could not appreciate the favor, much less render a return in kind for its bestowal.

Through the instrumentality of the ladies, assisted by our Committee, and by delegates, some of whom were clergymen sent by us for the purpose, the Government was induced to erect a Chapel for religious services. The building is over eighty feet in length and accommodates several hundred persons. In this Chapel meetings are held on Sunday for preaching, and as many as seven to ten prayer meetings and experience meetings have been held during the week. Often during these services the building has been crowded to overflowing by men, who before, either cared but little for religious worship, or denounced it as foolish and effeminate. These men have anxiously and earnestly inquired, what they must do to be saved, and with great eagerness, some of them have obeyed the directions given them, and with repentant tears and purposes of amendment, they have sought and found the way of life.

The Rev. G. H. Townsend and the Rev. Erastus Colton are now acting as Chaplains of the camp and hospital under our direction. Reports from those gentlemen show the necessity of their presence as well as afford a view of the important service they are rendering.

Social meetings are held in the Chapel and in the barracks and tents, during which, the Scriptures are read and conversed upon, and the men express their experience to one another and pledge themselves mutually in purposes of amendment. Many a tale of wickedness and penitence and prayer and amended life, has been told in these meetings and many a pledge has been given and received to pursue the better path.

The following letter from the Rev. G. H. Townsend tells an interesting story of labor and success among the varied characters of Camp Parole:

CAMP PAROLE, August 24, 1864.

G. S. GRIFFTH ESQ., *Chairman Md. Com. Christian Committee:*

DEAR SIR:—You doubtless are aware that the addition of some two thousand sick and wounded soldiers to this camp within a few weeks has greatly increased the care and responsibility of the Christian Commission here, devolving upon your agent an amount of labor and anxiety that causes him to feel at times, after exerting all his energies, that the work must still suffer for lack of service. I am happy to be enabled to report the spiritual condition of the camp as very encouraging. I have been here nearly three months, and have attended on an average as many as seven meetings per week in the Chapel, besides funerals and ward meetings, attending upon, and conversing and prayer with, and writing for the sick and wounded. The meetings have been very well attended. The Chapel, though some eighty feet or more in length, has often been so crowded that we have had to fill the aisles with extra seats. No week, I think, has passed without some soul being brought to Christ. And some weeks would average one or more each day who professed to find the Saviour. The Surgeons as well as other officers have been very kind, affording every needed facility for visiting and holding meetings in their several wards. Our social meetings are often seasons of great interest.

One says: "I have been a very great sinner. When at home my mother would pray and I would swear. I came to this camp very wicked and profane. But the other evening, while attending meeting here I thought this would never do, and I made up my mind to live a different life, to stop swearing and begin to pray; and I want you all to pray for me." A paroled man said: "When I was in a Rebel prison, without thinking much of my sins, I prayed earnestly to be delivered out of the hands ofthe Rebels, and the Lord heard my prayers and delivered me. Since I came to Camp Parole I have felt that I was a sinner, and I have been asking God to forgive my sins and He has done it, and I am happy." Another said: "I love my Bible. I learned to love it when, by Rebel hands, I daily expected to be led out and shot, as I was threatened, and as numbers of my comrades were. But I never loved it as I do now." One in substance, said: "I feel since I came to this Camp as though I had got at least half way to heaven. For I am sure that the transition from here to heaven cannot be much greater than from Richmond here." Another tremblingly arose and said: "This is the first time I ever attempted to speak in a religious meeting. I was brought up a Catholic; but I have been reading the Bible, which has shown me that I was a great sinner, and pointed me to the Saviour. I have come to that Saviour and he as forgiven me my sins." A German said: "When I came to this country at twenty-two years of age I had never seen a Bible. I obtained one, read it, and was led to renounce the errors of my life, and to embrace the pure gospel of Christ. My mind has been so enlightened by it that I want every body to read the Bible and see how much more intelligent and happy they will be."

### PRIVATE INTERVIEWS.

A wounded soldier came to my room one day saying: "When I enlisted, I belonged to the B— church, but I soon allowed myself to be led astray, and then withdrew from the church. Now I am very far away." I conversed and prayed with him, and then lent him a book on prayer. The next day he came again, his countenance lit up with a smile of joy, saying: "O Chaplain, I am so thankful for your counsel and for that book you lent me. It has been the means of bringing me back to the Saviour, and I once more have peace."

One day, a man apparently in deep concern about his soul, approaching me asked a private interview. I invited him to my room, when he stated that he had experienced religion since he joined the army and had been baptized. "But," said he, "I have been led away and lost my religion. I have been wishing for some time to come to see you, but was afraid. I have been praying, but God does not hear my prayer. What shall I do?" I conversed and prayed with him, and he prayed. The Lord heard his prayer, and he left rejoicing in hope. A Lieutenant, who had just been dishonorably dismissed from service, came to me for counsel and help. I conversed and prayed with him. He wept bitterly. But I fear it was more on account of disgrace incurred than sins committed. I told him plainly that while I deeply sympathized with him, I saw no help, unless he would cease to imbibe and begin to pray. He offered to pay me to go and see his father and some influential friends in his State. But I told him that the friend he needed most could be found without going out of the State. I fear he will make flesh his arm and inherit a curse.

### THE LONE ORPHAN.

Soon after I arrived here I observed in camp a sad but intelligent lad of some eleven summers, who proved to be the only child of a late wealthy lawyer in Jackson, Miss. His mother had died when he was but two years of age, leaving him the pet and pride of a fond father who would not allow his little Charlie to be separated from him, not even when doomed, for love of country, to a rebel prison, where, after eight months of solitude and privation, he died, leaving his little son unprotected and alone in the hands of enemies who had caused his own death. Charlie had just been sent with paroled prisoners to this camp. With the consent and advice of Col. R. I took him in charge, looked up his relatives and found for him in the family of a wealthy uncle in New York a hearty welcome and a pleasant home, where, in spite of the surroundings of wealth and the smiles of friends, Charlie will oft grow tearful and sad as he thinks of the cruel death of that affectionate father, whose remains are still in Rebel hands or planted in secession soil. May the Father of the fatherless protect and save him, so that inherited wealth may not hinder him from heaven.

### SAD BUT HOPEFUL.

A few days since, approaching a freight train from which more than one hundred sick and wounded soldiers had just been removed, I found lying alone in the straw nearly in a nude state, covered with filth and flies, a young soldier who at first appeared to be dead. Finding signs of life I applied stimulants until he revived so as to give his name and declare his faith and trust in Christ, and then sunk back into a state of unconsciousnes from which he never revived. I wrote to his father, a clergyman in Ohio, who called at my door a few evenings after and anxiously inquired after his son. Painful as it was I had to reply: "Your son is in his grave, or rather, I trust, in heaven." His voice trembled as he said; "This is the first breach death has been permitted to make in my family. I must be resigned. I am resigned. He was a pious boy. A son of great promise. Though not eighteen years of age he had entered his last year in college. He greatly excelled as a mathematician and linguist. He had only enlisted for one hundred days, and his time had nearly expired. I was counting the days when he would be home. Ah! but has he not gone home! Safely home! I must not complain. I would not have him back." We kneeled, and wept, and prayed together, and were greatly comforted.

I must not forget to mention that Rev. Brs. Tatlock and Colegrove were here about three weeks each during the summer, and rendered valuable and efficient services to the Christian Commission.

Your obedient servant,

G. H. TOWNSEND,

Agent U. S. C. C. Camp Parole, Md.

No Chaplain has been appointed by the Government for either the camp or the hospital. The Chaplain's services have been supplied by the Christian Commission. Rev. Messrs. G. R. Bent, I. O. Sloan, G. H. Townsend, Erastus Colton, Chas. Mallery, B. N. Hamilton, J. P. Merrill, J. Turbitt, C. Colegrove, J. D. Moore, M. T. Hill, J. Tatlock, have served at various periods. Messrs. Bent, Townsend and Colton have remained at the camp for lengthened periods, and have done much service in the management of religious services. The Rev. G. R. Bent as delegate and Chaplain of the Christian Commission, now our office agent, rendered very efficient service to this camp and its hospital. It was through his efforts that order and system were introduced in the religious services of both camp and its hospital. He conducted the meetings for worship and taught the men how to reverence God's sanctuary and to demean themselves towards each other as was becoming in persons living in a Christian land. Assisted by his inestimable lady, who was the courteous companion and helpmeet in his labors, he established a Sunday School which became an agency of great usefulness. The Bible class was taught by Mrs. Bent. Imagine a delicate and beautiful woman so full of desire to do good as to follow her husband to his field of labor among rude untutored men ; imagine such a woman surrounded by the uncultured subjects of her interests and instructing them in the elements of school study and in the truths of Christianity, pointing the listening objects of her anxious solicitude to Jesus the Saviour of sinners, and explaining to them the way of the soul's safety in the cross of Christ. Surely, in such imagination, the angel of Heaven's kindness appears in the communication of truth and counsels of love to the fallen,—the lowest among the fallen. And can it be believed that such ministrations shall be without effect. Such cannot be the result. It is impossible. God looks upon such scenes with approval and with purposes of blessing. The prayers of Mercy's angel ever offered for the lost, will be heard in Heaven and the answer will be returned in witnesses of success.

And what if the one so engaged, should fall a martyr to

her anxieties and labors? So did this noble woman. She persevered in her work, caring more for the souls of her charge than for herself, until she was stricken down by disease, when death made rapid work in the fall of his victim. Like a flower, when its beauty was most attractive and its fragrance the sweetest and most delightful, she faded and fell. A short illness was sufficient to cause her decline. She died in the camp, at her post of duty, and amid the hundreds to whom she had administered the instructions and consolations of religion. The death of the lovely martyr in the cause of humanity and of Christ, sent a thrill of most affectionate interest throughout the camp. Hardy men wept when they were told that the meek spirit had departed and the form they loved so well was left cold and still in death. They came for the last look upon the features they had so often witnessed in the animation of the spirit of religion, and when they beheld them calm and sweetly composed in death, it was impossible for them to restrain their grief, and many of them sobbed aloud in the bitterness of a sorrow that told that they deeply realized their irreparable loss. The dead still speaks. The impression made on many hearts cannot fade. It will be lasting. It will work still for Christ. The rough and hardy son of the camp will feel the force of her lovely example. It will nerve his arm in the battle. It will subdue his spirit in the camp and in social life. It will make him a better soldier and a better man. Live on sweet spirit, live on and labor on in thy home of Heaven. Thy work is not yet done. It is still in progress, and will yet bring many a penitent to the feet of Christ.

Such is the consolation that there is in Christ for the bereaved husband, who is still in the pursuit of his labors on behalf of the Commission. He left an important work behind him at Camp Parole to enter upon a still more important and more responsible position in the management of the affairs of our office. The business of the office has become so extensive as to render it necessary that the services of an agent should be secured. Mr. Bent is now performing this arduous agency, and finds as much as his hands can do and as fills his heart with deepest anxiety.

It was through the labors of Mr. Bent and his lady that a library of more than six hundred volumes was provided, and that books and tracts and religious newspapers to a very large extent were distributed among the men of the camp and the convalescents of the hospital. The library has received additions through the hands of Mr. Bent's successors in the service, and the work of distributing reading matter has been faithfully continued.

The Rev. O. M. McDowell, who has served the Commission in several important relations, and was for a time at Camp Parole, writes as follows in relation to the labors of Rev. Mr. Bent:

OFFICE OF U. S. CHRISTIAN COMMISSION.
*Baltimore, August 21st,* 1864.

By desire of Rev. G. R. Bent, General Agent of U. S. C. C. of Baltimore District, I beg leave to make the following statement: He is at present on a mission to Massachusetts:

The Rev. Mr. Bent was called to the work of the C. C. and took charge of Camp Parole in December 11th, 1863. He found no suitable place to carry on the work, but under his supervision, five good rooms were fitted up in good style. There had been no revival at this point. A spiritual dearth was prevailing when he took charge. Soon a revival commenced of great power and continued under his indefatigable labors until the roll showed 175 converted and reclaimed from sin. This result was reached before the following April. For the amounts received and disbursed at this place, see statistical report. The camp has been changed to Camp Convalescent, but will soon, probably, be called by its original name.

In the midst of his untiring devotion to the work and success, a cloud of affliction arose to darken the sky of his life. His wife, Mrs. C. A. Bent, who had interested herself in the S. S. department of this camp, was taken suddenly ill, March 1st, and after three days of suffering, departed this life for her home above. She was an affectionate wife and mother and a devotad colaborer. The affliction was so great and the desolation so complete, that our Brother dislikes to recur to this sad chapter in connection with this work at this point. As he was here some time, a much lengthier report would be justified. We close this report by the remark, that it is to be hoped that our Brother may detail some of the many interesting incidents that come under his personal notice.

O. M. McDOWELL.

A view of the present condition of the services of the Commission at the camp and hospital is afforded in a letter from the Rev. G. H. Townsend, recently received. The account of his encounter with a desperate character, and the manner in which, through God's assistance, the man of violence was reduced to the condition of a child will be read with interest.

CAMP PAROLE, *Maryland*, *August* 29, 1864.

DEAR BROTHER BENT:—I am happy to learn that you returned in safety from your visit to the early home, and present grave of your sainted wife. The fact that I occupy the very rooms where you spent so many happy hours together, during the last winter and spring, and lodge in the same bed from which she took her willing and triumphant flight to heaven is rather a source of *joy* than *gloom*. Is it not true that souls who are *united to Christ*, (*be they in the body or out*,) are also united to each other? If so, heaven cannot be far off. I was greatly disappointed in not seeing you when I visited Baltimore last. I trust you will not forget your repeated promise to visit this camp where, in former days your labors have been so greatly owned and blessed of God. As you are aware I was sent to Camp Parole last May somewhat against my wish, as I had previously set my face for the front. But now I see abundant reason for gratitude to God, as well as to the Christian Commission for directing my steps hither. For while it has thus far been one of the most laborious, it has also been one of the most happy and successful years of my life. I had not been one week in camp, before the Lord gave me a number of precious souls for my hire, and I think it safe to say that there has not been a week during the summer that some souls have not been brought to the Saviour. During the past month I have baptized twenty-eight, and six others have applied—not including those who have been hurried to the front—who have gone home on furloughs without being baptized, after expressing their desire. More than one hundred and twenty have joined the Soldiers Christian Association during the month. The work seems to be increasing in interest and power. Sometimes as many as forty have arisen requesting prayers, and twenty-five came forward one evening for conversation and prayer after the meeting had closed. More than one hundred tarried with them, until most of them found peace, and testified of the love of the Saviour. We hold meetings one hour every morning and every evening, except one, in the week. For a month or more I think no day has passed without some one being brought to Christ, and some days quite a number have professed to find pardon. Many ask and obtain private interviews with us, and a number have been converted, I trust, in our private room. I might give many individual cases of great interest, but have time for only one.

A wealthy Virginian who had been sent to this Camp, said to me one day, that there was no use of his trying to get religion, for if he had ever so much, he could not say three words without swearing. But soon after he began to attend the meetings, and three diffent times left the meeting in anger, thinking me personal in my remarks. The third time he stationed himself near the door, determined to knock me down when I came out. Ignorant of what was passing, I left the Chapel nearly the last one. Seeing a man standing alone in the dark, I approached him, took hold of his arm, and said, familiarly, "how are you getting on here?" He answered in a rather short but subdued manner, "not very well." I asked him to walk with me toward my quarters. As we passed along together, he said that he was a great sinner and feared there was no mercy for him. I did not recognize him until he referred to a previous conversation. I invited him into my room, where he informed me that during the Gilmor raid he had killed his own brother in the deadly conflict of battle, and was greatly troubled in mind in consequence of it. After much labor I succeeded in convincing him, that the killing of his brother whom he met in deadly strife—*a Rebel in arms*—furnished no obstacle in the way of his finding salvation. He bowed with us, wept, prayed, believed, and was saved. Now he can talk "three *words*," or, three *weeks* without swearing. He has joined the Soldiers Christian Association here, and is living for God.

Remember us in your prayers, and ask others to do so, for we stand in great need of help from God, to make us wise to win souls.

Brother E. Colton is furnishing timely and very efficient aid in the revival here. I think him peculiarly adapted to the work. We labor together in great harmony. He most undoubtedly has had souls as seals of his ministry in Camp Parole. I fear my strength would have failed before this, if he had not come to my aid. Long may he be spared to the church and to us.

Yours, fraternally,

G. H. Townsend,
Ag't U. S. C. C. & Act'g Chaplain,
Camp Parole, Maryland.

Rev. G. W. Bent, Gen'l Ag't U. S. C. C.

We append the narrative of his labors for six weeks by the Rev. Charles P. Mallery, of Philadelphia. His work will doubtless be long remembered by many among whom it was performed.

G. S. GRIFFITH, *President Maryland Branch C. C.*

On the 14th of April, I started for Annapolis, having received my out-fit of a blanket, haversack, badge, commission, &c., in company with several other delegates.

I was told to report myself at your office and was advised by you and Rev. G. R. Bent to go to Camp Parole, which I did, although I had started for Annapolis.

I found Camp Parole a commodious military fort with accommodations for seven thousand soldiers, although there were not that many there when I arrived, nor has there been that number there at any time during my service.

All of the buildings are frame—indeed I believe, there is but one tent on the grounds.

Each barrack, which contains one large room and one small office, can accommodate over one hundred men. The officers' buildings after the same pattern except that their barracks are divided into a number of small rooms. In one of these buildings the Christian Commission has its Head-Quarters. Here were its sleeping apartments, office and store-rooms.

It was our practice to start out with our haversacks over our shoulders, carrying books, papers, and tracts to the regiments of the Corps. One party would go in one direction and another in another.

In one of these excursions I called upon a regiment, in company with Mr. Color, a son of one of the Professors at Gettysburg College. We found the soldiers "at rest" in a field near their camp. We advanced to pay our respects to the Colonel, who was present, and to distribute reading matter among the men. As they had no Chaplain, we offered to supply them with a preacher, and were informed that such should be accepted "provided he had good common sense, a heart and a soul"—which qualifications seemed to be very necessary.

We did not always have the same reception—for we did not always deal with the same kind of men.

The hospital at Camp Parole consists of several large, clean, and airy buildings, averaging, when I was there, less than thirty patients each.

These buildings were well adapted to public service or individual conversation. Hospital ward No. 1, was used for the laying out of the dead, and also the funeral service was conducted there.

The first funeral at which I officiated was that of a boy of nineteen years, the next of a man three times as old.

The Reading-room was a long barrack like one of those used by the soldiers, except that the bunks were taken down. Reading and writing tables were there ; books, papers and magazines were furnished ; copy-books, letter-paper and envelopes were given, so that a soldier might profitably engage most of the day, for, being a paroled prisoner he was exempt from military duty until exchanged.

Part of this building was used for a Chapel, in which some meeting—either for preaching, prayer, or singing, was held almost every evening.

Two preaching services and a Bible class, and Sunday School were held on Lord's day.

Besides the work in the Chapel, there was the distribution in the camp, in the hospital, and to the soldiers leaving for their regiments. Before the cars would leave, I have gone through distributing reading matter as I went along, or throwing it to them from the outside.

I would also give a tract or two to soldiers who would call at the office for shirts, or handkerchiefs, or house wives, which was done often.

One day as I sat by the desk, Orderly Sergeant G———, came into the room. He was a German, and in broken English he told me that I had been the instrument, in God's hand, of his conversion. His countenance and actions, as he spoke, seemed to be those of one who had at last found a much desired object.

He had heard preaching in Germany, France and Switzerland, but never before had he heard the plan of salvation so satisfactorily set forth.

When he told me that he had been religiously brought up, and asked why it was he had not become a Christian before? He said that he had been taught that it was through his "deeds" that he was to be saved. Would that many more of our soldiers might let go such a delusion and trust in the only all-sufficient Saviour.

One day while in the hospital, I sat by the side of a soldier, as he related an incident or two, which occurred while he was in the hands of the enemy. I directed his thoughts to the all-important matter.

On a night after we held the conversation, I attended a prayer meeting in the room where he was. After service he called me to him and said, that what I had told him had led him to think on his way. May we so think as to cast every thought or word or work of his aside and trust in Christ alone.

One of the unpleasant—painfully unpleasant—duties, was that of answering letters of inquiry in reference to loved ones who had been captured and whose whereabouts were unknown. Perhaps they had died before they were exchanged, or were lying in some far off hospital, or perhaps in a soldier's graveyard they were buried, and the only thing to tell where they lay was the headboard marked "unknown."

I have served my "six weeks." Thankful am I, that I have been there, that my eyes have seen and my ears have heard the doings at Camp Parole. It will be a way-mark in my life, and I may be able hereafter to sit down, when my locks have grown grey and my voice is trembling, and tell of my experience there.

I may never meet again the soldiers to whom I have preached, and in whose ears I have spoken the glad tidings of salvation, but may they trust in that Saviour who alone can save, and I shall be happy.

Respectfully,

CHARLES P. MALLERY,
Ex-Delegate, C. C.

The subjoined statement of Rev. C. Turbitt affords a glance at the work of the camp and hospital which is gratifying and encouraging. Our Rev. brother occupied himself in his labors at the camp for two weeks when he left for another field. Doubtless he found the work as interesting and as important here as in any other department of his service.

CAMP PAROLE, *August* 15*th*, 1864.

G. S. GRIFFITH, ESQ., *Chairman Christian Commission, Baltimore:*

DEAR BROTHER:—Having spent some two weeks as Delegate of the Christian Commission, at Parole Camp, near Annapolis, Maryland, it must afford gratification to you, who have taken such a deep interest, and expended so liberally of your time, means, and labor in the noble cause, to learn that here, as in every other department of the field in which it has been my privilege to labor, a great and good work is going forward, admirably calculated to cheer the hearts of the benevolent every where.

Having on former occasions reported at some length, my operations in the service of the Commission in another field, and having been but a short time here, I purpose now to make only a very brief statement.

Every observant person, who has visited Parole Camp, must, I conceive, be fully satisfied, that both in a physical and moral aspect, it is a very interesting locality. Among the reflections awakened in his mind, is the vastly superior treatment received by our soldiers, to that received by troops of previous ages, especially of ancient times, and in other countries. What would the armies of ancient Greece and Rome, not to speak of less civilized nations, think of the punctilious attention paid to the material and spiritual comfort and welfare of our soldiery? The tide of benevolence, flowing in from all parts of our land, anticipates the wishes of our brave men, even down to the pins and pens, the nice note paper, the envelopes, the postage stamps, the comfort bags, and a host of other things too numerous to mention.

From the abundant stores of under garments you have been constantly sending us, we have dispensed freely in the hospital, and through the camp. Good flannel shirts, drawers, and socks, and even mittens, cravats and handkerchiefs, have not been withheld. No one considered deserving has been sent empty away; nor has there been any lack of delicacies in the shape of food for invalids in the hospital, the various wards of which are patterns of neatness and good order. A stranger entering these wards, can scarcely discover the slightest difference in the purity of the atmosphere, from that external to the building, whilst the inmates speak in rapturous terms of the comforts they enjoy, when contrasted with the miserable and cruel treatment they received whilst prisoners in the hands of the enemy at Belle Isle, and to which treatment we may trace the untimely death of not a few of them.

The Sanitary Commission have, under the superintendence of very estimable ladies, co-operated very abundantly and efficiently with your "Commission," in ministering especially to the physical comfort of the men. The surgeons are gentlemanly, faithful, and efficient. The officers and officials in Parole Camp, and in the 94th New York regiment, who guard the camp, are gentlemanly and courteous in their deportment; and best of all, some of them give evidence of being pious men. Under such a state of things, not only the hospital wards, but the whole camp, as you may readily anticipate, is characterized for the most punctilious neatness and good order.

But the most laudable and noble feature of the Christian Commission, and that which distinguishes it from some others, is, that whilst it by no means neglects the physical wants of our soldiers, but, like the good Samaritan, ministers abundantly to their bodily maladies, its special and principal mission, is to minister to the maladies of the mind. And how faithfully and efficiently has it labored, and what a glorious testimony has it given, to the heaven-born benevolence of the religion of the cross! and thus served, as we trust in no slight degree, to remove the scepticisms of the sceptic, and check the scoff of the infidel.

The usual routine of your delegate's duties consisted in his daily visiting, and delivering a short sermon or lecture, with the usual accompaniments, in as many different wards of the hospital. In addition to this, he engaged in preaching each evening in the chapel, and on all suitable occasions, conversing with numbers of the men on the subject of personal religion, and dispensing garments, &c., to the needy. In the duties of the Station, the Rev. Charles Mallery, a delegate of the Commission, cordially and promptly co-operated with me. While much solemnity often characterized the meetings, and personal conversation with the men, I have never discovered in Parole Camp, nor in any other part of the army where I have labored, a solitary individual speaking a disrespectful word against the Commission and its work. On the contrary, the universal sentiment seemed to be, that of unqualified commendation.

Amid all the horrors of this terrible war, God is affording His own people a glorious opportunity of illustrating the power of the Gospel, impelling them to noble deeds, and self-denying efforts for the benefit of their fellow-men. In this way the "wrath of man has already been made to praise Him, while the remainder of it he will, in due time, restrain." And if in future years, the retrospect of the sanguinary battle-fields, will call up painful emotions in many a household, those emotions will be greatly mitigated by the assurance, that many of their beloved ones, who fell on the battle-field, fell asleep also in the Saviour, guided to him in their dying moments by the ministrations of the "Christian Commission."

All the time, and toil, and means expended; all the services rendered, or sacrifices that have been made by the agents of the "Commission," have been a thousand-fold rewarded already by the good accomplished; and in consideration of this fact, we conceive, that God is at this time, in a very especial manner, calling on all our churches, and on all the benevolent of our land, to make renewed, and still greater persevering efforts, to alleviate, as much as it is possible, the sufferings of our brave men, who, in this terrible campaign, just at hand, will jeopardize their lives in struggling for the heaven-born rights of civil and religious liberty, for the present and coming generations.

And, Mr. Chairman, however great your toils, and trials, and sacrifices, in common with those of other noble men in this cause have been, in view of the blessings that have already crowned your labors, you have great reason to thank God for the past, and take courage for the future; "for as much as ye know that your labors shall not be in vain in the Lord."

J. TURBITT.

---

Col. Root, who is in command of the District of Annapolis, warmly approves the work of the Christian Commission. He has been an interested observer of the movements of our Chaplains and Delegates, and testifies of their usefulness from personal knowledge. It is gratifying to us to be approved by one so capable of estimating our service and so well qualified to judge of its character and usefulness.

CAMP PAROLE, NEAR ANNAPOLIS, MD.
*August 27th*, 1864.

G. S. GRIFFITH, ESQ., *Chairman Christian Commission, Baltimore, Md.:*

SIR:—I take pleasure in bearing testimony to the usefulness of the U. S. Christian Commission, at "Camp Parole."

Its agents have not only been zealous in their efforts to advance the welfare of the large number of troops at Camp Parole, but have established a just claim to the public confidence by the exercise of a careful discrimination in the issuing of the supplies with which generous people has entrusted them.

They have at all times evinced a proper regard for the necessary military "rules and regulations" of this command, and, in my opinion, have, by their personal influence and daily religious services, materially assisted in establishing and maintaining the admirable order and discipline prevalent at Camp Parole.

I remain, Sir, with respect and esteem,

Your obedient servant,

ADRIAN R. ROOT,
Col. 94th N. Y. Vet'n Vol's, Com. Dis. of Annapolis.

---

The following letter from Surgeon Gross, informs us of his being ordered to another field, and of course his valuable labors will be lost to the camp and hospital. We would express the hope that his successor may labor as faithfully and as harmoniously with the delegates of the Christian Commission as he has done:

U. S. A. HOSPITAL, CAMP PAROLE, NEAR ANNAPOLIS, MD.

*August* 31*st*, 1864.

DEAR SIR:—As I am about to give up my present position as Surgeon in charge of this hospital, having been ordered to the Department of the East, I believe it to be my duty to proffer my hearty thanks to you and to other members of the "U. S. Christian Commission," who have performed with becoming zeal their share of the labors necessary for the comfort of our brave armies.

During my term of service at Camp Parole, the inmates of the hospital have at times numbered as high as two thousand, (2,000). Your labors therefore have not been inconsiderable, and it would be useless to deny that a fair share of credit is due to yourself and colleagues for the good order and discipline that have constantly been maintained.

I am, Sir, your obedient servant,

F. H. GROSS,

Surgeon U. S. A., in charge.

REV. G. H. TOWNSEND, Agent U. S. C. C. Camp Parole.

---

The following testimonial to the faithfulness and efficiency of the service of the Commission will be read with interest by the friends of the soldier. The Provost Marshal writes like a practically experienced Christian, of which we would hope there may be many such in the army service:

PROVOST MARSHALS OFFICE, CAMP PAROLE, MD.

*August* 31*st*, 1864.

SIR:—I beg to be permitted to express to you my appreciation of your efforts and labors in this camp as a faithful and efficient agent of the U. S. Christian Commission, and also as an earnest, zealous servant of our Divine Master, "always abounding in the work of the Lord."

We have reasons for devout thankfulness that your labors are being blessed of Heaven, and that so many are being led by your teachings to examine into their condition without a hope in Christ, and are giving themselves to the Saviour.

You have my best wishes for your success, and may you

be permitted to see the fruit of your labors in the salvation of many souls. With esteem, yours truly,

ROYAL A. JOY,
Capt. 94th N. Y. Vols. Provost Marshal Camp Parole.

REV. G. H. TOWNSEND, Agent U. S. Chris. Com.

---

It is pleasant in a retrospect of our labors to find that they have been appreciated and warmly commended by officers who have been most closely connected with our Delegates and Chaplains in the service. In the midst of arduous and difficult labors, in which we for sometime engaged, it is refreshing and encouraging to find such evidences of respect and appreciation as the following:

G. S. GRIFFITH, ESQ., *Chairman U. S. Christian Commission:*

Our quarters being in immediate proximity with the rooms of the Christian Commission, we have taken occasion to watch its unobtrusive workings. We take great pleasure in bearing testimony to the nobly patriotic affairs of the Commission in endeavoring to realize the wants, spiritual and temporal, of the soldiers who are thrown together here. Those who contribute of their means to sustain this truly valuable Commission, can rest assured that, as far as our observation extends, their funds are most carefully and judiciously appropriated. The moral and religious bearing of the camp is truly remarkable, and in this connection it would not be doing justice, did we not mention the name of the indefatigable man of God, Rev. Mr. Townsend, who has had charge of the Commission's interests here for several months past. To him we are indebted for many acts of kindness and owe many obligations.

W. W. LINE, M. D., Baltimore, Md.
C. T. SIMPENS, Surg. 6th Md. Vols.
W. E. DAY, Surg. 117 U. S. Vols.
W. M. BABBITTE, Surg. 55 Mas. Vols.

The Baltimore Christian Association has sent committees to labor at Camp Parole, among which the name of the Rev. Thos. Coggins is prominent.

### Tilton Hospital.

Dr. E. J. Bailey, Surgeon in charge.

Capacity, 352. Patients, 189.

We have no direct report from any source relating to this hospital. From general notes, in which other hospitals are included, the present record is made. By these notes we are informed that the premises are in a good condition. The number of serious cases are small and the deaths but few. This fortunate condition is attributed to the effective supervision of the Medical Director of the Department, and the active co-operation of the Surgeon in charge with the other Surgeons who are assisting him in his medical and sanitary services as rendered to the several wards and other departments of the hospital.

Delegates have visited the hospital with stores and reading matter, which they have distributed as opportunity afforded. They have assisted in the performance of such services as are usually rendered by them. Their accounts of labors and successes, which have always been verbal, are uniform in the expression of approval, especially in relation to the medical service. Ladies of Wilmington visit the premises and render such aid as are admitted in their department. Delegates have witnessed with pleasure the means used by the ladies in the preparation of such food and delicacies as are granted to sick and wounded men and their delivery to the patients under the direction of the medical advisers.

### Point Lookout Hospital and Camp.

Rev. D. D. McKee, of the Presbyterian church, Chaplain.

Capacity of hospital 1,500. Patients 882. Ward masters and attendants 100. Admitted since September 1, 1864, 3,685. Discharged in same period, 2,817. Died 713, including Rebels.

*Post Hospital.*—Recently established. Capacity 25. Patients 2.

*Rebel Hospital.*—Rev. W. S. Leonard, of the Methodist E. church, Chaplain. Capacity 886. Patients 886. Sick in tents, &c., 360. Number of prisoners 7,100.

*Regimental Hospitals.*—Three in number. Capacity 60. Patients 40.

*Small Pox Hospital.*—Capacity 100. Patients 18. Number in hospital during the year 628.

Point Look Out is at the southern extremity of St. Mary's county, Maryland. The point is formed by the junction of the Chesapeake bay with the Potomac river. It looks out toward the sea, hence its name. The Point was called St. Michael's by Governor Leonard Calvert, in consequence of its being found by him on or near St. Michael's day. The point on the opposite, or Virginia side, was called by him St. Gregory's. The names were afterwards changed for others which were supposed to be more significant. The northern or Maryland point was named Point Lookout; the southern or Virginia point was called Smith's Point, because supposed to have been first seen by Captain John Smith in his expedition along the shores of the Chesapeake in that vicinity. Point Lookout extends out into the bay, and has the advantages of fine sea breezes. It is considered healthy on account of the purity and freshness of its atmosphere. It is supplied with fine bathing grounds. Its location is secure from invasion, and is probably one of the best in the State for the confinement of Rebel prisoners for which purpose it is used.

The Monitor Roanoke and twelve gunboats are stationed at the Point for its protection. The complement of officers and men of the Roanoke is three hundred. There is at present a number of the marines of the Roanoke on board sick. Their quarters are comfortable, and every necessary attention is afforded them.

We were in correspondence with the former Chaplain of the Point Lookout Hospital, Rev. J. A. Spooner, during the entire period of his occupancy of the post, which was nearly a year. From him we learned, and regret still to learn, that proper consideration is no tgiven by the officers in charge to services of religion. Apartments were appropriated to the storage of useless lumber which might have been thrown almost any where, to the purposes of a bowl-Ing alley and even to theatrical performances, either of which might have been converted into an excellent Chapel. At the present time our Committee has additional and much more grievous cause for complaint. After much effort, the 12th New Hampshire Regiment, which was stationed at the Point, succeeded in the erection of a Chapel which was used for the conducting of religious services until the regiment was ordered away, when the Chapel was presented to the Christian Commission and accepted. The officers have now taken possession of the Chapel, removed its pulpit and other chapel fixtures, and appropriated it to other uses. We are very well satisfied that the War Department will not sanction this action. We do not intend to enter complaint against any necessity that exists in the use of our premises, but we have no idea of their being used improperly. We make this statement in our report in order to show to the Government, to the officers of the Point Lookout station, and to our readers generally, the contrast presented between the action of the persons in charge of the post and the hearty co-operation and assistance our work has received in almost every other quarter. If objections are stated, let them be examined. If faults are found, let them be corrected. But let not an important and beneficial service be arrested.

The hospital and camp of Point Lookout compose one of the most important and responsible stations of our district, or of any district of the United States Christian Commission in the country. The station is appropriated to the confinement of Rebel prisoners. The number of prisoners is large and requires a considerable force of our own army to guard and protect them. Of the large number in confinement and their guards, there will always be a proportion on the sick records. These must be attended to in the hospitals. Some of the regiments stationed at the post have Chaplains, others have none. The Chaplain of the hospital, of which there is but one, has his hands and his heart full of his work. He needs all the assistance he can obtain from every source. In order to relieve him amid his arduous and oppressive labors, and to supply necessities that must always occur in a work so extensive, our Committee has sent delegates, clergymen, and others, chiefly clergymen, who have rendered the needed aid as far as their capabilities extended. There is a source of relief among the Rebels in their own provision of clergymen and others, for the management of their own religious services. They have day schools for the instruction of those who need it, and Sunday schools for religious instruction and improvement. In these agencies of morality and religion they must be assisted, and they naturally look to our Commission for this assistance. We have sent them books, tracts, and religious newspapers. The books and tracts are very kindly received, but they care but little for the newspapers. They contain so much matter that is offensive to them that they are often inclined to reject them altogether. This is natural enough. It has come to our knowledge, however, that some of them do read our religious newspapers, and we feel the importance and necessity of keeping them in the receipt of a sufficient supply. That they are receiving benefit from the reading there can be no doubt, and in the kind ministrations of our Chaplains and delegates the asperities of their opposition may be softened and from the consideration they express that the Commission's laborers are their friends, they may be led to the true condition of the loyal subject in the acceptance of the nationality and its Government as among their best and truest friends.

Among the delegates we have sent to Point Lookout we may enumerate as follows:

Reverends Andrew B. Cross, Roswell Porter, L. Hartsough, and Rev. R. C. Galbraith.

The Rev. A. B. Cross has continued his services, overlooking the entire work of camps and hospitals with but little intermission for several months. In weekly communication with our office he has been able to supply the necessities of post as they appear.

The Rev. L. Hartsough is at present laboring at the Point.

The following letter recently received affords a view of his work on the extended field over which it was distributed.

*Point Lookout, Aug.* 31*st*, 1864.

GENTLEMEN OF THE COMMITTEE:—I have been laboring among the troops stationed, and Rebels confined in camp and hospital. The number of prisoners here is 7,100. Several regiments are detailed to guard them. The sick are in the hospitals, and a few on board the Monitor Roanoke. I have preached on board the Roanoke once.

There are several regiments here without Chaplains. These regiments are here guarding prisoners. Great is the work, and I am trying to get it so arranged that every one can be reached as often as will be advisable.

You will not now wonder that I am so anxious to have our stores replenished. I was almost envious as I stood by the express boat and saw the vast amount of stores that the Sutlers were receiving and I must go away empty, and so many sick needing things that we have not got. A few I am fearful must die for the lack ere my orders can be filled. But do your best for us, praying, too, that God may honor my ministry here in the salvation of many dear souls.

Yours for the work,

L. HARTSOUGH.

---

The following letters were received from Rev. Messrs. Galbraith, and Baldwin, giving an account of their labors, &c., at the Point:

*Point Lookout, July* 19, 1864.

DEAR BROTHER GRIFFITH:—On the 8th instant, I came down the bay with a company of soldiers who were returning from Elmira whither they had been escorting prisoners. Found them very approachable. One of them told me that his regiment had been the most wicked in the service. But that after the battle of Stone River, in which it had been terribly cut up, the survivors became "moralized" in a remarkable manner, of which he was himself an example, giving proofs of being a good Christian man.

On Monday, this request came from the Christian Commission of the Ninth Corps, "Send us two ministers." Another brother with myself went. As we were crossing a field, a man hailed us with these words:—"I have been in the army three years; am about to be discharged; have never been wounded though. I have been in many battles. I feel that I ought to give my heart to Christ before I go home."

We are in great need of Bibles and New Testaments, English and German papers.

There is great occasion for preaching especially among the colored troops and penitent Rebels. I preached to the latter yesterday and supplied them with Bibles and papers.

There are here from about 1,500 to 2,000 patients in hospitals, and from 12 to 14,000 prisoners of war.

Yours, &c.,

R. C. GALBRAITH.

---

POINT LOOKOUT, *July 6th*, 1864.

BRO. G. R. BENT:

I arrived here last evening. I went to see Bro. Leonard, Chaplain McKee, and met Dr. Junkin, who, with myself, visited the rebel officers; they are very anxious for reading matter, and religious instruction.

I also visited the Invalid Corps of our troops. The Delegates had a prayer meeting on board last night. We need more delegates here. Dr. Junkin and myself are the only two left; he will leave to-morrow. Send anybody that will work.

I find the men eager for the little Hymn books; please to send some of them.

I give you a list of things needed. They are wines, brandies, canned fruit, oranges, lemons, sugar jellies, pickles, &c. We are in want of hymn books, prayer books, tracts, almanacs and religious newspapers.

I have had a request for a Bible Dictionary, if it is not out of our line; I could dispose of one very usefully. Brethren pray for my success. Yours truly,

CHAS. W. BALDWIN.

---

The Rev. Roswell Foster and the Rev. W. Van Wagner, have rendered such services at the Point as desire especial notice. From communications received, we derive the following information:

### REV. ROSWELL FOSTER.

Our Rev. Bro. Roswell Foster, who has been laboring at the Point, reports that in the time he has labored there he has held twenty public religious meetings—talked with seven hundred men—seen some converted and others inquiring what they must do to be saved—that he has rendered a grateful service to the sick in providing palatable sustenance for them by the assistance of his wife. He is much interested in the work, but regrets the necessity of leaving before his term of service expires in consequence of the illness of his wife.

### Rev. W. Van Wagner.

Several communications which we find on our file, contain commendatory notices of the services of this reverend brother. He has labored faithfully as one of our delegates, and it is with regret that we learn from himself that he had cause to complain of the exhibition of sectarian teaching and influence, of which he himself was the witness. It is his opinion, plainly expressed, that no sectarian distinctions should be admitted, and preferences allowed by the officers in charge of hospitals and camps. He faults clergymen and ladies for insinuating peculiar religious views, requiring certain forms of confession, performing certain ceremonies which he conceives to be inconsistent with the simple communication of Gospel truth to sick and dying men. He complains that he and other clergymen were thrust aside and not permitted to counsel with dying men who were subjected to the peculiar forms and ceremonies rather than instructed in the nature and obligations of the spiritual service.

The objections of our reverend friend in the relations mentioned, have been made by others, especially by the former Chaplain of the post, who was an Episcopal clergyman, and desired opportunities of affording religious services which he said were allowed to the clergymen and others referred to, while he was neither supplied with apartments in which to hold service, nor permitted to hold them even under certain proposed restrictions.

We can speak on behalf of our Delegate as an active, faithful laborer in his Lord's vineyard. He has, as far as allowed, visited from ward to ward in the hospital and counselled with patients in their spiritual relations. His labors have been approved and commended by his brethren, who have wrought with him and witnessed his ardent devotion to the cause of his Master.

---

**Fort Delaware.**

The location of Fort Delaware is on the island in the Delaware river near its entrance into the Delaware Bay, formerly well known as Pea Patch Island. The island was at one time regarded as a large pea patch. The name was derived from that circumstance. The area of the island is something less than one hundred acres. The fort occupies a large proportion of the land, the whole of which is appropriated to its use. The fort is about forty miles below Philadelphia, and is almost directly opposite Delaware City, a small town at the eastern terminus of the Chesapeake and Delaware Canal. It is about a mile from the Delaware shore and a mile and a half from that of New Jersey. Steamboats ply between Philadelphia, Wilmington, New Castle, Delaware City and the fort every day. The location is very pleasant in summer, open as it is to the winds on all sides. It is healthy, with the exception of its periodical visitation by intermittent fevers, which those who are careful in not exposing themselves can generally avoid.

Fort Delaware has been used, since there was occasion for it, as a place of confinement for political prisoners, rebel sympathizers and prisoners of war. It is occasionally used as a depot for the paroled of the Federal army. Political prisoners when allotted to apartments inside the fort have been allowed the privilege of walking on the outside, on which there are many very beautiful spots inviting the sojourner to their enjoyment.

General Shoepf, the present commander of the fort, resides on the outside of the fort. His residence is embowered among the foliage of trees and shrubbery and intertwining trails of grape and other vines. A number of residences occupy the island outside the fort, which are very beautiful and present to the visitor many attractions. We spent an hour very pleasantly with the family of the General. His excellent lady, who is an ornament to the most elevated circle of refined society, is the daughter of one of the most esteemed friends of our earlier years, the Rev. Wm. Kesley, a distinguished minister and one of the founders of the Methodist Protestant Church. The mother and sister of Mrs. Shoepf, happened to be on a visit to the family, which rendered our social enjoyment most agreeable and pleasant. In his home relations no man can be more happily situated than the General. The intelligence of the ladies department, to which he may retire in the evening, is sufficient to afford him a rich fund of enjoyment as a means of relief for the toils and responsibilities of the day.

The business relations of the fort are kept under the General's close supervision, and are regulated after the strictest order of military discipline.

A beautiful Chapel occupies one of the most prominent and attractive spots on the island. The structure is architectural and arrests the eye of the visitor, inducing a closer inspection in the promise of full remuneration for the effort. The plan of the Chapel was given by the General, by whose exertions it was erected. It is, as we were informed by the General, in imitation of a Hungarian edifice, which attracted his notice and pleased his fancy in his earlier years.

There are about eight thousand prisoners confined on the island. Their barracks are outside of the fort walls. They are protected by a high and close wooden fence. The officers have apartments separate from the privates. There is a number of political prisoners, some of them residents of Baltimore, confined in the barracks. Several regiments of Union soldiers are detailed as guards over the prisoners. The hospitals are situated a short distance from the barracks. The wards of the hospitals are as comfortable and kept as clean as any we have visited. The rebel sick occupy the same wards with the Union soldiers and receive the same attention.

There are two Chaplains connected with the fort. The

Rev. Mr. Way, of the Methodist Episcopal Church, is the Post Chaplain. The Rev. Mr. Paddock, of the Protestant Episcopal Church, has charge of the hospitals. Public services are held in the Chapel on Sundays and during the week. Public preaching and prayer meetings are frequent in such locations about the barracks as can be used for the purpose. Among the prisoners there are several preachers, who exercise a laudable Christian leadership over their companions. One of them, the Rev. Dr. Handy, is a man of very superior abilities. We were introduced to him and spent some time in conversation with him, and were satisfied of his purpose to use himself as industriously as possible in his labors for the spiritual advantages of his brethren in misfortune. His influence is almost unbounded among the prisoners, all of whom appear to look up to him for religious counsel and instruction. A large number of the prisoners have made an open profession of religion under his spiritual advisement. Every possible facility for the performance of religious services is afforded the Dr. and his associates by the officers of the post.

What is somewhat remarkable in the associations of these prisoners, is their establishment of schools for daily study and instruction. There are several excellent scholars among them, evidently men of superior standing, who are selected as teachers, and they receive all as their pupils who are willing to organize themselves into classes for the receipt of their instructions. Nearly all the branches of education, including those of the college, are pursued in these prison schools. We have had application for works in the higher Mathematics, and in Latin and Greek for use among the classes. We most heartily commend this exercise of talent and expenditure of time that might be otherwise unprofitably employed. A man's intelligence may be made a part of his religion, and it is so made when properly employed. The exercise of the higher intelligence in the religious service, affords the highest and most elevating means of religious enjoyment. The students of those prisoner schools and classes may be made wiser as well as better men by their daily application to systematic study. How much better and how much more profitably employed is the time thus occupied than that which is spent in other less humanizing, less ennobling pursuits? And how infinitely greater the difference between the character produced by such employment and that which results from the idle habit and the listless careless waste of the hours as they pass? Employment is man's duty. Employment is necessary for his health, for the prolongation of his life. Let the employment be of the proper kind and humanity must serve itself by doing the service to God that His laws demand.

The Rev. Erastus Colton served several weeks at the fort. He gives an interesting account of his labors in a letter recently received. The number of prisoners at the fort was much larger than usual during his visit:

FORT DELAWARE, *August 5th*, 1864.

MR. G. S. GRIFFITH, *Chairman*,
REV. G. R. BENT, *Agent U. S. C. C*, *Baltimore District:*

DEAR SIRS:—I herein make my first report. Coming here under your direction, to co-operate with the two Chaplains, the one, Chaplain Way, of the post, the other, Chaplain Paddock, of the hospital, I was very kindly received by them as well as by General Schoepf, who is in command. As soon as quartered, being introduced in the hospital and the barracks, to the prisoners both officers and co-operators, I went to work. I have mainly labored in the two barracks among the officers and privates and in the hospital, though I once carried reading matter to the Ohio regiment that is doing guard duty at this post.

As subsequently, Rev. Mr. Frazer, of Steubenville, Ohio, came in part to labor with that regiment, one company of which was from his place, in the want of a Chaplain, I ceased from action in that direction, except to supply some reading matter. Mr. Frazer came also under appointment from Philadelphia as a Delegate of the U. S. C. C., and bringing a box of excellent reading matter, which supplied said regiment and gave some to me for use in the barracks and the hospital. He preached for me several times in the privates barracks, and with good effect, while I was laboring under great hoarseness from a cold taken here by a sudden change in the weather. He preached to the regiment in their quarters and also in the Chapel on the Sabbath. I have preached in the Chapel once on each of the two Sabbaths that I have spent here to the Ohio men mainly; to many others also. In the officers barracks I have attended three of their daily prayer meetings at ten and a half o'clock; they were very spiritual and interesting, so much so that I longed to be with them every day, as an officer invited me to come. But the seven or eight thousand of privates demanded my services in their barracks, one of which takes place at the same hour in which the prayer meeting is held; of course I cannot attend them both.

Last spring several officers were converted, seventeen of whom joined the church, generally under Dr. Handy, a rebel prisoner and preacher. He informs me that these seventeen are growing in Grace, and are active in doing good. Others there are now serious, asking for prayers. Four rose in the meeting last evening and asked to be prayed for.

As the sun is hot and the meetings held out of doors, an awning is now sought by donations of the officers friends in Philadelphia and elsewhere. General Schoepf will have the awning put up when obtained, and under it the meetings will be held in the open yard. Great good is looked for. There is a "school of the *Prophets*" in this barracks of eight young men, under Dr. Handy, while an Education Society has been formed and several officers have pupils in the Greek language, in the Sciences, &c. I have procured from Philadelphia, books for some of the young to pursue their studies in Greek.

A decided religious, moral, educating, elevating and refining influence is most evidently being exerted in that barracks. There are several preachers in the barracks and in some divisions, as in Dr. Handy's. There is preaching every evening at sundown. A new prisoner preacher has lately been added,—a Baptist. I am exceedingly pleased with the state of things in that barracks; the men will be better fitted to return home when exchanged, or at the end of the war; and they will go with favorable impressions of us who seek to do them spiritual good. I have a brother, once resident in Baton Rouge, La., in the Rebel service, as *Quartermaster* under Johnson—a Captain here informed me of him. I am, anywhere among these officers, always most cordially received. If I could have an assistant, whom Chaplain Paddock has sought to obtain for me in Philadelphia, and I have written there for one—a six weeks Delegate, then another six weeks man, after the time of the first has expired, to act under me and with me, then I could oftener go into the officers barracks, and I could there labor more with the prisoners in the "citizens" barracks, where there are men ready to take the oath of allegiance, and I could assist the Chaplains in the hospital more than now. There is a great amount of hard work here to be done, and speedier and greater results may be produced at given points should the labors be oftener repeated. There is great labor necessary in the barracks where there are seven or eight thousand men.

I have been nearly twice around the divisions now numbering 21. The divisions contain from 100 to 470 men; those of the department that holds 100, being crippled men, and invalids generally. The divisions are from 200 and over to nearly 500 in number of men. It is hard preaching in a large division from the structure, many open windows, and noise outside, or in adjoining divisions. I have made myself hoarse several times; but by doctoring and exercise of my voice, and becoming accustomed to the place, I can now preach two regular sermons, which I do, one at 11 A. M., and one at 4 P. M. God is helping me in my good work. The men listen very attentively, sing from the hymn books I give them with true devotion, and co-operate every way in my endeavors. I am sometimes assisted in the prayers and in preaching by prisoner preachers, of whom there are several. After preaching I give out some reading for each man in the division, having, before leaving my room, counted out the requisite number of books, papers, &c. I make the Sergeants commanding the divisions the distributors, and such books as are put in for circulation I mark by writing on the cover, to *him* or *them*, as the case may be. This system, together with that of regular rotation or succession in the preaching services, works most admirably. All cheerfully co-operate. I am in perfect health.

One day, I preached to nine hundred men and gave reading to them all! Sometimes the interest is very great, reaching to tears. Could we hold repeated services at given points, or more, our meetings oftener, revivals and conversions would more frequently occur. Some conversions have already occurred, and several others are now inquiring of us, what to do to be saved? I have great hopes in my large Parish—this, of near eight thousand souls. One young man, hearing my first sermon, that evening at prayer-meeting, gave his heart to God. The next week he was taken sick and conveyed to the hospital, there he told me he was very, very happy, and was ready to work for his new master.

Besides tracts, papers, and little books, Bibles, Testaments and Hymn-books are given. In the hospital I labor as I can find time, having once and a half gone the rounds with the exception of the officers ward.

This is a most interesting and useful department of my labors. The Chaplains do most of their work here from one and a half to two hours in the morning, and continue a little time in the afternoon. Besides the books for the library, I have received one box reading matter from you, and the one found heresent to Mr. McDowell, and two boxes from Philadelphia, three boxes of Bibles and Testaments.

All of which is respectfully submitted.

Yours in the Gospel,

ERASTUS COLTON, D. C. C.

---

### Frederick City Hospital.

Rev. B. H. Crever, of the German Reformed church, Chaplain.

Capacity 1,316. Patients 886. Patients during the year 5,817. Discharged 34. Died 271. Rebels during the year 466. Rebels August 31st, 27.

The U. S. General Hospital at Frederick is situated on an eminence near the city suburbs. The site was occupied by the old barracks used for military purposes. The location is as healthy as any that could be obtained near Frederick, and this is equivalent to the declaration that it is as healthy as almost any location any where. We have visited the hospital and are aware of its position from personal inspection and its conveniences, as well as of some inconveniences, occasioned by the arrangement or misarrangement of some portions of the buildings. In repeated invasions, Frederick city and its vicinity has suffered much. The stores and private buildings of the city have been plundered on various occasions, when large amounts of property have been conveyed away. The proximity of the city to the Potomac, which is but a few miles distant, renders it liable to be raided upon whenever the occasion may be convenient for the purpose.

The Rev. Mr. Crever, Chaplain, is in daily attendance upon the hospital, and we have no doubt that from him the patients receive every needed attention, although we have no communication from him in relation to his labors. On a recent visit we learned that besides the services of the Sabbath, meetings were held during the week for exhortation and prayer. There is a library of several hundred volumes connected with the hospital.

From Mr. Gideon Bantz, one of our delegates, residing in Frederick, and now a member of our Committee, we have heard frequently in terms generally expressive of approbation and pleasure at the condition and management of the premises. Delegates in visiting the hospital have frequently met with the ladies of the city and of the adjacent country, some of whom are constant in their attendance upon the wards.

By the side of each other in the wards of the Frederick city hospital, the disabled of both the armies have been laid, and they have in the kindest and most liberal manner shared with each other the delicacies, &c., they have received. The number of patients has varied with the occasions that caused their conveyance to the premises, or their removal from them. When the battle has ensued after an invasion it has been necessary to clear the wards of those who were able to leave them to make room for the freshly wounded who claimed the services they had received.

Stores and reading matter have been sent from our warehouse and office, in liberal quantities, and we have received information of their faithful distribution among the suffering subjects of our concern.

---

### York Hospital.

The hospital of York is located on the precincts of the town in a commanding position. It occupies the large and convenient building erected for the use of a Female Seminary, and appropriated for several years to that purpose. Most of the wards are convenient—all of them are comfortable. The patients who are confined to their rooms enjoy the benefit of a free circulation of air, the building being exposed on all sides. Although the grounds of the hospital are limited, the convalescents have the view of large fields before them, and can exercise themselves at pleasure in walking over them, or engaging in such sports as they may fancy.

We have not been able to ascertain the capacity of the hospital, nor the number of patients actually accommodated in the wards. Our delegates, however, have visited the premises and assisted the Chaplain in his services. They have distributed religious and other books, tracts, and religious newspapers in large quantities.

On occasions of raids, and battles produced on their account, the hospital has been convenient of access, and the wounded have been conveyed there in larger numbers than usual. Reports that have reached us in relation to the condition and management of the premises have always been favorable, and we have every reason to believe the patients are comfortable and as contented as they are in any of the hospitals. A number of the clergy of the town visit the hospital and assist in such ministrations as are necessary both for their temporal and spiritual relief. There are ladies residing in the vicinity who render such aid as the sick and suffering require, and by whose presence and services the men are cheered and comforted. Convalescents of this hospital on their return to the front, in passing through our city, have called at our office and expressed their thanks for the favors they have received, and the hopes that they would be continued for the benefit of their successors, and of themselves, should they ever again be sufficiently unfortunate to need them.

---

### Fort Marshall.

This Fort was erected for the defence of Baltimore on the north side of the Patapsco river, Fort McHenry being on the south side of the northern fork or branch of the river ascending from the end of the peninsula occupied by Fort McHenry. Fort Marshall is some distance from the river on an eminence formerly known as Snake Hill. It is East of the city line, and in Baltimore county. The vicinity is called Canton, and is owned by the Canton Company of Baltimore.

Members of the Baltimore Christian Association have visited the fort and distributed reading matter furnished from our office. Rev. Mr. Coggins reports interesting conversations with the soldiers constituting the garrison and with the sick. He states he never visited a fort or hospital in which there was more eagerness manifested for the receipt of books, tracts and papers, and where the men were more anxious to talk on moral and religious subjects.

Ladies of the Relief Association have attended at the fort and rendered services to the sick. These ministrations have been kindly commented upon by officers of the fort, who have witnessed their labors among the disabled and the grateful manner in which they were received.

On one occasion, on Sunday morning, when members of the Baltimore Association visited the fort and expressed the desire to hold religious services with the men, the Lieutenant in charge expressed regret at not having received intelligence of the visit before so that he might have prepared for the services as desired. He proceeded immediately in the necessary preparation, and the services were held.

Why is it that the Christian mind is not more accustomed to its practical duties? Why is it, that there should be bodies of men living together in constant intercourse, and their residence circumscribed by lines enclosing but a small area, without provision for religious service? Just as needful as any thing provided for these in such relationship is the arrangement for God's worship. Libraries of well selected reading should be provided for every association of human intlligences, whether large or small, and provisions should always be made for the service that men should render to God in the public exercises of religion. Among any body of men, it may be supposed there may be at least one who may be sufficiently acquainted with such duties to engage in leading them. At least there must be one among such assembly that can read, and the gathering of the company for the reading of a few chapters of the Bible is an exercise that must be acceptable to God, and will be visited with His blessing.

Why is it that the officers in charge of forts, or of garrisons of men, stationed everywhere, do not consider these obligations and provide for their performance? And why is it, we may further ask, that the Government does not direct that religious services shall be performed in every military station by the Chaplain, if there be one, if not, by assembling the men for the reading of the Scriptures by the officer in charge, or by some one selected by him for the purpose. Such an order would be grateful to the Christian mind of the country, and would certainly be approved and blessed by the great Being in whose honor the exercise is directed.

---

### Fort Federal Hill.

There is not in or around Baltimore city a more formidable looking elevation than that presented on the north side of the abrupt and lofty eminence called Federal Hill. It is situated on the southern side of the basin of the Patapsco river, formed by wharves, which are very convenient for the river trade. The wharves bound the basin on Pratt and Light streets, Hughes' Quay and Bowley's wharf. Towards the east and south, the land slopes for a mile and a half until it reaches Fort McHenry, which is situated at the end of a peninsula, formed by the junction of the northern and middle branches of the river. Upon this hill there is now the fort which bears its name. It was erected just after the beginning of the war. An old building which will be remembered by many of the present generation, which stood on the summit near the edge of the hill, is the birth-place of Commodore Porter of the United States Navy of 1812.

The fort is constituted by an embankment of earth covered with grass, facing the streets of the city by which it is approached. Within the enclosure are comfortable quarters in wooden barracks, for the use of the soldiers stationed at the fort. The buildings form a hollow square, enclosing a beautiful lawn, which is used as a drill ground, and is very appropriate and convenient for the purpose.

The 131st Ohio Regiment occupies the premises at the present time. The regiment is entitled the Ohio National Guards. They are hundred days men, and of course will not long remain at the fort. Connected with the fort is a post hospital, which has been occupied by its full share of the sick. The Chaplain of the fort has had his hands full of work at times, and has well performed it. The location is high and healthy, but various causes have conspired to produce disease. The number of deaths, however, does not bear the usual comparison with the number of the sick. On several occasions the sick of the hospital have been supplied with delicacies and stimulants from our warehouse, and our Delegates and ourselves have visited the premises and witnessed the excellent condition of the same, together with the soldier-like discipline with which they are managed.

Both the Surgeon in charge and the Chaplain, have expressed their acknowledgments for the services we have rendered them in the supply of hospital stores and reading matter for the soldiers on duty in the garrison as well as those confined by sickness in the wards. The weekly supply of books, tracts, and papers is continued, and the recipients seem to be very grateful for the attention they thus receive.

There is a library at the fort consisting of between two and three hundred volumes, which was furnished by our Commission. This library is of great use to the occupants of the fort, many of whom without it would find many an hour to pass tediously over while unemployed and wearying themselves in the pursuit of amusement.

To Mrs. Alph. Hyatt, the Committee is indebted for valuable service in the preparation of delicacies for the sick of the fort, which have been personally administered, and for her continued kind attention to their necessities.

One of our Delegates at this fort, or perhaps we should say, one of our students in preparation for future work, is a lad between thirteen and fourteen years of age. His name is

John W. R. Sumwalt. He is one of the most regular of our laborers, calling at the office for his supplies and conveying and delivering them to the subjects of his interest. The case is an extraordinary one, and we present it as an example that may well be imitated by other youths of the same age and older. It must be remembered that this noble boy has his week's duties to perform in his school relations, and he comes regularly in the office on Saturday for his Sunday supply, of which he makes good use on Sunday. The following letter from our youthful delegate is printed without alteration. It expresses the experience of manhood in the work of religion:

FORT FEDERAL HILL, *Baltimore, Oct. 7th,* 1864.

G. S. GRIFFITH, Esq., *Chairman Maryland Branch U. S. C. C.:*

SIR:—The distribution of reading matter to the soldiers I regard as an important work to be done. I am myself engaged in it, under the auspices of the noble Commission, at Fort Federal Hill, and propose to give you a few incidents of the manner in which the papers, tracts, books, &c., are received. It being a camp of distribution, there are at times a great many soldiers waiting to be forwarded to their regiments. One Sunday last winter, while going round among the soldiers, I came across four men of the 5th Maryland Regiment, who asked me to bring them a lot of reading matter, two of whom wanted Testaments. I gave the two each a Testament and other reading matter, and requested them to write to me after being sent to their regiment. A few days after they were sent to the regiment at Fort Delaware, and on the 9th of last April, I received a letter from one to whom I had given a Testament, in which he stated that "through the kindness of myself and the minister at that place, his eyes had been opened to the sinfulness of his ways, but if Christ would help him lead a better life, he hoped at last to be worthy to sit at the right hand of God the Father." How interesting the sight as I enter the fort on the Sabbath, to see the men come running with, "please give me a paper." "How much are your papers." "This way with those papers," and numerous such phrases. One Sunday a number at the guard-house were calling me to "come that way," and I was pretty well surrounded by other men anxious to get a paper, when one who had received a paper said he would take some over to those at the guard-house. I gave him some and he started, but immediately turned around and said, "five cents a piece haint they?" I replied sir? when he repeated the question. "No sir," said I, "I give them to the soldiers." Very often have they come to me with money in their hands, asking for a paper and then offering the money as a return. I became engaged in conversation with one of them one Sabbath and he said, "The harvest truly is great, but the laborers are few." "You could not be engaged in a bettter work." Others have said "you are the first gentleman I have met in this city." The work I think does some good, and helps to promote the cause of Christ. Your fellow laborerer,

JNO. W. R. SUMWALT, *aged* 13 *years.*

Our young delegate has modestly recorded his age at the end of his letter, we suppose as a sort of apology for any evidence of immaturity it may present. There was no necessity for this. His communication bears as little evidence of immaturity as many of those written by older and more experienced laborers.

Should any of our young friends read this part of our report, we would recommend them to study and imitate the example of our little friend Sumwalt. And we would recommend to fathers and mothers who may come to the knowledge of this case, that they direct the attention of their children to such study. We say of this lad, that he is doing as much good on Sunday in his visits and counsels of religion to the soldiers of the fort as many older persons in the same service, and there are many other lads that may be taught and encouraged to go and do likewise.

Young Sumwalt has our most earnest prayers and best wishes for his prosperity and happiness in life. We pray that his manhood may be as profitable to himself in his personal character and relations as it promises to be to the objects of benevolence that may claim his service.

---

### Fort McHenry.

Rev. A. A. Reese, D. D., of the Methodist Episcopal church, Chaplain.

Fort McHenry occupies the end of a peninsula formed by the junction of the northern and middle branches of the Patapsco river. It juts far out into river and receives the breezes from the bay and river. The view from the fort is picturesque and beautiful, having on the one side the shore of Baltimore county, and on the other the shore of Anne Arundel county. The Marine Hospital appears on the Anne Arundel shore on the right, looking outward, and Fort Carroll immediately in front. The old fort held out successfully against the British invasion of 1812, when the bombs from the vessels of the enemy flew thick and fast over and about the enclosure. No spark from a shell could possibly have reached the magazine, which is buried deeply under ground, and entered by a labyrinthine passage to be traveled by no unintelligent agency.

It was, while confined a prisoner on board a British vessel off from the fort, that Frank Key, Esq., wrote his inimitable national song of the "STAR SPANGLED BANNER." He watched with the most excited interest the spot in the heavens occupied by the flag amid the shadows of the evening, and until the darkness of night hid every object from the view; and when the earliest tinge of the dawn appeared he was watching still and was overjoyed when he saw by the "Dawn's early light" the Flag o'er the "ramparts so gallantly streaming." The Flag has floated ever since from the staff planted on the eminence it has occupied for more than half a century.

General Morris, the commander of the garrison at the fort, is one of the most gentlemanly men as well as one of the ablest Generals of the army. His family resides in a cozy little cottage, over which Mrs. Morris, his excellent elegant lady holds as supreme control as he does over the garrison. The foot-prints of the first rate house-keeper are everywhere apparent over the residence of the General, and with splendid land and water views, the cozy premises, the lawn, the trees, the elevations bristling with ordnance, the activity everywhere present, the city near at hand, the almost everything that can render life comfortable and happy, the confinement of the fort life can hardly be realized.

The General exercises a constant supervision over his premises. He is aware of what is going on in every department. His authority seems to be supreme, while it is exercised with all the blandness of the home gentleman, and with much of the gentleness of the Christian. If we were doomed to imprisonment and were sure we would always be inclined to obedience and good temper, if we should not be most happy, we should certainly be the less unfortunate in having the General for our chief overseer. But we should think, wo betide us if we were refractory or disobedient. In our visits through the departments of the fort, including those devoted to the prisoners of war and political prisoners, the General accompanied us, and when we directed attention to the strength and solidity of certain cell-like apartments, he smilingly remarked, "These are for the rebellious among the Rebels." They were places of confinement for the refractory, and from the determined manner in which the General's remark was made, we involuntarily shrugged our shoulders at the thought that we had rather have the General for our supervisor outside of those strongly timbered premises.

We were complimented by the presence of the General through all the departments of the fort. The Chaplain being absent, we occupied a moment in his Chapel, a neat brick building in which religious services are conducted. "I am sorry, gentlemen," said the General, "that our Chaplain is away, but I assure you he knows his business, and is not backward in its performance. I believe he is now on a fishing expedition, and I assure you he is as good a fisher of men as he is of the finny tribes." We bowed to the compliment paid our worthy friend, the Doctor, and as we have not had the opportunity of communicating it personally, we take pleasure in mentioning it here.

In times of pressure the grounds of the fort are occupied by tents for the use of troops temporarily quartered on the premises. Rebel prisoners in large numbers have been placed there for convenience in emergent cases. We have visited and conversed with men thus conditioned, and have distributed books, tracts, and papers among them.

The hospital is a two story and attic building, located on the highest grounds within the fort enclosure. The wards are convenient and clean, and present an air of comfort only apparent in well kept institutions of the kind. The building is surrounded by a wide porch on each story, on which the convalesents, who are not able to walk out, can exercise themselves according to their ability. Hospital tents have been placed inside the fort walls and near the river for the the accommodation of the sick when the numbers were too large to be allotted apartments in the building. The sick among Rebel prisoners have had very comfortable quarters assigned them in their tents.

### Camp Bradford.

Camp Bradford is a Post Hospital. It is in the charge of Dr. J. T. Brown, Surgeon. It is capable of accommodating one thousand persons. The number of patients confined in the hospital has varied from ten to a hundred. It is located on North Charles street extended into Baltimore county on the grounds of the former State Agricultural Society, where the State, Cattle and miscellaneous Fairs were held for many years. It is distant about one-fourth of a mile from North avenue, the northern boundary of the city of Baltimore. The situation is high and healthy, and possesses many attractions from the beauty of the position and its proximity to some of the finest and most elegant residences and farms in Baltimore county. A field of several acres is in front of the barracks, is used as a drill ground, and there is quite a handsome grove in the rear. Its name is ordered in honor of Governor Bradford, whose residence is within two miles of the camp. Doubtless the excellent lady of the Governor was remembered when the title was given. Scarcely a lady of the times has been more active than she in the work usually performed by ladies in such emergencies as the present. Her service has been one of untiring activity on behalf of the sick and wounded soldiers of the hospitals. The camp was formerly known as Camp Cattle Grounds, and Camp Tyler.

On the morning of the Rebel raid while the Governor's house was burning, the Secretary of the Committee visited the camp and found a few men there who were left to guard the enclosure. Although few in number they were prepared for a spirited resistance should the enemy approach near enough to the premises for a skirmish.

The barracks recently erected are very comfortable and of sufficient permanency for an occupancy of twenty years. The camp has been used for various purposes. It was first occupied by the Pennsylvania regiments. It was afterwards a depot for drafted men. It is now appropriated to several uses, such as a depot for accepted substitutes and new recruits, and for a hospital for the invalids of the regiments quartered in the vicinity. On the breaking up of the Invalid's Hospital, which was located at the corner of North avenue and Charles street, the patients were removed to Camp Bradford.

The camp has never had a permanent Chaplain. At one time it was unofficially in the charge of the Rev. Dr. Piggot of Baltimore. The Secretary of the Committtee has frequently visited the camp in company with Dr. Piggot and engaged with him in the performance of religious worship. Subsequently other clergymen of the camp officiated, as they were desired to do so by the officers in command. Ever since its earliest establishment the Committee has visited the camp and sent delegates with hospital stores for the sick and with reading matter for distribution among the officers and men.

The ladies of the Relief Associations have attended constantly upon the camp and ministered as necessity required, to the wants of the disabled. For nearly a year, Mrs. Griffith and Mrs. Alph. Hyatt, had charge of the ladies department. They visited the sick of the hospital every day, and with their own hands, made up and administered the delicacies, the materials of which were furnished from our warehouse. The untiring activity and energy of these ladies were highly complimented by General Tyler when in command of the post. He remarked on one occasion, that he had never realized the devotion of woman in her service to suffering humanity to the extent that he had witnessed it in the unceasing labors of those ladies.

The present Surgeon in charge, Dr. Brown, is a gentleman of active supervising powers, and very attentive in every department of his service. It is his desire that the services of the Christian Commission shall be performed to the best possible advantage among the subjects of his charge.

The following letter is indicative of Surgeon Brown's characteristic service, as well as explanatory in relation to the condition and operations of his camp.

CAMP BRADFORD, NEAR BALTIMORE, MD.,
*August* 31*st*, 1864.

G. S. GRIFFITH, ESQ., *Chairman Maryland Division U. S. C. C.:*

DEAR SIR:—I have the honor to inform you that the average strength of this post is about 1,000, consisting of recruits, substitutes, etc., (white and colored) principally from Delaware and Maryland, with a guard of six companies, belonging to the 8th Massachusetts.

The average number sick daily is about fifty, one-half being in post hospital and the balance in quarters. The facilities for giving them proper care and treatment are now much better than they were four weeks since, though the new hospital and barracks are not yet completed.

We have received since my arrival, a number of articles from your esteemed Commission, for benefit of sick and destitute, both of delicacies and reading matter.

For the supply sent to the camp, please accept our many thanks. We are also indebted to Rev. Mr. Sewall, Chaplain of the 8th Massachustts V. M., for his very acceptable services and visits during the past six weeks on duty here, but must depend on your valuable Commission for religious services after his term expires.

Very respectfully your obedient servant,

J. T. BROWN,
Surgeon in charge of Post Hospitatal.

---

## Camp Carroll.

The location of Camp Carroll is in the southwestern precinct of Baltimore city. The title is derived from the Carroll residence. The ground occupied by the camp being part of the farm of the late Carroll family. The position is not very desirable, although the view towards the river on the southeast and of the city on the northeast, presents an agreeable and pleasant prospect. At the commencement of the year 1864, the camp was occupied by the 1st Connecticut Cavalry. Under the influence and direction of the Chaplain the officers and men of the regiment erected a wooden building, which they dedicated as a Chapel. In this building they assembled statedly for religious worship, and spent many a pleasant hour in such employment. In March the regiment was ordered away and the 1st Maryland was directed to occupy the position. When the 1st Connecticut was about to leave, they presented their Chapel building to the Christian Commission. When the 1st Maryland entered upon the occupancy of the camp, they brought with them a large number of sick and disabled men. The building was immediately converted into a hospital for their use. The beds, cooking apparatus and other necessary furniture were furnished by the Committee. Frequent and rapid changes occurred in the occupancy of the camp. No regiment remained long on the premises. It continued to be necessary to use the Chapel as a hospital during the spring and summer months. At times nearly every bed was occupied by a patient. During all the changes, the Christian Commission by its delegates and ladies of the associations continued to serve the patients of the hospital with such delicacies as they desired, and the whole regiment, including the sick, with reading matter. Great relief was afforded the sufferers by this attention, and many a hearty expression of gratitude has been heard by the agents of their relief.

A small library, the books of which were supplied by the Committee, was established at the camp. The books of this library were in constant use, and were rendered a source of great satisfaction to convalescents as well as to others who were not afflicted by sickness. Generals Lockwood and Kenly, after visiting the camp, expressed themselves highly gratified at the work the Commission was performing on behalf of the men of the regiments in its occupancy.

After the battle of Monocacy, a large number of the wounded of the Sixth Army Corps were crowded into the camp and hospital. Many of the men were almost entirely destitute of clothing. They were supplied by the Committee and were very grateful for the timely aid that was afforded.

Mrs. Alph. Hyatt, and other ladies attended the camp and ministered in their usual services to the sick and disabled of this hospital.

---

### Camp Bourney.

This camp is situated a short distance from the intersection of the northern boundary of Baltimore City and Madison avenue in Baltimore County. It is not far from Druid Hill Park. The camp is so thoroughly imbedded in an extensive grove as to be visible only in its immediate vicinity. It was formerly known as Camp Belger. We have visited the quarters of officers, Chaplain and men of the ranks throughout the camp, and were pleased to find every department convenient and comfortable. The quarters of the officers form a straight line and present the appearance of a well defined street. The camp is now occupied by colored troops. It is now called after General Bourney of the Colored Brigade. There is not a prouder, nor a happier association of men, white or colored, to be found anywhere than that occupying these quarters. They perform with cheerfulness any service that is required of them and operate in the drill with remarkable quickness, regularity and precision. During many hours of their employment, and when disengaged and in companies, they amuse themselves by singing various religious and military songs. They boast of their patriotism and express their willingness to sacrifice everything they possess, including life, in the service of their country and their flag. About the proudest man we ever saw was one that carried an American flag and placed it on the spot designated for its occupancy near his tent.

Delegates of the Christian Commission and ladies have frequently visited camp Bourney, for the purpose of rendering to its occupants any service they needed. Books and tracts and religious newspapers have been distributed among them, which they have always received with evidences of gratitude.

In conversation with one of the darkest colored of the men, a stout, strong and quite manly looking official, we asked what was his opinion of Abraham Lincoln. "In the work of emancipating the colored race," he answered, "Mr. Lincoln is above General Washington." He seemed to think General Washington had committed a great oversight in not performing this service, and thought the country would now be a hundred years ahead of what it is if he had effected the abolition of slavery throughout its territory. He believed he was the man that could have accomplished the object in the great power he possessed over the people.

### Invalid's Camp Hospital.

During a part of the past year there were several camps and batteries in the vicinity of Northern avenue and North Charles street. These camps and batteries were formally, if not officially, organized into a district and placed under the control of an officer. As is always the case when men are associated in large numbers, many of those of the camps and batteries were at various times so disabled as to require convenient and comfortable quarters and medical attendance. In order to accommodate the district in this relation, the Invalids' camp Hospital was established. Its position was one among the most healthy and interesting of the military locations, either within or around Baltimore City. The front line of the area occupied by the camp, is the boundary between the city and county of Baltimore. The hospital consisted of a number of tents, so arranged that they could be completely aired at any time, and that the air in greater or less quantities could be admitted into the apartments occupied by the patients. The medical and other stores were kept in two wooden buildings of octagonal form, and surrounded with air conductors. Flanking the camp at either end, they presented a business-like and quite attractive appearance.

This camp remained in existence but a few months when it was discontinued and the patients removed to camp Bradford. Dr. Manning, the Surgeon in charge, was always to be found at his post and in the discharge of his duty. Every portion of his camp was visited by him several times each day, and the most careful supervision was exercised over it. The Secretary of the Committee acknowledges important service received from the Doctor in his attendance on his youngest son, who was injured by a severe blow upon the head. His skill as a Surgeon, was tested in his successful management of the wound which resulted in the speedy recovery of the child. The sudden call upon the Doctor was promptly obeyed and in a very few moments his work was done, when he returned immediately to his camp. The Doctor's services will be long remembered by the family of the injured child.

The services to this camp, usually performed by ladies, was under the supervision of Mrs. S. F. Streeter, who visited the grounds daily, on several occasions several times a day. The Secretary of the Committee has frequently met Mrs. Streeter on her errand of benevolence, conveying to the sufferers the delicacies she had prepared. Her active and faithful services were continued until the breaking up of the camp.

---

### Fortifications Around Baltimore.

During the raid that was demoninated the Gilmor raid, which took place in July, it was deemed expedient by the Governor and the city authorities that defences should be provided in the precincts of every part of the city East, North, and West. The river on the South rendered fortifications unnecessary in that direction. These defences consisted of dikes and embankments forming generally two angles of a hollow square, in which bodies of men were placed with arms and ammunition. In the preparation of these temporary forts the voluntary service was insufficient, and it became necessary to detail citizens from the streets. In the pursuit of this purpose quite a number of persons who were esteemed as Southern sympathisers were detailed and obliged to perform service in loading drays and removal of stores from the Quartermaster's Department, &c.; very reluctantly was this impelled service rendered.—But neither refusals nor complaints were considered. The service was declared to be necessary, and the persons detailed, whether they were pleased with it or not, were obliged to contribute their portion of the work.

While engaged in this service, the persons detailed were supplied with such stores as they needed from our office and warehouse. Furniture wagons were hired and kept in constant use conveying the stores to the fortifications. The refreshments thus supplied were most gratefully received. In a number of instances the recipients rejoiced in the relief that prevented them from suffering with hunger. So sudden was the call, and so extensive the demand that the official supply, in a number of instances, did not reach the workmen in time to prevent the incipient pinchings of an unsatisfied appetite. The very moment the intelligence of this fact was communicated to us, we commenced the preparation of the needed supply, and in a very short time the desired relief was afforded. After the the fright was over a number of gentlemen called upon different members of the Committee and expressed their thankfulness for the timely aid that was interposed on their behalf.

Committees of gentlemen, clergymen, and others, were sent around among the fortifications and rendered aid as it was necessary to all they could reach in their visits.

The following statement from one of the Committees affords a view of the work they had in hand and the way they performed it:

BALTIMORE, *September* 1, 1864.

GENTLEMEN OF THE CHRISTIAN COMMISSION:—The Committee consisting of Rev. J. P. Carter and George N. Cressey, appointed on the 22d of July, to visit the Defences, &c. around Baltimore respectfully report:

That in the discharge of that duty, they found there had been made a very inadequate provision for the supply of the forces, called out, with rations. They visited the encampments and trenches on the northern, northwestern, and western limits of the city, and supplied abundantly, such articles as boiled hams, bread, crackers, cheese, condensed milk, tea, sugar, coffee, lemons, &c., to those whose scanty rations rendered this supplement particularly acceptable. After the forces were called in from the defences, your Committee continued their labor in visiting several hospitals, and the more permanent encampments, in order to supply any that might be sick, with such delicacies as could not be othwise obtained.

Among the Ohio troops stationed at Camp Bradford, they found many cases of great suffering from sickness. These cases, with others, which they found at several of the hospitals, they were happy to relieve temporarily, supplying the patients with such articles of delicate nourishment as are not provided by the Hospital Commissary, and which, the poor suffering men, as urgently need, as they do medicine and medical treatment. Your Committee are of the opinion, that the Christian Commission could not do a better work, than to obtain from the proper authorities, permission to supply regularly and permanently, to all our hospitals, *the much needed suitable nourishment*, for the sick and convalescent.

Your Committee further report, that in providing substantials for the body, they did not neglect spiritual food for the souls of the noble men, thus suffering for our country's sake. And your Committee are happy to state in conclusion, that in their office as delegates of the Christian Commission, they were in every instance, most kindly received; and the great work of the Commission in which they were engaged, was evidently duly appreciated.

All which is respectfully submitted, &c.

J. P. Carter,
Geo. N. Cressy.

## Magnolia.

Magnolia is a post station on the Philadelphia, Wilmington and Baltimore Railroad. It is distant about seventeen miles from Baltimore. The camp at Magnolia may be called a Camp of Transportation. It is a depot for the temporary sojourn of troops on transit from the more northern and eastern States through Pennsylvania and Maryland. At times there several regiments at the station. In almost all cases the regiments are supplied with Chaplains, who minister to the spiritual necessities of their several charges. Our delegates visit the encamping regiments with books, tracts, and religious newspapers, which are received by the men with evidences of thankfulness. During the time they are in waiting of marching orders, the time passes tediously by with some, especially after their curiosity is satisfied in their examinations of the surrounding premises.

In their interviews with the men the delegates have found many new recruits who were all eagerness and anxiety to make a survey of the wild and romantic country around them. By the orders of the several commands, they are not permitted to proceed far from their camps, and soon accomplish their purpose as far as it can be accomplished in visiting around. It is then that they need occupancy for their time, and are pleased to secure it in the conversation of the delegates and in reading the papers which they distribute among them. They are seen in large numbers, at times, seated under the trees, &c., sometimes singly, at other times in groups, reading the books, &c., delivered them. "What a nice little book," said one to a Delegate on the receipt of the soldier's prayer book, "What a nice little book to carry in my pocket and read as I have a chance. I shall read it until I shall know all that is in it." The conversation that followed was of quite an interesting character and led the Delegate to thankfulness that the opportunity had occurred of directing the thoughts of a young man to the employment of his leisure time in reading and study. The interview ended in the presentation of a pocket Testament to the young soldier with injunctions to make good use of it as it would afford him material for thought and study during all the leisure hours he might pass in all the future of his mortal life. The promise was given that the Testament should be so used.

### Harper's Ferry.

The situation of Harper's Ferry is on the bluff of a knob of the Blue Ridge, and is wild, picturesque, and interesting as that of any of the towns of the United States. It is on the Virginia side of the Potomac near its junction with the Shenandoah. The meeting of the rivers is at the base of the mountain near the place where they pass through the Ridge, which is nearly fifteen hundred feet in height, and slopes off on either side gradually from the summit. It is in Jefferson county, about fifty miles above Washington city. There are what are termed two towns, the upper and the lower. Together they contain about ten thousand inhabitants. The upper town is about three hundred feet above the lower, and overlooks both rivers, and has in view an extensive river and mountain scenery. Above the upper town is Camp Hill, a name derived probably from the fact of its having been occupied as an encampment during the war of 1812, or for purposes of military exercise and drill. It has long been used as a drill ground. On the East side of the town are the heights known as Loudon Heights, on the West are Bolivar Heights. The town derives its name from the owner of the Ferry, who in times not very long past ferried travelers over the river in a small barge, capable of containing a team of five or six horses and wagon, a horse or two, and a few foot passengers. We remember passing it when but a child in a perilous period, when the river was greatly swollen and running with great rapidity. The river is now spanned by a bridge nine hundred feet in length. Harper's Ferry was for many years the armory of the United States. Millions of small arms have been manufactured there.

There are several hospitals in and around Harper's Ferry, in which, there have been at one time from eight to ten thousand patients of the Union and Rebel armies. Large numbers of the wounded have continued to be placed in them. As fast as they have become convalescent they have been removed as necessity demanded to make room for others, who were brought in fresh from the battle-fields and from the points at which they were attacked while engaged on the transit from one place to another. The valley of the Shenandoah has been the scene of many battles and skirmishes and guerilla attacks, in which many of the Union troops as well as large numbers of the Rebels were killed and wounded. The town and vicinity has been several times captured by the Rebels, and as often recaptured by the Union troops.

As there are no Chaplains to field hospitals, nor to any but the General Hospitals and regiments, these places are supplied by the delegates of the Christian Commission. At all such points two delegates at a time have generally been sent and they have performed an extensive service to the suffering, on whose behalf they have labored.

From a number of our delegates we have received reports and letters exhibiting a view of their work among the thousands of the wounded that needed their assistance. With Surgeons and Chaplains they have labored in great harmony and with much success.

A company of excellent ladies of the Union Relief Association of Baltimore attend the hospital and camps at Harper's Ferry, and those of all the hospitals and camps along the Potomac. They take with them stores from the warehouse of the Christian Commission, and find supplies among our Chaplains and delegates, which they enjoy great satisfaction in preparing, converting into custards, jellies and conserves of various kinds, and administering to the afflicted subjects of their care. Scarcely a wounded man finds his way in and out of the hospital without receiving at some period during his confinement the kind attentions of these ladies. Mrs. Alph. Hyatt, Miss Ellen Small, Miss Emma Robins, Miss Harriet Southgate, and others, have rendered very efficient service to the invalids of Harper's Ferry.

Communications from our delegates at different periods afford a view of the progress of our work in the vicinity during the year. Rev. Dr. Strong writes in October, 1863.

*Harper's Ferry, October* 12, 1863.

G. S. Griffith, Esq., *Chairman U. S. Christian Commission, Baltimore:*

Dear Brother:—I have delayed answering your last that I might find time to visit the Maryland regiments in the vicinity. Last week I succeeded in making a call upon the Second Maryland, upon the summit of Maryland Heights, and also, the Tenth, which is lower down. It was my intention to have visited the Ninth which is stationed at Charlestown, on Friday, but the appearance of Rebels and a bloody skirmish in that vicinity a day or two before, led me to defer my visit there for the present. I did not find that the two former regiments are in particular need of anything except reading matter, which I distributed among them to some extent, and for which the men appeared to be grateful. The Second regiment upon the Heights are in a cold, bleak place, and must suffer more or less from the inclemency of the weather. Any little presents from their friends and benevolent people at home, I presume, would be gratefully received. But those who are much sick in these regiments which I have named are brought to this hospital and well cared for.

I am much obliged and grateful to you for the box of books, &c., which came to hand last week. The contents I am distributing as occasion demands, and as I have strength and time. There has been nothing of particular interest developed in the hospital since my last. Patients are coming almost every day, and convalescents are being returned to their respective regiments. I find a smaller proportion of those who have come in of late personally interested in Christ than at the first. On Sabbath, A. M., I distribute religious reading and converse with the sick either in the hospital here, or at Bolivar Heights, where the 34th Massachusetts are encamped. In the P. M., I preach in the first ward of the hospital here, which we use as a Chapel and reading room. I also conduct two prayer meetings a week. The last, which was on Friday evening of last week, was the most interesting of any we have had, a number of the soldiers taking part. I cannot perceive that there is any very marked interest at present, though I scarcely ever converse with a man who does not readily acknowledge the importance of religion, and that he ought to give his heart to God. What we greatly need is the presence of the Holy Spirit to convict and regenerate the soul, and to this end I trust we have your prayers and those of other Christian friends interested in the spiritual good of the noble defenders of our country.

We have for the present a sufficient supply of Testaments, Hymn books and tracts. I find that the soldiers in camp take quite a fancy to the Christian Banner. I could distribute five hundred copies, and more indeed, a month, if I had them, and with profit too. You sent me in the first box I received, a large supply of the August number. These I have distributed. If now I could have some of the September number I should be much obliged. The Parish Visitor is also quite acceptable. In the last box there was a goodly supply of the September number, and also of the American Messenger for the same month. If you could send me a lot of these of October number, they would be gladly received. Some of the latter in German would find earnest readers. Weekly religious papers of a late date can be distributed with profit. I should also like fifty copies or so, of "The Soldier from Home," also, as many or more of "Something for the Knapsack."

I have more than I can do. At the present two men could be most profitably employed at this station. It is hard work, but is a good work, and through the blessings of God will not be in vain.

Yours very truly,

D. A. Strong.

---

In January we received the following from our Chaplain the Rev. J. B. Poerner:

Harper's Ferry, *Va.*, *January* 11, 1864.

G. S. Griffth, Esq., *Chairman U. S. Christian Commission:*

Dear Sir:—To-day I called at the Head Quarters of Brig. General Sullivan and reported myself to him for duty.

He examined my papers and finding them in order, he directed his Adjutant to write a general pass for me, including a recommendation to all the officers of the regiments of his command to afford me the necessary facilities for the performance of my duty, preaching to the men, conversing with them, &c. He also requested me to write to you to send another minister to this post, as one is insufficient to minister to the men of his command, and in the vicinity. None of the regiments have Chaplains at present. The General promised to furnish us a house, where we could hold Divine service regularly.

I am sorry that you sent only six of our reports; I ought to have at least fifty. If you can spare me more, I would be very glad to have them, as I intend, with your permission, to give one to every commissioned officer of this post.

Mr. Jacob Kern has kindly offered me a room in which I may place matter and stores I receive, so that I may select and distribute them as soon as possible among the men of the different regiments.

Be kind enough and forward me as soon as possible from 150 to 200 English Testaments, and 150 to 200 English Hymn books, also 100 German Testaments, and please do not forget the reports.

Bandages, rags, linen, and lint are greatly needed, especially in the Regimental Hospital of Cole's cavalry, of which a number of men were wounded on Saturday night by an unexpected attack of 350 Rebels, composed of Mosby's and White's guerillas. The attack was made only one mile from here. Two were killed on the spot, and three died since, and were sent to their homes to-day, by Railroad.

I assisted to-day in carrying to the cars Adjutant Charles H. Richardson, of the 9th Maryland regiment. He was taken home by his parents to Baltimore. He was severely wounded in the thigh by a piece of shell, at the battle near Charlestown, Va., where so many of his regiment were taken prisoners by the Rebels.

We have had last week and yesterday very cold weather, several of the guards were frozen to death, and I suffered considerably from rheumatism in my left shoulder and arm. But to-day I am all right again.

I hope you will be kind enough to send us some delicacies, stockings, woolen shirts, &c.

Day before yesterday I visited the camp and hospital of Major Cole's cavalry. It is under the medical care of Surgeon Way, a resident of Philadelphia, Pennsylvania, a young, but kind hearted and Christian gentleman. I asked him if he was in want of anything besides reading matter. He asked for bandages, pillow cases, sheets and lint. Unfortunately I had none on had, but was glad to state to him that I had written to you and ordered just what he desired. Seeing that most of the wounded men were in clothes which were very much soiled, I requested the Major to send a man with me to my room, and I would send him shirts, drawers, stockings, &c.

Hearing this, he immediately sent a man with me to the Ferry. Their camp is on Loudon Heights, about two miles distant. I furnished for the men nine shirts, nine pairs of drawers, five pairs of stockings, four papers corn starch, two cans beef tea, two papers farina, and some papers and books for the use of the hospital.

Yesterday afternoon I visited the hospital again, and found quite a change in it; the soiled clothes had disappeared, and clean shirts, faces, and friendly countenances from Surgeons, officers and privates, smiled the heartily welcome for the friend who had relieved them. It affords me great pleasure to labor among these brave heroes. They are as grateful for friendly acts as they are brave.

Mosby, the leader of the murderous guerillas of the valley experienced a little of the bravery of these men. He lost four of his officers and a good number of his men, who were either killed or fatally wounded. It is said that his orders were, "*Show no mercy, give no quarters, we want only horses, and arms,*" *&c.*

Could you forward to me for some of our wounded men quilts, bedding, &c. They really need and deserve it. I do not forget the spirit of the brave defenders of our rights. A number of them as I have seen and heard are very profane. I will try with God's help, and by the power of His grace, to reform them. To accomplish this, I need a great measure of Divine Grace, and the assistance of the Holy Spirit. I hope I shall be able to carry out my plan in the reformation of these men. Will the Committee, the brethren and friends of the U. S. C. C. pray for me? I remember you all and the good work in which we are unitedly engaged, in my feeble, but sincere and honest prayers.

Very respectfully,

Your obedient servant,

JOHN B. POERNER,

Chap'n U. S. C. C.

---

The following from the Rev. John Turbit is dated in March, 1864:

G. S. GRIFFITH, Esq., *Chairman of the Committee U. S C, C.:*

DEAR SIR:—In a goodly number of the regiments I operated very extensively, in others my labors were necessarily much more limited. One hospital in Bolivar, to which your delegate paid special attention, contains ordinarily but few patients, consequently there were but few deaths. I had no Hospital Stores to distribute, nor did there appear to be any special need of any, as the patients have a special governmental allowance.

In those regiments that I have been able to explore the most thoroughly, I found a goodly number—in some a large number—of pious soldiers, who appreciate the efforts made for their spiritual interests, and many who, although not pious, when faithfully conversed with on the subject of personal religion, and the great uncertainty of life on the battle-field, far from home and dear friends, appeared not only serious, but in many instances deeply affected, and it is to be hoped that in not a few instances the impressions will be abiding.

Our religious meetings of a more or less public character have been held more or less frequently, as circumstances have permitted. There are various hindrances. The uncertainty of military movements have frequently knocked in the head all our plans for the time being, and prevented the fulfillment of many appointments that we had made. God, however, we believe, has been with us. We have had some very solemn and affecting scenes in our congregations. In Sandy Hook in particular, where your delegate has preached on several occasions, the people have had a religious meeting protracted for many weeks (probably over ten weeks) in which we doubt not the Spirit has been specially present, convincing and converting a large number of soldiers and citizens.

In taking occasion, as we frequently did in all the regiments, of speaking of the God-like spirit that originated the "Christian Commission" in connection with which so many of God's people are expending their money, and labor, and time, in providing for the temporal and spiritual welfare of the army, and in consideration of which the soldiers themselves should be specially interested in their own salvation, I don't recollect of an individnal, among the ungodly and profane, who evinced any reluctance to acknowledge the claims of the "Commissoin" on their gratitude.

Amid the fearful and multiform evils of the war, the testimony borne by your organization will be long and gratefully remembered, and its influence, I trust, extensively felt.

Iniquity, however, extensively abounds—card playing is very prevalent, the parties concerned generally attempting to palliate the offence by saying they play for amusement, not for money, consequently they don't consider it comes under the head of gambling.

Your delegate takes pleasure in reporting that the officials generally, in all the regiments where he has labored, have been very courteous and accommodating to him, and the longer he remains, and the more extensively he becomes acquainted with them, the more does he experience their courtesy and succomb in his work. This is a subject for thanks.

Your delegate, moreover, cordially concurs with Mr. Williams, the field agent, who was recently here, that Harper's Ferry should be the centre of operations for this region. Accordingly, since he left we have been fitting up the old Presbyterian Church, incurring but very little expense to the "Commission" as a depot for books, also to serve as a reading room, and for holding religious meetings. From this point neighboring delegates and governmental chaplains can receive a supply of reading matter.

In consideration then of what God has enabled you to do in times past and the prospect for the future, the "Commission" has great reason "to thank God and take courage." All which is very respectfully submitted.

JOHN TURBIT.

---

In July, 1864, Rev. Erastus Colton gives a view of the work at the Ferry:

HARPER'S FERRY, *July 5th*, 1864.

G. S. GRIFFITH, ESQ., *Chairman U. S. Christian Commission, Baltimore, Md.:*

DEAR SIR:—Detained as I am here for want of a pass to the fort, I give you some incidents for such use as you may deem advisable.

The work of the Christian Commission at Martinsburg, Va., has been a truly interesting one. The soldiers prize it highly, several saying to me: "We never really knew what the Christian Commission was till now. It is doing a great and good work! When we (one hundred days' men) return home we shall exert ourselves to have large sums raised for the Commission." The reading matter was very well received; conversation and remarks seemed to make a serious impression; the prayer meetings are well attended, and the singing was much enjoyed.

There was a great demand for hymn books. In one regiment I found that no hymn books had been circulated. I gave out a number, advised them all to sing, and to come and obtain of us all they wanted. In a few days I learned of a wonderful change in that body of men. They were all singing, much relieved of dullness, and very happy. I believe that singing, of a moral and religious nature, would do much to restrain from evil, to cheer, yea, to impress and convert. Especially is this true of the convalescent ones in the hospitals.

At the field hospital, of some two hundred patients, we held a meeting at 5 P. M. The children of the Methodist Church Sabbath School came over to sing. All were charmed, while some were affected to tears. One said, "he wept because it reminded him of home—of sisters and loved ones." Another said, "that one such meeting and the singing would do them more good than ten days' treatment of medicine."

A young man, having lost his arm, found Christ as his Saviour. He determined to live a different life. He almost felt thankful that God had taken his arm. Another young man said, "he had found Christ as his Saviour four months ago, was now very happy, wanted to attend prayer meeting, feared that he might lose his feelings, but wanted to keep them, carry them home and tell his friends what the Lord had done for his soul." He continued in this happy state.

In one of the hospitals I conversed with a wounded soldier—a Lieutenant. Seeing that he was tender in feelings, I said, "My friend, can't you believe on Christ, and entrust yourself wholly in His hands?" He answered, with a moistened eye, "I have been trying, but I cannot bring it about yet."

Meeting him, in another hospital, some three weeks afterwards, I found him very happy indeed in the Lord. Now it was "Christ Alone" with him. He would request me to hold a prayer meeting in his ward but for other sick ones. "When at home, I loved to go to meetlngs; but I never knew until now the real intent. Now the words of others in prayers and in exhortations express what is in my heart. Now the truth I read or hear, is precious to me." In prospect of death he is very happy, desiring prayer, reading, and conversation on the great theme. The change is a wonderful one. God be praised for this one case!

Yours in the Lord,

ERASTUS COLTON.

---

The following are brief notices of delegates:

HARPER'S FERRY, *July 30th*, 1864.

DEAR BROTHER BENT:—We walked here from Sandy Hook this morning in company with Brother Cooper, and occupied the former room of the Christian Commission.

Six boxes have come to hand, one containing shirts and drawers, one corn starch, one of wine, but this is only a drop in the bucket compared with the want of the men.

Waiting a speedy reply,

I remain yours, affectionately,

L. HANCKE.

---

BROTHER BENT:—Our brethren will need large supplies. Already one of the Surgeons of the 3d Division, Sixth

Army Corps, has called for stores. Reading matter for hospitals is an absolute necessity.

Our writing material will be exhausted by Monday.

In great haste, truly yours,

E. COOPER.

BROS. GRIFFITH and BENT.

---

### Sandy Hook.

Dr. Boone, Surgeon in charge of Hospital.

Capacity of Hospital, 1,000. Patients, 691. Patients in Hospital during the year, 6,442. Died, 57.

On the Maryland side of the Potomac, in Washington county, one mile below Harper's Ferry, immediately under the Maryland Heights, is Sandy Hook. It is probably so called from the hook like shape of the river, which makes a sweep around the projecting point of the mountain's base. There is an opening in the mountain near the hook, which leads to Pleasant Valley. The valley is indeed what its name indicates, one of the most pleasant valleys in the world. The mountain extends thirteen hundred feet above the town. The summit on which are the Maryland Heights is famous in the history of the present war on account of the attacks upon it, and the work frequently repeated of shelling the Rebels out of Harper's Ferry. The space between the river and the base of the mountain is less than one hundred feet, and within that space is the town, extending half a mile, and that length of the Chesapeake and Ohio Canal, which has one of its termini in Washington City, connecting with the Chesapeake Bay by the Patapsco river.

Pleasant Valley for some distance is occupied by camps, and several regiments of the Union army generally enjoy its pleasant walks and views. The Hospital occupies a healthy position, and from its situation and surrounding circumstances is almost continually changing its inmates. The freshly wounded, either in the skirmish or by the guerilla gang, are frequently brought in, and the convalescing, as soon as they can be removed, are transferred to other quarters more distant from the localities of battle.

Our Delegates are in constant attendance upon the hospital, and the camps, or Maryland Heights, and in Pleasant Valley. They give encouraging accounts of their labors among the subjects of their concern, and express with confidence the satisfaction they experience in the certainty of having done them good service.

Ladies from Baltimore are in frequent attendance upon the sick and wounded of the camps and hospitals. The delicacies of the Commission are prepared by them and administered in person to the sufferers. Many expressions of thankfulness follow these gentle ministers of God's favors, and many prayers are offered to Heaven for their protection and safety. Here also the ladies, whose names are mentioned in connection with the service at Harper's Ferry, have labored with great industry and success. One of them, Miss Robins, was injured by a fall while engaged in assisting the disabled soldiers.

We find the following card of thanks in the Baltimore American, which we transfer with pleasure to our report:

**A Card of Thanks.**

FIELD HOSPITAL, SANDY HOOK, MD.,
*September 15th*, 1864.

MESSRS. EDITORS BALTIMORE AMERICAN: —You will confer a favor by inserting in your paper the following card of thanks:

*To Mrs. Hyatt and the Ladies who lately accompanied her in a visit to the Field Hospital, near Sandy Hook, Md.:*

The Surgeon in charge, for himself and those associated with him, takes occasion thus publicly to express their sincerest thanks for those gentle ministrations of charity shown by them towards the sick and suffering soldiers under their care. That they were timely efficient, abounding in good, let this testimonial evidence, evoked by no other prompting than gratitude for noble benefactions. It remains but to offer a word of apology for this public allusion to acts which we know were performed in a spirit that brings from the Father who seeth in secret an open reward; and it is the justice that demands public commendation for services directed to the promotion of the public weal.

JERNINGHAM BOONE,
Surgeon in charge of Field Hospital.

11

Our correspondence affords a view of the work of the Christian Commission at Sandy Hook at several periods during the year. We extract as follows:

SANDY HOOK, *December 13th*, 1863.

G. S. GRIFFITH, ESQ.:

DEAR BROTHER:—I am happy and much encouraged now to know that Sandy Hook and its suburbs is my field of labor. The soldiers appear to be glad to receive religious services. They say, "We will help you all we can." I thank God that good has been done already. There is a happy revival going on in a school house half a mile from the hospital. The soldiers fill the house a full half hour before the time, six o'clock. All that come afterwards have to stand. There is not half room for those who attend. They sing delightfully. There were but two soldiers' hymn books in all the company until I supplied them. Brother Faulks, a Methodist minister, is here, and we labor together among the men. An invitation is generally given to all who desire to be prayed for to signify their desire. The moment the invitation is given a number rise on their feet and approach the anxious bench. In nearly all cases the effort is not in vain. Rejoicing hearts succeed the sorrowing tears, and the tale of the sound conversion is frequently proclaimed. Night after night the work is continued, and night after night some eight or ten profess a saving faith in Jesus Christ. On the railroad there are two companies of soldiers encamped. I visit them, and pass from one tent to another, and sing and pray with those in attendance. As I passed a tent I was quite respectfully invited to come in by a soldier who seemed to be concerned on account of his salvation. "I am a sinner," said he, "but my mother is a Christian, and I know I must be a Christian too." I told him what the Lord had done for poor fallen humanity, and for him and for me, and how Jesus loved to save sinners such as we. He said he knew that some of his comrades were converted. "I see the change," said he, "and I desire to receive the same blessing." I sung and prayed with him, and the tears came fast from his eyes. He said he felt happier then than he ever did in his life before.

In my visits to the hospital I go from ward to ward, read the Scriptures, and sing and pray. A young soldier, who was a Roman Catholic, asked me to give him a Testament, and I complied with his request, and he seemed to be very thankful for the gift. He said he would read it, and that he would pray to Jesus Christ, and would try to serve him. I supplied a number of soldiers with Testaments, which I got from the tent of the Chaplain. I received and distributed many other books. I gave away on Sunday all the German Testaments and religious papers I had. I gave them to a company composed of all Germans. Their camp is half a mile from the hospital. They expected me with the books, and several ran to meet me, and received them with glad hearts. Some of them commenced at once to read their books. They told me to come with more books and papers soon.

FRANCIS DARDIS.

---

*Sandy Hook, February* 30*th*, 1864.

G. S. GRIFFITH, ESQ.:

DEAR BROTHER:—We are now engaged in our field of labors assigned us by the agent, Brother Cole, and truly the Lord is with us and at work with the soldiers. We have had prayer meetings and social meetings; three of the men have been converted, and many more are inquiring, "What shall I do to be saved." We ask your prayers for us that God may continue His work among us.

Yours in the bonds of Christian love,

FRANCIS DARDIS.

---

SANDY HOOK, *July* 26*th*, 1864.

DEAR BROTHER:—Last Sabbath I was confined to my bed from over work, but God has brought me up again.

The hospital here contained about four hundred badly wounded and very sick men, and at Warrenton, two miles distant, there are two hundred more. You see how much there is to do and only one to perform it. Yesterday four bodies were placed in a soldiers grave and one more lies waiting the arrival of the bereaved wife.

I have never learned Pastoral Theology, as I am taught it daily in this place—nor have I ever been more happy.

Enclosed please find a note from Surgeon Boone, who has given me free access to the entire hospital.

Truly yours in the bond of a precious hope,

EDWARD COOPER.

G. S. GRIFFITH, ESQ.,
REV. G. R. BENT.

U. S. General Hospital, Sandy Hook, Md.

*August 31st*, 1864.

G. S. Griffith, Esq., *Chairman U. S. Christian Commission:*

Dear Sir:—Our work during the past week has extended mostly to the camps around the hospital. There are but a few hundred men in the hospital just now, and but a small proportion of them are what is here termed severe cases. They have all been visited several times during the week by Brother Curtis and Bracket, and brief conversations have been held with many of them. The hospital is now quite well supplied with necessary stores. The ladies department have afforded many a poor and suffering soldier nice delicacies and choice morsels which have formed a very welcome contrast to the usual fare of a soldier. For this kind attention the ladies will doubtless long be held in grateful remembrance.

Our field of labor out side of the hospital increases in magnitude. Pleasant Valley is now the head-quarters of the subsistence teams of this army, and has consequently brought many more soldiers within our more immediate reach. There are several new camps in this valley, containing in all about five thousand men.

On Loudon, Maryland, and Boliver Heights, are camps containing many wounded men.

The whole of these look to us for supplies in reading matter and the usual Christian Commission stores. All the camps and soldiers in this valley, so far as I can learn, are without Chaplains, making in all, as you see, a vast field for the Christian labor.

Yesterday Divine services were held at Bolivar Heights by Bro. Curtis, at Maryland Heights by Bro. Cross, at Camp Convalescent and Sandy Hook by Bros. Cross and Brady of 116 V. V. I., and at Dismounted Camp and the encampment of the 7th Pa. Cavalry, by Bro. Wood. All of which I believe were well attended and by good attention and interested prayer.

At Dismounted Camp some three or four hundred soldiers gathered closer and closer around the preacher while he talked to them in the rain which was pouring down in torrents. A new and encouraging field of Christian effort was opened at the camp of the 7th Pa. Bro. Bracket distributed reading matter and stationery and conversed with patients in all the wards of the hospital except a few which were visited in the evening by Bro. Wood.

Our distributions during the current week at a rough estimate, stands thus:—8 doz. Testaments, 700 Tracts, 650 little Books, 450 Papers, 6 doz. Hymn Books, 3 boxes envelopes, 25 quires Writing Paper, 3 boxes Essence of Ginger, 3 doz. bottles Blackberry Root, 2 doz. bottles Stimulants.

REV. J. B. POERNER,
*per* L. L. WOOD.

---

SANDY HOOK FIELD HOSPITAL,
*August* 31*st*, 1864.

G. S. GRIFFITH, ESQ.:

It gives me great pleasure to testify at this time to the great good and benefit which is constantly being done for the sick and wounded soldiers in this hospital by the Christian Commission, represented by their agents, Messrs. L. L. Wood and J. B. Poerner. These gentlemen are incessant and indefatigable in their labors among the suffering soldiers, administering physical comfort and spiritual cheer.

I have never before known a Commission since I have been connected with the army which has been so generally beneficial as this is here, nor at any time before have I known it to so completely and satisfactorily meet the noble end for which it was designed.

JOHN YOUNGLOVE,
Acting Assistant Surgeon, U. S. A.

---

## Point of Rocks.

About midway between Frederick city and Harper's Ferry on the Potomac river, the Baltimore and Ohio Railroad and the Chesapeake and Ohio Canal is the post village, extensively known in Maryland and Virginia as the "Point of Rocks." It is so named in consequence of a rocky jet of a spur of the Blue Ridge mountain extending out into the river, and which, at one time, sharpened to a point. Early in the history of the Railroad and Canal, both of which enterprises were in progress at the same time, it was found difficult to pass the point with but one of these important agencies of improvement. A law suit was entered which delayed the works for some years, when the happy expedient was determined upon of passing the point with both

Railroad and Canal. The work was commenced and the rock cut away to provide the necessary space for the accomplishment of the very desirable object. The labor was very extensive, as the present appearance of the premises bears prominent and permanent testimony. Although the point of the rock to be removed was very sharp, it soon extended itself on either side and widened for several hundred feet along the river. The rock was cut away into the mountain and now the rocky prominence rising some sixty to eighty feet above the river and extending hundreds of feet along its channel bears testimony to the greatness of the undertaking, and the skill and power of man in overcoming the difficulties that appear in the onward march of improvement.

The Point of Rocks has been the scene of many skirmishes and of much bloodshed, suffering and privation. Its situation on the Maryland shore, opposite territory for a long period in the occupancy of the enemy rendered it one of extreme danger. Its possessions in turns by the warring troops has nearly caused its destruction, The entire village has been converted into a hospital. Every house has been occupied in some way in the relief of the wounded and the dying, and in providing for the burying of the dead, or, having them removed to their former homes. Our delegates have done their work faithfully at the Point. While engaged in their benevolent ministrations the enemy has appeared, and they have been obliged to fly for safety, when the objects of their sympathy have been left to privations and more extended suffering. While busy in their work of war, besieging and plundering troops have had neither time nor disposition to turn aside to give attention, even in the delivery of a cup of water to the sufferer writhing in his agony, and famishing and dying on his bed of straw. Generally the Rebels have been able to hold the Point but a brief period when our troops, accompanied by our delegates, have returned to the performance of duty, not only to the disabled they had left in their retreat, but to the larger numbers accumulated in the sufferers the enemy was obliged to leave behind him. Sad tales of want and privation and suffering have been told on the re-occupancy of the village. Not a moment had the busy foe to give attention to the poor bed-ridden subjects of the war's misfortunes, and in some instances the sufferings of the wounded were continued through all the period of the absence of our troops. Some have been found dead, who no doubt had died from the lack of attention and nourishment. Such are the most deplorable casualties that occur in the hospitals.

With expressions of the most devout and heart-felt gratitude have the footsteps of the returning Delegates been hailed. "Thank the Lord for His goodness in sending you back," has been the often repeated expression of the languishing soldier as the Delegates approached the secluded spot on which he lay. The delegates may have reached the sufferer in time to save him, or to whisper the word of comfort to the passing spirit. In either case his work was accomplished, and God's blessing was doubtless with it.

The Point is very much exposed, and there may be many such changes unless the Government station troops enough to prevent it. Large quantities of stores are necessary for the supply of such emergencies. Two thousand wounded men are some times found in and near a village of less than a thousand inhabitants. The services of all the men and women, not only of the village, but of the surrounding country for miles have been called in requisition. Humanity has demanded the labor and it has been contributed in the relief of as severe cases of suffering as have occurred at any place where the wounded have been deposited. In many instances, but for our Delegates and stores, the privation and loss of life would have been much more deplorable than they actually were. Willing persons, gentlemen and ladies, have been found in the presence of the sufferers and without the means of relief and in an almost bewildered condition. They were anxious to perform the service desired of them, but the supplies were lacking and to stand by the side of a bleeding sufferer without the means required for his relief is more than even devoted and laborious and self-sacrificing humanity can endure. The best is all that can be done, and we trust to Providence and our friends for the supply of laborers and means to meet the emergencies.

---

### Monocacy Junction.

The work of the Commission at Monocacy Junction has been performed under many disadvantages. The courses of the railroad and the river intersecting and passing each other, one of the railroads crossing the river upon elevations considerably above the bed, the other intersecting it some distance above, with the undulating surface of the ground render the position of the battle ground as inconvenient as could be imagined, either for occupancy as a battle-field or for use in hospital provisions. As to the place and time of the battle, the emergency produced by the haste and confusion of both the attacked and attacking forces, allowed no manner of choice. The battle was fought apparently without any preparation on either side, save such as the necessities of the moment required. It seems to have been brought on and forced through in a hurry, and from the compulsion of circumstances. The movement was sudden, and the field of battle was soon cleared of its contending forces leaving the dead and wounded for the sympathies and care of a small party detailed for attendance upon them and of any persons who might happen to be near to lend a hand in the service.

The dead were soon disposed of. The badly wounded of both armies were taken up from their uncomfortable positions on the rough ground and amid growths of underbrush and weeds conveyed to places prepared hastily for their reception until they could be provided with more comfortable accommodations. Others were conveyed to Frederick and Baltimore cities where they were rendered as comfortable as possible in the wards of the hospitals.

The Delegates of the Commission who were in attendance were active in rendering such services as were necessary to the occasion. They were prepared with stores which they immediately proceeded to apply as they were needed, and could be received by the wounded men. Their services were rendered freely in and near the field of battle, and in accompanying and assisting in the removal of the wounded to the hospitals. Their services at the Junction, though brief, were much in demand, and in the rapid manner in which they were performed is remarked how much relief may be afforded to a large number of sufferers in a very brief period of time. Blessings upon them were as freely enunciated from Rebel-lips as they were from those of the Union soldiers, and they rejoiced in the measure of relief they were able to afford in the rapid and confused and severe, though brief emergency.

### Winchester.

About thirty miles from Harper's Ferry, and at the terminus of the Winchester and Potomac Railroad, is Winchester, a name famous in the history of the present war on account of its frequent captures or recaptures by the Union troops and Rebels. Before the war the town, which is the capital of Frederick County, Virginia, contained about five thousand inhabitants. It is beautifully situated in the northwestern portion of the great Valley of Virginia, seventy miles west and a little north of Washington City. The repeated raids made upon Winchester by the Rebels, and recaptures by the Federal army, have caused considerable damage to the town, notwithstanding which, it retains its former regular and substantial character and appearance, and is not as greatly affected as might be supposed by the reduction of the number of its inhabitants. Large hospital accommodations have at times been necessary in consequence of the number that have been wounded in the numerous skirmishes and battles that have occurred in the vicinity.

Whenever the town was occupied by the Union army our Delegates have been in attendance upon the hospitals and in the camps of the regiments quartered near, administering delicacies as they were needed and distributing reading matter among the men. During several months of the past year, it was found necessary to keep in continual employment in the vicinity, one or two Chaplains or Delegates who were clergymen, for the purpose of administering the comforts required by the sick and the consolations of religion to the dying. In several instances the persons engaged in this service made narrow escapes from capture, and almost always not without the loss of clothes and hospital stores, books and newspapers. The loss of the books and papers have not been regretted, as they contain much moral and religious instruction, which it was desirable the Rebels should read and which they doubtless did read with more or less profit. Captured men have expressed their pleasure in the receipt of such supplies when left behind in the flight for safety.

The people of Winchester have ministered as they had opportunity and ability to the sufferers of both armies. The ladies residing there have wrought with the Delegates of the Christian Commission in the performance of their labors among the wounded and dying. They have had their trials in the appeals of both friends and enemies for the exercise of their Christian sympathies. In but few instances have services been withheld by them which were needed for the relief of the bleeding victims of the battle-field who were depending in a great measure upon them for such ministrations as woman only can bestow. Some of them residing several miles from the scenes of conflict and from the town of Winchester have prepared at their homes such delicacies as they knew would be grateful to the subjects of their kind consideration which they have carried to the hospital, and after counsel with the Surgeon, administered to the relief of the patients. Instances have occurred in which parties of school girls, three or four in number, of not over ten or twelve years of age, have performed this service, walking as much as four miles to accomplish it.

The vicinity around Winchester presents a sad scene for the contemplation of the considerate mind and sympathizing heart. Beautiful lands once occupied by flourishing farms and rejoicing in the activity of busy and productive life, are now devoted to the purposes of the hospital in which wounded, bleeding and suffering humanity finds its lodgment, its agonies and its relief either by the soft hands of interesting sympathizing friends or the relentless iron hand of death. The consideration of numbers in regard to the hospital capacity, it is as difficult as it is unnecessary to estimate. The space and agencies that accommodated the ten, has at times been occupied by the twenty. The emergency has crowded the wards that were arranged and caused the number to be doubled. In the hurry of the removal, men have been laid close by the side of each other and have expressed their joy in being able to teach their fellow sufferers at their sides, and converse with them as they had strength to do it as brethren in the same sad bonds of affliction. The very necessity of placing close by the side of each other the wounded, of the field and which caused grief to those who were engaged in the service, was found to be a source of satisfaction and pleasure to the subjects of their anxious and afflictive ministrations. In such proximity the sufferers have been seen in their exchange of such restoratives and agencies of refreshment as have been placed in their hands. "Touch this to your lips," said a Delegate to a man with one arm, "and place it near the lips of your friend by your side who has no arms." The order was obeyed with an earnestness that witnessed an anxiety on behalf of the brother sufferer almost equal to that felt by the one assisting in the relief. When the period arrived for the removal of the sufferers to a more comfortable situation, one was discovered to be a Union soldier and the other a Rebel, and the fact was known to both of them. So near in its moral effect is the hard bed of earth on which the bleeding victim of the battle-field is laid, to that other deeper bed, the grave, where all find equality, that it covers the bloody purpose of the enemy and reveals the sympathy of friendship which the man of suffering experiences on account of his brother in the afflictive issue of a common misfortune. Truly there is in humanity, that which would impel it in the pursuit of the better purpose in the sympathy of relief and kindness, if it were not obscured by the conflicting interests of personal desire and selfishness on which the same humanity crosses and abuses its heritage of life. Let these instances of generous sympathy which occur among men, that have drawn each others blood upon the battle-field be told. Let them be caused to appear as evidences that beneath the troubled billows of anger and strife and blood, there are waters of peace and of quiet assurance, that are beautiful and attractive, and would minister to the happiness of mankind were they permitted to show themselves in their guise of love upon the surface. Let them be remembered as the testimonials of the better condition produced by civilization and religion, and the sympathy of man for his fellow, may not only be excited on occasions of human suffering but they may operate in the prevention of even the possibility of war.

---

### Martinsburg.

The town of Martinsburg is on Tuscarora creek, on the line of the Baltimore and Ohio Railroad, in Berkely county, Va. It is a thriving town of some three thousand inhabitants. The Railroad Company have a number of machine shops in Martinsburg, in which there are sometimes a number of valuable and costly locomotives and other cars. The Government made it a depot of army stores on account of the convenience for transportation to the seat of war. On this and other accounts, the place is rendered attractive to the Rebels, who have several times taken possession of it, burned the locomotives and other cars, and conveyed away or destroyed the Government stores. The inhabitants of the town have suffered very much in consequence of the raids of the enemy, who have never obtained possession of the town without doing some damage to private property.

Hospitals have been established at Martinsburg, and it has been used as a depot for the transportation of such of the wounded soldiers as could be removed.

The Committee has visited Martinsburg immediately after a bloody battle in its vicinity, and beheld the wounded as they were brought in, seven or eight hundred each day for several days, some of them dreadfully mangled, and crying out in agony for relief. The number of Surgeons in attendance, though sufficient for an extended emergency, was not sufficient for the immediate relief of the hundreds and thousands that have been suddenly thrown on their hands. Those in attendance have labored industriously in their horrid work of amputating limbs and probing and bandaging wounds. It is surprising with what coolness and deliberation their service has been performed as they piled around them large stacks of human legs and arms and feet.

The Delegates of the Commission have been on hand on the occasion of every battle. Many of them have assisted the Surgeons in their bloody and disagreeable work. All of them have ministered to the physical and spiritual necessities of the injured men. Supplies have been sent by us on every occasion of disaster, and we have heard how faithfully and wisely they have been administered. Ladies of the neighborhood have been very active in rendering aid to the sufferers. As in other places they have prepared delicacies at home and brought them in *their own* hands for delivery to those who needed them. Like the ladies of Winchester, those of Martinsburg and its vicinity have wrought faithfully and arduously in their work of relief, and many an afflicted subject of their sympathies has uttered blessings upon them for their kindly interposed and timely relief. The records of the future world will tell of these sacrifices and labors on behalf of their bleeding, suffering fellows in humanity's common bonds.

The following correspondence affords a glance at the work that has been performed in Martinsburg, and its vicinity.

MARTINSBURG, VA., *November* 11, 1863.

G S. GRIFFITH, ESQ., *Chairman Christian Commission:*

DEAR BROTHER:—The box of reading matter received from you a few days ago was acknowledged by brother Patterson. They were a nice assortment of books, papers, tracts, &c. They have been distributed through the different regiments of this command. Since I have been receiving books from your society, Corporal Humphrey, a member of company B, has been appointed a delegate of the Commission in Philadelphia, and I have been receiving books from that society. As I do not wish to call for more reading than I can distribute I delayed writing until the present. We have met with great success in the distribution of those books, &c. We feel that our efforts to do good are not in vain. We begin to see the fruits of our labors. Corporal Humphrey is holding prayer-meetings in the different companies. The tent is always crowded. Our brother soldiers seems to attend them with interest. After it closes, when they are retiring to their respective tents, I could hear them remark "that was a good meeting. It reminds me of the prayer-meetings I used to attend when at home." Others would remark, "I am going to lead a different life from this hour." We intend to continue these meetings, hoping that great good may result from them. In our visits through the different regiments here we find too many soldiers who are yet out of the ark of safety—who have never enjoyed that peace of mind with God that would make them happy and joyous in this world, and that one to which we are fast approaching. We talk with them upon the importance of being prepared to meet their God.

Some of them remark they know it is their duty to become Christians. It is so hard for them to be a true follower of Christ while in the army, that they will put it off till they return home at the close of the war.

But ah, my fellow-soldier, God may call you from this world before you return home. Then you will wish you had have listened to his teachings, and obeyed them. Oh that God would awaken the unconverted soldier and bring him to Christ before it is too late.

Parents have a great work to do in preserving the moral integrity of their sons, while in the army. They should not forget to write to them, after giving them Christian advice, urging them to become Christians, or to hold fast to the profession they made when they left home. They should not forget to pray for their soldier boy that is far from them.

May every soldier that returns home at the close of this war, return with their character pure and spotless. How joyful will those parents be who greet their sons in possession of that precious boon.

You will please send me another box of books. Thanking you kindly for what I have received from you, I will close.

Respectfully yours,

GEORGE F. BROWN.

---

MARTINSBURG, WEST VIRGINIA, *March* 14, 1864.

G. S. GRIFFITH, *Esq., Chairman U. S. Christian Commission:*

DEAR BROTHER:—I will try to give you a short account of my work at this station.

I commenced in the beginning of February in the camps and hospitals, in company with Rev. Mr. Heyser, (Army Missionary of the American Tract Society.) We visited daily together a camp and supplied the men with Testaments, Hymn-books, and other reading matter, which were received with the greatest eagerness, especially Hymn-books, and religious newspapers. We conversed with the officers and privates on religion, whenever an opportunity has offered us. We preached to them during the week and on every Sabbath forenoon and afternoon, both in English and German.

The audiences were generally not very large, as in most of the cases a great many were out on scouting expeditions, or just returned from them. They were of course too tired to attend service. Those who, however, were present, were generally very attentive.

Last Saturday a week, I visited two camps, 18th Connecticut Volunteer Infantry, to whom I preached in English in the Court-house, where they were stationed as Provost Guard. I explained to them the necessity of being ready to meet the Son of Man, when it should please Him to call them home from their earthly pilgrimage; and pointed out to them as forcibly as I could the means of grace, by which we only can be prepared to meet His call. I exhorted them to use and apply these means, now, while they are in a state of health and activity, &c.

After my services was over, a German soldier of the regiment came to me and grasped my hand, thanking me for the counsel I gave him. He promised me that he would attend my service in the German language. He related to me that he heard me preach on Sabbath before in German, which had been the first sermon he had heard in his native tongue since he emigrated to this country, which is over seven years. He asked me also for a German Bible, in order to send it home to his wife and children, as he had never had an opportunity of buying one.

To-day I have to preach twice, at 2½ and 7, P. M., first in English and then in German. Our work is prosperous everywhere; the Chaplains, soldiers and officers feel that we work for their bodily and spiritual interest, and give us every encouragement.

Last Wednesday I went over to Hagerstown to review the field of our labor among the military there. I found one company of 116th Ohio Volunteers doing Provost duty, and about 250 men of the 12th Pennsylvania cavalry, who guard and care for the horses, and all their camp equipage, &c., during the furlough of the veterans of that regiment.

I distributed Hymn-books and other reading matter amongst them, which were accepted gratefully.

Among other visits, I made several. Rev. Bro. Evans, (Lutheran pastor,) who related to me that he had from seven to eight boxes of hospital stores on hand, containing dried fruits, condensed milk, a few bottles of stimulants, shirts, drawers, and also linen, lint and bandages.

His intention was to send them on to Philadelphia, but I told him that he could save that trouble and expense to the Christian Commission if he would deliver them over into our hands. If agreeable to the Committee we will take charge of them and distribute them as usual among those who need them.

Very respectfully, your Brother,
John B. Brown,
Chaplain Christian Commission.

---

**Valley of the Shenandoah.**

The Valley of the Shenandoah lies southwestwardly from Harpers's Ferry, its northwestern terminus. The river, which is wild and beautiful, runs through it in two forks, the northern and southern, which unite a few miles north of Front Royal. The length of the river is about one hundred miles, bounding and passing through Jefferson, Loudon, Clark, Fauquier, Warren, Page, Shenandoah, Rockingham and Augusta counties. The valley, which is variable in width, and winds among the mountains, extends along the river through several of the counties named, at times almost filling the gap that passes between the mountains and then opening into an area of considerable extent. It is accessable to the Valley of the James river and to Richmond between mountain ridges and mountain gaps, which are wild and intricate and sometimes passable only with difficulty. Along this valley the rebels, in guerilla bands and larger forces, have worked their way ever since the beginning of the war. By watching favorable opportunities they have made successful attacks on Winchester, Harper's Ferry, Martinsburg, Point of Rocks, Frederick city and other places, all of which they have several times captured and plundered.

The valley, from Winchester to Harper's Ferry, has been occupied in frequent changes by Union and Rebel troops, and scenes of terrific slaughter have occurred in the contests for its possession. The camps extend through this portion of the valley, and hospitals have been erected near Harper's Ferry. The camps occupied by regiments from the different northern States, have been frequently and continuously visited by our delegates who have rendered the usual aid to Chaplains in the distribution of books, tracts and newspapers, holding meetings for preaching and prayer, and exhorting and comforting the sick and wounded. An extended amount of labor has been performed in this way.

Large quantities of hospital stores and reading matter have been sent to the valley, and every possible attention has been given to the necessities of the soldiers as they have appeared. The number of Rebels that have at different times received our ministrations in the valley is large. In all cases of invasion, their forces have been driven back when the principal part of their dead and wounded have fallen into the hands of the Union forces. Thousands have been buried by our troops and thousands more in their wounded condition have received the ministrations of our Delegates and of some of the ladies of the association who have ventured along the dangerous pathway of war and performed the required service for the sufferers. Among the most devoted of these gentle ministers of God's favor to the sick and wounded, are Mrs. and Miss Jane B. Moore and Mrs. Hyatt. These ladies have labored along the line of the Potomac and through the valley to the southern side of Winchester, and they have ministered effectual and successful services, which have saved many lives.

### Near Petersburg.

At the beginning of the war Petersburg was a very beautiful port town of about eighteen thousand inhabitants. It is situated on the south side of the Appomattox river in Dinwiddie county. It is twenty-two miles south of Richmond and ten from City Point, which is near the confluence of the Appomattox with the James river. It was connected with Richmond by the Great Southern Railroad and with City Point by the Appomattox Railroad. A short distance above the city are the Falls of the Appomattox, around which there is a canal by which small vessels ascend the river nearly a hundred miles. The water-power supplied by these Falls is considerable. Included in the borough of Petersburg are the ruins of the old town of Blandford, which at one time was much larger than Petersburg and commanded the trade and possessed the wealth and influence of the vicinity. But little remains of Blandford except the old Church, the venerable condition of which reminds one of the picturesque ruins of some of the older cities of the world.

"Near Petersburg" is the line of fortifications and trenches occupied by the besieging army, which are about four miles from the town. These fortifications have been, and continue to be, the points of exhibition for some of the most ingenious stratagems and dangerous conflicts of the war. The eagerness of the Union troops to possess the town, and the necessity forced upon the Rebels of using every agency of protection in their power, renders the vicinity a scene of unceasing watchfulness and activity. The fortifications of both armies, consist of earthworks forming intrenchments, behind which, the thousands of able, spirited and resolute men are watching and improving the opportunities that are presented of working the terrible machinery of attack and defence. The Union troops have continued in the advance, fortifying themselves as they proceeded until they have reached their present interesting and perilous position. They are now watching their opportunities and employing them as they appear in the accomplishment of their determined purpose of securing the victory and the capture of the town.

Temporary hospitals for the accommodation and protection of the disabled are arranged in the rear of every corps. In these hospitals, and from them to the trenches, in which there are always large numbers of men that are exhausted from continuous watchfulness and labor, the Delegates of the Christian Commission are always found moving forward in their work of relief and religion. Refreshments for both body and spirit are furnished in the time of greatest need to those who are the most anxious to receive them. There is refreshment in an apple, a peach or the bite of a pickle under such circumstances, that is inconceivable to persons who have never witnessed the condition of men that are waiting and working and watching with unceasing industry and anxiety, and in the face of the terrrible engineers of destruction ever frowning fearfully in their view.

There are moments amid those scenes of peril in which the men need and desire employment and refreshment for their minds and spirits. It is during these moments that the delegate finds his opportunity to converse with the subject of his solicitude and to read a passage from the Bible or some other book or from the tracts or newspapers. Scarcely an opportunity of this kind is allowed to pass unimproved. Upon the movements of every little group of men, some Delegate is watching, and when a favorable moment appears, he ventures forward with his means of refreshment for the body and his word of instruction, of encouragement and consolation for the weary mind and spirit. The conversation, the reading, sometimes the singing and the prayer are results of the interview, which very seldom fail in the receipt of God's blessing to the edification of all engaged in the sacred, solemn and soul reviving services. It is in such a moment that the soul of the soldier is impressed with a proper view of its responsibilities to God, to mankind, and to itself, and lessons of heavenly wisdom and counsel are afforded, never otherwise experienced.

Thus the Delegates of the Commission face the dangers of the siege in order to convey the means of relief, and with them the message of the Gospel to the toil-worn and weary watcher of the trenches. in numerous instances of which we have heard, the tear of sympathetic interest and of deeper seated religious affection, has traced its passage to the eye, and over the sun-tanned cheek, and found its way to the soil which it moistened in the evidence of the patriot's devotion to his country, his love for his family, and his reverence for the services of religion.

Supplies in very large quantities have been sent from our warehouse by Delegates bearing our commission, who have conveyed them to the places of their labor, and with their own hands they were administered in the moments of greatest necessity to the men who were greatly in need of them, and who have received them with such evidences of pleasure and gratitude as humanity in the time of its necessity only can exhibit.

It is worth something to hear the courageous and earnest Delegate tell how he stood and sat and knelt in the trench, while the busy evidence of preparation for the attack was apparent in the movements of the enemy, as the bayonet would appear above the parapet and the huge mortar of destruction seem to be changing its position; and then the flash and the roar, and the flying exploding shell, and the necessity of watching the scattering fragments of the missile less one of them should fall in perilous proximity to the person and cause disaster. At such a time is prayer of no avail? Is it not well that the minister of God should be near in the period of such peril, and that he should pray that humanity in its bravery, and exposure, and danger might be preserved from the threatening destruction? If there be truth in the intelligence received through the volume of Divine Revelation, there is more to be expected from the prayer than from the other agencies of defence. There can be no well founded doubt that thousands of lives are spared in answer to prayer, if not offered by the imperiled man himself, it may be by the friend that witnesses his condition, and in a calmer frame of mind than his, presents the petition in his behalf.

While the men of war are engaged in their perilous enterprise, forced upon them in the necessity of defence, they should not forget to pray to God for the success they seek under the direction and protection of His providence. And while the army is in the field, the church should do its duty in its place of prayer, and the Divine interposition should be continually implored that the honor and integrity of the nation may be preserved, and the lives of its citizens spared. While we are providing the materials of relief and comfort for our brethren in the field, our prayers should be in perpetual offering. They should ever be ascending like incense into the Great Presence and the descent of blessing should ever be in anticipation. In proportion as we are faithful in this department of the service, we may expect the Divine intervention and favor, and the relief we most anxiously desire.

---

### Bermuda Hundred.

On the Appomattox, above its confluence with the James river, and on the opposite side from City Point is the locality known as Bermuda Hundred. The operations of the Commission, through its agents and Delegates, have been carried on at Bermuda Hundred in its connection with City Point. Conveniences were afforded in the arrangement which circumstances suggested and the movements of the army were directed accordingly. The services of the Commission were rendered as the necessities appeared in the operations of the army. Wherever there are camps and hospitals there is need for our labors, and those labors are performed as the needs are rendered apparent.

In the statements that have been made by delegates, Bermuda Hundred has always been so intimately associated with City Point that no specific information has been afforded in relation to their labors there. Our supplies, however, with the labors of our Delegates have been appropriated to the use and relief of necessities as they have appeared, and in large proportions they have been administered to the immense multitudes that have occupied, and are still occupying the vicinity from Bermuda Hundred and City Point to the trenches near Petersburg. The trenches and fortifications of the army extend from fifteen to twenty miles. All along this distance portions of the vast army of the Potomac are stationed. The base of supply for this multitude of men is City Point, with its adjunct Bermuda

Hundred. Busy scenes present themselves at this base. All through the day the living masses are in motion, and throughout the night the movements of guards and attendants upon the sick and wounded are continued.

---

### Fortress Monroe.

This fortress, which has become celebrated in the history of the present war, is situated at a point formed by a curve in the James river near its junction with the Chesapeake bay. The obtuse peninsula affords two sides for defence from the river. The space occupied by the Government for purpose of defence, drill, hospital, service, &c., is sixty acres. Over this extent are spread the fortifications, buildings, garden patches, &c., presenting walks in various directions, some of which are very pleasant and attractive.

A Chapel was built in December, 1863, for the use of the regiments stationed at the Fortress. It was erected under the direction of the Rev. James Marshall, Chaplain, and dedicated to religious services two days after Christmas. Five clergymen of different denominations engaged in the dedication ceremonies. Officers, Surgeons and private soldiers attended and engaged together in the services. Every one appeared to be pleased at having a place of worship on the premises. Besides the Chapel there is a building which was erected for the use of a library and a reading-room. A Sunday school is conducted in the Chapel which is very well attended. Bible lessons are studied by the soldier pupils which are recited to soldier teachers with a very high degree of mutual enjoyment. Bibles, Testaments, and other books were supplied from our office, on account of which, many thanks were expressed by both teachers and pupils. Great delight is experienced in these Sunday engagements, and our brave soldier friends send us kind and Christian greetings in which their gratitude is feelingly expressed.

An excellent idea is entertained by the Chaplain of sending the men home after the war with sufficient interest and experience to render them successful Sunday school teachers and superintendents. To this end many are engaged in teaching, and they are making satisfactory proficiency in the pusuit.

Large quantities of stores of various kinds have been sent by us to the Fortress for the accommodation of the sick and wounded of the hospital. These stores have been thankfully received and frequent desires have been expressed that the ability would be afforded of making return services. The will thus apparent in the desire of the patients, exhibits a kind feeling towards those who have assisted them in the time of their trials that may be remembered by them with gratitude all the days of their lives.

For some time after General Grant commenced his march for Richmond, Fortress Monroe was the forwarding depot for our supplies, and the point at which our Delegates gathered their stores for their onward progress to the point. Heavy cargoes of freight, and, perhaps, a thousand Agents and Delegates of the Commission have been transported by this conveyance. The wharf at the Fortress has presented frequent busy scenes in the moving of passengers and freight in the necessary exchange of conveyance.

To Moore N. Falls, Esq., President of the Bay Line Transportation Company, for his gentlemanly courtesy and uniform kindness in obliging us, and to the Company over which he presides, the Committee take pleasure in acknowledging very valuable and important services.

The following letter from Chaplain Marshall indicates the service which the Commission is assisting him in performing:

CHESAPEAKE GENERAL HOSPITAL,
NEAR FORT MONROE, *January* 6, 1864.

MR. G. S. GRIFFITH, *Chairman Chris. Com. Maryland Branch:*

MY DEAR SIR:—I am greatly obliged to you for your kindness to me while in Baltimore. I obtained nearly every thing necessary for our purposes. Our Chapel was dedicated December 27, 1863. The dedication was very pleasant and gratifying to all present. The house was crowded. Many strangers were present. Four other ministers aided me in the exercises—Rev. Mr. Palen, formerly of Hampton hospital, since tranferred to Balfour hospital, at Portsmouth, Va.; Rev. E. N. Crane, Superintendent of Work of Christian Commission, from Eastern Virginia, now stationed at Naval hospital, Portsmouth, Va.; Rev. Mr. Hager, Chaplain 118th New York volunteers, now at Newport News; and Rev. Mr. Moffit, of Pennsylvania, Missionary among the negroes. Baptists, Presbyterians, Congregationalists and Methodists were represented. I invited Mr. Bowen, Unitarian, of Baltimore, also, Rev. Mr. Chevers, Post Chaplain, an Episcopalian, and Father O'Keefe, Catholic—who courteously declined because of engagements at Norfolk. I was desirous each denomination should be represented, as nearly all contributed to the Chapel. The day was delightful; and I think our soldiers here will long remember the day and the occasion. Many said it was the most home-like day they had enjoyed since leaving home. Fifty-seven persons partook of the Lord's Supper. Surgeons in charge knelt with the soldiers at the feet of Jesus and partook of the emblems of the Saviour's death. The influence has been most salutary. We now truly have the Sanctuary among us. It is like the Tabernacle in the wilderness. General Butler granted an order for material for a library and reading room, and that is now finished and joins the Chapel like a session room to a church. Our advantages are great.

Last Sabbath I organized a Soldiers' Sabbath school. About fifty were present. We organized into classes, and the exercises were quite interesting. The soldiers seemed pleased. Our object is to make it a Normal School—qualifying these men for teachers and superintendents when they go home.

The Bibles you sent me are now in great demand. Their value is great to these men, who study the Old Testament as well as the New. They want a Bible in hand continually; references are so frequent to the Old Testament. Our soldiers feel very grateful to you, and the friends of the Christian Commission through you, for thus supplying them with the whole of God's word. What oceans of seed the Christian Commission scatters! That society will reap a great harvest in this world, but what wonderful results only eternity can reveal. So great a seeding will gather many at last to shout the "Harvest Home." I believe the soldiers greatly appreciate what is doing for them through such agencies. They will be the friends of such organizations as the Christain Commission. They will give time and money to carry on in future what the Christian public, through its agency, are now building up.

We daily see the fruits of this universal shower of religious truth poured into every group of men and soldiers throughout the nation. Chaplains and Delegates and Christian soldiers and Christian women are sowing broadcast Bibles, Testaments, religious books, miscellaneous tracts and papers, such as you sent us, and they are favorably praying the Spirit of God may bless the efforts thus made to build up Zion and break down the structures of Satan, so prevalent. May God's blessing attend all your efforts to help the Chaplaincy carry on its work and to plant the truth where no other means seem available! With Argus eyes and Briennian arms your Commission sees the wants everywhere, and then reaches out the help so greatly needed to give heart and life to the cause of our blessed Master.

Most truly,

JAMES MARSHALL.

---

### City Point.

Near the junction of the James and Appomattox rivers, about thirty-five miles southeast of Richmond, is the Post village of City Point. The landing is on the James river. Inland vessels of large size are employed between the village and other ports on the river. The village is about ten miles east a little north from Petersburg, with which it is connected by the Appomattox Railroad. The camp at City Point is about two miles from town, extending nearly two miles along the Appomattox, beginning about a mile and a half from its mouth, on the South bank, which is elevated considerably above the river. Between the camp and the river is the road that leads to the army at the front. The road is in constant use, and in the dry summer is one of the dustiest in the world. Forty acres of land are covered by the camp. A number of battles took place in the progress of the army to City Point, and when the town was first occupied by our troops in search of quarters for the wounded, it required nearly all the houses and barns to accommodate them. It was but the second day after, when the work of locating this largest hospital ever erected was commenced. In a brief period, not much longer than is required to tell the tale, the huge hospital was ready for the brave men who were to occupy it. They were brought in by thousands and deposited in the comfortable accommodations provided for them. The tents are regularly arranged and the busy line abounding in the avenue, and which consists merely of attendants upon the tent-wards present the appearance of quite an extensive business town.

The tents of tbe Christian Commission are fifteen in number. They consist of regular rows, with tents in the rear and on the side accommodating the arrangement to the surface and the convenience of the department. The tents are appropriated as reading and writing-rooms, post-office, store, offices, cooking, dining and sleeping apartments. Far in the rear are booths for horses. The material of the tents is the same that was used as the Chapel tents of the winter quarters. Some of the sleeping tents are thirty by fifteen feet, office, and reading tents are of the same dimensions. The cooking tent, which is erected on ground rising above the front, is fifty feet by thirty. It is furnished with four large caldrons holding forty-five gallons each. The caldrons are raised on furnaces, and are provided with tubs, &c., for use in the preparation of lemonade, milk punch, &c.

The camp is provided with Chapels for religious services, some of which are occupied every day and night in the week, and all of them on Sunday. The Delegates of the Christian Commission are usually in attendance in sufficient numbers to afford the needed assistance to the Chaplains in relieving the temporal and spiritual necessities of the sick and wounded men. The number generally in attendance is about fifty. The relief afforded by these men to the sick and wounded sufferers is not to be measured by any figures used in the computation of human affairs. Thousands of those whose lives have been saved through their agency have been returned to their places in the ranks, who would in all probability be underneath the sod. They are now the hale hearty men and brave soldiers of the army who were the suffering subjects of the hospital. Through the timely service rendered them in the critical hour of their necessity, are now restored to health and energy, and active service in behalf of their country.

---

**The Steam Fire Engine.**

This, as we have before stated in our summary at the beginning of this report, is one of the steam Fire Engines of Baltimore city. The Rev. A. B. Cross, who is constantly in motion, in the active service of the Commission, observed with great interest and feeling, the clouds of dust that were constantly rising from the road, and from all parts of the camp, driving through the tents in the warm summer days, covering the beds and the faces of the patients, collecting in their food and annoying them to the last degree. The suggestion of the remedy was promptly made. His mind reverted to the steam Fire Engines of Baltimore, and one of them was the very thing for the purpose. The idea was made known to General Grant, and Mr. Cross was forthwith despatched to Baltimore to borrow, if possible, the needed agency of relief. Mayor Chapman, as we have stated, was prompt in his reply, as he always is, when the country, or humanity, or suffering soldiers call for his aid. He ordered the Engine to be placed in readiness for removal, and in as as short a period as it could be conveyed to its destination it was taken there and set to work. Never was a greater blessing afforded sick and suffering men.—Twenty-two hundred feet of hose were attached to the Engine and water was thrown throughout the camp and along the road completely laying the dust and affording coolness and refreshing moisture to the atmosphere. The thousands of bleeding men upon their beds breathed freer and easier, and took in refreshment for languid systems and more languid hearts from the generous supply.

The Engine has been kept in active operation from the moment of its location on the premises. By the order of General Grant large tanks have been provided for the use of of the camp, and these are kept constantly supplied with fresh and refreshing water. The Engine, though it was first supplied by the Commission, was taken in hand by the Government. It now has its corps of Engineers and attendants, and is one of the most useful and actively operating agencies of the army. The water supplied by the Engine is from the deep water in the channel of the river and of course is purer and better than could be procured near the shore.

---

**Our Team for Land Conveyance.**

No less in the case of our large team of six horses and wagon was necessity the mother of invention, than it was in the supply of the Steam Fire Engine. Our stores were sent to Fortress Monroe and thence to City Point, where they remained for some days waiting the means of transportation. Apprized of the fact by letters and despatches, we proceeded at once to the purchase of the team. It was found to be of great advantage in effecting the desired object. Large quantities of stores were conveyed by this agency from City Point and Bermuda Hundred to the Front. The certainty of this conveyance, amid the confusion and danger of the period was a consideration not to be lightly esteemed. It was not the time for delay in the transportation of hospital supplies. The battle-fields were supplying the subjects of our interest and care by thousands. Bleeding men were calling for help and our Delegates were near to afford it as far as their own personal ministrations were concerned. They could assist in removing the wounded to places of safety and comparative comfort, and they could counsel them in the hour of their trial and necessity. But they needed the refreshing agencies which we had packed and sent, and which were detained on their passage in the lack of the means of conveyance. It was not the time to hope and wait and urge the quickened motions of the usual modes of transportation. As quick as thought suggested the movement, measures were provided for its accomplishment. The team was soon in hand, and at the first possible moment it was at City Point and in process of loading with its precious freight.

Its first arrival at the Front was hailed with demonstrations of joy. There was no time that the team could be allowed to remain idle, and it was consequently kept in brisk motion until the extreme pressure of the demand was relieved, when it was ordered for more regular and less frequent journeys. Many a blessing from the hearts of relieved sufferers and from those of gratified Delegates followed the team in its travels, and doubtless there are men living and able to continue their service to their country who could hardly have survived if the timely aid it contributed had not been afforded.

Delegates are constantly in motion in their passage to and from City Point. Reports are daily made at our office and means and supplies furnished. Cheering accounts of the success of their labors are in perpetual circulation. They tell us of nearly an hundred meetings for religious service in a single day at the camp. They tell us of religious revivals, of conversions, of recoveries, of deep and ardent and soul stirring devotional exercises, of labors and successes of almost every character as they accord with our pursuits and purposes. From the statements received, the impression is produced that thousands of the men of the ranks and sufferers of the hospitals become much more concerned in regard to their spiritual condition than they have ever done at home. In view of the dangers that surround them and the difficulties they are obliged to contend against, they experience a depth of interest and feeling altogether unusual. At such a period, a word from the Chaplain or Delegate in relation to their spiritual necessities is a word in season, and in most cases it has its effect upon the understanding and will of the subject. It were duty, well performed, to keep in this field so ripe for the harvest, sufficient labors to work it succesfully.

---

### Mount Savage.

The town of Mount Savage is in Alleghany county, about eight or ten miles from Cumberland. It is situated in a slope of a mountain. The situation is healthy, and the resort of invalids at certain seasons of the year. Near the town is a hospital, which has been occupied by a large number of the troops in sickness or in consequence of wounds received in battle. Delegates and ladies have attended the sufferers with stores and books and papers from our supply rooms. A number of the neighbors residing in the vicinity of the hospital at Mount Savage, have contributed supplies of vegetables and other necessaries, and ministered as they had opportunity to the wants of the disabled men.

---

### Cumberland.

The City of Cumberland, in Alleghany county, is situated at the base of one of the Alleghany mountains, on the left bank of the Potomac river, and at the western terminus of the Baltimore and Ohio Railroad and of the Chesapeake and Ohio Canal. It is about one hundred and eighty miles from the City of Baltimore. It has considerable trade by the Railroad and Canal and by the National road, of which it is the eastern terminus. The population is about eight thousand. The proximity of Cumberland to the Potomac and the Railroad has exposed it to invasion by the rebels who have visited it for plunder on several occasions as well as for the purpose of securing advantages in the movements of their army. The Railroad in the vicinity has been frequently damaged, and many lives have been lost and a large number wounded in the skirmishes that have taken place.

The number of the wounded rendered it necessary that a hospital should be established and continued in use in the city. Several regiments of the army are usually quartered in the neighborhood. Our Delegates have attended the hospital and visited the regiments, distributing stores, books, tracts and religious papers, holding meetings for preaching and prayer, and assisting the Chaplains generally in their work.

Several of the ladies who are rendering service to the Commission have visited Cumberland and the hospitals adjacent, and have ministered to the necessities of the suffering.

### Clarysville.

Clarysville is a village of Alleghany county, in the vicinity of Cumberland. Near the village is the hospital that bears its name. At one time there were fourteen hundred patients in the hospital. The number at this time is nine hundred. Delegates have visited the premises and ministered to the necessities of the patients. Mr. O. Perinchief, a gentleman residing in the neighborhood has acted as Delegate and performed acceptable service in the reception and distribution of our stores and in attendance upon the sick and wounded. Supplies needed by the men were collected in the vicinity of the hospital. The neighbors were kind and contributed what they could to the cause. Others with Mr. Perinchief labored on behalf of the sufferers in the supply of such vegetables as could be secured. A Chapel for religious worship is called for and is said to be very much desired by the patients. The convalescents are called out to service in the open air, and those confined in the wards are attended in their beds. The provision of a Chapel would materially subserve the cause of religion and do good service to the men. Were it in our power the desire should be satisfied in the erection of a suitable building for Chapel purposes. Reading matter has been distributed among the men, which they have gladly received and expressed the wish for further and enlarged supplies.

---

### Maryland State Fair.

The Maryland State Fair was held in the large hall of the Maryland Institute. It was commenced on Monday evening, April 18th, and closed Saturday evening April 30th.

The proposition that a Fair should be held for the benefit of the Christian and Sanitary Commissions, came from certain ladies of Baltimore City. The first suggestion was made by Mrs. C. J. Bowen, wife of the Rev. T. J. Bowen, Chaplain of the National Hospital. It occurred in a conversation between herself and Mrs. Alexander Turnbull. The proposition as considered by these ladies, was limited to the aid of the Sanitary Commission, and when submitted to Mrs. Alph. Hyatt, it was amended by the association of the Christian with the Sanitary Commission, the Christian Commission to have the precedence. It was in this form that the suggestion was presented to the Maryland Committee, who received it with favor and promised every possible assistance to the enterprize. The expenses of the necessary preparation were proffered by the Committee and accepted. In furtherance of the object, a meeting of ladies was called, at which the proposition was discussed and approved, and the Maryland State Fair Association organized. Lady officers were at first selected, but as the enterprize appeared to be too formidable for their unassisted labors, it was agreed that a number of gentlemen should be chosen, by whom the lady officials should be aided in the duties appertaining to their respective offices. The board of direction thus constituted is as follows:

*President*, MRS. GOV. BRADFORD, assisted by WM. J. ALBERT, ESQ.

*Treasurer*, MRS. ALPH. HYATT, assisted by HENRY JANES, ESQ.

*Recording Secretary*, MRS. CAMILLUS KIDDER, assisted by JAMES CAREY COALE, ESQ.

*Correspondiug Secretary*, MRS. ALMIRA LINCOLN PHELPS, assisted by JAMES CAREY COALE, ESQ.

EXECUTIVE COMMITTEE.

MRS. ALEX. TURNBULL, assisted by GEN. JOHN S. BERRY.

MRS. C. J. BOWEN, assisted by JOS. H. MEREDITH, ESQ.

MRS. A. LINCOLN PHELPS, assisted by GERARD T. HOPKINS, ESQ.

MRS. WM. J. ALBERT, assisted by JAMES CAREY COALE, ESQ.

MRS. ALPH. HYATT, assisted by THOS. J. MORRIS, ESQ.

MRS. CAMILLUS KIDDER, assisted by GEO. GILDERSLEAVE, ESQ.

MRS. JAMES D. MASON, assisted by JAMES W. TYSON, ESQ.

MRS. JOHN S. BERRY, assisted by JAMES D. MASON, ESQ.

MRS. CHARLES SPILCKER, assisted by REV. JOHN W. RANDOLPH.

*Ladies Committee of Reception*, MRS. ROYAL T. CHURCH.

*Finance Committee*, THOS. SWANN, ESQ.

*Committee on Fine Arts,* GEO. B. COALE, ESQ., Chairman.

*Committee on Rooms and Decorations,* WOODWARD ABRAHAMS, ESQ., Chairman.

*Committee on Order,* SEBASTIAN F. STREETER, ESQ., Chairman.

*Committee on Lectures,* HON. HUGH L. BOND, Chairman.

The work of preparation was continued through several weeks, during which the ladies labored with assiduous activity animated by the hearty zeal which loyalty alone can inspire. The difficulties surmounted by them were of the most formidable character. But they were not to be deterred in the performance of the great enterprize by any obstacles that might appear before them. Ladies of most of the counties submitted proposals for admission into the Fair Association and were admitted. The counties represented are Alleghany, Anne Arundel, Baltimore, Carroll, Cecil, Dorchester, Frederick, Harford, Howard, Kent, Montgomery, Talbot, Washington, Worcester.

Besides the tables representing the respective counties, there were others as follows:

Madison Home Circle, National Tables, Fishing Ponds, West's and Newton Hospitals, Central Union Relief, Children's, Scotch Association, Strawbridge, Union Slipper Circle, East Baltimore and Patterson Park, Photographs and Books, West end and North Baltimore, German Asssociation, Cinderella, Union Knitting Circle, Jacob's Well, New England Association, Fortune Teller, Eve's Express, City Post Office, New Era, Floral Temple, Book Table, Art Table, Yacht, New England Kitchen.

The Fishing Ponds were ponds in which visiters were permitted to fish with silver hooks or their equivalent in Post Office or other currency. Jacob's Well supplied excellent Lemonade. Eve's Express conveyed packages, letters, &c., to persons to whom they were addressed, for which the price was paid. The New Era was a newspaper published for the fair by N. Snethen, Esq. The amount realized by its publication during twelve nights and an extra, was over a thousand dollars. Floral Temple, was a magnificent table of flowers. The Yacht was a fishing boat manned by young sailors.

The New England Kitchen was a very large Kitchen with all its utensils and characteristic paraphanalia. The ladies were dressed in the style of their mothers of the Revolution. The Kitchen supplied refreshments by which several thousand dollars were realized.

The Fair was one of the most brilliant and beautiful exhibitions ever witnessed in this country. More extended efforts have been presented, by which more space has been covered, greater crowds accommodated and more money realized, but for display in taste, elegance and beauty, the Maryland State Fair has never been excelled or equalled. Never was there a greater or more attractive display of elegant ladies. The least that can be said of them is, they were beautiful in person, tastefully dressed and elegant in every movement. There need be no fear entertained that their grouping in the crowded hall will soon be excelled in beauty, grace and tasteful ornamentation.

It was truly heart cheering to witness the grand display and to associate it with the grander ideal of benevolence that wrought it up for the relief of the sufferers of the hospitals who needed and deserved all the attention it could secure and all the comforts its means and agencies could provide. The moral effect of the scene and its associations is not to be described. To undertake the description were folly. The grand Tableaux it presents is that in which age, and youth, and beauty, and grace, and wealth and moderate condition, and even poverty, with official station, and fame, and intelligence, and common life, all appear with their contributions to the common store from which the desired relief is to be realized. The common fund becomes a sacred treasure sanctified to the noble and glorious purpose of mitigating and relieving the sufferings of humanity, encountered and endured on behalf of the proudest and most exalted nationality that ever existed. It was in the names of civilization and patriotism and religion that the great enterprize was started and to their cause as represented by the bleeding objects of the battle-fields and afflicted inmates of the hospitals will the fruits of its labors be applied.

The nationality was well represented in the effort to work up the voluntary enterprize of the people in the greatest and grandest scheme of merely human benevolence the world ever witnessed. The Fair was opened with exercises becoming the occasion. Prayer was offered by the Right Rev. W. R. Whitingham, D. D., Bishop of the Protestant Episcopal Church in Maryland. A national hymn was then sung, after which Gov. Bradford formally opened the Fair by an address appropriate to the occasion. The address of the Governor was followed by addresses by his excellency, Abraham Lincoln, President of the United States and General Wallace, military commander of the district. Mr. Wilson G. Horner, then sung the popular song "We're coming Father Abraham."

At the conclusion of the opening ceremonies, the immense throng by which the Hall was crowded, proceeded on its promenade in a rapid view of the ladies and their tables and other sale arrangements. The business part of the busy scene soon commenced, when the funds and articles of sale passed through the process of changing hands. The goods were sold duriug the progress of the twelve days and nights, and the funds returned in an amount which exceeded EIGHTY THOUSAND DOLLARS.

The Secretaries of the various departments of the United States Government visited the Fair, and with other distinguished gentlemen addressed the vast audiences in attendance.

If our limits would admit of it, we should be glad to give an extended notice of the effort of the ladies, embracing in detail the history of the tables, &c., and the labors of the fair saleswomen representing the city and counties, with delegations from other States. But when we say that the record of their names alone would cover several pages of our report, we are sure we shall not be blamed for the omission, especially when we state that we are obliged to leave out considerable matter that we have prepared. It must not be regarded as invidious, however, if we speak distinctively of the most beautiful ornament of the Hall, "the Floral Temple" of Mrs. Hyatt, and the most unique specimen of representative life on exhibition in one of the large upper rooms in the form of the "New England Kitchen." By the delicate and beautiful representatives of their mothers of the Revolution, the most palatable and refreshing dishes were served up in the Kitchen, and if any visitor went away with his hunger unsatisfied, the fault was all his own, and we have no sympathy for him in any sufferings that might have been occasioned thereby. Several matronly forms of over seventy years were the observed of thousands of observers as they mingled with their younger and more agile companions of the occasion, all attired in the costume of the ancient worthies of the revolutionary era. It was sometimes difficult to distinguish the maidens from the matrons, so well did each personate the character they represented in the person of the wives and mothers of the heroes of the olden times. The activity and grace with which the elders did the honors of the occasion, were only equalled by the dignity and stateliness with which the youngers imitated the ancient character.

The Fair in its perfection and completion was highly creditablt to our fair townswomen and countrywomen. The benfits it has been the means of conferring upon the sufferers of the battle-fields and hospitals, have caused the invocation of many a blessing upon the heads of the gentle and thoughtful and laborious contributors to its success. May those blessings be fully realized and may those who share them be encouraged by them to future labors on behalf of their afflicted and needy countrymen. From present prospects, battles have yet to be fought and maimed men have yet to be brought from the fields to the hospitals, and sympathies and labors have yet to be mingled in providing the means of relief and comfort for them. We doubt not future calls for aid to our Commission will meet with a ready response from the homes of many of our fair co-laborers in our Christian service. Through the gentlemanly Treasurer of the Association the Committee acknowedges the receipt of forty thousand one hundred and forty-six dollars and fifty cents.

**The National Book.**

The most prominent of the literary features of the Fair was the National Book entitled, "Our Country," projected, edited, and published by Mrs. Almira Lincoln Phelps, Corresponding Secretary of the Maryland State Fair Association. The book is composed of original articles, in prose and verse, contributed by distinguished American writers. It is dedicated to the mothers, wives, and sisters of the loyal States, whose sons, husbands, and brothers are periling their lives in the cause of their country. The contributors are Hon. Edward Everett, of Massachusetts; J. H. Alexexander, L. L. D., of Maryland; Rt. Rev. T. M. Clark, of Rhode Island; Mrs. L. H. Sigourney, of Connecticut; James Wallace, of Maryland Volunteers; Rev. Thos. Hill, D. D., of Massachusetts; Rev. John Lord, Connecticut; Rev. A. C. Coxe, D. D., N. York; Allan D. Brown, U. S. N., Vermont; Mrs. Emma Willard, New York; Rev. A. P. Peabody, Massachusetts; Major B. Mayer, Maryland; Mrs. S. J. Hale, Pennsylvania; Mrs. E. Ellett, New York; Col. Charles E. Phelps, Maryland Volunteers; Rt. Rev. G. W. Burgess, Maine; Miss Anna H. Dorsey, Washington City; Ex-Governor Washburn, Massachusetts; Mrs. Sophia M. Eckley, Massachusetts; Hon. J. P. Kennedy, Maryland; Lieutenant E. F. Fisher, New York; Charles E. Norton, Esq., Massachusetts; Mrs. Celia M. Burr, Ohio; Mrs. C. B. F. Landrum, New York; Thos. E. Vanbibber, Esq., Maryland; E. J. Ellicott, Esq., Maryland; Miss Martha Quincy, Massachusetts; Chancellor Kitts, Maryland; Mrs. C. A. Hopkinson, Massachusetts; Miss C. G. DeValin, Maryland; Rev. T. D. Huntington, Massachusetts; Rev. W. H. Muhlenburg, D. D., New York; Mrs. Lincoln Phelps, Maryland; Rev. J. N. M'Jilton, D. D., Maryland; Dr. John Ordonaux, New York.

From the table of contents, as above, a fair judgment may be elicited of the value of the work. Its literary character is of the highest order, and it will no doubt circulate far beyond the times and localities of the Fair. The sales of the book realized over a thousand dollars for the funds of the Fair, and it is expected that a much greater sum will be afforded through its increasing popularity, which extends with the ever widening circle of its readers and admirers. Appropriate as it is for the centre table and the library, and as a testimonial for the times, it is eminently worthy of the occasion to which it is indebted for existence, and may be rendered a source of continued revenue to the Christian Commission.

### Fair at Chambersburg.

The ladies of Chambersburg held a Fair in July last, in behalf of the United States Christian Commission. It was well patronized by the people of the town and its vicinity. The amount realized was over three thousand dollars, which amount was paid into the Treasury of the Central office at Philadelphia. The result shows what can be done for a good cause by a few earnest-minded, persevering women. At the request of some of the ladies an appeal was made by our Committee to our fellow-citizens which secured contributions in aid of the enterprize.

Animated by the purpose of doing service in the cause of suffering humanity, the ladies persevered in this noble undertaking, overcoming all the difficulties that appeared in their way. Their success was fully equal to their expectations, and they enjoyed the satisfaction of presenting a handsome contribution towards the relief of the disabled soldiers and marines of the hospitals. Were the good example of the ladies of Chambersburg imitated by those of the numerous towns of the loyal states large accessions would be made to the Treasury of the Commission.

### Fair at Clearspring.

To the ladies of Clearspring, a village of Washington county, the Committee is indebted for the proceeds of a Fair held by them in March, 1864. The amount realized is five hundred and twenty-two dollars, which was paid into our

Treasury. A letter of acknowledgement was addressed to Miss Eliza J. Powers, President; Miss Maggie S. Dorrance, Vice President, Miss Sallie Edelen, Treasurer, and Miss Hannah M. Hale, Secretary.

The management of the Fair Association through the period of preparation and sale of the articles produced at the Fair reflects great credit upon the ladies. They have entled themselves to the thanks of the Committee, and of every friend of humanity, for their zeal and industry in securing a valuable contribution to our funds. In thus commending their earnest and successful labors, we here express the hope that the ladies of other villages and towns of our State may be induced to imitate their praiseworthy example.

---

### Burning of Chambersburg.

On the 30th of July, but a short time after the ladies held their Fair, the town of Chambersburg was entered by a number of Rebels, and after being plundered to a considerable extent, it was set on fire, and over two hundred and sixty houses destroyed. A number of public buildings, including churches and hotels were mingled in the ruin. By this unprovoked and unnecessary act of revenge, a large number of families were rendered homeless, some of them penniless. The aid of our Committee was solicited in providing funds for the relief of the needy among the sufferers. We responded at once to the call, in the use of the means within our control for the desired work. A subscription was opened at our office, on behalf of which appeals were made to our fellow-citizens through the newspapers. The amount realized in a few days was $3,261 40, which amount was forthwith paid into the Treasury of the Relief Committee at Chambersburg. Other smaller amounts were afterwards received which were transmitted to the Committe, by whom they were duly acknowledged.

**Ladies Auxiliary Christian Commission.**

It has been deemed advisable and proper by the United States Christian Commission that Ladies' Auxiliary Associasions should be organized in every congregation of religious worshippers admitting the same. The first of these associations was organized in Concert Hall, Philadelphia, on the 4th of May, 1864. The churches represented are the Baptist, New School Presbyterian, Moravian, Dutch Reformed, Methodist Episcopal, Reformed Presbyterian, German Reformed, United Presbyterian, Protestant Episcopal, Congregationalist, Lutheran, Old School Presbyterian.

A second meeting of the Association was held May 31, for completing the arrangements of the first, when, so actively had the ladies entered upon the work that a subscription was presented amounting to three thousand two hundred and seventy-four dollars.

It is desirable that Ladies' Auxiliary Christian Commissions should be organized in congregations throughout our District, and clergymen and others interested have been desired to favor the object. We have reason to believe that our appeal will meet with a general response, and that a large number of Ladies' Associations will become auxiliary to our Committee. The membership fee recommended is one dollar a year for each member.

The ladies of San Francisco, California, have acted promptly and efficiently in response to the call of the Commission. They have organized a Ladies' Christian Commission, with a membership fee of five dollars for ladies and ten dollars of gentlemen. At their first meeting a thousand dollars were subscribed.

The membership fee recommended by the Central office at Philadelphia is so small that children may become subscribers. In many families who have the ability, it would be well to have all the children recorded as members of the United States Christian Commission. It is an excellent opportunity to start the younger members of families in the enterprize of benevolence. They may become distinguished in after life in such pursuits, by being introduced thus early into the field.

**Public Meetings.**

Three public meetings have been held in Baltimore city during the year. The interest of our fellow-citizens in the work of the Christian Commission was witnessed on these occasions by the crowded audiences that were in attendance, and the earnest solicitude manifested on behalf of our mission of love and benevolence. Beneficial results were realized by those meetings in directing the public mind to our cause and encouraging its liberal sentiment in its behalf. Benefits were realized, not only in exciting additional favor towards our humane enterprize and encouraging liberal views in regard to its pursuits, but also in securing contributions to our funds. We have found it profitable to communicate information to the public as frequently as possible in the publication of our operations and necessities, and we have scarcely made a movement in this way that has not developed facts of highly interesting nature as well as opened avenues for the future extension of our plans, and the realization of greater success. We have held but few public meetings on account of the difficulties attending such efforts in providing suitable places and attractive programmes. On each occasion of our public services new interests were excited and new encouragements afforded of extending our labors.

Thanksgiving services were held on the usual Annual Thanksgiving of the 26th of November, 1863, and Fast day services on the occasion of the National Fast, August 4, 1864.

The meeting of the 26th of November 1863, was held in the Light street Methodist Episcopal church. Addresses were delivered by Judge H. L. Bond, who presided as chairman in the absence of Mr. Griffith, Rev. E. R. Eschbach, of the German Reformed church, Rev. T. Storke, of the Lutheran church, Rev. Geo. P. Hays, of the Presbyterian church, and Rev. I. P. Cook, of the Methodist E. church. Prayers were offered by the Rev. Thomas Sewell, D. D., of the Methodist Episcopal church, Rev. G. P. Nice, of the Baptist church, and the Rev. Wm. Bruce, of the Presbyterian church.

On the evening of the National Fast day, August 4, 1864,

a meeting was held in Exeter street Methodist Episcopal church. The Chairman of our Committee, G. S. Griffith, Esq., occupied the Chair. Addresses were delivered by Mr. Griffith, Rev. J. McKendree Reily, D. D., Rev. G. R. Bent, Rev. Andrew B. Cross and J. B. Stillson, Esq. These gentlemen are all active and efficient co-laborers with the Committee in the great work of the Commission.

The choirs of the churches on both occasions produced most excellent music. The crowded audiences of both occasions appeared to be highly pleased with the exercises, giving evidence of their interest by remaining until the late hour of closing the services.

The third public meeting held by the Committee was the Anniversary. It was held in St. John's Methodist Protestant church, Liberty street. At this meeting a general report of the labors of the Committee during the year was read by the Secretary. Addresses were delivered by the Rev. Dr. Shaaf, of the German Reformed church, New York, and the Rev. Lemuel Moss, of the Baptist church, Secretary of the Home Organization of the Christian Commission.

The exercises were interspersed with excellent singing by the choir of the church. The addresses were of a high order of talent, containing lessons of patriotism, and religion, and encouragement for the work of the Commission.

In these successful efforts to interest the public in behalf of our work, the Committee are encouraged to perseverance in the necessary and difficult work they have in hand. Not the least matter of interest in the use of the public meetings is the securing of the Divine blessing upon our humble efforts to relieve the necessities of our suffering fellow-men, and to labor in the name of Christ for their salvation. If we may expect God's blesings on any labor, surely it is that in which we engage for the relief of the suffering body and the safety of the immortal spirit of man.

---

### The American Bible Society.

It is with gratitude and pleasure that we record the acknowledgments of the Committee for the enlarged contributions of the American Bible Society in Bibles and Testaments. By the liberal favors of the Society we have been enabled to circulate thousands of copies of the WORD OF GOD among the representatives of every class of life as they have been assembled in the ranks of the army and on the vessels of the navy.

Many of the men in whose hands the sacred volumes were placed had never read a page of their inspired truths, nor had they ever felt the least concern in relation to their Divine counsels and instructions. Through their agency the knowledge and comforts of religion have been carried to the battle-fields, and the dying soldier has realized the benefits afforded by their intelligence and exulted in the triumph they afforded him in his passage to his rest. Souls have thus been saved that will rejoice in bliss forever. Others, still of earth, are enjoying the satisfaction of serving God in the dedication of faithful lives to Him and the hope of realizing the estate of higher happiness the departed have reached but a little while before them.

Truly the blessings of thousands of our fellow-men who "were ready to perish" will be realized in the future usefulness of an institution which has labored, and is still laboring so faithfully and efficiently in the effort to enlighten and save the souls that might otherwise continue in darkness and perish.

In ignorance of God and of his claims upon the obedient services of every one of His intelligent creatures might multitudes of men live and die in the absence of the Divine pages circulated by the American Bible Society. Such had been the condition of thousands of battle-fields without this timely intervention.

---

### Church Action.

On several occasions when ecclesiastical bodies have assembled in annual council for the consideration of their church relations, we have endeavored to procure favorable action in the form of resolutions recommending the work of the Christian Commission to the patronage of the ministers and members of the respective bodies. In a few instances we have succeeded in eliciting expressions of most favorable consideration, and the passage of resolutions as desired. On two occasions, the General Synod of the German Reformed churches thus favored the Commission. The ecclesiastical councils of the Presbyterian and Lutheran, and other churches, have ordered that the cause of the Commission be presented to the congregations under their control, recommending such aid as they might be able and willing to contribute in furtherance of the measure of humanity as presented in our circulars and general appeal to the public.

The Bishop of the Protestant Episcopal church of Maryland, recommended to the clergy of the diocese the devout observance of the day of Thanksgiving and Prayer, and the contributions of the offerings to God in the form of alms "for the relief of the sick and wounded sufferers by the war."

In consideration of the commendatory notices, by church authorities, we hope we may be remembered on occasions of Divine worship, and other occasions by the congregations and individuals connected with the same, and that we may receive large contributions from them to our treasury.

The following report and resolution were adopted by the General Synod of the German Reformed church, held in Pittsburg.

REPORT.

A communication has been received from Messrs. Griffith, Hays, and M'Jilton, on behalf of the United States Christian Commission, of the District of Maryland, stating their great need of funds for the supply of hospital stores, blankets, &c., for the sick and wounded soldiers and sailors of the hospitals, and asking the clergy to take up collections in aid of those objects on Thanksgiving day.

RESOLUTION.

*Resolved,* That we heartily approve of the cause of the Christian Commission in the United States, and that it be recommended to the pastors of all our churches to lift collections on Thanksgiving Day, or as soon after as expedient for the noble enterprize, and forward the amounts collected to the Rooms of the Christian Commission, Baltimore street, Baltimore Maryland, or to any other Committee connected with the Christian Commission.

---

### Baltimore Christian Association.

Throughout our report in connection with hospitals and other points of labor will be found the names of members of the Baltimore Christian Association. Sixty-three of nearly one hundred, composing the Association, have been commissioned as Delegates. They have visited the camps and hospitals from Cumberland to the front near Richmond, and rendered great service to the cause. The services of these gentlemen are the more valuable on account of their large experience in visiting the sick and ministering to the necessitous of every character. Among the hospitals and public institutions of the city, nearly all the members of the Association are in the habit of visiting. They assist the Chaplains in holding prayer-meetings, and praying by the bedsides of the patients, &c.

We have been assured by Chaplains and Surgeons of hospitals that the services of the members of this Association could not be omitted without detriment to the cause of religion among the sufferers of the wards and the convalescing under their charge. The monthly meetings of the Association are held regularly when reports of most interesting character are presented. There is scarcely a service in which persons of a religious character can engage that is more profitable to the community than is that rendered by the Baltimore Christian Association.

---

### Maryland Soldiers Home.

There is an Association chartered by the Maryland Legislature for the purpose of providing an Asylum for the permanently disabled soldiers of the war who have no means of support. The number of these after the war will be considerable. Several have appeared at our rooms desiring relief. Others have been driven to the extremity of street begging. Others again have been obliged to seek a home in the Almshouse. It is desirable that some permanent provision should be made for these persons. The Secretary of our Committee is the President of the Association, having this work of benevolence on hand. It is designed that land shall be purchased in the vicinity of Baltimore city, upon which buildings shall be erected for the permanent accommodation and support of these unfortunate persons. At present, accommodations are provided for twenty to twenty-five by the erection of a frame building on the bed of an unopened square of Oregon street, between Franklin and Mulberry streets. Permission was given by the Mayor for the occupancy of the ground, which it is supposed will not be required for the use of the street for several years to come. The hospital building is one of the most complete and comfortable of its kind that has been erected. It is plastered and painted, and altogether as serviceable and as durable as an ordinary frame dwelling. This is as necessary a work as has interested our Committee, and it has our most earnest prayers for its success and usefulness.

---

### Services of Dr. F. E. B. Hintze.

We have found it necessary in the prosecution of our labors outside of the hospitals and camps, to call in medical aid on behalf of Delegates while passing through the city, refugees in distress, whom we have assisted in necessity, the families ot absent soldiers and others discharged from the service. In nearly every case we have called for the attendance of our friend, Dr. F. E. B. Hintze, and although he has retired from the practice of his profession, he has, with his usual readiness and promptness responded to our calls. In other than professional services we have been favored by the Doctor's assistance, and it is due to him that the Committee should make this acknowledgment of the application of his distinguished abilities in the service of the Commission.

### Services of Dr. Jos. C. Bensinger.

Dr. Jos. C. Bensinger, of Catonsville, Maryland, was twice in our service as a Delegate. He rendered very important assistance in the exercise of his medical ability to Surgeons of the army. The following letter was received from him after his return from his first service:

G. S. Griffith, Esq., *Chairman of the Committee U. S. C. C.:*

Dear Sir:—I left Baltimore on June 28th, at 5½ P. M., for City Point, Va., arrived there about 6 P. M., June 29th, after stopping a short time at Fort Monroe.

Reported to Surgeon E. B. Dalton, chief Medical Officer, June 30th. Was, by request, assigned to the Sixth Corps, having previously worked in that corps. Assistant Surgeon McDonald, chief Surgeon of the corps, assigned me to Hospital B., with Surgeon Saunders. Our patients numbered upon an average, one hundred and twenty, there being constantly removals and additions. The time I remained there I performed the routine duties; attending to the sick and wounded, dressing, prescribing diet, &c.; assisting in removals, &c. A few of our Surgeons and Delegates being taken sick, I also took charge of them. Left for Baltimore July 13th, arrived home July 15th; my visit having only the more fully impressed me with the conviction of the inestimable good the U. S. Christian Commission accomplishes.

I remain very respectfully, ever yours to command in this Christian work,

Jos. C. Bensinger, M. D.,

---

### Services of Mrs. C. A. C. Norris.

Among the leading women that have labored in the service of our Commission, we have held in high estimation, Mrs. C. A. C. Norris, of Boston. The valuable services rendered by this lady are extensively known and appreciated. At West's Building Hospital, she labored a long time with assiduous application. Her active service among the ladies of the New England Kitchen of the Maryland State Fair will not soon be forgotten. While at West's Building Hospital there was no case of necessity that escaped her notice, and her ministrations to the sufferers were most promptly and efficiently applied. Possessing perfectly the confidence of the Surgeons of the hospital, she has moved among the wards dispensing her services as they were needed in the relief of the disabled objects of her sympathy and care. Many a basket has been filled at our rooms which she has herself carried to the scene of her labors and dispensed the contents with her own hands to the sufferers. May the life of this noble lady long be spared for the exercise of her distinguished benevolence.

---

### Services of Mrs. J. C. Moore and her Daughter, Miss Jane B. Moore.

These ladies have been in the service of suffering humanity since a short time after the commencement of the war. They have generally selected as their points of labor such places as were most destitute of the services they were ever ready to render. During the past year they have endured many privations and hardships, and labored most faithfully and efficiently among the camps and hospitals of the army of the Potomac. They are now in the Shenandoah Valley, where they are ministering in their benevolent services to the sick and wounded of the camps and hospitals. Under the protection and by the permission and request of General Grant, they prepared the delicacies they had provided through the the contributions of their friends and delivered them to the suffering men, who would otherwise have been deprived of the services of which they were greatly in need. Officers and men of the army beheld the labors and endurances of these noble women with amazement, and were induced to render them every assistance in their power. They proceeded as near the trenches as it was possible for them to go, and under the notice and approval of the most distinguished of the army officials, administered their nicely prepared provisions and stimulants to the patients entrusted to their care.

Like services with those performed in the army of the Potomac, was rendered to that of the Valley of the Shenandoah, under the supervision and with the approval of General Sheridan. The following letter recently received from Miss Moore, tells a much better story than we can of the dangers and hardships endured and services rendered by these self-sacrificing, devoted and truly patriotic women.

EIGHTH CORPS HOSPITAL,
WINCHESTER, VA., *August* 31, 1864.

REV. J. N. M'JILTON, D.D.:

DEAR SIR:—On my return from daily distribution in Sheridan Hospital I received your kind letter, and hasten to thank you for the generous assistance and encouragement I have ever met with from you, in a task whose difficulties are known to few, and if aught from my pen can benefit the suffering, or appeal in their behalf, it shall not be wanting. Early in the spring we visited Wheeling, and collected some thirty boxes of stores and delicacies for the troops in the Valley, receiving also from Mr. Stewart a large assortment of books, leaflets, paper, &c. With these we visited General Siegel's army, near Winchester, supplying the 12th West Va., the 1st Wheeling Battery, Snow's Maryland Battery, the 1st Va., the 54th Penn., 18th Conn., 34th Mass., and other regiments, with Hymn-books, papers, soldier's books, pickles, stationery, &c. The army received marching orders before we left, and we had the satisfaction of bringing a mail of our own collection, (knapsacks and writing material having been sent to the rear) of thirteen hundred letters, some of them doubtless, the *last* the writers ever penned.

In May, by the advice of the Surgeon General, we took a large collection of stores up the James river, remaining ten weeks in the hospitals of the 10th and 18th Corps, at Point of Rocks, on the Appomattox. After the battle of May the 20th, many of the wounded were brought here, and to not a few of these we supplied as well as others could supply, the places of mothers and sisters far away. In our little room, filled as it was with boxes, barrels, and cooking utensils, the Delegates had one delightful soldier's prayer-meeting, attended by some fifty of our patients. In the grave-yard at the "Point," sleep many who were then the objects of our care. When the mine was exploded, and the disastrous charge made before Petersburg, a wide field was offered in the field hospitals of the 9th corps, within some two miles of Petersburg, and a tent being furnished us, through the kindness of the Medical Director, Dr. Prince, at General Burnside's request, we devoted ourselves more particularly to the relief of the sick and wounded of Gen. Ferrero's Division, (colored) and mostly from Maryland. The horrors of Gettysburg did not surpass those of that day—even yet I recall those woods, thickly strewn with the mangled and dying, some with arm and leg off, one with both eyes gone, some insensible, and others moaning, in an agony of pain. Only half an hour had elapsed since they had been wounded, and the war of musketry close by, sounding awfully in our ears, as halting our ambulance, Rev. Mr. Boole, of the Commission, my mother and self, made pail after pail of milk punch, and distributed it, with handkerchiefs, bandages, canned peaches, wine, crackers, &c., to the sufferers. "I have not seen a lady for months," said one poor boy, who was ready to weep over the disasters of the day, "and it does seem sweet to see one in this awful place." Colored citizens of Baltimore cried to us to give them "only one cracker," and our hearts melted when the appeal was enforced by their directing our attention to the "stump" of an amputated arm, or leg. In the box there proved to be a few stray tracts, and books, and these were handed to those who could read. "Are those Testaments?" said a colored soldier, "do please give me one. I tried so hard, as I lay wounded on the field, to reach one, that had dropped from a dead soldier's pocket, but my wounds were so painful I could not crawl far enough." What a spectacle the Gospel of Peace so earnestly called for, in a spot more resembling hell than aught else on earth! As I moved in the midst of these appalling horrors, I heard many groans and prayers, one just brought from the "table" was saying with all the fervor of a departing soul, "I shall never see my home again, but Lord, don't you forget me." Death revelled in their midst, and few had time to number or notice his victims. How delighted they were to know that we would bear their messages home to their native city, our much loved Baltimore.

As we hurried to and fro, a group of newly organized colored musicians, collected in the woods, and struck up, "My Maryland." We had not time then to thank them, but do it now. In this hospital we remained two weeks, ministering to their temporal wants, as well as writing letters, which most of them could not do themselves. Many of these are well worthy of publication; one with five severe wounds, wrote to his wife, "You must take things as they are. I am a soldier. *Keep the faith*"—and then passed away.

Through the assistance of Mr. Caton, a Delegate from Ohio, we were enabled to do much good, and the eagerness of the 30th and 39th U. S. colored regiment, in the Fourth Division, for reading and spelling books, cannot be described. They literally hungered and thirsted after instructions. And some carried books of large size through many a weary march. When I refused them to those who could not read, they looked up pleadingly, saying, "But I 'wants' to learn. I'se tryin all I can." Never shall I forget the words of one, brought in sun-struck, and laid on the earth, in the midst of great discomfort. I asked where his friends were, "Lady," said he, "my wife is somewhar, and my mother is somewhar, but whar, I don't know." He seemed to feel his condition deeply; but a moment after, Jesus was mentioned. "Oh," said the poor untutored African, his eyes beaming as he spoke, "*You* may have all this world, but give *me* JESUS."

And rarely have I heard such fervent, heart-felt prayers, as the man poured forth, in behalf of our distracted and bleeding land. Would that all Christians prayed thus!

Before going to the 9th Corps, the deadly malaria, so fatal in this region during the summer months, and frequent riding without regular food, from early morning until late at night, laid me on a sick bed, and I was removed at the suggestion of Dr. Pratt, of a Maine regiment, on board the hospital boat, "Matilda," lying in James river. Dr. Pratt was the Surgeon in charge, and through his care, though certainly not by his advice, I went again to the hospitals nearer Petersburg. In the 1st Maryland Dismounted Cavalry, at Deep Bottom, I found a number of sick, who preferred remaining there to being removed to Point of Rocks. They were needy and uncomfortable, and milk, tomatoes, jelly, stationery, &c., were very acceptable. The 1st, 4th, 7th and 8th Maryland regiments, we found in the "Maryland Brigade" of the Fifth Corps, and, says one, "may you be rewarded by the deep gratitude of thankful soldiers." Here, as in other Maryland regiments, we distributed Testaments, Hymn-books, papers, books, stationery, canned and dried fruits, condensed milk, handkerchiefs, &c. The 5th Maryland received Testaments and Hymn-books very joyfully, and many of the forms that gathered round our ambulance, on that shadowless, burning plain, were so altered by exposure and hardships, that they would scarcely have been recognized at home. We could hardly refrain from tears, when in an opening in a dense wood, frequently shelled by the enemy, and on the very spot where a soldier had been killed two days before, the small remnant of the gallant 2nd and 3rd Maryland regiments, now, as one said, "a mere handful of men" surrounded us, and expressed their satisfaction that some one from their State was looking after their interests in an especial manner. Money could not purchase the precious letters we since have received from them.

"The Hymn-book you left," writes one, "has solaced many a lonely hour." "I greatly prize the Testament, especially as it was given by your hand." "We pray for you, that God may bless you, morning and night, and we thank God who put it into your heart to come among us."

Mr. Caton and myself had a narrow escape. Hearing that many of the colored soldiers from ignorance in writing, and directing, were unable to send their money safely to their friends, I offered to carry it in person, and deliver it freely, for those whose families resided in Baltimore, Some two thousand dollars, a number of watches, letters, likenesses, &c., were thus entrusted to our care, and conveyed to their friends. Some articles belonged to the fallen, and were received in tearful grief—the distress of one poor woman, whose husband had been killed, I shall never forget. One, whose arm was gone, wrote, "The night before, when I heard we was going into a fight, I went out by myself and prayed, and the only Best Friend I thought of, was the LORD."

Whilst receiving and directing the envelopes, which enclosed their payments, the Rebels opened a new and powerful battery upon us, and shell after shell whizzed through the air. We did not imagine ourselves in danger, until all at once a death-like stillness rested on the group, we in the ambulance did not see that on the ground beneath our wagon, and even under the horses, men were crouching for shelter; but we did hear the unearthly screeching of a shell, and with mute, pale faces waited for it to explode. But it passed directly over our heads, and we were safe. Half an hour after we left, several exploded on that very spot.

We had previous received every kindness and assistance from Lieutenant General Grant, by whose special favor we were allowed to remain "Front" in General Burnside' Corps, and the anxiety thus shown by the Commander of our armies to have the wounded receive all the attention in his power, to our mind covers him with more honor than victories such as Vicksburg. By the way, the barrel of pickles furnished us through Mr. Bent, was taken in the midst of a drenching rain, to some of General Sheridan's weary raiders as they were encamped at Haxall's Landing on James, river. The brave and chivalrous Col. Preston, of the 1st Vermont cavalry, tin cup in hand, dealt them out to his tired men, meeting our thanks with the reply, "No ladies, I feel that I cannot do too much for soldiers." And then he proposed, and they all gave. three hearty cheers for their friends in Baltimore."

But a short time after, riding in the cars, I saw chronicled in the morning paper, the heavy loss of the 1st Vermont, and the death of the noble Colonel leading a charge at Coal Harbor.

Just before one of the battles of the Valley, we reached Winchester, and through the kindness of Dr. Manown, the *Christian* Surgeon of the Fourteenth Va., were furnished a room, &c., on Braddock street, near the West Va. or 8th Corps Hospitals. The afternoon of the 21st, we spent preparing pails of milk punch for the long trains of wounded coming in army wagons from the "Front."

Just about dark, they arrived, and we set to work supplying those on the street. It was a strange warlike scene—dark night settling over Virginia roads; mud, cavalry and wagons—the *last* freighted with mangled, bleeding, but *precious* burdens. The night was raw and chilly, but we flitted to and fro, with flaming candles, and by the invaluable assistance of my faithful Brooklyn orderly, James Buckridge, supplied several hundreds. By and by we came to those containing the "Rebels," and the question was asked, "shall we supply them?" "Certainly," was my reply, "we have never made any distinctions, and as *Christians*, never shall." The sufferers had a night's ride of twenty-two miles to Martinsburg before them. "But that punch did us a heap of good," said one, afterwards. Next night we supplied the wounded in forty seven wagons, though two of their agonized victims were dead when they arrived. The whole town seems to be full of hospitals, the Churches and many private dwellings being crowded, as well as the numerous tents of Sheridan, which, through the kindness of Capt. Mann, the courteous Quartermaster, we have been able to visit daily, and with constant supplies. In one ward is Isaac Price, of the Fifteenth Va., a soldier of thirty-eight years of age, with a wife and nine children, the eldest of whom, a lad of nineteen, is in the Tenth Va. But the greatest of calamities seems to have fallen upon him, for both his arms have been amputated, yet he is cheerful and patient, always greeting us with a happy smile.

On the Church floor lay young Sergt. Smith, from N. J., shot through the lungs, and so agonized by the delirium of pain, that he vainly sought to tell us his father's name. What agony was in his tones as he repeatedly exclaimed, "*Oh I can't tell my father's name!*" God grant that in the days of health he had made a loving friend of His Heavenly Father, and went to be with him forever! "Thanks be unto God for that, I know and feel its truth!" exclaimed a

Pennsylvania soldier named Jones, dying away from a destitute family, when I read to him of "that fountain"

"Plunged beneath whose flood
Sinners lose all their guilty stains."

"What shall I read to you?" I asked Eli Davis, a member of the Fourteenth Va., mortally wounded. "I'm not much acquainted with books, and have no preference." But blessed be God, he was acquainted with Jesus, who revealed Himself to him as he lay there, wounded and without any outward agency, drew him to Himself. But the sweet prayer,

"Leave, oh leave me not alone,
Still support and comfort me!"

found an echo in his heart, and when I read those lines of a favorite hymn,

"We speak of the realms of the blest,
That country so bright and so fair,
And oft are its glories confessed;
*But what must it be to be there!*"

his face shone, he was very near that glory, "and," said he, "I long to go! I want to go to my Jesus." For weeks Gilbert Buchanan of the Tenth Va., has been my daily care. Earnestly he desired to live; he was so young and it was hard to die without the sight of father or mother, whom I had written to to come and see their dying son. Oh what a sad case his was! how sick as he was, he counted the miles and the length of the journey, and then died without the sight of a familiar face.

Every day a little package of letters, written for the sick and dying, by my mother, goes into the mail box, and what histories they reveal!

When you give a package of stationery to the Commission, dear reader, do you ever think what messages will be written upon each page? Some parent will hear of the death of the first or youngest born; some stricken wife learn that strangers cared for and closed the eyes of a dying husband, while to others tidings of safety will be gladly sent.

Do not then withhold your offering.

One more incident from the many, and I close.

I want to show how a little girl's gift was bestowed, and to whom. Among some articles received by me from the Baltimore Commission, was a handsome Needle Bag, of soft red, white, and blue material, enclosing a few pieces of candy and a Carte de Visite of the giver. A note dated Gettysburg, Pa., February 25th, accompanied it and read as follows:

DEAR SOLDIER:—I can't do much for you, as I am a very little girl, but I think about you and pray for you too. I hope you are good and pray for yourself. When we had the battle here, I saw how you had to suffer, and I pity you. I carried things to the sick soldiers, and, if you were here, would do it for you. I send my picture that you may see how small I am. Good bye.

LITTLE CARRIE FAHNESTOCK.

Perhaps Carrie thought she would never hear of her offering again. We shall see. On the Church floor lay a bright black eyed boy, named George Hill, a dear little fellow whom our good Dr. Manown carried in his arms from the wagon, the night the wounded came in. "It's a child's weight," said the Dr., as he tenderly guarded the maimed hero, "And I'm only a child," answered the clear treble voice. Where could Carrie have found a fitter recipient for her present. This is Georgie's reply:

WARD 7, SHERIDAN HOSPITAL,
*November 5th*, 1864.

DEAR LITTLE CARRIE:—I am quite a little boy, and my name is Georgie Hill, Co. K, 13th West Virginia. I have been a soldier boy fourteen months, and was wounded in the leg with a minnie ball on the 19th of October, near Cedar creek, Va. I was carried to Newtown, and lay in a tent, and on the 20th, the Dr. took my right leg off. My father is dead, but I have a mother, three brothers and one sister in Mason Co., Va. Three of my brothers are dead, all soldiers, one died in the Mexican War, one at the siege of Vicksburg and one in the hospital at Gallapolis, Ohio. Mrs. and Miss Moore, who were at Gettysburg after the battle, are here taking care of us, and Miss Moore gave me your dear little present. She told me I must keep it as long as I live, to remember the time I lay wounded on the Church floor in Winchester, and I will. Yesterday they brought me to this hospital where the sick are all in tents, and I find mine very cold this windy day. I don't like it half so well as a house, and if I could, would not have left the warm Church. I was afraid Miss Moore would not know what tent I was in here, and so I should miss the nice things she brings round, but she found me to-day right in her ward. She got me a little puzzle box with seven pieces of wood, and if you know how, you can make squares, triangles, and funny figures. At first I could not put them all back into the box. I shall play with it when I go home, before I get my wooden leg, and am able to run round. We do suffer a great deal. One poor boy died next to me in the Church. He was in so much pain, he could not tell where he lived nor his father's name. He was shot through the lungs and could hardly breathe. I heard him cry, "Oh! Lord help me! I can't tell my father's name!" I have not been home for fourteen months, and don't know when I shall get there. I have not heard from my mother for two months. Either she does not get my letters or I don't get hers, I don't know which. I am going to eat the candy after dinner—(I had some difficulty in convincing him of the propriety of waiting.) A lady brought me some pudding but it has lemon in it, and I don't like lemon, so I keep looking at the candy. Miss Moore asks if there is anything else I want to say. But I never wrote to you before, so you must excuse me, good bye Carrie.

Your little friend,

GEORGE HILL.

I hope Carrie will do more for the soldiers. I cannot close without acknowledging the kind assistance of Mr. Brackett, the Delegate from Maine, in charge of the station, who has furnished us with such articles as were at the Commission room. To Dr. Brock, also, I am indebted, as well as the suffering soldiers. May the time soon come when we shall no more need to perform such acts of mercy! That the blessing of God may rest indeed and in truth, upon all who have aided us in our labor of Christian love, is my most earnest prayer, and upon none more than yourself.

I remain dear Sir, yours very truly,

JANE BOSWELL MOORE.

# REPORTS OF DELEGATES.

## Report of Rev. O. M. McDowall.

*August* 15, 1864.

G. S. Griffith, Esq.:

Sir:—I beg leave to report that during my two first months connexion with the work of the Christian Commission, my labors have been somewhat scattered, attending to a variety of matters connected with the progress and work of the Commission, such as destributing religious reading to the soldiers, visiting the hospitals, camps, forts, and regiments, conversing with the sick, and praying for the dying—preaching and addressing the people upon the interest of their souls, and upon the work and wants of the Commission. A good degree of interest has everywhere been visible, some conversions have taken place, and the sick and wounded appear anxious for reading, conversation and prayer. My reception everywhere has been cordial, my work pleasant, and with some success.

To be somewhat more specific, my labors consist of twenty-five visits to hospitals, seven to U. S. ships; twenty-four addresses, nine sermons, two hundred conversations and five prayer-meetings attended. My acquaintance with the Chairman and general Agent, Rev. G. R. Bent, has been to me very pleasant. Time will never efface from my heart the kind manner of my reception, and the pleasant relation the writer has sustained to all the Delegates with whom he has become acquainted. Should my health be sufficient, I shall be most happy to continue to labor for so good a cause.

Permit me to add a few incidents that have come under my own observation. One day an officer met me, and seeing my badge, he remarked, "you belong to the Christian Commission." Yes, said I, but my friend what do you know about this work? "Why," said he, "I was wounded on the Potomac, at Harrison Landing, and in the Wilderness, and the Delegates of the Christian Commission picked me up, dressed my wounds and saved me; and besides I went to the war a very wicked young man, and through their influence I have been led to Christ," and, said he, "I am going back, and I may fall wounded the fourth time, and I shall want some one to care for me, so here is five dollars for the Christian Commission."

While at the front recently, I staid with Chaplain Hunt, of the 112th Pennsylvania Heavy Artillery. He related to me the effect of a conversation and tract. While we were posted upon a hill to witness the play of some batteries, some young men were profane, and the Chaplain reproved them, and I followed with some advice. The next day one young man was led to reflect upon his sinfulness, and finding just at this time one of the Christian Commission tracts in his tent, he read it twelve times, and then came to the Chaplain to confess his errors, and asked what he must do to be saved. While there, there were others who were asking what they must do to be saved. The voluntary testimony of some of the Chaplains has been furnished me that boys with whom I labored, afterwards died trusting in the Saviour. A person cannot go through the hospitals as a Delegate without hearing our noble, suffering boys exclaim, "God bless the Christian Commission." The Delegates picked me up, but for them I must have died." The sick are thoughtful and many of them are prayerful. A large majority of our soldiers have once been Sabbath school scholars. When at the 18th Corps, before Petersburg, one young man was wounded and his arm was amputated, and in a little while he was heard singing, "The Sunday School, that blessed place," &c. He was a Christian, and in his sufferings he thought of his Sunday school.

Another Sunday school scholar who had neglected his soul was about to die in the same room, and he said to the Delegate, "I want Christ," and his dying breath was prayer.

Many other incidents might be given. Suffice it to say, that it is my firm belief that the Christian Commission is saving thousands of lives and thousands of souls.

Yours, truly,

O. M. McDowall.

---

## Report of Rev. E. Loomis.

G. S. Griffith, Esq.:

Dear Brother:—When I arrived at Martinsburg, Jan. 26th, a force of 8,000 or 10,000 troops were at the post. The Cavalry were in winter quarters, but daily sending out heavy pickets, and at frequent intervals dispatching considerable bodies in scouting parties for an absence of several days.

The Infantry also were changing places, and moved to distant points frequently.

The field was, however, regarded as one of peculiar promise for Zion.

A series of meetings had been held in the Methodist Church by Chaplains Brady, of the 116th O. V. M., and Ferris, of the 123d O. V. M. These meetings had been largely attended by both citizens and soldiers, and about two hundred conversions reported.

After the return of Averill's Division from the raid in West Virginia, these Chaplains, with others from recently returned regiments, opened another series of meetings for soldiers in the German Reformed Church. These meetings for a time were crowded, and gave promise of an abundant harvest.

But just before I came to Martinsburg, an order was issued forbidding soldiers leaving camp in the evening without written permission. The effect of this order was to reduce the attendance and check the interest.

The meetings were, however, continued for a period, and your Delegates were welcomed as fellow-workers with the Chaplains. The interest revived. At some meetings about twelve would express a desire for the progress of Christians. Several were hopefully converted. These meetings were continued about five weeks, and then terminated in consequence of a military order prohibiting the absence of men from camp after roll-call.

About this time the canvass covers came to hand, and the work of fitting up regimental Chapels was finished.

Preparations for fun were being made when marching orders broke up the camps for which three of them were intended, and removed the men from our influence.

Two of them were erected and opened for religious services In one of them, that in the camp of the 14th Pa. Cavalry, Chaplain Osborne, meetings have been held to this time every evening—often crowds of great interest. In consequence, the moral aspect of the camp has been greatly improved and numbers it is believed have been led to Christ.

A soldiers Reading Room was opened in the Brick Hotel near the Railroad, and there continued through the months of February and March. April 1st, it was removed to the Grand Jury room of the Court House, a spacious and accessible room in the centre of the town, yet sufficiently retired and quiet for our purpose.

By the liberality of publishers our table has been furnished with daily papers from Baltimore, Philadelphia, and New York, with a semi-weekly from Boston, and with several of the choicest weekly and monthly papers and magazines. We have had also a large assortment of religious papers.

The Methodist Episcopal and Baptist publishing Boards have made valuable grants of books for the library, to which have been added valuable additions from individuals. Writing materials also have been furnished gratuitouslv, and freely used at our table by the soldiers.

From 1500 to 2500 religious newspapers have been distributed weekly from our rooms, besides the constant distributions of Bibles and Testaments, books and tracts, which have gladdened the hospitals and tents of thousands.

Our intercourse with the Chaplains has been fraternal and cordial. They have received large and frequent supplies of reading matter, and in warmest terms expressed their obligations to the Christian Commission. We have been welcomed at the weekly Chaplains' meetings, and in various ways have wrought pleasantly together as mutual helpers in a common cause.

We have frequently visited, with papers and tracts, the prisoners of the guard-house and the patients of the Post Hospital. The hospital has been an interesting field of labor. It has been a privilege to be recognized by lonely desponding patients as a friend, to receive the interested attention of the careless, to direct the enquiring, to soothe

the last hours of the dying, and to hear the expressed faith of some awaking to a new life.

At the time of the capture of the supply train from New Creek and pursuit by our forces, March 2d, I joined a body of reinforcements passing through Martinsburg in order to secure such help from the Christian Commission as the exigencies of situation might demand. On this trip I visited the Chaplains and troops at Cumberland, and arrived at New Creek in time to receive early intelligence in relation to the pursuing expedition.

March 12th—Acting under your instructions, I also made a tour of observation on the western line of the Baltimore and Ohio Railroad. I went as far as Grafton, and visited and held preaching services at the barracks and the hospital.

Associated with me at Martinsburg at different periods were J. B. Poerner, Rev. M. M. Langley, Rev. A. G. Loomis and Brothers C. O. Kneopper and J. V. Ebbinghans, the last two were students from the Theological Seminary, Mercersburg.

Brother Poerner, assisted by Brother Ebbinghans, labored among their countrymen, the Germans, of whom there were several in every regiment, and some companies and battalions were composed almost entirely of those who listened eagerly to men able to use the tongue of the *Fatherland.*

Those brethren also held services in the German language in the German Reformed Church, Sabbath afternoons, for the benefit of both citizens and soldiers.

Brother Langley, having become specially interested in the 34th Massachusetts, at Harper's Ferry, followed the regiment to Martinsburg, and during the brief remainder of his term of service toiled diligently with them. He was rewarded in seeing a Chapel tent of the Christian Commission erected in their camp, in delightful evidence of the quickning energy of the Holy Spirit in the meetings thus held, and in the gathering of a regimental church, to which six were admitted by baptism, and others on profession of their faith.

Brother A. G. Loomis continued the work after Brother Langley's departure with not a little watchfulness and diligence, removing the Chapel on the receipt of *marching orders* by the regiment, and again setting it up when the orders were countermanded—and again, almost immediately taking it down again when the regiment removed.

Brother A. G. Loomis also followed the regiment to Harper's Ferry, and wrought among them there till the expiration of his term of service.

Brother Kneopper has been a valuable co-laborer in camp and hospitals, and with Brother Ebbinghans remained on the ground after my departure.

Our work has been seriously interrupted by the illness of two of our number, which has not only suspended their own labors, but divided the care of some of the brethren for a season.

I review my own work, humbled that results have been so small in comparison with what has seemed necessary and expedient; yet thankful that I have been permitted to engage in the blessed service, and that, as I believe, a measure of grace and prosperity has not been denied me.

Respectfully yours,

E. Loomis.

## Report of Rev. I. O. Sloan.

ANNAPOLIS, MARYLAND,
*September* 1, 1864.

The present report of my labors at Annapolis, as an agent of the Christian Commission, will embrace the last six months. My efforts in behalf of our suffering soldiers have mainly been devoted to those in the Naval School Hospital. Occasionally stores have been supplied to Division hospital, No. 2 now in charge of Surgeon Palmer. The work here, as always under this benevolent and Christian organization, has been to me such as brings a present, cheering reward. It is enough to hear the expressions of gratitude from these brave suffering men, and their oft repeated prayer "God bless the Christian Commission," to repay for anything we may do to help and comfort them. All who have not to face the bullets, endure the long marches, be subject to the privations and hardships incident to a life in the army, are under every obligation to labor to ameliorate their condition. Whatever we do for them is not so much a sacrifice or free will offering on our part as the discharge of a claim they have upon us, and upon every lover of his country. The service rendered to him who saves my life, or befriends me in deep distress is not regarded as an evidence of disinterested benevolence, or as confering a favor. Far from it. It is the expression of my gratitude for the benefit they have conferred on me. The danger encountered, the willing aid afforded, and the relief experienced, have awakened feelings that prompt to serve as evidence of my appreciation of what they have done. Thus we feel while working as an agent of your noble Commission. And frequently in the distribution of stores, as we have heard the remark, when a soldier has come for a shirt, a pair of drawers, or some other article, showing by his appearance, enfeebled and emaciated, that he needs relief—"I do not like to beg, and I would not ask for these things if I could get my pay, or if my descriptive list was here so that I could draw from the Government." We have replied, "You are not begging, my brave boy. These things are not mine, but for you and all your comrades who are suffering, and toiling and fighting to preserve the Union of all our States. Don't thank me. Don't thank the Christian Commission or any other agency. You have a *right* to any thing you require for your comfort from any Commission or Association in the army." And was not our reply a true one.

"Your prompt and liberal response to every request for stores is in evidence of the feelings you entertain for those suffering heroes. There is no point within the range of the numerous hospitals scattered over the land of more importance than this one, and none to which the fathers, mothers, sisters and friends of the soldier, who falls into the hands of the Southern authorities, look with more interest. Because they are all brought here, when released. We have seen many boat loads arrive.

As soon as it is announced that the New York is coming we hasten down to the wharf to welcome and aid the brave suffering ones on board.

On the arrival of any boat, when present in the hospital, we have made it a duty to be there and to remain until all were removed, endeavoring to do all we could to comfort and cheer these emaciated and almost starved men. Every facility is afforded one in this work by the officers on the boat, Major Mulford and Dr. Frey, and by the kind hearted excellent Surgeon, with his efficient and worthy assistants in charge of this hospital. Indeed we could say much in praise of the exhibition of benevolence, and the prompt action taken by each of these officers in behalf of our men when they arrive from Richmond. But men who act from a sense of duty, and prompted by humane feelings, do not desire, or ask for praise. They readily say "we have only done that which it was our duty to do." Let it be enough to say that in the management of these hospitals, in the attention given to all who enter as patients, the dearest relative could find no cause for complaint. And in this statement we speak of what we know, and testify to what we have seen.

In several instances their condition was beyond description. With few exceptions they were in the last stages of starvation. We do not believe the South can supply our soldiers who fall into their hands with as large a supply, and as great a variety of food, as we can to their men whom we hold as prisoners. But making all due allowances for the exhausted condition of the Confederacy, there is, after all, a most palpable evidence of neglect and wanton determination on the part of the authorities in the South, to forever prevent all whom they take as prisoners, from taking the field again. They can treat them better and more humanely than they do.

Much has been written and published about the returned prisoners, and so far from being an exaggeration, it does not come up to the reality. In many cases it was just the breathing skeleton, dying after they reached the ward. Sometimes when they were put on the stretcher to remove them from the boat, we have detained the bearers on the wharf, until we endeavored to gather from their own lips their name and regiment, and post-office address at home, knowing that in a few hours, they would close their eyes on all the scenes of earth.

The Christian Commission commands the admiration and receives the praise of all in this hospital.

In this remark we would by no means seek to convey the impression that other benevolent organizations are not at work here. The Sanitary Commission have their agents, and liberally administer to the wants of the suffering. There is also much aid afforded by the Ladies' Relief Association of Annapolis, who have, we believe, since the first establishment of hospitals at this place, been silently but effectively laboring for the relief and comfort of the wounded and sick soldiers. Each one of these institutions finds abundant opportunities for the exercise of their benevolent designs. And every lover of his country and friend of the soldier will say of each, "God bless you, and God speed you in the noble work in which you are engaged."

We have now, in the Naval School, two distinct hospitals—one for officers and one for privates. Both are, however, under the management and control of the same medical officers. At this time we have about 350 officers as patients, and the rest enlisted men, making in all, at least, 1700 under medical treatment. The capacity of this hospital is, I am told, 1700. That is, this number of patients can be comfortably accommodated. The capacity of the hospital at St John's College is 700. At the present time they have over this number. Tents have been put up in the yard to admit those who could not, for want of room, be placed in the buildings. It affords us pleasure to be able to state, that all the officers in connection with each of these hospitals are men faithful in the discharge of their duties, manifesting a deep interest and sympathy in the cases of suffering placed under their charge. The friends of the soldiers who enter as patients here may rest assured that they receive every attention possible. Every thing that they need for their comfort and is conducive to their recovery is provided. They could not be better provided for, or even as well, at home.

But you want facts and items of interest of particular cases.

John P., a member of the 118th regiment New York Volunteers, was received from the flag of truce boat in August. He had been a prisoner in Richmond four or five months. He was a young man of about eighteen or nineteen years of age. While we were on the boat, soon after she reached the wharf, looking around at the condition of the several hundred brought away from that dismal and much dreaded place, "the Libby," Major Mulford called our attention to this case. As he moved the blanket that covered the poor suffering boy we were startled, although we had seen so many specimens of the life of a Union soldier in Richmond before. Before us was a most complete reality of a living skeleton. Every bone in the body seemed devoid of the least particle of flesh. And it was not the result of sickness, but the result of utter neglect and a want of food. How was it possible that life and speech could be found there? And yet there was the manifestation of the most cheerful, hopeful spirit that we had witnessed in any case on the boat. Major Mulford requested that he should be carefully removed, and special attention given to him in the hospital. He manifested great interest in him, as he does in all our released prisoners. It is fortunate that we have such a man entrusted with the management and care of our men received from the hands of the rebel authorities.

We took this young man's name, company and regiment, and had him carefully removed to one of the wards in the hospital. He lived about ten days after he entered. We cannot forget his earnest hopeful look or his reply, as we said to him the next day after he came, "John, notwithstanding you have suffered a great deal, no doubt you feel that God has been good and merciful to you." His eyes filling with tears, he said: "If He hadn't been I wouldn't be here, I could only trust in Him." As soon as his father learned that he was here he came and remained with him. The news that his son was alive was startling indeed, but still joyful news. For at home he had been mourned as dead for several months, and a funeral sermon preached. He died, we trust, as those of whom it is said, "Blessed are the dead who die in the Lord."

On several occasions three, four, and even six, have died on the passage up from Fortress Monroe. The names of these men have not always been obtained. Often they were so far reduced when received on the boat that they could not tell their names. It is sad to think that the bereaved and sorrowing friends at home will never learn any tidings about them. Anxiety and suspense are often worse to bear than the dread reality. Letters of inquiry have come to us about such and such a boy, who was taken prisoner, but we could not write back any thing to allay their anxiety.

But if these beloved sons, fathers and brothers are never discovered—where they died, how they died, and where buried, let the mourning friends at home remember that they perished in behalf of our noble Union. Their names will stand upon the roll of honor, along with the tens of thousands fallen in the same cause. Their noble deeds, sacrifices and sufferings are not unknown. They are gone—mustered out by the order of Heaven, but not forgotten. As they passed away we imagine a prayer for our country lingered on their lips.

Darwin S., of the 1st New Hampshire Cavalry, was another of our released prisoners. His condition was almost as bad when received into the hospital as the case already described. He was about nineteen years of age, reduced to a skeleton we had no hope that he would recover. He was a prisoner about four months. We felt a peculiar interest in him, he was so patient, uncomplaining and willing to hear of Jesus and his love for sinners. While telling him of the love of God, he often would say, "Yes, my time has come; it is all up with me, but Jesus will not turn me away." He loved to hear the Christian minister pray at his bed side. And the stricken father who was with him several days before his death would kneel often at his side, and with his spirit crushed and overwhelmed pour out a prayer to God in behalf of his dear boy. Ah! this war brings tears to many an eye! to eyes unaccustomed to weep. And what heart could remain unmoved, while hundreds and thousands of noble generous spirits, the youth, the flower of the nation, lay maimed, limbless, and pierced with the fatal bullet, all around! This young man did not live many days after his father came. The day on which he died a kind lady, whose efforts, sincs the war began, have been voluntarily devoted to the suffering soldiers, Miss M. C. Hall, of Washington, visited his tent, and sat for some time by his couch. After conversing with him, and endeavoring to comfort him with the precious promises of the Scriptures, she sung for him that sweet hymn which tells of the mansions of rest.

"In the Christian's home in glory."

He endeavored to muster all his remaining strength to unite his voice in singing this hymn. And it was evident that he felt and rejoiced in the sentiments expressed in the words of it. He believed that there was a home in glory for him—a rest for his weary soul. He is gone. The language of the afflicted father was, "I am comforted, and can bless God for the evidence which he gave of going to that rest prepared for the people of God."

Lewis B., belonging to a Maryland regiment, had been to some of the evening meetings held in the wards. Here he began to think of becoming a Christian. One evening, after the meeting, Chaplain R., who was present with us, spoke to him as he was going to his room, on this all important subject. He found he was deeply impressed with a sense of his sins. At our meeting on the following evening in one of the tents, we mentioned that a young man, the night before, had expressed a desire to be a Christian, and asked that all would pray for him. We did not know he was near, but it appears he was outside of the tent and heard the remark. He immediately came in and said, "I am that young man. I feel that I am a sinner against God, and hope you will all pray that He will forgive my sins and change my evil heart." Each day as we saw him after this, we found he was deeply in earnest. The burden of his sins pressed heavily upon him. He came frequently to my room to tell me of his distress, and how he could not sleep—his sins appeared so great, he must, he said, be lost. Nursing some wounded officers he could scarcely attend to his duties. He wanted to be on his knees all the time, crying to God for mercy. Early one morniug he arose and fell on his knees to pray. His distress was so great that all in the tent, although not Christians, felt the greatest sympathy for him. He was not ashamed to tell them what was the matter. Some one came and told me about him, and I sent word for him to come to my room. I prayed with him, and pointed him to Jesus, the Lamb of God slain for sinners. And here we trust he found peace. He has since enjoyed the presence of God, and has great delight in his service. May God keep him and bestow his graces upon him, in all the terrible scenes before him in this war.

We rejoice in being able to tell you that many of the afflicted and wounded ones brought to this hospital have found the pearl of great price. Co-operating with the Chaplain of the hospital, Rev. Mr. Henries, we have endeavored to hold religious services through the different wards as often as we had opportunity. Sometimes three, four, and six of these meetings have been held during the week; and on Sabbath mornings religious reading, papers, tracts, &c., are distributed with as many services among the patients as the time before dinner will allow us to hold.

In the afternoon and evening services are held in the chapel by the Chaplain. This is a large field of labor. Brother Henries has twice the amount of work that should be allotted to any one man. He is constantly at work doing what he can for the comfort and relief of the patients.

We shall never forget our visits to the bed-side of poor G. He was one of the returned prisoners. When the prospect of recovery seemed but slight, he began to think in earnest of death, and a preparation to meet God. The declaration of God's word soon presented themselves to his mind in all their vivid authoritative and inspired force. Eternity was just in view. "And if the righteous scarcely be saved, where shall the ungodly and the sinner appear?" We never witnessed a soul so agonized on account of sin. His calls for God to have mercy were heartrending. The nurse said he was nervous and excited. But we knew that God, by His Holy Spirit, was at work upon that heart. It was not mere excitement. It was not the fear of physical death. He had gone through hardships and sufferings worse than death. God had shown him what sin was. And his whole soul was overwhelmed. We sat on the side of his couch and tried to point him to Christ. He said: "Oh I have been such a great sinner! I can't tell you what a sinner I have been! And now I must die and meet God-- meet that God who is so good, and has borne with me so long! How shall I meet him? Oh tell me! how shall I meet him?" We repeated many precious passages of Scripture. "He that cometh unto me I will in no wise cast out. Though your sins be as scarlet they shall be as white as snow—though they be red like crimson, they shall be as wool Believe on the Lord Jesus Christ and thou shalt be saved." We prayed with him. In the prayer he frequently joined audibly, beseeching God to hear and answer.

One great cause of distress to him was the care of a brother who was in the army, and who was not a Christian. He frequently besought God to awaken him and convict him of sin. Twice he asked me to pray for that brother. I failed to get from him the regiment and company to which his brother belonged. I want to write to him, and tell him the deep concern which his departed brother manifested for him in his last moments. He prayed and agonized with God that his brother might be converted. We feel that God will hear that earnest dying prayer. Before he died he became calm. Whether Jesus was seen and apprehended by him or not we cannot tell. We hope he was. A Christian lady who was present on one occasion when we visited him, two days before he died, sung those beautiful words:

"How sweet the name of Jesus sounds
In a believer's ear;
It soothes his sorrows, heals his wounds,
And drives away his fear."

He seemed to take great comfort in the truth contained in the Hymn. God has received him, we trust, to the mansions of eternal rest.

Two other patients were in the room with poor G. They saw how anxious he was about his soul. But we could not see that they felt any concern. In one of them, an interesting young man, and apparently a bright intelligent youth, who was sitting up in his bed, said he would soon be able to go about, and he hoped to get a furlough to go home. But death is near when we least expect him. In less than two weeks both those men were numbered with the dead.

The same cold narrow house to which G. had gone was to be their abode. To put off preparation for death until the last sickness comes, oh how unwise! A few hours ago I went to see one of the last prisoners that came from Richmond. He was near his end, and is probably now gone to the spirit world. While talking with him, and urging him to trust in Jesus, he said: "Oh I ought to have attended to that subject before now—in life and in health was the time." Yes! How true it is, life is the time to make our peace with God. Oh! why should any soul put off this work to a dying hour?

Many of the prayer-meetings held in the various wards and in the Chapels, have been exceedingly interesting, and profitable to all present. It is to be lamented that so few officers congregated here as patients, not unable, however, to go about, ever attend these meetings. How cheering and encouraging to every Christian to see an officer in the army standing up boldly for Jesus! The influence of such a stand is incalculable upon the men. The most hardened are moved by it. Not long since, at one of our meetings, three officers who were present, for out of several hundred we have a few who attend, arose and testified to the power and blessedness of religion. A Chaplain present, as soon as they had spoken, got up and said, he thanked God whenever he heard the voice of an officer in a religious meeting, telling of the goodness of God and earnestly urging sinners to come to Christ. Oh, what an army we should have if all our officers were God-fearing men! How it would bring hope and confidence to every loyal heart, when there is a belief that "the Lord reigns." His remarks were earnest, and received a hearty response from all present.

We have some noble Christian men in the army, and eternity only can tell how much their prayers and example have tended to success on many a hard fought battle-field. But alas! alas! how many "who have no fear of God before their eyes!" We rejoice and bless God for the Christian element in our army, small, though it be compared with the great mass. God hears prayer, and his righteous indignation and judgments are withheld often, at the earnest pleadings of a few, who recognized Him as the Sovereign of the universe, and the One in whose hand, are the destinies of nations and individuals.

About two weeks since when the remark was made, that we should be happy to hear any who were present speak for God, and his great Salvation, a Captain got up and said, "My friends, I cannot leave this meeting without making some remarks. To-day I received a kind and affectionate letter from my wife. After going on to state how anxious she felt about me and about my safety in the present campaign, she concluded by saying, 'I have come to the determination to live a different life. I think religion is the chief thing that we ought to attend to, and I mean to seek this, the pearl of great price. Will you not join me—and should we not both now give our hearts to the Lord?'" "My friends," he continued, "I have determined to unite with my wife, in this good purpose, that we may both walk together in the way of the Lord. Will you not all help me by your prayers?"

This young friend and officer, we trust, will not give up these good resolutions, but in the strength of Christ, will go on, growing daily in the knowledge and grace of God, until at last, he and his beloved companion, with all who are dear to them, shall find an eternal home in the mansions of glory.

We have never met with any one among the numerous patients that have from time to time, been in this hospital, who have refused religious reading matter. The inquiry has generally been, "Can't you bring us something to read?" As I go through the wards I find many reading their Testaments. A few days ago as I went around with a supply of the religious weekly papers, I said to one whom I found busily engaged in reading this good Book—"ah, you have the best of all reading—that's the book of Books, and I trust you love to read it." "Yes, Chaplain, I do love to read it. That little Testament I have carried with me since I have been in the army, now near three years. I can't tell you how many times I have read it through, but every time I do read it, I find something new in it. I don't know any money that could by that little Book." From all our experience among the soldiers in our army, we do not feel discouraged or alarmed about the men who shall return to civil life when the war is over. Seed has been sown by the Christian Commission, which will spring up and bear fruit to the glory of God among hundreds and thousands of these brave boys. Many, who before they came into the army, had never read a chapter in the New Testament, or any portion of the Bible, are now familiar with every part of it.

A few days ago, one came to me and said, "Can't you give me a Bible? I have read the Testament through and through so often, that now I want to read the Old Testament." Yes, I can give you a Bible. Did you ever read this good Book before you came into the army? "No, not a word," Well, how do you like it? "Oh, I love to read it—I had often heard of the Bible, but never thought it was so interesting before." "My word shall not return unto me void, but it shall accomplish that which I please, and it shall prosper in the thing whereto I sent it."

A few days ago I sat by the couch of one seriously ill—a Lieutenant in a Tennessee regiment. He is from one of the Tennessee counties, loyal to the Government of the United States. We have little hope of his recovery. But he is happy in trusting in the promises of Christ. He is not afraid to meet death. Yesterday while sitting by his side, he said, "I have had many happy moments since I have been sick. God's promises are all true. He will never leave or forsake us. I can testify to that. Whatever is His will concerning me I know I am safe. He will do with me what seems best in His sight. I leave all with Him.

"All with the Eternal Friend,
On whom my hopes of heaven depend.
I leave—assured he knoweth best,
And in the end, I'll reach the promised rest."

Blessed promise to all who trust in Him. He will never leave nor forsake his children. Even in the valley and shadow of death he is with them.

Not long since a Chaplain stated in one of our prayer-meetings that the happiest period of his life had been during his stay in this hospital. Never before had he realized so much of God's goodness, or felt in his heart so much of the love of God. God had so revealed himself to him that he could *never* again doubt his promises.

Leonard W. H——, Comp'y G, 106 N. Y. Vols., was wounded on the 9th of July, at Monocacy bridge. He came to our hospital about a week after he was wounded. His wound was a very severe one, and while sick and suffering, he was led to think of religion and his need of a hope in the Saviour. He gave his heart to the Lord, and as we trust, is now, truly a new creature in Christ Jesus. To-day in a conversation with him, he spoke of his hope in Christ. He said that "he felt happy in the Lord, and that he believed there was a reality in the religion of the Gospel, and he would not, with God's help, turn aside from the good faith on which he had entered. The Chaplain baptized him. And we feel that he is truly a child of God, happy in the faith of Jesus.

Be assured the Christian Commission is greatly appreciated at this post. Many boys from your own State, Maryland, have been aided with stores from the liberal supplies sent us from Baltimore.

"God bless the Christian Commission" is the universal expression of the suffering in the army.

Yours truly,

I. O. Sloan,
Agent U. S. C. C. of Md.

---

## Report of Rev. Edward Cooper.

Sandy Hook, *August* 20, 1864.

G. S. Griffith, Esq., *Chairman U. S. Christian Commission:*

Dear Sir:—Your note requesting a report of my labors in the work of the United States Christian Commission, came to hand in due course of mail, and I haste amid the interruptions incident to our Head-quarters to respond to your call.

I received my commission from the Cincinnati Branch of the United States Christian Commission on the 21st of June, and proceeded to the Kanawha valley. The regiments in that vicinity had started a few days previous to my arrival to meet the forces of the raid through the Shenandoah valley, leaving but small detachments of dismounted cavalry, and a small number of convalescents at the Post of Charleston.

A few companies of the Ohio National Guards were stationed at the fortification on the line of Gauly Bridge, and the number in the hospitals was much less than usual. Two faithful Chaplains were attending to the moral and spiritual wants of the men, making a prudent use of the supplies furnished by the Cincinnati Branch of the Commission. As my mission was undertaken with special reference to Ohio soldiers, though not restricted to any class or locality in my efforts to do good, when I ascertained that large numbers were employed in guarding the Baltimore and Ohio Railroad, and for the fortifications in the valley contiguous to it, I continued my journey to Martinsburg, Va.

The Ohio National Guards wherever found, were conspicuous in their correct behaviour, and many of them were nobly resisting the baneful influences of the wicked and profane.

At Martinsburg I found two worthy brethren, with tents well stored by the Baltimore agency, and an ample field for a large corps of active and energetic Delegates. The hospitals were filled with the sick and the wounded, and the adjacent camps represented almost every regiment in General Hunter's army. The demoralizing influences generated among so many hundred in daily suspense in regard to expected orders, were very much restricted by the distribution of religious books and papers, made with personal admonitions and words of cheer and encouragememt by the Delegates of the Christian Commission.

Our labors at Martinsburg were soon interrupted by the approach of the Rebels and the consequent order for the evacuation of the place, late in the evening of the 2d of July. The reading matter and other property of the Commission were hastily stored among Union families, who had taken great interest in providing for the sick and wounded, and who had co-operated with the Delegates, for safe keeping, and to be subject to the same exigences as their own property. The perishable articles, wines and fruits, were freely distributed among the sick and wounded on Sabbath morning, as it was deemed prudent to make even a lavish use of these stores among our own suffering men, rather than incur the risk of their falling into the hands of the enemy or wasted by long storage. These restorants as well as the socks, towels, and handkerchiefs, were gratefully received by these men as they were placed along the railroad and in the cars.

About an hour before the Rebel column approached the environs of the place the train freighted with about 700 sick and wounded was put in motion, leaving a few men too feeble to be moved in the care of one Surgeon, and the devoted Christian ladies, who had given substantial and decided evidence of their love for the Union. Proceeding with this train, I ministered to the wants of the suffering as best I could under the circumstances. We arrived at Frederick late in the afternoon, and the next day the train proceded to Camp Parole, where they were kindly received at a late hour of the night. I then reported in person to the Maryland Committee, and having been commissioned to Sandy Hook and Harper's Ferry, I left at half past 4 o'clock, P. M., July 6, for my work. The train, on account of skirmishing at Point of Rocks, went to Frederick. The next day I reported to General Wallace, at Monocacy, and in the afternoon witnessed the engagement on the Hagerstown road.

On the morning of the 8th, through the courtesy of General Howe, I took the military train for Sandy Hook. Immediately after my arrival, I collected what property of the Commission could be found and began to serve the sick, weary and wounded, using the very limited means at my disposal to the best advantage.

For nearly two weeks communication with Baltimore was broken, and hence no supplies could be obtained except a few articles purchased here.

The wounded were brought in faster than preparations could be made for them, and day and night the energies of Surgeons and Delegates of both the Sanitary and Christian Commissions were taxed to their utmost abilities-

On the 25th of July, among other valuable donations, a car load of ice was received from you and turned over to the hospital. It came at a most auspicious time, when the weather was intensely hot, the dust almost suffocating, and the wards crowded with men severely wounded, and many cases of amputated limbs in danger of becoming gangrenous. The effluvia from decomposition was becoming so offensive as to endanger the health of the attendants, and intense apprehension was felt for those whose duty required their constant presence with the suffering inmates of the hospitals. The application of ice, with the use of purifying agents, soon changed the atmosphere, and cool beverages gave joy to many hundreds of poor sufferers. No benefaction reached so many persons as that car load of ice. The expenditure may have seemed large and extravagant, but it lasted about a month, and was enjoyed by more than 3,000 persons during that period. A little calculation will show that *this necessity* was made a *cheap luxury* for many.

Another benefaction, reaching a much larger number of persons in the army and out of it, is the free and liberal distribution of writing materials for correspondence. The soldier, whether in the camp or hospital, is always gratified and benefitted by communicating freely with the dear ones at home, while millions of anxious friends and relations participate in the joy of an intercourse that could not be kept up without the agency of the Christian Commission. The personal suggestions, which the occasion invites, enables the Delegates in bestowing the paper to drop "words fitly spoken," which are really "Apples of gold in pictures of silver" to the heart of the soldier melting with thoughts of his distant home.

Religious papers have been most eagerly sought, and generally are read until they are worn out, one being exchanged for another. Nor less acceptable are the attractive small books, so excellent in their adaptation to the circumstances and condition of soldiers, and so liberally furnished by the Christian Commission.

The Hymn-books are also an agency of great good in substituting Sacred Song in the camps for the falsely called amusements that bring temptations and lead to the formation of vicious habits. They are also needed on occasions of public worship, enabling many more to participate in the exercises. In these, as well as sanitary supplies, the Christian Commission meets such wants as the Government can neither prevent nor provide for by its own agencies. It is the good Samaritan of the Church, and has claims upon its membership and the benevolent, that admit of no denial without entire disregard of the noblest impulses of the heart. The streams, which flow from so many and such distant sources into one common treasury, carry still further the blessings of this noble work.

When, from all sections of all the loyal States, are found in each army and made the subjects of the Commission's pious care. Hence every contribution made to this cause enlarges and binds together millions of loyal and Christian hearts.

The army of the Middle Department is comprised of several corps, with an unusually large number of exhausted and wornout men, for whom less provision has been made for sanitary, moral, and spiritual wants than in any other portion of our country. The privations have been made more oppressive and painful by the exhausting marches of the late raid by General Hunter, and by the pursuit of the Rebels in their recent invasion of Maryland. The necessity of holding these valleys, and the probability of severe conflicts in this region, indicate clearly that immediate and incessant efforts should me made to resuscitate and encourage soldiers upon whose bravery and success so much depends. In the present status of the army and dispositions for the hospitals, no place is more important for carrying out the benevolent plans of the Christian Commission in this Department, than at Sandy Hook. This Division hospital at this point, has increased its capacity from two wards to twenty-three, in the past five weeks, and yet hundreds were compelled to lie under shelter tents on the surrounding hill sides. From seven to eight hundred have been brought in each week, and sent away to General Hospitals as rapidly as their condition would allow. The convalescent camp contains from 1,500 to 1,800 men for treatment and rest. The number of this class change each day by fresh arrivals and departures, and hence what is done for them must not be delayed. In close proximity are camps of dismounted cavalry, awaiting equipments and orders to the front. Also, men on duty along the railroad, Maryland Heights, and the surrounding fortifications. This point is therefore a centre from which your benefaction which radiate to a wide circumference of the most needy in the army.

When it is considered that no Chaplains are appointed to Division hospitals, that the men are brought in from the battle-field in their worst condition, that here the sick men from the road-side and the camps are washed and clothed in clean garments, and that very many of them are faint, weary, and suffering for nourishment, some small conception of the constant pressure may be formed by an outside observer; but the reality cannot be comprehended, and eternity alone will reveal the good accomplished.

With a view to exhibit the character of our work, I will describe the labors of the Delegates on the arrival of a train of sick and wounded men.

For example, on the 15th instant, at a little past 11 o'clock, the ambulances began to enter the area of the hospital. As the men were taken from them, we passed around, bottle and cup in hand, to give each man, who for thirteen hours had been borne along the road, a sip of wine with words of sympathy and welcome. After they were wasbed, clothed, and placed in clean beds, a cup of coffee and a cracker were passed to each by the *attachees* of the hospital, and all were left in charge of careful nurses for the rest of the night. In this manner hours are spent in ministering to their comfort on each arrival, and a way to their hearts is readily gained for religious conversation on subsequent visits.

On every proper occasion we aim to have public worship, and whenever detachments of regiments or personal friends from a distance are in attendance, religious services, conducted by one of the ministerial Delegates, accompanying the burial of the dead. Another duty to be frequently performed is the delicate one of writing letters for the sick and wounded to their companions and relations, often being the last message sent to them. This confidential and tender trust requires great prudence, refined taste and elevated piety, as an opportunity of setting forth the preciousness of the Gospel is thus given that might employ an angel's powers.

Many of the most affecting scenes of an hospital grow out of such correspondence, in a desire to conceal the real condition of the poor sufferer, and get prepared a loving heart afar off, for the distress he would gladly spare it. Said one, "write a good long religious letter to my wife—tell her I am badly wounded, but not that my leg has been amputated. I cannot fill her soul with grief, therefore say that I am doing as well as could be expected."

On another occasion he said: "I have been a backslider, but by the grace of God I will follow my Lord closer on one leg than I ever did on two. Surely God has been very gracious to me in sending this wound, for it is to be a perpetual admonition for me to keep nearer to the cross." "I can run the Christian race yet." A whole volume of similar incidents might be given in the experience of a few weeks.

The generosity, or what might be called disinterested benevolence, often exhibited by soldiers, seldom finds a parallel in human experience. There are innumerable instances of selfishness, and the vulgarity it creates, to be seen in one's intercourse with the army; but there are also conspicuous and delightful exceptions to the rule. Often in passing through the wards with a limited supply of something craved by all, I have been told "to give it to some one else who needs it more." One very remarkable instance of self-denial that came under my observation is worthy of a record in gold, and I give for the encouragement of any who may profit by such an example. Among the many who were broken down and emaciated by the long and tedious march from Lynchburg over the mountain ranges to the Kanawha, and brought from thence into Pleasant Valley, in the emergency of the rebel raids, without rest and destitute of clothing, was a minister of the Gospel from Ohio, who had enlisted as a private soldier, and, to use his own words, who felt "proud to serve in that capacity."

There was so much fortitude and self-denial, so much cheerfulness in his demeanor, notwithstanding the almost frightful appearance of a countenance that mirrored forth suffering from hunger and an emaciated form, with evident premonitions of insanity, that I felt anxious to supply him with articles so necessary to his health and comfort; but he declined the offer, saying "that he could not receive them unless it was in my power to furnish his comrades with the same;" "that if he should accept them he would excite their envy, and lose his influence over those whom he had counselled to be contented, and for whose spiritual welfare his heart yearned." Said he, "in a few days we shall be clothed by the Government, and I prefer to wait and be treated as my companions will be." His glazed eye told more than his words, and we parted. I met him several times, and always found him uncomplaining and submissive to the severity of his privations.

When rested and furnished with clothing, he said with an air of triumph, "the Government for which we fight will treat us justly." Such patriotism is seldom found, even in the army.

The intercourse of a human heart with those in distress receives and imparts sympathy that chastens and refines the feelings.

"If you would have me weep, begin the strain;
Then I shall feel your sorrows, feel your pain."

The sorrowing soldier, who weeps in gratitude for kindness and sympathy, will excite the same emotions in the heart of his benefactor, and thus teach him "that it is more blessed to give than to receive." Hence all who labor faithfully for the Christian Commission come away improved by their experience, and better qualified to discharge the duties of the pastoral office in that portion of the vineyard assigned them by the Master. The arteries of this noble benevolence are thus made to run through all our churches, whose ministers engage for a few weeks in this work, and the current flows back to bless the people. It is like "the sweet south wind, breathing upon a bank of violets, stealing and giving odor."

Therefore pour in your wealth into the Commissioner's treasury, give your ministers leave of absence for this work, and let your prayers ascend daily to a throne of grace in behalf of this Gospel charity, and He "who rewardeth not as man," and blesses the giver of a cup of water in the name of a disciple, will bring back blessings a hundred fold.

It may be proper, in conclusion, to state, that great wisdom and decision are necessary in the distribution of our stores.

The most unworthy are often the most persistent in their appeals, and everything contributed to a shirk and laggard aids in the demoralization of an army, and abstracts just so much from the meritorious and needy. The tendency to be too confiding and too lavish in giving, especially when Delegates first enter upon the work, is almost universal; but experience and prudence will soon qualify a close observer to discriminate and sift the character and claims of applicants.

And now, dear brethren, allow me to say in conclnsion, I love this work and all sincerely engaged in it, and my prayer is continually, that God will, by His Spirit and His rich abounding grace, guide and sustain you and all commissioned by you, in this practical exemplification of the Gospel of Christ.

Fraternally,

EDWARD COOPER.

---

## Report of Rev. C. Colegrove.

G. S. GRIFFITH, ESQ., *Chairman U. S. Christian Commission, Baltimore:*

OCTOBER 8, 1864.

The undersigned has the honor to submit the following report: After eight weeks sickness, I find myself still almost too debilitated to write, but I feel unwilling to withhold any longer some account of my labors from the Commission. On arriving at Baltimore, July 8, and reporting to you, I was assigned to Camp Parole, near Annapolis, Maryland. One evening, on the steps of the Chapel of the Naval Hospital, I conversed with a young captain of the 183d Pennsylvania, who while deprecating fear or anxiety in regard to death, or the hardships and perils of the battle, confessed that *one thing* gave him uneasiness, and that was *the state after death.* I responded to the effect that such solicitude was rational, and I tried to commend to him the one resource and means of safety and consolation, viz., *looking to Jesus.* I pray that good may result. The more, in view of a very sad detail of a Vermont officer a short time previous, of great losses in his regiment in the recent fighting under Grant in Virginia, especially the loss of intimate personal friends.

Prayer meeting this evening, July 15th—Brother Paine of the Sanitory Commission leading. It is indeed a place of interest, where these men from all states, gone forth in the nation's defence, sing and pray and speak, engaging zealously in the worship of God. The exercises throughout are generally intelligent, earnest and devout.

Distributed reading matter yesterday, and to-day also gave out the Pardoned Soldier, the Black Valley R. R., a curious and significant representation of the woes of intemperance, and other tracts to a battalion of men (say 300) just going to Washington to Camp Distribution, to be forwarded to their various regiments.

I went through Hospital A, wards 1 and 2, distributing, and here and there saying a word of exhortation. Found one man from Pennsylvania, who shed tears copiously in conversation, evidently very tender. He confesses past neglect of God, but since the war he desires to return and trust in Almighty grace.

At his request, purchased some lemons at the sutler's, and brought them to him.

Another sick man, and pious, from Massachusetts, I have several times seen. Both wish me to write and ask some dear one at home to come and see them. I shall write this evening. Another, youthful looking and modest man, from Fredonia, New York, interested me. He was a member of the 112th New York, under poor killed Colonel Drake. He says the Colonel was very forward, mounting rebel entrenchments, though previously wounded in the head, and was subsequently shot in the abdomen, dying in a few hours. (Colonel Drake was formerly pastor of the Paptist Church in Westfleld, New York.)

Gave some reading matter to men in front of the guard-house, and others.

Got some rice gratis, at cook-house, near the Chapel. Rice, blackberries, crackers, tea, and a little meat with pickles, though all in a homely style, are abundantly satisfactory. Let the praise be given to the Giver.

Sabbath, 5 P. M.—Preached in the Chapel this morning, from Romans v. 1. "Wherefore being justified by faith," &c. Just before service, was requested by Dr. Brown, formerly of 94th regiment New York, to attend the funeral service of two men drowned yesterday at

Annapolis. Service held at Ward 4, Hospital A, consisting of reading Scripture, exhortation and prayer. United States flag was wrapped around the two coffins. How suddenly were these two young men ushered into eternity! They were re-enlisted veterans, just returned to camp after (I think) a thirty-five days' furlough each. Excellent soldiers they were, I hear; but alas, I fear unprepared for the great change. We accompanied the dead to the place of interment, with military order, and a farewell volley was fired over the graves. How thickly lie the dead in that cemetery! How impressive the sight of those steep mounds of red earth, rising in close order, each with its little white head-board, telling in language so sadly eloquent of the fearful and fiery ordeal through which the nation is passing. It is the harvest time of the Reaper Death! Perhaps a thousand dead lie here. I have written to the friends of the men.

Evening—Preached in the Chapel to night. Good congregation and good freedom in utterance. Closed with prayer meeting—time well improved, some of the men expecting to leave in the morning. At the close a man requested to speak with me. He is almost heart-broken at the reported death of his brother, who is said to have sank exhausted, Saturday, July 9, at the battle of the Monocacy. Poor man! He wept freely, being not only keenly distressed with this affliction, but also suffering some qualms of conscience in regard to the Scriptural allowableness or right of war, or fighting at all. I tried to comfort and edify him as well as I could.

Had a conversation with Dr. ———, a young surgeon, intelligent, but unconverted. He has been through battles and dangers in Grant's campaign. It was an interesting interview. Hope it may do good. Saw brother Kelly again, of Sabbath night's interview, and rejoiced to see him cheered with the news that his brother is alive, although a prisoner. The praise is the Lord's.

Tuesday, 6 P. M., July 19.—Distributed religious papers through nearly twenty wards, and also to cars just starting off with soldiers, (perhaps 150 of them.) Also procured of the paymaster nearly $300 for absent soldiers, at their request, to be forwarded to them when I learn their address. Also have assisted in unloading and unpacking stores for Christian Commission, such as hospital stores, &c. Work not yet done, and will take part of the day to-morrow.

Wednesday, 20th.—Attended prayer meeting last evening. Good congregation of saints. Came home tired and a little dispirited. Brother Townsend, who has been a short time absent, returned last night. He is poorly with diarrhœa.

6 P. M.—Went to Annapolis to pay D E. Price his money. Tried to obtain pay for another soldier. Finally took him, got a pass, and was successful. Paymaster, Major Wilson, a kind man. Talked with negroes that dig graves in the cemetery. They say they are Methodists. Exhorted them to duty. Exhorted swearing boys to forbear their oaths. Got back tired. Found Baptist brother Bacon, of Toumansburg here to get men furloughed. Glad of his society.

Thursday—Helped an Irishwoman from New York to find her wounded son in Hospital A, Ward 1.

Called on Colonel Root at his headquarters, and also on his mother at her room. Suggested to the Colonel whether he might not give the cause of religion more aid. by signifying at least a personal wish that the soldiers in Camp as a body should attend Divine service on the Sabbath, or to that effect. To which I was sorry to hear him give a negative answer, and the more as he is known to be a professed Christian. Still I may misjudge in regard to his duty. Received applications from four soldiers at Alexandria for money to be collected and sent. Money ready for two. Distributed papers in some wards and at the guard-house. Propose to commence *ward preaching* to-morrow with brother Townsend.

Friday, 10 A. M.—Prayer meeting last night. Service in a ward, the second from this building this morning, forty or fifty present. Brother Townsend spoke.

Saturday, 10 A. M.—Yesterday went to Annapolis to obtain pay for two men.

At evening attended prayer meeting. Brother Bacon is gone home with his men. Glad of his success. After meeting last evening had an opportunity to renew conversation with the young surgeon (and a companion also, cultivated and intelligent) on some of the great themes of the Gospel, though sorry to discover, and obliged to combat some tendencies to infidelity. They may soon be at the post of danger, doing active field duty again. I pray for their illumination and salvation. This morning attended prayer meeting at Chapel at 8.

Afternoon—This morning distributed tracts through twelve wards, and letters to write.

Sunday, July 24.—Preached this morning in the Chapel, with great difficulty through infirmity. Heard brother Paine (Sanitary Commission) in the afternoon. Then a good conference. Affected by the remarks of brother W. H. Ball, of S. W. Virginia, an apparently humble Christian, who left his Southern home to fight for the Union, leaving his family behind, from whom he has heard not a word in more than three years.

Reading to-day Matthew Mead's "Almost Christian Discovered."

Brother Townsend preached a vigorous sermon in the evening.

Monday—Rainy, and rain very welcome, but rather difficult to get about. Felt discouraged last night. Prayed earnestly. Comforted a little with a work called "The Blood of Jesus." Send $40 by Express to McGrath, Arlington Heights.

Afternoon—Distributed tracts and papers in about eighteen wards. Prayer meeting in the evening. Had liberty and comfort to say a few words.

Tuesday—Went through some wards having a little religious conversation. The same in the afternoon. Found a backslider, a Baptist, from Ohio. Counselled him to duty. Evening prayer. Inquirer at the close, who had conversation with brother Townsend.

Wednesday—Ward meeting at 8 o'clock; ward, No. 28. Brother Evans spoke. Prayed to close. Wounded boy from Jamestown sat at my side. He would like to be a Christian. I pointed him to the Lord. Visited two wards. Found a New Hampshire soldier, a

Christian and re-enlisted veteran, whose wife lay sick at home with consumption. Ventured some words of consolation, as I saw how deeply he seemed to feel this affliction.

Tried to instruct another, who on being interrogated, dwelt on the "difficnlty of being a Christian." Conversed with two next door men, one having a harassing and perhaps dangerous cough, and the other a bullet in his back, which entered at the jaw. Preached this evening. Text, "Submit yourselves therefore to God." Thought and longed to submit more thoroughly myself. The Lord grant it. Brother Townsend followed with forcible remarks.

Thursday, July 28.—Meeting in Ward 34 at 8 A. M. Brother Townsend talked well. Conversed with an East Tennessee boy, and commended him to Christ, and with four others at some length. Call by some soldiers for meeting at 3 P. M. for prayer and conference at the Chapel.

Friday forenoon—Distributed 475 religious papers through thirty-four wards. Intensely hot and dusty. A trial of patience and strength. Evening prayer meeting.

Saturday—Prayer meeting at 8 A. M. Distributed 130 papers through Parole barracks. Distributed 100 papers in Hospital A, and religious conversation. Thermometer 98 in shade.

Sabbath, July 31.—Extreme heat. Brother Townsend preached at 10½ A. M. Brother Evans at 3 P. M. Myself in the evening. Brother Townsend and self distributed papers to companies of New York National Guard, just arrived. Am poorly in health, and feel compelled to leave.

If not considered out of place, I should like to speak of the overwhelming importance of the *religious fidelity of officers.* How difficult to estimate the responsibility of those who stand in positions of influence so peculiar! Who can tell what an impetus their personal attendance on meetings for Divine worship of officers *professing Christianity* would give to the cause of Christ, in the camp and in the field? and on the other hand, who can estimate the injury done by their habitual absence? will it suffice to plead mere private integrity at the bar of God as an excuse for inaction? or as a substitute for a known and active Christian interest among the men they command? The officers' presence and co-operation at *prayer meeting* for example would so manifestly be for the glory of God, that a moment's discussion of the subject is unnecessary. *This is a theme of special and peculiar importance.*

I am induced to say a word of the undoubted utility of *ward meetings.* Although not much was done in this direction during my stay at Camp Parole, yet a commencement was made, and I am happy to speak of the ready and evidently efficient adaptation of my colleague, the Rev. Mr. Townsend, to this, as well as almost every kind of religious labor among the soldiers.

The chief consideration and encouragement to *ward meetings* is the opportunity thus afforded for reaching the men scarcely otherwise accessible. At least the Gospel is brought to the lame and sick and listless and indifferent, and profane men of every class, who *seldom or never attend meeting in the Chapel* when time can be given or appropriated from other labors. I can but regard this as an important instrumentality of good.

C. COLEGROVE.

---

## Report of Rev. Cyril Pearl.

SIX WEEKS WITH THE SOLDIERS OF THE UNION.

G. S. GRIFFITH, *Esq., Chairman U. S. Christian Commission:*

DEAR SIR AND BROTHER:—In accordance with your instructions I give you a report of the labors of six weeks in the service of the United States Christian Commission. I reached this place by the P.M. train. I received the needed passes from the Provost Marshals, and the general commanding allowing me to visit all parts of the Division. After conference with the Medical Director, I decided, by his advice, to report at the Division Hospital at Sandy Hook, and on my way met brother John Turbitt from the State of New York, who had been laboring some weeks in this field, and gave him my letter of introduction from brother Williams. I also met at Sandy Hook brother Francis Durdis, a lay member of the Methodist Episcopal Church from Philadelphia, who had been laboring some weeks in that part of the field. Meeting a cordial reception from the surgeon and other officers of the hospital, I engaged to preach at the dining hall, Sabbath, P. M., and had supper in season to go with some recent converts to prayer meeting at a private house at the base of the mountain. Sabbath the 7th was a day of deep interest. At ten o'clock, by request of brother Durdis, I met and opened the Sabbath school in the Stone school house which he had assisted to organize the Sabbath previous; addressed the children and soldiers again at the close. At one o'clock, I also addressed those assembled for class meeting at the same place. At four o'clock preached to the convalescent patients at Division hospital, and distributed reading matter among them. Attended service at the Stone school house in the evening, and listened to a sermon by Rev. John Turbitt, on the Spirit of Adoption "whereby we cry "Abba Father." I addressed the congregation at the close. On Monday, brother Durdis left for his home in Philadelphia, leaving only brother T. and myself to labor in a field with some 16,000 soldiers scattered over a circuit of some six miles radius, with parts of regiments ten or twelve miles distant.

A small box of books and papers arriving for brother Durdis at the time of his leaving, he turned over to me with which to commence distribution. Calling on brother Turbitt, he went with me upon Maryland Heights where I made the acquaintance of officers in command of forts and regiments at various points, and the next day I commenced the work of supply. A revival of religion had been for some weeks in progress at Sandy Hook under the labors of circuit preachers of

Baltimore Conference, and nearly one hundred soldiers had experienced a hope of being saved. Many of these had come down from the mountain almost every night for eight weeks. This seemed to render it very desirable to sow the seed with liberal hand.

The box left me by brother Durdis lasted me but part of a week, and the eagerness for reading matter on the Heights made it very hard for me to say I have no more to distribute. Three other small boxes were sent me in the first three weeks, but I needed four times that amount to meet the demand. Visiting Halltown, as well as camp Hill, Bolivar Heights, the road to Sharpsburg, as, also, Weverton, Knoxville, and Berlin, with troops at all these places, it was soon evident that it would be impossible to supply them adequately without a larger number of laborers, and a more complete organization. This state of things led me to write you so urgently for books at the close of two weeks. I wrote to brother Damond, of Boston, as he had requested, and sent the letter through the Philadelphia office to be read there. I also wrote to friends in Maine for sanitary stores needed at the Division Hospital, which appeal was sent to the Philadelphia office, and thence to Baltimore to be supplied.

After a full survey of the field and its needs, and consultation with the military and medical department here, failing to receive any counsel or instructions from Baltimore or elsewhere, I could not hesitate to follow what seemed to me the imperative inclinations of Providence trusting his direction and not doubting the approval of the Commission in the work so clearly necessary. Brother Williams, when here, had obtained verbal permission, as I understood, to take, repair, and use the Presbyterian church for purposes of the Commission, and brother Turbitt commenced the work of cleaning it out during the week after my arrival. It was quite evident that while the church could be roughly fitted up for meetings, Sabbath schools, &c., and perhaps a reading room, or depository for the Sabbath school, and the soldiers in the immediate vicinnity, it could not well be fitted to answer all the purposes of the Commission. There was needed a convenient room for general depository and distribution to Chaplains and Delegates, a home for Delegates, where they could meet for counsel, rest and refreshments, and where they could receive soldiers who might desire to counsel with them in retirement. The old church was in a sad plight to be transformed so as to answer these purposes and not defeat the object of religious worship, Sabbath school lectures, &c. The part of the house near the door was drenched with water every driving rain storm. The gallery floor torn out, and the cupola open on all sides, books could not be safe in that part without a large outlay. If the opposite end were re-covered, then the whole floor must be traversed by every box and every visitor. Saturday being especially the day for Chaplains to get supplies, the church must be in a bad condition for the Sabbath. The old church vestry having been used as a stable both by Rebel and Union soldiers, the house was overrun with huge rats which infest Shenandoah street more than any other part of the place. It was imposible to warm the whole building during cold weather, and there was no place for lodging, rest, or retirement. Then it would be a severe labor to get heavy boxes up the stone steps and into the church.

These and other reasons led me to make diligent search and confer freely with the military and medical authorities as to location. Preferring a place near the express office and the railway station I searched in vain for a suitable building which we could use with reasonable hope of not being obliged to vacate on any sudden emergency or caprice. The Ordnance Master directed me to Government building No. 20, on High street. This was in bad condition. Doors, stairs, and windows torn out, as well as casements, closets, and bare boards, and all parts of the plastering defaced with black and unsightly images. But the walls of massive stone, and the roof and floors were nearly in a good condition. Labor, lime, and water would, however, renovate it, and friends of our cause on the ground offered to aid us in fitting it up if I would give them an address on Washington's birthday.

While deliberating, a colored man offered me a shanty for $10, which had cost him about $50, but the Government required its removal, and he desired to aid our cause. This offer decided my course as the materials would close up windows and doors, make rough doors, shelves, seats, &c., and as it was nearly impossible to get boards here for any purpose, I could not feel justified in losing the opportunity. In four hours we had the materials in the building and a guard was detailed to protect it till we could enclose it and take possession. The purchase of the shanty was on the 18th of February, and on the 26th, I was able to make my home in the building, with all our stock of books arranged on convenient shelves.

At this stage we were visited by brother Cole, the General Field Agent, who, though at first a little disturbed by the boldness and suddenness of the movement, after careful consideration, decided to carry out the plan proposed, appointed Rev. M. M. Langley, Station Agent, and divided the field of labor into five departments as having to each Delegate his field.

Our force then consisted of Rev. John Turbitt, who had been longest in the field, Rev. M. M. Langley, who came the next week after my arrival, brother Durdis, who returned from Philadelphia on the 27th, and brother Wright, a licensed exhorter in the M. E. Church, who came with him.

The Sabbath following preached at the prison at 9 o'clock; heard brother Langley at the church at half-past 10; school and service for the colored people at 1; preached at church at 3, P. M. This brings my report to the time covered by my report of March, to brother Langley, forwarded to you on the 18th.

At this period it was determined that I should visit Washington city for the purpose of receiving aid from the Government, if possible, in fitting up a place for worship.

The closing week was one of intense, but delightful labor, as our building was so far fitted up that one could live comfortably in one of the chambers, leaving the office free from all inconvenience. Calls for reading matter increased rapidly, as also for sanitary stores, some boxes of which came from Philadelphia in time to relieve much suffering at the Division Hospital, and in various regiments. We have now a depository building most ample and convenient for all the purposes of the Commission, though fitted up in "rough and ready" style. The office room, which has now been successfully used for nearly four weeks, is well adapted to that use. Being small it is easily warmed and kept in order and very convenient of access. For two weeks it was also used as my sleeping and living room, but now we have a large airy room in the story above, with rough board stairs, good fireplace, rough closet, door, four half-windows, the sash of which is loaned us by a Trustee of the Lutheran church, the glass put in with tacks, so as to be easily removed when no longer needed for our use.

The Chaplain of the 18th Connecticut regiment shared this home with me until he could fit his own quarters, then a sick soldier took his place while waiting for his discharge. There are twenty-four board and plank seats in the church also furnished and fitted by me after our seats were called for and removed by the Government, these are sufficient for seating over two hundred persons. We have used it four Sabbaths for public worship twice and three times each day. Our white congregation have ranged from forty to sixty persons, and our colored Sabbath school and service from fifty to one hundred and twenty.

Our closing Sabbath was one of deep interest, manifestng in both congregations increasing tenderness and earnest interest. Both services were followed by the communion. About twenty communicants in the white congregation and twenty-five in the colored.

The desire of the colored people for a day school is most earnest and persistent. I have, by their request, written to New York in this matter. The progress in learning letters and simple words in the last two Sabbaths was of the most encouraging character. It is greatly to be desired that they shall be cared for by the Commission till other provisions shall be made.

The closing week of my mission was the most laborious and successful in the work of distribution, and public meetings.

The services for Sabbath, March 20, were for prisoners in Lockwood House, at 8 o'clock. Preaching in ward of Rebel prisoners at 9. To Union prisoners for offences against society, or rules of war, quarter before 10. At Brick church half-past 10, followed by communion. Colored Sabbath school at 1, P. M. Preaching to them and communion service at 2. Closing visits at the several wards in Division Hospital at half-past 4. Distribution of German papers to the German Battery in the absence of brother Durdis. Farewell sermon at Sandy Hook stone school-house at 7.

In presenting this report your Delegate desires to acknowledge with devout gratitude the hand of Providence in sustaining him through more than six weeks of the most laborious and exhausting work of this kind. He desires also to acknowledge gratefully the uniform courtesy and efficient co-operation of the commanding Generals, and subordinate officers, both of the Post and the Division. Such acknowledgments are due also to the Quartermasters, Ordnance officers,

Medical authorities of all the hospitals and regiments. To the soldiers and citizens I owe much in the successful prosecution of my labors. By the courtesy of the Post under the direction of General Wheaten, I was at all times furnished with horses to visit distant regiments, equally an aggregate of near 150 miles, and also the use of teams at all times in removing materials for fitting up our buildings. To the Railroads from Maine to the front beyond Washington, the Commission is indebted for free passes, and on the Baltimore and Ohio Railroad for half fares. So that in traveling nearly 1,700 miles by Railroad the sum did not exceed $7.00. The work of the Commission in some twenty or more regiments and parts of regiments required walking more than 200 miles in the six weeks, thus making a distance of more than 2,000 miles, at an expense of less than $8.00 to the Christian Commission. Courtesies of Telegraph officers also were a saving to the Commission.

By continuing labors three days beyond the six weeks, seven Sabbaths were embraced in the mission. Upon these Sabbaths, I preached from three to seven times, making an aggregate of 32 sermons on the Sabbaths, and eight on week days, evenings. I gave also five patriotic speeches and three lectures on Temperance. These services were at Sandy Hook, Weverton, Knoxville, Berlin, at the Division Hospital on Maryland Heights, in the old church at Harper's Ferry, at the Guardhouse on Hall's Island, to both Rebel and Union prisoners; at Bolivar and Halltown, at Washington and Bullock station. I assisted in six prayer meetings and class meetings, besides several brief services I held at the hospital wards. Officiated also at eight funerals, three weddings, and seven baptisms. My coneregations varied from 30 to 300 in attendance. I had occasion to visit and converse with more than four hundred patients in several hospitals, including Regimental, Division and General hospitals. Wrote letters for four, and furnished papers and envelopes to more than one hundred in camps, hospitals and prisons.

The first three weeks there was a great lack of reading matter. I had but three boxes containing about eight bushels, but no invoices; and the papers, tracts, and small books, were distributed uncounted. The destitution had been such that I needed four times the amount to supply the demand. The Testaments and song books in these, with those that were subsequently received and distributed by me, would make an aggregate of four Bibles, six hundred and fifty English, and two hundred and fifty German Testaments, and five hundred and fifty Army Hymns.

The last three weeks my distributions were 220 volumes in twelve small libraries bound, 1,250 small books given, with 3,700 newspapers and 10,155 pages of tracts. We needed 600 or 800 more newspapers, and 500 Testaments on the last Saturday to meet orders made at one station.

At Sandy Hook an interesting revival was in progress when I reached there, and continued during my mission. More than one hundred soldiers, and a considerable number of citizens profess conversion. Many of these soldiers were accustomed to come down from their quarters on Maryland Heights six nights in the week, for some six weeks, while a protracted meeting was in progress. And after its close, our evening lectures were almost uniformly crowded. Some new cases of hope occurred almost every evening. The officers of the regiments that shared most largely in this revival bore united testimony to the great improvement of these men, and of their regiments as the results of the revival. Many of the cases were very remarkable, and in general the converts appeared extremely well. An interesting revival was also in progress in the 139th Pennsylvania volunteers, as, also, the 102d regiment. A Connecticut regiment, the 18th, came in from Martinsburg near the close of my stay, bringing an interesting account of the revival in that place, in which some 300 soldiers had professed conversion.

It may be well supposed that I leave the field of interesting labor deeply impressed with the vastness and value of the work upon the hands of the Christian Commission.

Yours, truly and fraternally,

CYRIL PEARL.

---

## Report of Rev. Isaac Cole.

BALTIMORE, *June* 1, 1864.

G. S. GRIFFITH, ESQ., *Chairman U. S. Christian Commission, Baltimore:*

DEAR SIR:—Under the auspices of the Christian Commission, I left Baltimore on Monday, May 16th, 1864, for Fredericksburg, Va. In the afternoon of the same day, I arrived at Washington, D. C. There I reported to the Christian Commission of that city. I was Informed that the War Department had refused to grant passes to any more to go to the front as it was believed that enough had gone for present conveniences. I spent two days in Washington visiting the hospitals in that place. I was glad to find those institutions so neat and comfortable, and every attention paid to the suffering soldiers.

On Thursday, I was informed that passes had been granted me and others to proceed to Fredericksburg. On Friday, we started early in the morning, and reached Belle Plain about 2 o'clock, P. M. At 3 o'clock, we started on foot for the place of our destination, about 10 miles distant. After walking about six miles, I became so wearied that I asked permission to ride in a Government wagon, which request was granted. We arrived at Fredericksburg about night fall. On Saturday morning, after a refreshing sleep, we received our appointments to the several hospitals. The Surgeon of the "Garcelon Hospital" requested me to take charge of a ward, which I did, and immediately entered on the duties assigned me, viz., dressing wounds, and distributing among the sufferers such articles of diet and refreshment as were furnished by the Christian Commission.

I did not, however, confine my labors exclusively to that department, but visited other hospitals, and did what I could to relieve all that required my assistance. The city was a grand hospital. Every store, church, and nearly every dwelling, was house of refuge for the wounded and dying. There was enough for all to do. The Christian Commission stood firm at their post. The suffering soldiers often expressed their gratitude for the benefits received at their hands—and many said, how much more would we have suffered had it not been for the Christian Commission.

We not only attended to their physical wants, but their spiritual necessities were not neglected. It was truly gratifying to see how attentively they would listen to any one who had anything to say on the subject of religion. The poor sufferers seem to feel that there was something wanted more than meats and drinks and dressing of wounds to control their minds. Whatever might be the moanings and groanings of the sufferers when prayer was offered, or a word of exhortation given, or hymn sung, all were silent, and the most respectful attention given.

I visited several that were in a dying condition. Some I found ready for the change that awaited them. I said to one who was supposed to be dying, do you think Christ would receive you into heaven if you were to die to-night? He replied, "Yes." I prayed with him and retired. Before I left him he requested me to write to his wife and inform her of his condition which I did.

I insert a copy of her answer.

New York, *May* 20, 1864.

Rev. Isaac Cole:

Dear Sir:—This is an acknowledgment of your kindness dated Washington, May 18, 1864, for which I am very thankful to you. May God reward you for your kindness and acts of mercy. I will address my husband immediately.

Bridget Brooks.

Thus we are paid for our labors of love.

The following interview was had with a young man in a dying condition. He was 18 years old, and belonged to one of the Ohio regiments. At first he was in great distress about his soul, praying and calling upon his Saviour for mercy. He had spent the morning in prayer. After which he became calm. He said he had been a bad boy at home and was sorry for it. He had an excellent praying mother. She had often prayed for him—and tried to win him to Jesus; but that he was self-willed and wicked. He then said he felt that he had peace with God, and attributed it to the influences of his mother's prayers. Say to mother that I now know that I shall meet her in heaven. Say, also, to my dear little sisters and brothers, I die happy. And he did so die.

What blessed intelligence to communicate to his affectionate and pious mother.

Were all the interesting cases which occur on the battle-field and in the hospitals collected and printed, *volumes would be made.*

I am pleased to say that whilst our own soldiers claimed the first attentions of the Christian Commission, yet the Confederate wounded were not neglected. They received the same attention as the Federal wounded. And thus did we obey the instructions of the merciful Jesus. "Love your enemies, bless them that curse you, *do good* to them that hate you, and pray for them which despitefully use you and persecute you."

The Christian Commission is a noble institution and worthy of the patronage of all. I regard it as another benevolent institution owing its origin to the benificent Spirit of the Gospel which teaches us to make provision for the necessities of humanity as they are developed.

May God continue to prosper you in your kind and generous enterprise until there shall be no further need of your efforts. And may the time speedily come when wars shall cease, and Christ the Prince of Peace shall reign over the kingdoms of this world.

Yours in the bonds of Christian love,

ISAAC COLE.

---

## Report of Rev. G. R. Bent.

BALTIMORE, *December* 3, 1864.

G. S. GRIFFITH, ESQ., *Chairman U. S. Christian Commission Baltimore District:*

DEAR SIR:—As a Station Agent for the U. S. Christian Commission, Camp Parole, near Annapolis, Maryland, I commenced my labors, aided by my companion, December 14, 1863, after all my requests had been responded to by the generous and Christian officer commanding the post, Colonel A. Root. I had good quarters for my family, and went to our good work in the name of the Lord.

God did help us, and sinners were converted, and backsliders were reclaimed, until about 160 joined the Soldiers' Christian Association of Camp Parole. We had to co-operate with us in our good work, Revs. S. P. Merrill, J. D. Moore, J. Turbitt, Professor Barron, of Anderson, Massachusetts.

All the above brethren were noble Christian men, and displayed great aptness in the work. The camp became orderly, and the men happier and wiser. because God was pleased to refresh us from on high. Officers and soldiers were kind and courteous. We distributed hospital stores from January 1st to April 14.

On the 14th of February, 1864, I baptized 17 persons, and on February 28, four persons. My dear wife was happy and successful in her efforts to do good to all, and especially to the sick in the hospital;

and until March 1st, was untiring in her efforts, when in the Providence of God, she was stricken down with fever, and in a few days she closed her eys to all earthly things, "and ceased at once to work and live," "she rests from her labors and her works do follow her," and her dust slumbers in its native dust in Mendon, Massachusetts, the home of her childhood—while I still linger with my dear little daughter. We hope to meet her ere long beyond the swellings of the tide, where the sound of war ceases forever.

The Christian Commission at Camp Parole has been ably represented since I left, and my connection with the Baltimore Committee has been most pleasant since April 14th. Our labors have been arduous, and my experience and observation prove that God has raised up noble men to carry on this noblest of Institutions in the Baltimore District as well as elsewhere.

I remain yours, truly,

G. R. BENT,
General Ag't U. S. C. C.,
Baltimore District.

---

### Letter of Dr. S. A. Kessler.

*August* 20, 1864.

G. S. GRIFFITH, ESQ.:

It is with the most unfeigned satisfaction that I take up my feeble pen for the purpose of rendering witness to the invariable kindness exhibited by the Christian Commission, its Agents and Delegates, towards the suffering inmates of our hospital. To dwell here upon the noble aims and works of that body would be utterly superfluous. Its deeds are known, felt, and appreciated through the whole length and breadth of our land, from the Atlantic to far Pacific; from the snow clad hills of Maine to the sunny shores of the Gulf: and even beyond the limits of the Union, all over the civilized world. They are written in indellible characters of steel and granite upon the pages of history: they are proud and lofty monuments of the dreadful civil war desolating our country, but purifying our institutions and elevating our people. They display the grandeur and excellence of a nation, that, in spite of untold miseries and misfortunes, cares with almost prodigal liberalty for the martyrs of a holy cause. Indeed, the Christian spirit of the loyal people of the United States has rendered more sacred yet the cause of the Union, Constitution and Liberty. The struggle forced upon us by traitors and rebels has redeemed, purified and elevated this nation.

From a small, insignificant beginning, prompted by the benevolence and patriotism of a few, the Christian Commission and its kindred sister, the Sanitary Commission, have risen to great institutions, whose blessings are felt upon every field of battle and at the bedside of every soldier who bleeds and suffers for the triumph of this kind and free Government. Wherever the sound of cannon and musketry roar, wherever the furious battle-cry rends the air, wherever the agonies of the wounded and dying ascend to heaven, there the brothers and sisters of these charitable orders minister to the suffering heroes. They people all abodes of sickness and pains, and carry comforts and delicacies to the men who contracted disease and received wounds in defence of their country. The dark history of this civil war, with all its cruel sacrifices in blood, treasure and prosperity is brightened and softened by the charity and devotion of these good Samaritans. They shed radient lustre upon the land of their birth and court the admiration of all mankind.

During my brief connection with the service I have become pretty familiar with system adopted by the Christian Commission in relation to the great purposes for which it was called into life, and it is but justice to declare that there exists no other organization in the world which has achieved grander results with the limited means at its command. And I think I am equally justified in the utterance of my conviction, that the Committee of Maryland, headed by its kind and consciencious Chairman, and aided by truly excellent Delegates, is second to none in the country, and highly deserving of the lasting gratitude of all good and true men.

Every new arrival of sick and wounded soldiers in our hospital was signalized by the unremitting efforts of the Christian Commission for their relief and comfort, and with ready and ever open hands were distributed among them refreshments, delicacies and luxuries. From day to day they were visited by kind Delegates laden with baskets containing choice fruits, and cordials, and restoratives, books and periodicals, paper and envelopes, handkerchiefs and wrappers, socks and slippers, and everything that was calculated to promote the well being of mind and body. I take great pleasure mentioning here especially the unceasing kindness of Mrs. Norris, who labored faithfully for the good of our patients. Hundreds will remember her gratefully for the many tokens of sympathy she bestowed upon them. The munificence of the Christian and Sanitary Commissions, and local Relief Associations, combined with the excellent measures and provisions of the Government, render the condition of our sick and wounded soldiers as comfortable as possible within the sphere of human power.

The military hospital system of the United States, although in its infancy, as compared with that of other countries, which support large standing armies, bids fair to contend successfully for the laurel; and next to the humane exertions of the Government and its special agent, the Medical Department, to render it perfect, the efforts of those charitable bodies which sprang from the patriotism, benevolence and sympathy of the people have a large share in its improvement. Thus they aid in making the military hospitals of the United States not only worthy of this great and noble country, but first in excellence—monuments of pride and honor throughout the whole world as the famous "*Hotel des Invalides*" is the pride of France. God bless their noble efforts and the objects of their benevolence.

DR. A. KESSLER,
United States General Hospital,
West's Building Baltimore.

## Report of Rev. L. L. Wood.

BURLINGTON, VT., *Aug. 30th*, 1864.

G. S. GRIFFITH, ESQ., *Chairman Christian Commission:*

DEAR SIR:—The following is a report of my labors while engaged in the work of the Christian Commission:

When I arrived at the General Field Hospital at Sandy Hook, Md., the agency of the Christian Commission, which had not been long established at that point, was under the direction of Rev. Edward Cooper, Chaplain of the Eighth Ohio Cavalry, who soon after joined his regiment, leaving the field in charge of Chaplain J. B. Koerner, whose faithful labors in the work of the Christian Commission are already too well known to require a single word of commendation from me. Afterwards, Br. Koerner's health failing him, the field was left in my charge during the few weeks that I remained in the work. The agency was a new one. The number of Delegates being small, and our stores and facilities for the work being very limited, we were not at first in the systematic order and efficiency so characteristic of the Christian Commission generally.

We tried to attend to all the wants of those in the hospital and devoted what time and attention we could to the thousands in the various camps about the hospital needing physical and spiritual aid.

Those in the hospital we washed, clothed and fed, lifted them in and out of the ambulances; wrote, read and prayed for them; gave them stationery and reading matter; and performed every act of kindness we could for them. At first the hospital contained 1,000 beds, afterwards 1,300 beds. These were constantly occupied and vacated, as fast as the patients could possibly be moved to Frederick, Baltimore, and elsewhere, sometimes as often as twice in one week.

Thus we were constantly brought in contact with these hundreds and thousands of soldiers constantly passing through the hospital, for whom we could do but a trifle perhaps; yet who knows but that some of these many thousand tracts and books distributed, kind acts performed and words of kindness and admonition may have been the sowing of good seed, which shall yet bear fruit in the kingdom of our Redeemer.

My own *modus operandi* at the hospital was, after doing the necessary duties at the office, to take my memorandum and pass through the various wards holding very brief conversations with the patients, making inquiry concerning both their physical and spiritual condition whenever it was practicable to do so; taking notice of all their wants and noting down those cases of necessity which we could and should supply; writing and doing whatever we could for them. At the close of the day would carry or send up those things of which I had made a memorandum. If a case required immediate attention, would either go or send a nurse with an order to the office at once. The next day beginning where I left off and proceeding as before. In the mean time would often be interrupted to visit the dying or attend to something or other. Sometimes it would occupy a week to complete a single round in this manner. It was a slow process but a thorough one.

On the Sabbath our distributions consisted mostly of reading matter and stationery. Many a countenance would brighten as we distributed to each a Christian Commission envelope, with its pretty little design of a carrier dove bearing its glad tidings, containing a sheet of paper and perhaps a little book or tract. Even those who were neither able to write nor dictate a letter, would want one tucked under their pillows, it was so suggestive of home and pleasant thoughts. In this way we often found an easy avenue to the soldiers heart.

I can say that in all my intercouse with the soldiers, both by night and by day, I never received a repulsive word or look from any one to whom I addressed a word concerning the interest of his immortal soul. But I found a good many Christian lights "under a bushel."

The ladies department, so ably conducted by Mrs. Hyatt and other ladies of Baltimore, performed a most efficient work in their tender care of the "low diet men" and other acts of kindness in which they had our hearty sympathy and co-operation, and for which they did and ever will receive the blessing of many a suffering patriot as well as of him wbo has said that even he who gives "a cup of cold water to one of these little ones, shall in no wise lose his reward."

It gives me pleasure also to say that the invariable kindness of Dr. Boone, Surgeon in charge of the hospital, and all the Surgeons and others in authority, deserve honorable notice.

We visited the various camps about the hospital as often as we could, and held religious services in them whenever it was possible to do so.

At the village of Sandy Hook, religious meetings were held every evening and during the day on Sabbath. They were attended with considerable interest and were mostly under the charge of Bro. E. W. Brady, Chaplain of the 116th Ohio, who was with us most of the time and rendered valuable assistance.

At Camp Convalescent, some of the time there were over two thousand soldiers. Bro. R. C. Stephens' of Guildhall, Vt., labored here very successfully during his brief stay with us. Just previous to the battle of Winchester, this camp had become reduced to about two hundred. But we had interesting meetings there. The Christian element had begun to develop itself, and they held meetings of themselves when we could not meet with them. Some thirty were anxiously enquiring the way of life; backsliders of years standing were returning to their first love and souls were being saved.

Other camps in the vicinity were without Chaplains, but as they were several miles away, it was only occasionally that we felt like walking to and from them after working incessantly all day, as our meetings were held in the evening, except on the Sabbath. We had no means of conveyance whatever. At first we were obliged to walk to Harper's Ferry and other places to transact our business. We then borrowed horses of the officers about the hospital till we got tired of it. Afterwards, on application to Capt. Flagg, post Quartermaster, we were kindly furnished with a horse, which was of great service.

On Sunday we usually held divine services in as many places as our number of Delegates would permit. Some going to the various camps in Pleasant Valley, others to Maryland Heights, and others still to Boliver Heights, till they had Chaplains at the latter place, and two or there remaining at the hospital to take care of the office and talk with the patients, as it was not thought best to hold public services in the hospital.

One Sabbath I visited Dismounted Camp, some three or four miles up Pleasant Valley. We had an interesting meeting. A violent shower disturbed us some in the midst of the discourse, but I kept on talking and hundreds of the eagerly listening soldiers gathered closer and closer around me in the open air, while the rain was descending in torrents. It showed an eagerness for religious truth and afforded a good lesson to the less patriotic ones at home who are so afraid of a rainy Sabbath as not to attend worship even under cover.

The same afternoon I visited another camp recently established, not far from Dismounted. Formed a very agreeable acquaintance with the commander, and after learning that they had no Chaplain, and that they had had no religious meetings for some months, I proposed that we have service that P. M. The commander very gratefully received the proposition, but could not second it, as he said his men had become so abandoned and had expressed themselves so hostile to anything of the kind that he feared any attempt to hold service would meet with a failure unless the men were compelled to attend. But in compliance with my wishes he caused the Church call to be sounded, but, as he expected, it met with no response from the camp. Then, with his permission, I mingled with the soldiers a little, got into conversation with them, found some singers and commenced singing some familiar hymn in which they joined, and soon had gathered around me as attentive and interesting an audience as I ever addressed; I left them anxious for me to come again.

At another time I rode out to another camp in the evening. It was too late to have a meeting when I got there, but the soldiers gathered around and I distributed my haversack of papers, Testaments, &c., which, however, was but an atom for all that crowd, eagerly extending their hands and exclaiming, "give me a prayer book, Chaplain," "give me a Testament, &c." I quieted them with the promise to bring them more soon. But was not permitted to redeem my promise, as the advancing army immediately called our attention in another direction. I then proposed that we sing some of those good old hymns so often heard at home. All the soldiers joined, and as I looked over that vast mass of soldiers crowding thickly around on every side, I could not resist the temptation of addressing them for a few minutes from my horse. As I rode away the air was ringing with hymns of praise, where a short time previous it was filled with implications and oaths. I hastened forward to call at another camp on my way home, where I had held a meeting the evening previous and promised to call this evening, if they would begin the meeting before I came. I feared lest the meeting would be over long before I got there. But, as I drew near I again heard songs of praise rising heavenward on the clear air of that beautiful moonlight night. After a short exhortation and another hymn, a goodly number manifested their desire to become Christians by standing up. I arrived home a little after ten o'clock with a light and happy heart. This was my last visit. The next day I went to the front. But I venture to say that the numerous camps about us and the headquarters of the army trains near by would have been large and interesting fields of Christian effort, and had our force of Delegates been ample enough to hold regular religious meetings in them, they would also undoubtedly have been fruitful fields. Often would we find ourselves hastening to an appointment, when, perhaps for the first time during the day, it would suddenly occur to mind that a text was necessary. But on arrival at camp, the Lord would seem to suggest an appropriate text and subject. The wind would sometimes blow out the candle and we could neither see to find the text nor read a passage of Scripture. But we could sing and pray and talk in the dark, and it was a very interesting scene, hundreds of attentive soldiers sitting on the ground all about the speaker in the dark. Notwithstanding the great demoralization in many parts of our armies, the soldier as a general thing, is attentive and susceptible to religious truth. My own experience in cases where I little expected it, convinced me of this. Often I was saluted by some wounded soldier lying about the battle-field or in the hospital. On giving an inquiring look or word, they would say "don't you know me Chaplain, don't you remember that talk; I heard you preach at such and such a camp, you gave me a Testament, &c. I little thought then that I should be here in this condition," &c., &c. The effects of Christian efforts are often more readily apparent in the army than at home.

By an order from Gen. Sheridan to clear and enlarge the hospital at Sandy Hook, we had reason to expect some movement of an unusual character. Accordingly I sent you word that we should in all probability require an immediate supply of men and stores. Taking advantage of the quiet at the hospital, I hastened to the front where I arrived Saturday night. The next morning proceeded at once, according to the suggestion of one of your committee, who visited us a short time previous, viz: to ascertain as far as I could, the spiritual condition of the army and the practicability of sending out some supplies of reading matter.

I had proceeded the whole length of the army and met as many Chaplains and officers as possible, and had made an estimate of about how many Delegates it would be practicable to send as substitutes for Chaplains, and whom, I was informed by the officers, would be cordially welcomed in those regiments where there were no Chaplains. The army was in such an unsettled state that the wounded were all sent in to the General Field hospital, and there seemed to be no particular demand for Christian Commission stores, except reading matter, which the whole army was craving. At two of the clock that following night the army moved. The order came to move first while we were having service in what is called the Vermont Brigade. It was soon after countermanded however, but came again at half past one the next morning. We had no knowledge of where we were going when we started. The army moved on until about six and a half o'clock A. M., when it met the enemy about two miles out side of Winchester. The fighting begun immediately and was incessant all day, but truly terrific in the P. M. At noon the Regimental and Brigade Hospital where I was, was considered unsafe. It was in a little ravine on the field of battle. The enemy were firing some of the time over our heads to those out side of us, and the shot and shell were bursting and falling all about us. We then moved down to the Division Hospital just off the field where we were less exposed. Though the minnies fell among us quite freely a part of the time, but we were too busy with the wounded to pay them much attention. The wounded came in faster than the Surgeons could attend to them. Bringing what little knowledge of the business I had to bear upon the occasion, I borrowed scissors of one Doctor, lint and bandages of another, adhesive plaster, &c., of another, and made myself as useful as I could, dressing some fifty wounds during the P. M. From the Division Hospital the wounded were taken in ambulances back to the Corps Hospitals. At night, after riding over the battle-field where our heroes had made those terrible charges which told the story of that bloody day, and visiting a few that remained on the field still, I went back to the hospital of the 6th Corps.

The loss in wounded was necessarily very severe. There were between three and four thousand wounded and one thousand one hundred of them were at the 6th Corps Hospital. There was of course extreme suffering. But I had become so exhausted that I could hold out no longer and fell asleep in the midst of the indescribable misery. I shared the blankets of a kind Chaplain, but the night air was very chilly, and when I awoke in the morning, suffering from the cold, I thought what must the poor wounded soldier have suffered who were obliged to be all night on the cold damp ground without any covering.

Early one morning an order came for the Surgeons to follow the army, which had then begun its victorious march up the Valley, driving the enemy before it, and take the tents and all the instruments and medicines, leaving the wounded as a military necessity, to be taken into the town as fast as the few ambulances could be spared from the advancing army to carry them.

Thus they were obliged to leave the wounded without food or care. With the exception of a few cases of operations during the previous P. M., they had received no medical treatment and a quarter part of the wounds had not been dressed at all. Dr. J. D. Thompson, of the 77th N. Y., was left in charge. Dr. Thompson showed me every kindness and offered me every facility in his power, both here and in his hospital at the town of Winchester; but, having nothing to do with, he could give the suffering no medical treatment whatever. Everything of a medical or surgical character had been taken off in the dispensary wagon, leaving neither stimulants to support the sinking nor anodynes to mittigate the suffering. One bottle of morphene was fortunately overlooked. But it was of little account for such a multitude. I begged the last of it from the Dr. the first night There were two Chaplains there most of the time, but they were unable to attend to the wounded of their own regiments even, and the greater part of the wounded had to lie uncared for.

My first work was to try to protect the worst cases from the heat of the sun, which gave indications of being very severe. Having procured an axe at a Confederate house near by, I got a convalescent soldier to use it for me as my right arm had been useless for several days. We then got the helpless cases together as much as we could, drove down stakes at their heads, covering them with blankets, bushes, hay and whatever we could. It was but a feeble protection from the excessive heat and cold of the days and nights at that time. But the noble martyrs felt grateful for it feeble as it was. This was occupied till the middle of the P. M. Then I turned my attention towards feeding them. They had nothing to eat since the morning they went into the fight. When they begun the march they had five days rations in their haversacks. But when a wounded soldier is brought off the field during the battle, his straps are usually cut from his back. A few haversacks, however, had been brought off, and in these I found coffee and hard tack enough to feed them nearly all once around. I found a man to cook the coffee and then carried it round. Those who were able helped themselves, and those who were helpless I gave a little hard tack and poured some hot coffee into their dish or canteen, where they were minus a dish. Those who had neither canteen or dish, shared from their partners. With what little assistance I could get, I had emptied the last coffee pot between eleven and twelve o'clock that night, having served nearly all the helpless ones. After spending a couple of hours with the dying, I fell asleep again, more in obedience to the stern force of nature than of the spirit.

The next morning the Dr. found me about a bottle and a half of whiskey, which I dispensed in very small portions to the lowest cases, as far as it would go. The rest of the day was spent in carrying water, trying to keep the flies from the wounds and affording spiritual consolation. It was a hard case. Oh how much I would have given for some of our Christian Commission stores and the assistance of the Delegates! But there was no communication from me to them, and the circumstances were irremediable. The noble fellows understood this and with few exceptions would even die without a murmur. Often did I kneel by their side in the dark and silent hour of midnight and take their last message to loved ones far away at home. At one time during the battle of Monday, P. M., our stock of bandages became exhausted. I took a bandage from my own arm and even used the soldiers handkerchiefs and shirts till our stock was again replenished. I thought that was extreme destitution. But it bore no comparison to this. I had yet to see the real horrors of war.

The last load of wounded was taken off late Wednesday night. There were about four hundred in the whole train, and it became necessary for them to remain in the ambulances during the night after they arrived at the hospital in Winchester, it being too late to make room for them that night, making three days and nights that many of them lay in this deplorable condition.

Winchester was flooded with both Rebel and Union wounded, and still they came pouring in from the front. Some were obliged to lie in the fetid atmosphere waiting their turn for medical treatment for days after they arrived, till their wounds became fly blown and the maggots grown to full size and literally covered their body.

Came down to the hospital at Sandy Hook with the first train containing seven hundred and one wounded. Ambulances could not be spared in sufficient numbers from the army, and the wounded were put into the returning army trains. It occupied a day and night coming down and unloading, yet the poor fellows endured it like heroes, though the dreadful jolting of those great army wagons must have continually reminded them that they were reclining on anything but "flowery beds of ease." From Halltown I hastened on and gave notice of their approach at the hospital where they had a good warm breakfast prepared for them, which must have been acceptable indeed after their severe fare of the past week.

Coming down, during the night I was reduced to the singular extremity of sleeping on horse-back, which, at that time, seemed as sweet sleep as I ever enjoyed. I came in healthy, hearty, sleepy, crocky, bloody and lousy, and presented myself safe and sound to the brethren, who, for several days had supposed me gobbled up by guerrillas which infest the whole Valley.

About a dozen Delegates with stores went on as soon as possible; some to remain and establish an agency at Winchester, others to follow the army.

Nothing but necessity would have compelled me to leave the work at that period, but, having already staid longer than I intended, I soon reluctantly left the field. My heart is still in the work and my prayers for it.

Justice compels me to make favorable mention of the faithful labors of brothers Curtis and Brackett, who, I trust are still in the glorious work. Likewise of all the dear brethren associated with us in the noble cause. Yours most respectfully,

L. L. Wood.

---

## Report of J. B. Stillson, Esq.

Baltimore, *August 3d*, 1864.

G. S. Griffith, Esq., *President Maryland Branch U. S. C. C.:*

Dear Sir:—In accordance with your request, permit me to say, the work of the Christian Commission in the hospitals, camps, and forts, and at the docks and rail cars, during the past year, in this city and vicinity, has been steadily pursued by the committees assigned to the several localities, with gratifying results.

It is not perhaps too much to say, that substantial relief and comfort have been daily administered, in some form, and every opportunity sought to relieve the sufferings of soldiers, and impart spiritual counsel and encouragement.

The sick, the wounded, and the dying have uniformly been the special objects of attention, and no efforts have been spared to carry out, in the practical detail, the grand central idea of this most blessed agency, in providing for the souls and bodies of men.

The members of the Commission, in conjunction with the worthy Chaplains, have maintained weekly prayer-meetings in the hospitals, for the special benefit of the convalescents and invalid corps, and have distributed tracts and papers, and other religious reading, at the forts and camps. It affords us sincere pleasure to be able to say, these meetings and efforts have been greatly blessed, as a means of grace, to many souls, and eminently promotive of good morals and religion among the soldiers.

In several of the hospitals a revival of religious interest has been enjoyed, and many starving prodigals encouraged to return to their "Father's house, where there is bread enough and to spare."

The potency of the gospel, in its infinite adaptations to meet and alleviate the miseries of a sin-ruined world, have been gloriously manifested in many instances, in the triumphant death of patriot soldiers, who, even in the dying hour, have been pointed to the loving Jesus, and, by his grace, led to experience, with rapturous joy, the saving efficacy of his most precious blood.

Perhaps, not a day has passed since the commission began its early labors in this field, but some real-life incident has transpired, to cheer and thrill the heart, and fortify the faith of those engaged in these labors of love.

Entering the hospital, we kneel beside the dying couch of some poor mother's son, who has "fallen in the fight." His moaning wails touch sensitive chords in the heart. His words are incoherent. Now! he is at the home of his childhood. He calls—"*Mother! mother!! Do you not hear? Will you not come?*" Alas! mother did not hear. She could not come. But there is one at his side that will do all and more than a mother could do for her dying boy, under the circumstances.

Laying our hand upon his forehead, and speaking his name gently, he opens his eyes wildly, as if waking from a dream.

Consciousness returns. The dread future is just before him. He trembles as he draws near the "dark valley." No ray of light falls upon his wounded spirit. Fearful forebodings agonize his soul. A life of sinful indulgence comes rushing upon him from the forgotten past. Memory, truthful and unerring, arrays before him the dark catalogue of his transgressions. Despair, with an iron grasp, seizes the dying sinner, and would hurl his deathless soul into the pit of deepest wo! But here stands the Christian brother. He knows it all, and realizes the conflict raging within. He comes with an infallible cure: the "Balm of Gilead" is in his hands. He soothes the wounded spirit; he tells the story of the cross; he points to the Lamb of God, who invites all to the gospel feast, "without money and without price." Oh, how timely! The new Light from above dispels the darkness. The lost is found—the sinner is saved, and earth and heaven rejoice together.

This is no imaginary sketch, but an occurrence the living witnesses will remember with undying delight.

Once again, pass with us through the wards of another hospital. Behold the anxious countenances of the pale sufferers, as the words of Christian kindness and sympathy fall soothingly upon their ears and hearts!

"Are you a Christian man?"

With a look of indescribable penetration, as though he would know by what authority you ask the significant question, he fixes his gaze upon you, and, ere he can answer, tears come unbidden, and the deep fountain of his soul is stirred.

You wait for a reply. It comes in tones of tender sadness. "*No, I am not; but I wish I was. I ought to have been a Christian. My mother has warned me, and prayed for me many years, ever since I can remember. I have a praying wife and children; but somehow I have kept putting off and putting off preparation for death until now. I am broken, and mangled, and dying, without hope. Oh, God! be merciful to me a sinner*," was his piteous cry.

We tried to point him to the loving Saviour, and offered prayer in his behalf, and urged him to "pray on."

"*Oh*," said he, "*I have no heart to go to God now, and offer him the miserable end of a miserable life*." With sorrowful reflections, we turned to other scenes and duties; but the memory of this scene will never cease to impress us with the importance of giving the fatlings of our flock, with our best years and faculties, to God.

I have recited the above life-incidents solely for the purpose of giving a glimpse of the Commission's labors, and inciting, it may be, some to greater earnestness and fidelity in this ample field of Christian usefulness.

For many months before the Christian Commission was organized for its work, it was the writer's privilege and duty to leave home and friends, to do what he could in the field and in the hospitals of the Potomac army, by way of comforting the sick and dying, and encouraging the young men of the army "to do well," and maintain the honor and purity of their early manhood, despite the vices and temptations swarming the track of war.

Every day's effort brought encouragement, and every day's experience since has magnified the essential greatness and glory of the plan and aims of the Christian Commission. Volumes would be required to record a tithe of its doings. Eternity only will disclose the grandeur and magnificence of its triumphs, and secure to the faithful workers the imperishable rewards of "well doing."

May the time speedily come, when this noble brotherhood shall no longer be required to expend their vast material and moral power on fields of blood, but concentrate their forces in a more delightful labor, for the world's enlightenment and redemption.

### POWER OF PRAYER.

Enoch K. Miller, of the 108th N. Y. Volunteers, was sadly wounded at Gettysburg through the left lung, and when found by one of the Christian Commission, was thought to be in a dying state. His wound was dressed, stimulants and suitable food given him and he was tenderly nursed as were also hundreds of others. Miller was a Christian boy; at the time of his enlistment was pursuing his studies for the ministry in the theologicial school at Rochester, N. Y. Under the kind nursing of the Commission he soon began to improve—notwithstanding the fact that a minnie ball had passed entirely through his body, penetrating the lower part of the lung. About two days after the battle he was transferred, with other convalescent soldiers, to the hospital at Annapolis. Shortly after his arrival there he had a relapse and "went into deleriums," and for the space of three weeks, was thought to be dying, his physician regarding his case as hopeless.

But on a certain Sabbath his reason returned and he began to get well, to the joyful surprise of all.

After a few weeks he obtained a furlough to visit friends in Western N. Y., where he learned from his pastor the interesting fact that at the very time and hour his reason was restored, the Church to which he belonged, was engaged in a meeting for prayer, expressly appointed on the P. M. of the Communion Sabbath to pray for the young men who had gone out from the Church and Sabbath School to defend and maintain the honor and integrity of their country.

Earnest and importunate prayer was offered for these young patriots, and Miller was prayed for by name, knowing, as they did, his critical condition.

His life has been spared and God has evidently a work for him to do. Since his recovery he spent some months in the Invalid Corps and rendered very valuable service to the Christian Commission at Annapolis, as many can witness.

Since then Miller has been licensed to preach the Gospel, and is now a Chaplain in the navy, doing, no doubt, a precious work for Jesus.

How many like him will ascribe the preservation of their lives to the timely ministrations of this Christian agency. The multiplied trophies of grace won by the fidelity of their labors of love eternity alone will reveal.

### THE AGED SOLDIER AND HIS DYING SON.

After a long night of suffering and toil, the glad light of the coming day began to stroke the east.

The morning I had observed was always hailed with a peculiar satisfaction by the suffering. The sadly wounded more especially would often ask during the night hours, "how long before the morning will come?" as if impressed with the thought that with the morning beams would also come deliverance. There seems to exist a kind of constitutional tendency with the afflicted to associate darkness with sorrow and light with deliverance.

At a very early hour an old Confederate soldier, nearly seventy years of age, having two flesh wounds, one in the arm and the other in the leg, beckoned me to come to him as though he would inquire, "Watchman what of the night?" I had often ministered to his wants and had as often been forcibly impressed with the general and patriarchal look and manner of the old man. His head was bald and his look venerable, while the expression of his countenance indicated a peaceful and trusting heart.

With voice subdued and gentle as a child, he spoke of his son, his only son, Thomas, who was in the fight, and "whom he feared was either killed or wounded."

Learning his company and regiment, I began to make inquiry for Thomas, and it was not long before I found him, about one hundred yards distant from his father with two wounds, one in the arm and the other in the bowels, and mortal.

Thomas expressed great anxiety for his father, and inquired at once, "is my father living?" Being answered in the affirmative, he said quickly, "Oh, I wish I could see him once more!"

I told him his wish should be gratified, and procuring assistance I bore him to the side of his father.

As they were brought face to face, tears, burning tears, flowed freely ere a word was spoken. The old man's greeting was simply, "Thomas, my son"—he could not speak more, and Thomas in reply said, "my father are you badly wounded?" When informed that his father's wounds were not serious, a smile of thankfulness lighted up his face for a moment. The father recovering from the first gush of a parents love and sympathy, inquired, "Thomas are your wounds serious?" "Yes! I fear they are mortal," answered the sinking and dying boy. I pointed Thomas to the Lamb of God who taketh away the sin of the world, and offered prayer and passed on to other cases of suffering equally sad and touching.

That day, as before, every temporal want was supplied, but the fatal shaft had reached its mark, and Thomas, ere the midnight hour, slept his last sleep.

Subdued and broken hearted, the old patriarch wept and mourned as did Jacob of old, for his darling boy Joseph, and said, "would that I might also depart."

I am now alone, all alone in the world. I followed three sons to the war, and now, alas! they all sleep in death. "Will not my gray hairs go down with sorrow to the grave?" I have no one to call me "father." My wife and children are in heaven and I am weary of life; my aching limbs and fainting heart admonish me that the time is short. I tried to comfort him with the precious assurances of the gospel, that "our light affliction, which is but for a moment, worketh for us a far more exceeding and eternal weight of glory." A few days after the cloud that seemed so impenetrable then, was scattered before the brightness of the rising Son of righteousness and the old man rejoiced in confiding faith that "He doeth all things well."

As he became better, he freely communicated to me the facts of his history. He said he had always loved the Union and had only followed his sons in the Confederate army because he had no home. "Not a day has passed," said he, "but I have prayed God to give success to the Union arms, and save our country from the ruin that threatens her destruction."

Several instances occurred where similar testimony was given by dying men in the Confederate ranks.

### THE OLD HERO OF GETTYSBURG—HIS WONDERFUL PRESERVATION—THE CHRISTIAN COMMISSION, &C.

John C. Burns, a man of temporal habits and of upright and unpretending life, was born in Burlington county, State of New Jersey,

September 5th, 1783, and at the time of the battle, was near seventy years old.

Much has been written concerning him since the fight, but very little that has not involved both fiction and error.

As a member of the Christian Commission it was my privilege to know personally of his wounds and deeds. It may not therefore be out of place to record, briefly, some of the facts and incidents that have given rise to a wide spread interest in his history.

From the beginning he deplored the war and "was concerned for his country." For several months he did service in Gen. Banks' command when he was at Harper's Ferry, and only withdrew from the army because age and infirmity compelled him.

Having no sons he felt specially called, as an individual, to do all in his power to aid his country in this crisis, as he had formerly done in the war of 1812. Hence, when it became evident that Hill, with 40,000 Rebel troops, was approaching Gettysburg, and that a battle was iminent, he resolved at all hazards, to aid in driving back the invading foe. He could not fight alone, and hence, without delay, prepared himself with rifle and ammunition for the first collision, and reported himself *on the field ready for service* on the morning of the first day's fight.

It will now be my aim to give the old soldier's statements of facts and events substantially as he narrated them to me.

"My heart," said he, "was made sorrowful, when I saw so many of the citizens about the streets on the morning of the battle, who evinced less concern for their country than for their personal effects. I fought for my country in 1812, and then learned to love it, and I have loved and honored it, I believe, with an honest affection to this day. I was sorry for this apathy, and I was sorry also that I had no sons to help fight the Rebels, but I was glad too when I remembered that I was still strong and could help fight them myself.

Without delay I borrowed a rifle and provided myself with powder and ball, as I was accustomed to do when in younger days I hunted the wolf and the deer along these same mountains and valleys so recently swarming with Rebels against our good government—the best government in the world.

I dressed myself for the fight in the same blue coat, and vest, and corderoys I wore in the war of 1812, and which I had sacredly kept as memorials of other days when I had fought and bled in defence of liberty and right.

Thus equipped with as strong a heart and as steady a nerve as I ever possessed, I turned my willing feet to where our troops were forming into line of battle.

Without ceremony I reported myself, I think, to Gen. Wister, who commanded the 2nd, 6th and 7th Winconsin Regiments and the 19th Indiana, and 24th Michigan, composing the "Iron Brigade." Approaching him I said, "General! I fought for my country in 1812 and I want to fight for it again to-day." The General looked at me keenly from head to foot, and seeing I was in earnest, extended his hand and said, "God bless the old soldier, he shall have a chance." I entered the ranks of the 7th Wisconsin, and right well did the old Rifle speak and work that day.

Never did I draw a bead with steadier aim on the deer of the mountains than on those Rebel leaders. Vacant saddles attested the work of the unerring missiles. I had not fought long, however, before a ball from the enemy struck my left side. I did not fall, though at first inclined to, for the shock was severe. It is no time thought I, "to look at wounds," I must fight while life and strength remain.

I resumed my work and continued to fire successfully for sometime, when I was again hit by a minnie ball near the groin, the shock was terrible, but I did not fall.

I now felt the blood running and I expected my end was near.

With an effort I lifted my gun quite readily and thought as before, I can still fight, and "this is no time to look at wounds," and with a determined purpose to strike to the last, I continued to load and fire.

Loading quickly, I poured shot after shot upon the Rebel leaders.

It seemed to me that my aim was never more deliberate or steadier on buck or doe in the best days of my manhood.

Soon thereafter, another ball pierced my left leg about midway between the ankle and the knee. This was a fearful wound to me, but I very soon recovered my feet, when I found that no bones were broken.

Once more I thought "this is no time to look at wounds." I must fight while I have strength to load and lift my gun. Then did the old rifle do well and quick its last work. It spoke in tones the living may not forget.

But my firing was of short duration. The battle raged hotter and hotter, scattering our noble boys with every volley like autumn leaves before the hurricane's blast.

Another ball penetrated my left arm a few inches below the elbow. Then my work was done, I could no longer hold my gun. I felt that my time was short. The blood was flowing freely from my wounds.

Darkness came stealing over my senses, and fainting, I fell, to remember no more until the first day's battle was closed and I a prisoner within the enemy's lines. When consciousness returned I began to consider my condition as a prisoner, and not being a soldier proper, it occurred to me I would not be entitled to the treatment due prisoners of war, and therefore might be killed without ceremony. With my well hand I succeeded with my pocket knife in burying in the ground my ammunition, and then crept away as far as I could from my gun. Shortly after a Rebel officer approached me and said gruffly, "old boy what brought you here."

I made no reply. "I know," said he, "and I'll have your case attended to shortly." I laid upon the field that night without any attention, thirsty and feverish with wounds inflamed and painful, but not bleeding much. The next morning, by the kindness of a neighbor who recognized me, I was brought to my house, where my wounds were dressed and every needed care and comfort supplied.

It was not long, however, before the Rebel officer traced me out and again threatened my life for fighting—not as a soldier, but as a citizen. About an hour later in the day, the same officer returned, accompanied by a soldier, and questioned me closely respecting the part I took in the fight.

Being weak and much exhausted, I resolved not to answer his question and hence tell him no lies.

The soldier passed aronnd my bed and seemed to be looking intently at some object outside the window that looked toward the Rebel lines and also toward a house occupied by the Rebel sharpshooters.

Soon they left me with a renewal of the threat that "they would attend to my case." About an hour after this interview a ball from the house occupied by the sharpshooters, a third of a mile distant, was fired through a pane of the window opposite my bed, just grazing my breast and burying itself in the partition wall near me."

In view of these wonderful escapes, it may be well to revert briefly to the incidents of this narration, simply for the purpose of tracing in it the hand of the Lord in thus saving from serious injury the old soldier's life and limbs five separate times.

The first ball that struck his side was turned from his body without injury to his person by the intervention of a pair of old fashioned spectacles in his vest pocket. The second struck a truss, worn for an abdominal injury, and glanced off, cutting away the flesh from his thigh about two inches below the top of the hip bone. The third ball passed through his leg between the large and small bones without injuring either bones or arteries. The fourth ball passed through the fleshy part of the left arm below the elbow, also without breaking or rupturing arteries. Finally, as a crowning climax to these hair breadth escapes, showing most clearly the special care of Providence over his children—the murderous plans of the enemy to kill him in his own dwelling—were also signally thwarted. Just before the ball was fired through the window, the old man had become weary of lying on his side and had turned for relief on his back. Thus the ball that would have killed him lying on his side, did him no injury.

I was deeply impressed with his simple story, and could not but realize the marked intervention of the Divine hand in his preservation.

While pointing out to him God's care and goodness in thus preserving him, tears of gratitude fell freely, and I could not but feel that the venerable patriot and hero then and there made a hearty and honest consecration of himself to God, as in prayer we commended him to the dying love of Jesus and read for his encouragement portions of the sacred word.

This is but one of many cases that come to my knowledge, warming my heart and strengthening my faith during the labors of nearly a month with the wounded and dying at Gettysburg. The ways of the Lord in His dealings with men, in several instances, were strange and unaccountable, and of such a character as to quicken His children to duty and lead them to an abiding confidence and trust in the wisdom of His plans.

Will not the precious, though painful experience of the agents of the Christian Commission amid scenes of carnage and death when related to the people at home, do much to enlarge the sympathies and expand the benevolence of the masses and ultimately prove the means, under God, of a glorious "advance movement," in the work of evangelizing the world.

I most confidently believe a new era has already dawned in the history of the Church. Christian men and women in all parts of the land are now making unusual sacrifices of health and time and money to promote the cause and happiness of a common humanity, and such as were never before made by any nation or people since the dawn of governments.

This Christ-like work—this living for others and not for ourselves, has undermined and broken down, to a large extent, the heaven-high barriers of selfishness that for long years of our national life have stretched in towering proportions across the track of Christian progress. "*The world moves.*" Humanity rises in the scale of values as it becomes more unselfish and Christ-like. When the glad day of our country's deliverance dawns, and peace once more smiles on a land redeemed and saved, then the history of the United States Christian Commission will be written—written it may be on fleshly tablets, but presenting a record powerful for good and more enduring in renown than those chiseled on the proudest monuments of granite or bronze in ancient or modern times. *Whole hearted giving and whole hearted labor* God requires, specially requires in this age of achievement. An imperfect offering He never did nor never can accept. It is a stench in His nostrels. The clarion-calls for generous sacrifices come trooping from every quarter. The sufferings of fathers, husbands and brothers, on the battle-fields and in the hospitals, appeal with ten thousand voices for aid and relief—for the little delicacies and home comforts indispensable to the sick room and the restoration of health.

"The earth is the Lord's and the fullness thereof."

Only as stewards will God permit us to accumulate and hold riches. When mercenary ambitions give the reins to selfishness, then may we fear, then there is cause indeed for great alarm lest He say as to one of old, "*Thou fool, this night thy soul shall be required of thee—then, whose shall those things be which thou hast provided.*" "It is more blessed to give than to receive."

The generations of yet unborn will bless God for the Christian Commission, because it will appear more evident then than now that it was a wonderful agency, under Providence, for correcting the evils of selfishness—one of our national sins—and promoting the blessed spirit of Christian benevolence and Gospel good-will in its stead.

May its treasury be speedily and constantly replenished with the large means necessary to the fulfilment of its glorious mission.

### THE DYING SOLDIER.

"T'is sweet to die
When Jesus is nigh."

"Are you the man that sang and prayed last night?" asked a dying soldier just at the break of morning. I was one of them, was the reply. Taking my hand in his he pressed it warmly and said with tearful eyes, "God bless you my brother." "It was so sweet."

"It soothed my aching heart so much that the night did not seem half so long as the one before." A heavenly smile irradiated his countenance and told of inward peace. "I did not think," he continued, "that I should ever hear the voice of prayer and praise again in time," "but oh! how precious." "It brought peace and heaven to my soul." "It fell on my crushed and bleeding heart as the dew that descended on the mountains of Zion."

We breathed a short prayer for the dying Christian soldier and left him with ministering angels waiting to convoy his freed spirit to the land of unfading brightness where garments rolled in blood are never seen and where there is rest for weary souls. An hour afterwards we passed on our rounds the spot thus made sacred with the heavenly light of dying grace. We lingered but a moment to close his eyes and wrap around his manly form the soldier's shroud.

His countenance, pale and serene, was touchingly beautiful in death.

The lines of sorrow that shaded his face when we first saw him, were no longer visible. They had given place to an expression of peaceful resignation that spoke plainer than words of his triumphant victory over death and sin.

We gave him a Christian burial and dropped a tear of sorrow as we remembered the aged mother far away, who for long years had indulged fond hopes for her darling boy, never to be realized.

God bless the stricken mother was our heartfel prayer as she reads the letter of Christian sympathy announcing the death, in Christ, of her only son.

## Sergeant Pennoyer, 111 N. Y. S. V.—Truth Stranger than Fiction.

A Union soldier mortally wounded in the head by the fragment of a shell, expressed a desire to become a Christian. After supplying his physical wants he was pointed to the loving Saviour and urged to accept Him without delay as a friend in every time of trouble, and the only source of help either for the living or the dying. We commended him in prayer to the love and mercy of Jesus.

His wound was so serious that our communication with him was strictly of a religlous character and such as to encourage us to believe that he embraced the offered Christ by a living faith.

A few hours before his death he was asked if he would not like a drop of wine. "Yes!" he replied, earnestly, "may I not take it as a Sacrament?" Do you wish to, was the inquiry—"yes I do," he replied—whereupon Chaplain Murphy of the 111th N. Y. V. administered the wine as a Sacrament.

A few hours later I came round in my circuit and his peaceful spirit had gone to the God who gave it.

We gave him a Christian burial in a soldier's shroud and laid him in a soldier's grave at the foot of a Wild Cherry tree, marking his name distinctly on a head board. I cut six buttons from his coat and sent them with an appropriate letter of condolence to his excellent and afflicted mother. For some days I had ministered to his wants without knowing his name, and it was only a few hours before he died that I learned the fact that in his early boyhood he had been an inmate of my own family and had often knelt around the family altar and been the subject of many prayers.

Truly the ways of Providence are mysterious and past finding out.

Yours, &c.,

J. B. STILLSON.

---

## Report of Rev. J. B. Poerner.

U. S. CHRISTIAN COMMISSION, AT THE U. S. GENERAL FIELD HOSPITAL,
SANDY HOOK, *Maryland, August* 18, 1864.

G. S. GRIFFITH, ESQ., *Chairman U. S. C. C. of Maryland:*

As it is your special request to me to furnish you a statement of my work in the U. S. C. C., I will try to give you a short description of it, and will commence at once, with my work at Gettysburg, of which I never had an opportunity to tell on account of my protracted sickness last year.

I arrived at Gettysburg, on the 6th of July, 1863, and was at once detailed on duty to the 11th Corps Hospital, then under the superintendence of Mr. James Grant, of Philadelphia who labored with one and other Delegates among about eighteen hundred patients, of whom about from five or six hundred were in a most pitiable and distressed condition.

On account of the heavy rains which poured down in streams upon our camp from the 4th to 9th of July, the whole field, but especially the level and lower parts of it, became in a certain sense a perfect lake in which the poor fellows laid, in their little shelter tents, two by two, literally covered in mud and rotten hay or straw, from three to five inches deep. I went to work at once, and with the consent of the Surgeon in charge, Dr. Armstrong, proceeded with a squad of men through the surrounding country in search for lumber, but as I could not find any, I went on to Gettysburg aud engaged all the empty boxes, barrels, and hogsheads, took them apart, and forwarded them to our 11th Corps camp. Another squad of men were sent to the woods to cut rails and forked pins, and after hauling them to our camp, commenced building up couches, and thus relieved that large number of suffering men from a muddy and watery grave, and just as fast as we built up and raised our wounded, we were furnished with comfortable hospital tents with which to cover them.

I continued in my work for four weeks, when I was ordered from the field by both brothers Griffith and Boardman on account of perfect exhaustion, which finally proved a hard attack of typhoid fever, from which I suffered two months in my bed, and one month after I was able to leave it before I was able to return to the benevolent work of the Christian Commission.

During my fourth week's work at the 11th Corps hospital, we held daily Divine services, at different places, in the streets of our camp, so as to enable every man within the tents to listen to the singing of hymns, prayers, and preaching of God's Word. The good which has been accomplished by the services Eternity alone will reveal.

Many of the sufferers were made glad by the physical and spiritual aid they received from the Christian Commission through the hands, hearts, kind words, and earnest, as well as consoling entreaties of its Delegates.

On the 14th of November I commenced work at the office, 77 West Baltimore street, and assisted as agent in receiving and forwarding hospital stores, &c., and other miscellaneous work, till the 5th of January, 1864, when I left for Harper's Ferry and Martinsburg, Va., according to order of the Committee. There I commenced my labors at once in company with brother Loomis, of Littleton, Massachusetts, in the regiments of 1st Virginia cavalry, 2d Virginia cavalry, 3d Virginia cavalry, 5th Virginia cavalry, 7th Virginia cavalry, 14th Pennsylvania cavalry, 12th Pennsylvania cavalry, 5th U. S. Regular artillery, companies B and L, 116th O. V. I., 123d O. V. I., 18th Connecticut V. I., 24th Massachnsetts V. I., &c. &c. We distributed during the winter season, systematically, all kinds of reading matter, writing material, and assisted in keeping up religious meetings, in which a large number of soldiers from the above named regiments became interested, and upwards of 400 soldiers became hopefully converted, according to the universal testimony of the Chaplains and Delegates of the Christian Commission.

On the 28th of March, I received my appointment from the Committee of Maryland to act as Agent at Harper's Ferry, and went forthwith to enter on my duties at said station. My first work there was, to order large supplies of soldier's reading matter of every description, for the regular weekly distribution among the different regiments and parts of regiments at Harper's Ferry, Sandy Hook, &c. These orders were promptly filled, as also those for stationery, and we had not only the pleasure of drawing many soldiers to our small Reading Room (which had been established before my arrival by Rev. brother Langley and other Delegates,) but pointed many of them to Jesus, by our conversation with, and our prayers for them. Thus, I labored with the brethren Boardman, Johnson, Durdis, Wright and H. G. Loomis among troops of this army, till the 13th of May, when I received a telegram, requesting me to come home immediately, on account of very dangerous illness of my dear youngest daughter. I left everything in the hands of brothers Boardman and Durdis, with the request to forward our tents, unnecessary blankets, and other stores to Baltimore.

After I had been led through the deepest bereavements by the Allmighty and All-wise hand of Divine Providence, in the loss of my eldest daughter, having lost two sons in a little over two years before I returned again to the blessed work of benevolence in the service of the U. S. Christian Commission on the 20th of July, and was ordered to go to Sandy Hook, Maryland, to labor there mutually with Rev. Edward Cooper, Chaplain 8th Ohio volunteer cavalry, who labored there since the 2nd of July in the capacity of Station Agent U. S. Christian Commission.

I commenced my work at once there, in the General Field Hospital, convalescent camp, at Harper's Ferry and Bolivar Heights, and found everywhere such a hunger after the Word of God, that I felt very sorry that I was not able to fill all the requests made for Testaments, Hymnbooks, &c., but especially for all kinds of clothing, stockings, &c. But, thank God, our applications for large supplies of reading and writing materrials, delicacies, stimulants, &c., were again promptly filled, according to the wisdom and ability of the Christian Commission at Baltimore, and as fast as we received them they were distributed as judiciously and economically as possible.

Another proof of the blessings resting upon our labors were manifested by the anxiety for the preached Word of God, and the continued request for our prayers by hundreds of men, in behalf of their soul's salvation, and the anxious inquiry—"What must I do to be saved?"

Much good has been done, through the instrumentality of the Delegates of the Christian Commission and Chaplains Cooper, 8th O. V. C.; Walker, 18th Connecticut V. I.; Brady 116th O. V. I., and others, but a great deal more good could have been done if we had had the most necessary means of transporting our supplies on horseback and wagons, to all the regiments connected with the army under command of General Sheridan, consisting of the 8th, 6th, and 19th Corps, besides the many cavalry regiments connected with the above corps.

Our work has been very hard, it is true, but the helpless and destitute condition of sufferers, constrained us to labor during the last skirmishes with untiring zeal and energy in order to relieve the wounded, who were brought in from the battle-field into our General Field Hospitals at Sandy Hook, Maryland.

Good Christian, energetic and healthy men, to labor as Delegates of the Christian Commission, and among them a number who are able to speak, read and write both English and German, are greatly wanted, besides a large quanty of hospital stores of every description, reading and writing material.

N. B. L. L. Wood, Esq., of Vermont, Rev. Stevens, of Vermont, Rev. Curtis, of Elkton, Maryland, and Mr. Brackett, of Maine, labored at Sandy Hook, as Delegates of the Christian Commission in August aud September, 1864.

Your humble brother, and obedient servant,
JOHN BERNARD POERNER,
Chaplain and Field Agent, U. S. C. C.

---

## Statistical Table of Receipts and Disbursements.

| | |
|---|---|
| Number of cases purchased and made up at our office from September 1, 1863 to September 1, 1864.................................... | 2,555 |
| Number of cases contributed by central office, Philadelphia, through Geo. H. Stuart, Esq... | 1,340 |
| Number of cases contributed from Pennsylvania and other points........................... | 223 |
| Whole number of cases distributed...... | 4,118 |

| | |
|---|---|
| Number of distressed families assisted, whose husbands, brothers and sons were in the army. | 265 |
| Bibles and Testaments distributed............ | 12,350 |
| Library books distributed.................. | 1,560 |
| American Messenger and other Religious papers. | 205,300 |
| Soldiers' books.......................... | 170,253 |
| Soldiers' Hymn-books..................... | 18,100 |
| Pages of tracts.......................... | 3,600,000 |
| Christian Ministers and Laymen commissioned to minister to men on battle-fields and camps, hospitals and ships..................... | 85 |
| Persons connected with the Baltimore Christian Association, and laboring in our District not considered Delegates.................... | 63 |
| Religious meetings held during the year separate from Chaplain's services.............. | 1495 |
| Public meetings held..................... | 3 |

| | |
|---|---|
| Balance on hand September 1, 1863........ | $759 01 |
| Amount of receipts during the year........ | 57,212 98 |
| | $57,971 99 |
| Amount expended through the year.......... | 33,876 02 |
| Balance on hand......................... | $24,095 97 |

| | | |
|---|---|---|
| The value of the stores distributed is........ | | $175,000 00 |
| The amount credited to transportation, and time occupied in the service of Delegates is twenty-nine thousand dollars as follows: | | |
| Northern Central Railroad................ | | |
| Philadelphia and W. Railroad.............. | | |
| Adams' Express Company............. } Baltimore and Ohio Railroad........... } Telegraph despatches................. } | $14,000 00 | |
| Delegates time valued at................. | $15,000 00 | |
| | | $29,000 00 |
| | | $204,000 00 |

### Balance on Hand.

The balance on hand was exhibited on the day the report was made up, but the demands upon it were so extensive that it was greatly reduced in a few days. By the time this report reaches the reader, the whole amount will have been exhausted, and at least three times the amount will be needed to meet engagements of the most pressing nature.

## Speech of Rev. Dr. P. Schaff,

*Delivered at the Anniversary of the Maryland Branch of the U. S. Christian Commission, held in St. John's Methodist Protestant Church, Sept.* 26, 1864.

Facts and figures such as you have just heard from the Secretary's report, are the best arguments, and speak louder than words. "By their fruits ye shall know them." The United States Christian Commission need not fear this test. Its doings are before the world, and they command the respect of every true patriot and christian. The United States Christian Commission and its twin sister, the United States Sanitary Commission, represent the reign of mercy in the midst of wrath, and will furnish one of the brightest chapters in the dark history of this war for the maintenance of our American nationality and self-governing institutions. Kindness is as old as human nature, and charity as old as Christianity. Charity has always done its quiet, modest, self-denying work in war as well as in peace. Florence Nightingale is the true heroine of the Crimean war, and her name will be blessed when the names of Generals Raglan and Smith, Canrobert and Pelissier are forgotten. "The poor you have always with you," says the Saviour, and so the fountains of charity that poured from the heart of Christ will never fail. But never before has Christian charity been organized and systematized on so large a scale for the benefit of an army or navy in time of war, as in the civil war of America. Its rise and rapid progress is marvellous before our eyes. There is hardly a town or village in the loyal States which has not made some contribution either to the Christian or Sanitary Commission, or both; and the interest is growing as the field enlarges. I never was in the service of the Christian Commission, and speak of it here only as a friendly outside observer who has watched its operations in the home offices at New York, Philadelphia and Baltimore, on the battlefields of Antietam and Gettysburg, in the hospitals of Maryland and Pennsylvania, and I can truly say that I admire and love it for its Christ-like work.

The object of the United States Christian Commission is to save the souls and to relieve the sufferings of our American soldiers and seamen, and thus to perform, in the midst of this raging war, the office of the good Samaritan, in imitation of the example of Him who went about doing good to the bodies and souls of men. The instrumentalities employed are the distribution of camp and hospital stores, Bibles and Testaments, (generously granted in immense quantities by the American Bible Society,) suitable tracts, religious newspapers of various denominations, and the living preaching of the Gospel. The agents are Christian ministers and laymen, animated by the love of Christ and of souls for whom He shed his blood. The Commission follows the army and navy in all their movements, and makes its influence felt in almost every camp and military hospital, even in the extreme front of the marching or fighting troops. It enjoys special facilities for transportation and communication, and has the hearty commendation of our highest civil and military authorities. The ruling motive of the Commission is that charity which is the highest of the Christian graces, which blesses friend and foe, and is never weary in well doing. I know men in Baltimore, Philadelphia and New York who devote nearly their whole time, together with a large amount of their income, to this noble work, and consider it a luxury to do so, well knowing that "it is more blessed to give than to receive."

The United States Christian Commission consecrate the war to holy purposes, and turn its horrors into blessings for thousands of our soldiers and sailors who, by the instrumentality of this institution, find the Saviour whom they had lost or never known at home. It restrains the profanity, intemperance, Sabbath profanation, licentiousness, gambling and other vices so fearfully prevalent in our as in every other army, and imparts moral strength and vigor to it; for the best Christian and citizen, in Washington's opinion, makes the best soldier; he who is true to his God is also most true to his country. It heaps coals of fire upon our enemies, who are or ought to be as well treated and provided for as our own soldiers whenever they fall into the hands of Christian charity, which, like the good Samaritan, regards every sufferer as our neighbor, without regard to his race, creed or position. On the battle-field of Gettysburg a confederate officer, after having been rescued, with many of his men, from filth, starvation and agony, by the self-denying labors of the agents of the Christian Commission, addressed them at last in these remarkable words: "You Yankees are strange people; you fight us like devils in battle, and treat us like angels after battle. I shall never take up arms against you again." There can be no doubt that hundreds and thousands of wounded and captive confederates will always gratefully remember the acts of kindness shown them. Thus the labors of this institution must prove one of the most efficient means for bringing about a final reconciliation of the two hostile sections of the country.

The United States Christian Commission is engaged not only in a good, but also in a successful work. It is enlisted under the star spangled banner, surmounted by the higher and holier banner of the cross, which bears the inscription: "By this sign thou wilt conquer!" Truth may, indeed, be crushed and crucified, but it will rise again. Our cause is getting stronger every day, while the rebellion is getting weaker. We have the vast superiority in men and in means. It is true we should never forget that the fortunes of war are the most uncertain of all fortunes, and that the race is not always to the swift, nor the battle to the strong, but the Lord giveth victory. Little Greece defeated the hosts of Persia, which outnumbered them ten or twenty to one. Switzerland successfully maintained its republican freedom for five hundred years against the repeated assaults of Austria and France. Holland achieved its independence against the powerful kingdom of Spain. But I base my confidence in ultimate success, not so much on our *material* strength, which may fail, as on *moral* grounds, of which I shall present you a few:

### 1. THE RIGHTEOUSNESS OF OUR CAUSE.

This is not a war of conquest and aggression, (if it were I would not defend it for a moment,) but a war of self-defence of our country against its domestic foes, who, whatever may have been the amount of provocation, were certainly not justified to appeal from reason to passion, from argument to blood, from the ballot to the bullet, and to destroy those self-governing republican institutions which their fathers helped to build up, and which have been their pride and protection as well as our own. *It is a war of union against disunion, of nationality against dismemberment, of government against rebellion, of loyalty against treason, of freedom against slavery, of the rights of the people against the spirit of cast, of the progressive tendency of the modern age against a relic of mediæval feudalism.* Aristocratic pride and disappointed political ambition are at the bottom of this rebellion, and pride goes before the fall: "whom the gods wish to destroy, they first make mad." That there was no just cause for this rebellion, we need no better testimony than that of the rebel Vice President, Alexander Stephens, in his almost prophetic speech delivered shortly before the secession of Georgia. It is the strongest argument against this rebellion, and when he joined the movement he acted against his better judgment.

### 2. THE YOUTH OF THIS NATION.

God does not permit a nation to perish before it has accomplished that mission for which he called it into existence. The untimely destruction of a nation so youthful, so promising, so pregnant with future destinies, before the first century of its birth, would be without a single parallel in the history of our race. If this country has no future, I do not know where to look for a future of secular and ecclesiastical history on the face of the globe.

But it may be said that the country and nation is large enough for two, and if need be for a half a dozen republics. This is true as to extent of territory and natural resources, not as to the configuration of our country. If we except the mighty wall of the Rocky Mountains, which has nothing to do with the controversy between the North and the South, the territory of the United States seems predestined by nature and nature's God to be one undivided whole. The absence of a geographical line of separation between North and South, East and West, (except the Pacific coast,) the course of our mighty rivers, the increasing facilities of communication, the essential unity of language, laws, and religion, from Maine to Florida, from New York to San Francisco, seem to indicate that this country is destined in the providence of God, to enjoy freedom in unity, and unity in freedom. Separation would only be a breeder of border wars and endless discord, prepare for us the fate of the divided republics of Central and South America, and deprive us of all power before the eyes of Europe.

### 3. THE VAST NUMBER OF GOOD AND GODLY PEOPLE IN THE COUNTRY WHO ARE FIGHTING, LABORING, AND PRAYING FOR THE RESTORATION AND REFORMATION OF THE UNION.

If God was willing to save even Sodom and Gomorrah for five righteous persons, will he not save this hopeful and Christian nation for ten thousand times ten thousand of his children in this Christian land? I believe that Christianity flourish at least as much, if not more here than in any part of the world, and this for the very reason that it is not forced upon the people by the Government, but left free to every man's conscience and conviction. Religion, like commerce, eloquence, and many of the first blessings of a nation, thrives best in the atmosphere of freedom.

Christianity has largely entered into this war. This is shown in the labors of the Christian Commission. Our Government itself, has, more than ever before, felt and publicly acknowledged our dependence on God for success in this mighty contest, and repeatedly called upon the people to humble themselves for their sins, and to thank Him for our victories. General McClellan and President Lincoln have issued army orders against the needless profanation of the Lord's Day during the war, such as never issued from any of the European Governments, although they are united to the Church. These, and other public documents clearly testify before the world that we are a Christian people, and that our Government, though separate from the Church, is not separated from religion, but bows reverently before the Almighty Ruler of nations. I hope the time is not far off when some more express recognition of this Great Head will be embodied in our National Constitution. This will be one of the many good results which mnst ultimately come out of this war by the all-ruling providence of Him, who turns even the wrath of man to his own glory.

4. I might easily multiply reasons on which I base my hope of final success, if time would permit. But we should remember that the *military* settlement of this great national contest is only one part of the task before us, which must be completed by the longer and more difficult work of the *political* and *social* settlement. A Union to be held together for all time to come by military force, is not worth fighting for, and would involve the ruin of our self-governing republican institutions. We want a *moral* Union, held together by the strong ties of mutual interest, respect, and friendship. We will not sacrifice our liberties for union, but union and liberty, one and inseparable. We desire to make friends and allies of our Southern enemies. This cannot be done by war. Our army and navy can, and I hope will, ere long, put down the armed force of the rebellion. But here its work ceases. Then comes the *political* settlement of the many complicated questions involved in, and rising out of this gigantic conflict, such as the terms of peace and re-union, the question of State rights, of the future condition of the negro race, of the amendment of the Constitution, &c. This requires the highest order of *statesmanship*, such as we have not, as yet. But the war raised its own Generals, and so the crisis will call out a generation of *statesmen* who are governed by principle, not expediency; who care for their country first, their party next, and themselves last and least, while the multitude of our smart *politicians* care for themselves first and most, for their party next, and for their country last.

Alongside with this political settlement, however, we need a *social* settlement, or an actual reconciliation of feeling and moral re-union of

North and South. This seems at first to be a hopeless task. But it can be brought about by the diffusion of truly *Christian charity*. Now the contending sections hate each other with an almost deadly hatred. But it must be remembered that it is so, more or less, in all civil wars, and that hatred is inverted love. The very intensity of this hatred shows the capacity of an equally intense friendship and love. It is moreover not so much a personal hatred, as a *sectional* animosity. The Rebel picket calls over to the Federal picket: "Yank, have you got some coffee or sugar? The Federal soldier replies: "Reb, or (Johnny,) have you got some tobacco?" And so they exchange these little offices of kindness, and even give each other fair warning when they begin to shoot. I conversed with many wounded Rebels and found them very friendly and grateful for every little attention. The common soldiers and the people of the South can be reconciled, I am confident, whatever may be said of the small minority of their present leaders, who are fast falling in the conflict. But it requires a high degree of Christian kindness, forbearance and generosity on our part. And I hope this will be exercised to the fullest extent after the military force of the rebellion has been broken down. The victor can afford to be generous and ought to delight in it. This will be the noblest triumph of our Government, if it succeed in this work of moral and social re-union.

But just here the labors of the Christian Commission will be powerfully felt. For, as already remarked, they extend to the Rebel soldiers and prisoners as well as our own, as far as they come within the reach of its agents. Such labors of love cannot and will not be forgotten by the Southern soldiers. They remove prejudices, gain confidence, inspire respect, secure gratitude, and constitute a strong cement of re-union. Christian charity is the greatest hero after all: it can disarm and reconcile an enemy without shedding one drop of blood.

Hence the work of the Christian Commission appeals to your patriotic as well as your Christian sympathies. He who supports it supports the cause of Christian charity; the cause of his country; the cause of Union and re-union on a lasting foundation, and secures a share in the grateful remembrance of our children and children's children who will reap the benefit of this terrible baptism of blood through which we are now passing. For as the blood of martyrs was the seed of the Church, so the blood of patriots will be the seed of the republic; a republic founded in the recognition of the universal rights and eternal destinies of men.

## Committee of Maryland District.

Several additions have recently been made to the Committee of Maryland. The Committee as at present organized is as follows:

G. S. GRIFFITH, Chairman, *Baltimore.*
REV. GEO. P. HAYS, Treasurer, *Baltimore.*
REV. J. N. M'JILTON, Secretary, D. D., *Baltimore.*
REV. T. STORK, D. D., *Baltimore.*
REV. ISAAC P. COOK, *Baltimore.*
CHAS. W. RIDGELY, ESQ., *Baltimore.*
REV. R. C. GALBRAITH, *Govanstown, Baltimore County.*
GIDEON BANTZ, ESQ., *Frederick City.*
REV. ROBERT H. WILLIAMS, *Frederick City.*
REV. J. D. CURTIS, *Elkton, Cecil County.*
REV. J. EVANS, *Hagerstown, Maryland.*
REV. HENRY C. WESTWOOD, *Maryland.*
DAVID E. SMALL, ESQ., *York, Pennsylvania.*
CHAS. A. MORRIS, ESQ., *York, Pennsylvania.*
REV. G. R. BENT, General Agent, *Baltimore Md.*
J. R. MILLER, Gen'l Field Ag't for the District.

---

## Conclusion.

The report of the Committee has been extended much beyond the limit assigned it when its preparation was commenced. And now, at its close, we find there is much interesting and valuable information that we are obliged to omit. The Secretary has prepared nearly a hundred pagess which cannot be used, and there are many incidents reported by Delegates which it would have afforded pleasure to have inserted, had it been possible. The address of the Rev. Dr. Schaff, at the anniversary meeting, is regarded as matter relevant to our purpose; and setting forth, as it does, the patriotic as well as the moral and religious features of our Commission, it appears to be a proper paper with which to bring our report to a close.

Respectfully submitted,

J. N. M'JILTON,
*Sec. Com. of Md. U. S. C. C.*

# DONATIONS.

Donations have been received during the year as follows:—

| | |
|---|---|
| H. W. Drakely | $1257 50 |
| Ladies Fair, Clearspring, Washington Co., Md | 522 50 |
| G. S. Griffith | 1000 00 |
| Kimberly Brothers | 8 62 |
| Otterbein Chapel of the United Brethren in Christ | 26 54 |
| Churchville through Rev. Mr. Williams | 3 00 |
| Poor Lady through Rev. Geo. P. Hays | 1 00 |
| Union Lady of Virginia | 3 00 |
| Cash | 1 25 |
| Rev. Mr. Wolf, German Reformed Church | 10 00 |
| Thomas Armstrong | 25 00 |
| Jesse Tyson | 10 00 |
| Mrs. C. S. Houseman | 1 00 |
| Rev. H. C. Cushing | 1 21 |
| Mrs. E. Hambleton | 1 00 |
| G. D. C | 1 00 |
| L. P | 1 00 |
| R. C. G | 2 00 |
| R. Snowden | 1 00 |
| Mrs. E. Allen | 50 |
| J. S. W | 3 00 |
| G | 1 00 |
| Male Grammar School No. 2 | 4 17 |
| Male Grammar School No. 6 | 2 37 |
| Rev. Mr. Quinan | 25 |
| Net Receipts of Concert | 31 32 |
| Mr. Weeks through Mr. Brown | 5 00 |
| American Office, through Mr. Fulton | 1000 00 |
| Hanover Pennsylvania Soldiers Aid Society | 120 00 |
| American Office, through Mr. Fulton | 104 00 |
| J. T. Kelso | 5 00 |
| Wm. C. Conine | 20 00 |
| George F. Brown | 2 50 |
| Rev. J. T. Stuchell | 2 00 |
| G. W. Sumwalt | 1 00 |
| Moravian Church, Lehigh Co., Pa., through J. B. P | 14 93 |
| Evangelical Church, Lehigh Co., Penn., through J. B. P | 9 50 |

| | |
|---|---|
| Schwenkfelder Church, through J. B. P. | 28 86 |
| Mrs.. Flores & Miss Dubb's, Hassensock, Lehigh Co., Pennsylvania, through J. B. P. | 5 45 |
| Dr. Samuel Dickey. | 5 00 |
| E. A. Dalrymple. | 5 00 |
| George M'K. Teal. | 2 50 |
| Miss M. R. Rankin. | 14 40 |
| P. W., for prisoners in Richmond. | 20 00 |
| Ladies of Taneytown, Carroll Co. | 30 00 |
| D. Meyers. | 10 00 |
| Mrs. Rowe. | 1 00 |
| Mr. & Mrs. Geo. W. Tyler. | 20 00 |
| N. & B. | 25 00 |
| Frank Morton. | 2 00 |
| Grand Division Sons of Temperance. | 20 00 |
| Collection and subscription at the meeting at Light Street M. E. Church. | 276 00 |
| Second Presbyterian Church. | 30 00 |
| Fourth Presbyterian Church. | 6 50 |
| Govans Chapel, through Rev. Galbreith. | 20 00 |
| Monument Street M. E. Church. | 55 00 |
| Trinity Church, through Rev. Geo. A. Leakin. | 21 19 |
| German Reformed Church, through Rev. E. R. Eschbach. | 30 00 |
| United Presbyterian Church, through Rev. Mr. Bruce. | 25 38 |
| Mount Zion P. E. Church, through Rev. McJilton. | 10 89 |
| Mrs. E. P. S. | 10 00 |
| Reformed Presbyterian Church, through Jas. Wright. | 25 00 |
| Luthern Church, Hummellstown, through E. Huber. | 11 70 |
| English Luthern Church, Cumberland. | 30 00 |
| High Street Baptist Church. | 15 00 |
| Miss M. L. T. | 5 00 |
| Columbia Street M. E. Church. | 20 75 |
| William Street M. E. Church. | 26 00 |
| Franklin Street M. E. Church. | 26 60 |
| Harford Avenue M. E. Church. | 20 00 |
| Contribution from Exeter Street Church. | 22 00 |
| English Lutheran Church, Selingnore. | 20 00 |
| M. E. Church, Clearspring. | 11 00 |
| German Reform Church, London, Franklin county, Penn. | 9 00 |
| Lutheran Church, Middletown. | 12 00 |
| St. Marks Eng. Luth. Church, (Dr. Stork,). | 55 00 |
| Mrs. E. B. Stork. | 10 00 |
| Caroline Street Church, through Rev. C. B. Tippit. | 138 01 |
| Rev. Mr. Leinbach, German Reformed Church. | 14 00 |
| Rev. Mr. Height, Blair county, Penn. | 10 00 |
| J. W. B., a Soldier. | 50 |
| Collection at Wesley Chapel, Baltimore, Capt. Levin Jones, \$200-- Balance Collection \$31.50. | 231 50 |
| Rev. Ethan Allen. | 1 00 |
| Adam Hellersman. | 1 00 |

| | |
|---|---|
| M. E. Church, Havre de Grace | 50 00 |
| Lutheran Congregation | 36 20 |
| Orchard Street Colored Church | 4 08 |
| Gratztown Congregation, Killinger, Pa. | 16 00 |
| Samuel Buck | 2 00 |
| Miss Lucy A. Hahn | 5 00 |
| Lower Chancelford Church | 41 00 |
| Broadway M. E. Church | 91 00 |
| Lutheran Congregation, Middletown Valley | 19 25 |
| Andrew Grey | 20 00 |
| Ger. Ref. Church, Easton, Penn., Rev. J. Beck | 65 00 |
| Lutheran Congregation, Salem, Ohio | 18 00 |
| Capt Bossler, through Rev. Geo. Wolf | 5 00 |
| First German Reformed Church, Chambersburg | 73 00 |
| M. E. Church Chestertown | 95 00 |
| Rev. G. H. Mildorf, Buckettsville | 10 00 |
| Lockhaven M. E. Church | 21 00 |
| Lutheran Church, Mechanicstown | 11 00 |
| A few friends, by E. C. W | 7 42 |
| By reports, V. Diffey | 1 25 |
| Two M. E. Churches, Williamsport | 23 70 |
| Presbyterian Congregation, Alexandria, Penn. | 18 00 |
| M. E. Church, Union Square | 36 00 |
| Christ Church, Owensville | 18 10 |
| Evangelical Lutheran Church, Duncanville | 22 00 |
| Asbury Street Congregation, (colored) | 17 50 |
| Emmettsburg Congregation | 50 00 |
| Cavetown Congregation | 20 50 |
| Rev. J. M. M. Gravill's English Lutheran Church | 10 00 |
| Martin Hawley | 100 00 |
| Congregation, Rochester, Beaver county | 4 00 |
| Jefferson Street M. E. Church | 14 00 |
| M. E. Church, Cumberland | 27 65 |
| Mrs. R. J. Brest | 5 00 |
| Evan. Lutheran Church, Dillsburg | 14 00 |
| Lutheran Reformed Congregation, Hummelstown | 9 80 |
| Josephine Gorsert | 25 |
| Logansville, Clinton county, Penn | 2 00 |
| Mr. G. N. Lusher | 3 00 |
| Paradise Charge, Limestoneville | 21 60 |
| English Lutheran Church, Minersville | 10 00 |
| M. E. Church, Chestertown | 50 00 |
| Union Square M. E. Church | 2 00 |
| Adam R. Height, Tirone City | 3 00 |
| J. W. Frey, Banner Valley, Iowa | 4 30 |
| M. E. Church, Elkton | 22 00 |
| Rev. Daniel Cunning, Taneytown | 2 91 |
| P. E. Church of Ascension | 13 00 |
| Evang. Lutheran Church, Duncansville | 14 00 |
| German Ref. Congregation, Blain | 21 25 |

| | |
|---|---|
| Second Eng. Lutheran Church | 20 00 |
| All Souls German Ref. Mission | 60 00 |
| M. Knight | 1 00 |
| Geo. W. Hensell, Ger. Ref. Church | 8 65 |
| M. P. Church, Chestertown | 10 00 |
| M. P. C. | 3 10 |
| German Evangelical Reformed Church | 64 20 |
| Luth. German Ref. Methodist United Breth | 80 00 |
| A. Hoen & Co. | 10 00 |
| Church of Holy Innocence | 70 |
| Isaac Gerhart | 1 00 |
| Rev. C. A. Reed | 1 75 |
| Lutheran Church, Westminster | 15 40 |
| First Evang. Luth. Church | 27 00 |
| Black Hole Valley Cong. | 100 50 |
| Yellow Creek Charge | 8 65 |
| German Reformed Lutheran Congregation, Shrewsburg | 53 50 |
| Dr. Zeck, Emmettsburg | 5 00 |
| German Reformed Church, Rural Village | 9 30 |
| Presbyterian Congregation, Town Creek | 75 00 |
| German Ref. Congregation, Clearspring | 15 50 |
| Lutheran Congregation, Argusville | 8 45 |
| Caroline Street M. E. Church | 3 00 |
| Rev. E. W. Wolf, German Ref. Church | 23 00 |
| German Ref. Church, Rev. S. G. Wagner | 10 00 |
| German Ref. Church, Owensville | 17 20 |
| Welch Run Church, Mercersburg | 11 00 |
| Rev. H. Williams, Chesterville | 1 00 |
| Paxton Church, Rev. A. D. Mitchell | 23 25 |
| Lower Chanceford Church | 1 00 |
| Mrs. Hyatt | 1 00 |
| Mrs. Wilber | 2 00 |
| George C. Smith | 1 00 |
| Gentleman in N. Y. Car | 1 00 |
| Mrs. Attenburg | 3 00 |
| Luth. Ger. Ref. Meth. and United Brethren | 4 00 |
| Danville Charge | 17 10 |
| St. Mary's Church, Dauphin county, Pa. | 3 25 |
| Presbyterian Church, Taneytown | 12 00 |
| Evangelical Lutheran, Johnston, Pa. | 3 85 |
| Capt. D. P. Thurston, Gen. Lockwood's Staff | 100 00 |
| " " " " " | 26 00 |
| German Ref. Church, Landisburg | 5 00 |
| A. G. | 10 00 |
| Wm. M. Deatrich | 8 12 |
| H. Daniel | 5 00 |
| A. Mower, Ashland county, Ohio | 5 00 |
| Messrs. Carter & Co. Daily Gazette | 8 25 |
| George F. Brown | 1 00 |
| German Ref. Church, Stugville | 40 00 |

| | |
|---|---|
| David Fishell | 2 00 |
| Hon. Mr. Fiery, Washington county, through Mr. Silverwood | 5 00 |
| Rev. J. B. Kiuest | 22 50 |
| German Ref. Church, Rimersburg, through Rev. Joseph H. Apple | 2 60 |
| Rev. B. Knepper, in books | 6 50 |
| Mrs. S. R. F., of Chambersburg | 10 00 |
| Miss Amelia Hertzell, of Myerstown, in papers | 2 00 |
| Mr. S. Barber | 10 00 |
| Sarah Shull, Marian, Pa | 10 00 |
| German Ref. Church, Troutville | 15 00 |
| Wm. S. Cross & Bros | 10 67 |
| Dr. J. N. Johnson | 100 00 |
| Wm. Harper Beays | 6 00 |
| Dr. J. Murry, Centreville, Maryland | 5 00 |
| Miss H. C. Cockey | 1 25 |
| Wm. B. Waugh | 2 00 |
| Wm. Talbot, U. S. Receiving Ship | 5 00 |
| Rev. Wm. Jones | 3 20 |
| W. G. Maxwell | 10 00 |
| Greene & Yoe | 25 00 |
| Wm. G. Maxwell | 29 00 |
| W. H. W | 5 00 |
| John Sheckles | 10 00 |
| Wm. C. Conine | 20 00 |
| Thos. S. Alexander, Attorney | 50 00 |
| N. M. Storks | 2 00 |
| Mrs. W. L. T. | 10 00 |
| A soldier friend | 5 00 |
| Through Rev. O. M. McDowell | 200 00 |
| Cash | 83 |
| Ellen and Henry Finley | 5 00 |
| Refunded by Rev. M. Waugh | 75 |
| Mrs. E. F | 5 00 |
| J. M. Grant | 2 00 |
| Donation from Reuter & Sons | 25 00 |
| Wm. Woodward, cor. Hanover and German streets | 20 00 |
| Henry Schillinger | 5 00 |
| Rev. R. C. Galbraith | 5 50 |
| B. H. L., of Baltimore | 25 00 |
| Draft from Rev. O. M. McDowell | 500 00 |
| Draft from Rev. L. Hartsough | 39 52 |
| Check from Rev. Geo. Wolff, for German Reformed Church, Meyerstown, Pa | 77 10 |
| From J. Garrett, Scotland, Pennsylvania | 8 50 |
| Received of H. Heckerman | 14 25 |
| Received of Mrs. Dickey, Philadelphia | 3 00 |
| Collection through Rev. Mr. McDowell | 120 15 |
| David Neff, Reading, Pennsylvania | 5 00 |
| Tyler & Bro | 6 82 |

| | |
|---|---|
| John Michael, Union M. House.......................... | 7 00 |
| A friend.............................................. | 10 00 |
| Columbia street M. E. Church, through Rev. John M. Start | 15 57 |
| Whatcoat Chapel, through Rev. J. B. Reese.............. | 3 25 |
| Jefferson street M. E. Church.......................... | 13 05 |
| Monument street Church, through Rev. R. Hinkle......... | 41 00 |
| Charles street Church.................................. | 57 70 |
| Church of Holy Innocents, Protestant Episcopal......... | 75 |
| Check from Samuel B. Caldwell.......................... | 9 30 |
| Light street Church Collection......................... | 88 73 |
| East Baltimore M. E. Church, through Rev. James Curns.. | 10 00 |
| M. E. Church, Frederick City, through Rev. Mr. Downs... | 9 00 |
| Check from Port Deposit, Md, M. E. Church.............. | 50 00 |
| High street M. E. Church, Baltimore, Md................ | 76 15 |
| J. F. M., Baltimore, Md................................ | 1 00 |
| Rev. C. T. Hoffmier, McConnelsburg, Pa................. | 11 00 |
| Strawbridge M. E. Church, through Rev. S. W. Price...... | 6 50 |
| Courtland, N. Y. Collection through Rev. L. Hartsough.... | 14 00 |
| E. W. Hayward, Uxbridge, Massachuseets................. | 50 00 |
| Rev. Mr. Aldwin, Baptist Church, Wilksborough, Penn.... | 7 10 |
| William street M. E. Church............................ | 8 00 |
| Cash from sale of Old Iron............................. | 2 25 |
| Mrs. McKnight, through O. M. McDowell.................. | 5 00 |
| Eutaw M. E. Church, through Rev. J. A. McCauley........ | 65 00 |
| R. A. B................................................ | 1 00 |
| Lieut. Chas. W. Potwin, Co. A. 159th Reg. O. Vol........ | 40 00 |
| Mrs. Sarah Olinger, through S. J. Berlin................ | 5 00 |
| Mr. Morton............................................. | 1 00 |
| Mr. Carter............................................. | 1 00 |
| Thos. Higbee, Treas. U. S. C. C. Peoria, Ill., for J. Tompkins, | 50 00 |
| Mr. Musson............................................. | 5 00 |
| Maryland State Fair, Henry Janes, Esq., Treas.......... | 40,000 00 |
| Samuel F. Bacon, for Church in Newark, Valley Co., N. Y. | 11 00 |
| Received from Rev. A. E. Gibson of the Broadway M. E. Church, Baltimore................................ | 39 41 |
| From Central Office, Philadelphia, through George H. Stuart, Esq.................................................. | 7502 21 |
| Total.................................... | $57,212 98 |

# CONSTITUTION

OF THE

# BALTIMORE CHRISTIAN ASSOCIATION,

AUXILIARY TO THE

## UNITED STATES CHRISTIAN COMMISSION.

---

ARTICLE I.

The Society shall be distinguished by the title of "The Baltimore Christian Association, Auxiliary to the United States Christian Commission." The object of the Association shall be to afford both Physical and Spiritual aid to the sick and wounded soldiers, as well as to disseminate religious truth among military camps and hospitals.

ARTICLE II.

This Society shall be constituted of male members of all Evangelical Churches in good standing, of twenty-one years and upwards, who are strictly loyal to the Government of the United States, and heartily opposed to the wicked rebellion now in progress.

ARTICLE III.

The officers of this Society shall consist of a President, Vice-President, Secretary, Treasurer and seven Directors, who shall be elected by the Society for the term of one year, and shall constitute a Board for the transaction of business.

ARTICLE IV.

The regular meetings of the Association shall be held on the second Tuesday of each month. Special meetings may be called by the President at any time,

# BY-LAWS.

First.—The President, or, in his absence, the Vice-President, shall preside at all meetings of the Society. Seven members shall constitute a quorum. The President or presiding officer shall preserve order, regulate the proceedings, and give the casting vote when necessary.

Second.—The Secretary shall keep a record of the proceedings at each meeting, and read the same at the opening of the subsequent meeting; he shall have the custody of the Constitution and By-Laws, receive the signatures of new members, and shall give notice of proposed meetings, either special or regular.

Third.—The Treasurer shall receive and hold for the use of the Society all donations in money, and shall pay such bills or orders only as are countersigned by the President. He shall from time to time make a statement of the receipts and disbursements, and the amount in the Treasury.

Fourth.—It shall be the duty of the officers and members of this Association to visit military camps and hospitals, and while there converse with the soldiers on religious subjects, distribute religious and other proper reading matter, hold meetings for prayer, experience, &c. and in any other way operate so as to promote Evangelical piety among the soldiers. Each member of the Association shall keep a memorandum of his labors, and give a written report of the same at each monthly meeting.

Fifth.—No alteration or amendment shall be made to the Constitution unless one month's notice be given previous to the time at which it is acted upon, and then only by the concurrence of two-thirds of the members present.

## BALTIMORE CHRISTIAN ASSOCIATION,

## Auxiliary to the United States Christian Commission.

PRESIDENT.

G. S. GRIFFITH.

Vice-President.

W. F. CARY.

Secretary.

J. HENCK.

Treasurer.

J. N. M'JILTON.

DIRECTORS.

JOHN N. BROWN,
Rev. THOMAS COGGINS,
SYLVESTER SANNER,
WM. SILVERWOOD,
Rev. JOHN KULLING,
JAMES MORFORD,
JACOB YEISLEY,
CHAS. FRASKO,
Dr. W. BURLINGAME,
Dr. HENRY S. HUNT,
W. H. HARRISON,
Rev. F. W. BRAUNS,
" R. SPENCER VINTON,
GEO. N. CRESSY,
Rev. GRIFFITH OWEN,
E. R. HORNER,
S. S. STEVENS,
J. H. HERPEL,
J. T. KELSO,
J. B. STILLSON,
J. H. WESTWOOD,
W. A. WISONG,
Rev. F. A. MARINE,
WM. L. GARRITEE,
Rev. T. W. SIMPSON,
" T. H. QUINAN,
" R. R. WELLS,
" S. GUITEAU,
" S. W. PRICE,
" THOS. MYERS,
" J. P. CARTER,
J. M. GRANT,
LEWIS RAYMO,
W. H. MITTAN,
WM. B. CANFIELD,
GEO. F. ZIMMERMAN,
Rev. J. B. POERNER,
JOSEPH LINCOLN,
Rev. J. T. VANBURKALOW,
" GEO. P. HAYS,
" GEO. A. LEAKIN,
" ANDREW B. CROSS,
" E. M. BUCK,
" J. T. STUCHELL,
W. BAKER,
Rev. GEO. M. PURVIANCE,
ANDREW HARRIGAN,
ANDREW MERKER,
S. BEALE,
GEO. W. SUMWALT,
DAVID MAXWELL,
J. A. PECK,
WM. RUDOLPH,
JOHN L. REED,
Rev. SAMUEL WILSON,
S. W. CORNER,
Rev. I. P. COOK,
" G. R. BENT,
WM. BOYER,
Rev. JOHN MUSSON,
J. POTTER,
G. DAVIS,
JAS. BALLOCH.

# CONTENTS.

# THE WAR

AND THE

# CHRISTIAN COMMISSION.

BY ANDREW B. CROSS.

1865.

# CONTENTS.

# PRISONS AND PRISONERS OF WAR.

---

## RICHMOND—ANDERSONVILLE—FORT DELAWARE—WALLABOCHT BAY.

The wounded from the battle of Gettysburg had scarcely been housed in comfortable quarters for the winter, when reports came, by various modes of communication, that our men who had been captured at Gettysburg, and other places, were suffering in the prisons of Belle Island, Libby, Castle Thunder, &c., at Richmond, for want of food, clothing and shelter.

It was hard to entertain the idea that it could be true of men who had enjoyed the blessings of civilization and christianity, and who profess to have attained to a standard of humanity, civilization and chivalry beyond any of their Northern brethren. To charge such a crime upon them, for milder language is not becoming, we were very unwilling. Yet after examining into the matter with all the care, attention and impartiality possible—comparing the statements and editorials in their papers with written communications from prisoners in prison, and the personal verbal testimony of men who were privates and officers, men whom we personally knew—we were left without a shadow of doubt upon the subject. Being eye-witness to the condition of those that were admitted at Annapolis from the steamer New York, from Richmond, on May 2d, 1864, also of those admitted to West's Building Hospital, on the 18th of April, we can testify that their condition was all that is sta'ed in the report of Mr. Wade, on May 9th, and that the photographs of the persons were correct

When the miserable commissary was denounced in their Congress by *Mr. Foote* as a cruel wretch, disgracing the Confederacy, robbing and murdering by inches the prisoners—when they permitted provisions and clothing to be forwarded, it was an admission on the part of the Rebel Government of the truth of the statements to a very large degree.

Convinced of the fact, and finding a door open, we gave what diligence we could in endeavoring to secure and send forward to our men in prison such articles of food, clothing, &c., as would help to make them comfortable. At first they were freely received, and in part, if not wholly, distributed. Then it was objected that they could not distribute what the Government had sent, but would that of the Commissions—then none except individual packages. When reduced to this, we took the names of individuals, and dividing the goods into moderate sized boxes,

2

forwarded them to individuals, many of whom we were thankful on knowing that they received them. Others to whom boxes were sent, not only did not receive them, but from some we have learned that when they were released for exchange, on passing out, saw boxes directed to them, with the goods in some cases removed, and in others spoiled.

To what extent our papers were guilty of exasperating them by gross representations and violent denunciations of their conduct, we cannot tell. It certainly was a duty to point out this gross neglect, resulting in starvation, when their papers admitted, urged and justified it; and must have been gross when Mr. Foote, one of their Congress, felt called upon by his humanity to denounce it publicly in that body.

The history of this starvation is one of the darkest pictures of this rebellion. To capture men in war, to shoot them down in battle, to require of them even exertion to procure their food and clothing, to let them live even on rougher fare, might be admitted as an accompaniment of war. To withhold proper food when they have it—not to furnish it in quantity when they have abundance, to admit their want and open a door to receive food and clothing—then when furnished, to shift and shuffle from one point to another, to have some pretext to continue the work of starvation, exposure and death—and then for the editors of their papers to gloat over it and glory in it, is one of the most horrible things which has occurred since this horrible war was commenced, and admits of no apology. To have men suffering from want of clothing, and withhold clothing furnished to them without cost; to have men starving and dying, and let provisions rot before their eyes without letting them be given; to let their fellow-men, prisoners in their hands, for whose lives they were responsible to God, die thus, is an outrage on humanity, such as the world has scarcely ever seen, and is evidence of the strongest kind, to us, that their cause is of that character that God could not and would not prosper.

In times of excitement, we are in great danger of losing sight of proper and correct principles—in a storm a sea captain may lose his reckoning; in a battle, amid smoke or fog, soldiers and officers may lose their place and be captured—the confusion of the contest may break order and discipline; in time of civil and warm political contests, men lose sight of individual rights, correct principles, and forget and neglect the duties they owe to one another; but no man has a right, no people have a right to sanction inhumanity—to pursue it with a plan and purpose. What incident in the life of the cruel Nero is more indicative of his savage temper, and indifference to human rights, than that during a general famine, when many were perishing for want of food, he ordered a ship from Egypt, the granary of Italy, with a load of sand for the use of wrestlers, that he might be amused in the contest?

Among the vessel loads of our returned prisoners were men whom we had known for many years. Those in the photograph plates were true, but there were worse cases. No report can convey the impression which a man would have who saw them upon the boats.

The people of the South, in general, are not to be charged with this cruelty, for in many cases we have heard from our prisoners that acts of kindness and attention to their wants have been shown in ways which speak for their humanity and ingenuity in helping them; neither would we charge it upon officers of standing or rank in State, or the army. The neglect the withholding and the cruelty which has placed such a picture of horrors before the world, is principally due to the officers in charge of those prisons, who have acted as commanders, provost marshals, keepers, guards and commissaries, with negligent surgeons. We would not, however, by any means, excuse the criminality against God and humanity, which in the higher officers of State permitted these men so to act, or the Government which would withhold help, or when help was offered and brought by their consent, would suffer the same to go to waste, while the men died for want. If they did not in person examine, they should have had reliable men; if neither, what excuse can they make? They could not be ignorant.

We are the more explicit on this point, and make the complaint with somewhat of right, personally, because we have endeavored to have the Rebel wounded in our hands cared for in proper manner, as a duty we owe to God, to humanity, and to our nation. The Rebel wounded at Gettysburg, and in our hospitals, were taken care of as well as our own, by surgeons of the Government, and by the delegates of our Commission.

*Wounded and prisoners* constitute two great classes in war. In this, the contest is to settle the permanency of republican institutions—the right and power of self-government—the hope of liberty in the world; whether man shall be man as made in the image of God, with rights and hopes for this world, or whether he is to be enslaved, oppressed and down-trodden under the heels of despotic power—that absolutism which craft, taking advantage of ignorance, combined under satanic influence, with power, has interfered between man and his Creator—between man and the blessings which God has entitled him to, and made him the mere creature of their will and pleasure, instead of man in the image of God, sitting beneath his own vine and fig tree, with no power to molest him.

Sprung upon the people of this nation as this war was in the early part of 1861, all the facilities which belonged to the Government removed by the cunning of traitorous officers, with the permission or neglect, if not connivance of James Buchanan, the Chief Executive, the energy of the nation, its reserved power had to be called forth, and provision made for its defence. It has been done on a scale of grandeur and magnificence. For thirty years the Southern leaders had been preparing. When they made their first moves they were the strongest. When their rebellion was thoroughly inaugurated they were in their strength. The national arms and munitions of war, which then were as nothing, have gradually been growing into a perfectness in numbers and strength until the present time.

In the progress of our Government's provision no department has been more carefully and permanently advanced than that which belongs to the *wounded and prisoners*. Beginning without hospitals and prisons, indeed without surgeons, for what were the few army surgeons to the demand? When we called the second day after a battle upon a Medical Director to ask him to telegraph for fifty or one hundred surgeons, he answered "We had enough for our wounded." Several days after the Surgeon General called for fifty to one hundred. Men could not realize the magnitude of the war, and just in the proportion of that did we need surgeons, hospitals and prisons, with all the appendages necessary to a humane caring for of the lives of our own men and of the enemy as they should fall into our hands.

Torture is not an element of war. With all its horrors and sufferings and deaths, a real soldier would feel dishonored and degraded if he let his humanity leave him for the impulse and spirit of a demon. On the battle field, while the musketry has been one continued crash and the artillery one deafening roar as men advanced against the enemy, a man has been known to stop and give a drink of water from his canteen to a wounded enemy. At Point Lookout we preached from a Testament belonging to one of the Rebel prisoners, in which he had written, "*Given to me by the Enemy on the field of battle, at Gettysburg.*"

In the Peninsular war, when the English and French had been in deadly conflict, the English army overpowered, had retreated across a river, the French pursuing to its edge They had succeeded, and were passing over a rising ground on the opposite side to escape the sharpshooters of the French, who were now occupying the ground which they left. The bugles sounded for a move, when some one observed that a woman, the wife of one of the soldiers, in the confusion and haste had been left on the opposite shore, and was standing with arms outstretched imploring help. The noise of the stream and the roar of musketry drowned her cries. What was to be done? How can she be saved? While the army turned to behold her one general feeling of interest was awakened. Suddenly the ranks opened, and a man pushed forth on horseback. Pressing the spurs into his horse he dashed into the stream. The storm of bullets from the French army fell as hail around him, yet on he pressed, stemming the flood, and reached the shore where she stood. Seizing her with his strong hand he lifted her upon his horse. Turning his head he rushed again into the river. The French now, for the first time, saw for what he had braved their army single-handed. Dropping their muskets to the ground, and taking off their caps, with one huzza they joined the English army upon the other side in paying their tribute to the humanity and philanthropy of the Scotch nobleman who had perilled his life for the saving of another.

This spirit has not left the men in the army on either side in this dreadful contest. Oftentimes when the officers of the Rebel army will permit, their pickets hail our men with as much freedom and cordiality as if there was no strife between them. They will trade tobacco and sugar and papers, &c., until ordered to cease, and even then will notify our men that they may be on the watch. There are some green spots now and then in the desolations of war which show where human kindness can soften the pillow and soothe the dying hour even of an enemy in arms.

We are thankful that amid the terrible horrors of this war there are agencies at work in addition to the regular provision of the Government, in concert, and heartily co-operative with all those surgeons or men of the medical fraternity who are seeking to alleviate the pains, bind up the wounds and minister food and nourishment to the wounded and dying on the battle-fields and in the hospitals—to speak words of comfort to their souls, pointing them to Jesus Christ, the Saviour of sinners, receiving and sending their dying messages to parents and kindred, and relieving those at home by letting them know of their place and condition.

To accomplish such ends much labor and self-denial has often to be endured. Care and caution has to be observed, lest in a desire to do good a philanthropic individual does not come undesignedly in the way of an officer, whose instincts are his pay, his rank, and his personal convenience, or who may have some private pique with some individual or society, or who may feel that enough is done by the Government and physicians without any meddling philanthropist.

No government ever did more for its wounded and prisoners than has been done by our Government. Never were officers in charge of an army, or surgeons in charge of hospital departments, more attentive to their men than men who are connected with our army; yet from Lieutenant General Grant down—we may say from the President, himself, down—there has been an appreciation of that kind of labor and attention which in a thousand ways has helped to mitigate the severity and horrors of war.

In the surgeons' department, where the only jealousy arises and where little things either without design or by mistake, or through inexperience and want of knowledge of men and the world, have given offence, we take pleasure in saying that almost uniformly this kind of labor has been received gratefully, kindly, and in many cases sought for and co-operated with to such a degree that you would forget that he was an officer under pay and with authority, and feel that he was like one of yourselves, seeking only to do good to his fellow man.

If there be one thing in the army more to be dreaded, and condemned than any other, it is *the use of intoxicating drinks* in officers, surgeons and privates. If there be a man upon earth who should be a sober man, cool, calm and collected, it is the man who goes himself and leads others into battle. He risks not only his own life, but his men and his cause. So of the man who undertakes to attend upon the sick and wounded after a battle. The time was when to be almost drunk was an essential to a sea captain, an engineer, a commander, a private soldier and a preservative to a surgeon. But the sunken ships, drowned passengers, exploded engines, scalded victims, frightful conflicts of railroad cars, captured officers and men by blunders, and the bad management and neglect in the cases of wounded men, resulting from drink, have demanded sober men.

Stimulants that are needed for wounded men; strong drink which according to scripture, is to be given to men who are ready to perish, is not necessary for men who are well and properly cared for. The testimony of commanders of armies, of surgeons of long experience in war and in countries where fevers and chills are common, is against the use. 1. A man sells to make money by it. 2. A man drinks because he loves it and desires to have it near him.

With some surgeons we have noticed the bottles from the dispensary with the label *Spiritus Frumenti* are a sort of sovereign panacea. We with pleasure record the conduct of others, when their wounded men have come in and spirituous liquors have been proffered, have rejected it and sought for hot coffee. In the hurry and pressure often incidental to war, especially during and after an engagement, *neglect* and *oversight* of many things is almost a necessity, orders that pertain to the efficiency and success of the army must be carried out without delay and without regard to persons or cost. At such a time no sane man will interfere to hinder the same, but when at ease, with leisure, inattention and neglect are unjustifiable.

After a battle, the first thing is to save life, make as comfortable as you can the wounded and make secure the prisoners.

The same thing which called for enlarged and humane exertions toward the wounded, from the large number of prisoners in this war, called for places of security. Our government has provided Fort Delaware, Point Lookout, Johnson's Island, David's Island, &c.

The whole system of imprisonment in its best forms is not attended with the humanity it should. We find in our State prisons until lately where no passions are called out, merely the keeping safe of criminals, neglect and often severity. Abroad it has been far worse. The Prison History of Europe until exposed by Howard was a horrible disgrace to human nature. Where passions are inflamed on either side and men are placed over prisoners, who have neither humanity, coolness, courage nor management—the treatment of prisoners will be without consideration and without humanity. Oftentimes these prisons and burial grounds exhibit the brutality of officers, surgeons and we might add of nurses in charge.

In the month of November, 1863, while engaged in sending to our prisoners at Richmond, some person called at the commission room and said that we had better look into the condition of the rebel prisoners at Fort Delaware. On Friday, December 3rd, we went to New Castle and on Saturday 4th to Fort Delaware. We spent Saturday afternoon, Sabbath and Monday morning looking carefully into the condition, a report of which was published in the Baltimore American of December 10. From it we extract as follows:

"Fort Delaware is situated on an island in the Delaware river, directly opposite to Delaware city, the point where the Chesapeake and Delaware Canal opens into the Delaware river.

The island is about three-quarters of a mile from Delaware City, about one-half mile from the Jersey shore, and contains about seventy-five acres of land. It was formerly called the *Pea Patch*, and now, at times, gets the old name. The ground is flat, and at high tides would overflow, but an embankment is made all around it, higher than the tide at any time rises. On the east side of the island is a lock by which the river is admitted into the moat which surrounds the fort. From this also there are several smaller canals, which drain the island, and passing through with the rise and fall of the tide, carry away any filth or putrid water which might and must gather around a large fortification with so many persons in and about it.

The fort is built of solid granite stone on the outside, with brick casemates and garrison houses within its enclosure. These casemates are three stories high. All the buildings and fort seem to have been put up in a very substantial manner.

The rebel prisoners occupy barracks outside of the fort and on the northwest corner of the island. Each of these has three rows of *bunks* on each side, with an isle about 8 to 9 feet wide. The bunks on each side being 5 to 7 feet deep, would make the barrack about 18 to 20 feet wide, and about 200 to 250 feet long. In each of these are four to five large coal stoves, with cylinders, which would hold at least a bushel of coal at a time. The Hospital Department is as good as any of our soldiers could wish for, and their rooms comfortable unless their men neglect to keep up the fires. They have hand-barrows and carts, &c., with which the prisoners amuse themselves in hauling coal, which is furnished in abundance, so that if they do not keep them warm it is their own fault.

Sabbath morning, the 5th, was exceedingly cold—the very kind of a day to see if they were suffering. From our observation of them, as well as our own feelings, we could give no other statement than that they were as comfortable as it is customary for our soldiers to be in their barracks.

At 10 o'clock we preached in the quarters of the artillery inside of the fort; at 11 in one of the hospitals. As we came out we noticed the prisoners making to the cook-house. We went down and through it to see what fare they had. Here was good bread—sweet, well-baked, and better than we have eaten a hundred times in other places—and plenty of it.

The meat for dinner was good shoulders, and we think hams. The men around expressed their opinion that it was good meat.

While standing among them we asked them if they would like to have preaching. They readily assented, and circulated the notice among their companions. We went out and selected a spot in the barrack yard, which was protected from the wind, and where the sun shone. Here were gathered in a few minutes almost one thousand men, who stood listening attentively for over half an hour that we talked to them. and then seemed unwilling to part, begging us to come and preach to them again or send some one.

In the hospital cook-house the fare was very good, all looked cheerful.

We went to the fort to look into the condition of the rebel prisoners, so that, if they were in any suffering condition, we might seek a remedy, and if we found them cared for as we believed that we might hold it up as a reason why our soldiers in Libby, Castle Thunder, and Belle Island should have what they were entitled to, even from rebels.

Brutus said to his fellow conspirators against Ceasar's life—

"Let's kill him boldly, but not wrathfully ;
Let's carve him as a dish fit for the Gods,
Not hew him as a carcass fit for hounds."

Men who fought as those did under Lee at Gettysburg are degraded before the world, when the officers of their Government will treat the prisoners that they took with inhumanity. So our Government would be justly the contempt of the world, if we by neglect or ill-treatment wasted away in prison the lives of those we have taken. While in war and battle we use every appliance with all skill and energy—to the wounded and prisoner let us show the magnanimity—the humanity of men. We ask nothing more for any of our men at Richmond than we give their men at Fort Delaware. If they can't do it for them, allow us to aid them in doing it.

All the spare time between the services we used in inquiring into the condition of all the men there, especially that of the rebel sick and prisoners. Concerning all, we would say that they are well cared for, and that this is the answer of every one to whom we spoke, excepting that the prisoners have not as much preaching as they would like, nor as much reading matter, the Chaplains confining themselves mainly to the garrison and those in the hospital.

Under General Schoepf the barracks and everything around partake of order, cleanliness and comfort. He requires the prisoners to be taken out in the fresh air and walked about during which time their part of the barracks are cleaned and white-washed; blankets, clothing, &c., all brought out and aired. This is health to the prisoners, and, of course, economy to the Government; it is cheaper to the Government to give the vegetables and fruits, which are wholesome, than to pay for the medicines and attention to them when sick.

The conduct of the rebel government to our soldiers in their prisons at Richmond, awakens up in the hearts of many, the spirit of retaliation and revenge. God forbid that it should be attempted against any of their privates who are prisoners in our hands! That inhumanity of man to his fellow man, which

"Has made countless millions mourn,"

does not belong to the spirit of our Government. If the rebel government will so basely treat our men, as we know they have done at Richmond, don't let our souls come into their assembly, or practice their cruel deeds.

Surgeons and Chaplains from Libby, who have spent nights with us on their return, urge that we be kind to the prisoners among us. War in any way is terrible. Don't let it be aggravated by the meanness and malice which would prey like vultures upon the wounded and prisoners.

Christianity requires of us to feed the hungry, clothe the naked, give drink to the thirsty, visit the sick and the prisoner, not to gloat on his unfortunate condition, but to try and do him good, ministering compassionately."

Coming from Fort Delaware we met in the cars a young man of 17th Connecticut, who was in Barlow's division of the 11th corps, wounded the first day at battle of Gettysburg. He was wounded north of the town and brought to the German Reformed church hospital by the rebels who then held the town. This church was *General Ewell's headquarters*, or observatory, it being the best point about Gettysburg to see the movements of his men on the north and east. From it almost every man of his corps attacking on cemetery hill could be seen He heard Ewell when the Louisiana men fell back, abuse them as cowards. The aids and men who were on guard, while looking at the attack remarked that General Lee had said to his officers that our "right centre must be taken if it cost two-thirds of the men." The desperation of the attack gives weight to this remark.

After this visit we continued to do what we could in the sending of provisions of food and clothing to our men in Richmond. The reports from there daily harrowed up the feelings of every humane man. Freezing and starvation seemed to be the two chief sources of torture. We feel a loathing to record the statements we had from so many persons of those dismal months. Would that it were blotted from the history of man. But it is an index of the spirit of rebellion which is itself cruel.

*Libby prison,* where our officers were mostly confined, is a row of brick buildings on the canal, facing the James river, three stories high, formerly used as a tobacco warehouse. The rooms are about one hundred feet long and forty wide In six of these rooms, 1,200 officers, from General Neal Dow to a second lieutenant, remained, with no other space for eating sleeping taking exercise, cooking or washing. Not two feet by ten to a man, out of which was to be taken room to pass, cook, wash and dry.

Two men, Major and Richard Turner, had charge, one as officer, the other as inspector of the building. No one was allowed to go within three feet of the windows, which reduced their space about one-sixth, or two by eight and a half feet. The appearance of one near the window, was sure to induce a shot from the sentry, which occurred almost hourly. Lieutenant Huggins was shot at, when standing eight feet from the window.

One of the officers who escaped in the *tunnel* assured us that the accounts we had of the suffering by cold, withholding of food, &c., were by no means exaggerated. The only correction which he would make was in regard to the corn meal, of which he did not think the cob was generally ground, but that the corn, bran and all without sifting was given out to them, but that it was often with crusts so hard and thick that they could not eat one-half of it, and the allowance for the day was one of these pieces about three inches by four and about two inches thick. One of these rations he left with us, but frequently we have seen the same when our men have come up in the truce boat.

Sometimes they were tantalized with the sight of the boxes sent to them which were piled up—but occasionally the contents were thrown to them in such a way that they were mixed together and ruined. Gen. Dow and others speak of the reception of articles and attention which indicate a different treatment at other times to some of the officers.

The Rev John Hussey, of Ohio, who was taken prisoner while attending upon our wounded at Chicamauga, spent seven weeks in Libby. On his way to Richmond, passing through Atlanta, he saw Judge John C Gaut, of East Tennessee, hand-cuffed, and at Richmond, in Libby, Dr. R. Humphreys, of Jonesboro', East Tennessee, Mr. Hardin, of Virginia, living opposite Fredericksburg, about sixty-five years of age *without a shirt,* only a woman's shawl over his shoulders. He also saw children in the prison held as hostages to compel their fathers who had avoided the conscription, to present themselves.

*Belle Island* is in view of Libby, in the James river. Trees and rocks are upon part of it The portion on which our prisoners, privates, were kept is almost entirely of sand, low and barren even of shrubs. About five or six acres are ditched and earth thrown up about three feet, on which about forty feet apart, are the guards. Within this are rows of tents, which poor in themselves, shelter but few of those in the camp. Thousands had no shelter of any kind. It was before the eyes of the people of Richmond. The President and Cabinet, with the Congress and Senate of the confederacy were within a few minutes' walk of it.

The men having been stripped in part of their clothing, deprived of their money, which is the common charge, without shelter along that bleak river, often enveloped in its pestilential fog, with but a little fire here and there, while thousands who cannot approach, are shivering around, or trying to keep their blood in circulation by keeping themselves in motion day and night. The severity of the frost of last winter was so great, that nearly all the ice houses around and down the James river were filled. Thousands of men trying like hogs to get together in such numbers as to keep themselves warm, the outer ones occasionally changing place with some more favored, at different hours of the night; in other cases the outside ones frozen to death. An occurrence of almost every day during the winter. No amount of clothing will keep a man warm who is deprived of food.

### STATEMENT OF J M'ILVAINE.

"I belong to the ninth Maryland; was taken prisoner at Charlestown, Virginia, October 18, 1863; marched to Staunton 24th, there until Monday 26th; about 9 A. M. took cars for Richmond; got there about daybreak 27th; marched to tobacco warehouse, stayed to November 1, about 1½ o'clock; about 450 were in the cellar. The ground was wet all the time from a hydrant which leaked on the ground. The warehouse was four stories high, full of prisoners; bars in the windows, but no glass. Got wheat bread about size of a rusk twice a-day with a piece of meat not equal to one-fourth of our rations, and the bread not equal to two hard tack. The meat stunk so we could hardly take it. The guards used to hallo in to us—'Yankees, how does horse meat eat?'

"To Belle Island November 1. No shelter of any kind; nothing but naked earth until last of January, when five hundred went away. We got into an old tent which sheltered us from the wind, but not from the rain. Our overcoats, blankets, shoes and dress coats and money were taken from us at Charlestown as soon as we were taken. Over one thousand dollars was taken from our regiment. They said when we were paroled they would give it back, but they never gave a dollar, and said they never would; they would do just as our government did.

"About ten thousand were there at Christmas. In each corner of the square, holes were dug for drinking water. The ground was so low that water came at about one and a half feet from the top of the ground. During the day so many were allowed to go outside of the ditch next to the river about twenty to thirty feet, but a great many of the men were not able who were suffering from diarrhœa. The gates were closed about sun down. Sometimes the water in these holes out of which we were to drink would be as filthy as in holes of a barn-yard.

"The first month we got one piece of corn bread and such meat as we got in the warehouse. After that no meat, corn bread twice a day, unless some of the guard reported us, then we could get only one piece and sometimes none. The average of deaths must have been twenty to thirty a day, and they have laid unburied for days, five men lay unburied for nine days."

### STATEMENT OF REV. W. H. TIFFANY.

Rev. William H. Tiffany, M. E. church, Charlton, Saratoga county, N. Y., as delegate chaplain of the United States Christian Commission, on the Blackstone; W. C. Berry, of Stamford, Conn., Captain. Left Fortress Monroe November 8th, in company with the fleet of seventeen vessels, for Savannah. There were no prisoners on the Blackstone going south. Saw on the George Leary, a lot of about four to five hundred, who seemed in good spirits and condition, and apparently well clothed. We arrived at Hilton Head on the ——, we left it on November 20, arrived at Venus point eight or nine miles northeast of Savannah, in river that evening; on 21st we loaded five hundred and sixty-five of our men. Col. Mulford said, as we had no berths, he would give us the best of the returning prisoners. There were at least twenty in the first stages of fever, and fit subjects for the hospital, yet all walked on board. There were six or seven we feared could not live, but by careful nursing they were brought to Annapolis and carried ashore. After we had landed our men, we went out to the Atlantic which drew too much water to get to the dock, and took her men. There seemed about the same number of men; of these there were seven who had died on the passage, one died while we were carrying him to the wharf, and two appeared to be dying as they were carried ashore. The prisoners on board the Atlantic appeared in a pitiable condition, while fifty or sixty carried on an upper deck were in a horrible condition, living, dying skeletons, filthy with vermin, and *nearly, if not quite a dozen naked and with no covering but the blanket furnished by our government.* Of the fifty or sixty, they were mostly so weak that I had to lift their heads to get them in a different position. One of these asked me to help him to turn over, the bones had worn through his skin. Part of the crew of the B. helped me to put on shirts and drawers, furnished by the Christian Commission, on those naked.

The fifty or sixty did not speak harshly or vindictively, but sadly and mournfully of their cruel treatment by the South. In regard to food they were kept on short allowance on the most trifling excuse and persecuted in various ways. Some of them had money which they hid in their bread and meat. When a young man from Norwich, Conn., came on board the Blackstone at Savannah, he said he had eaten nothing but raw salt meat for several days, had a terrible diarrhœa, and wanted some food suitable to his case.

Of the captain, W. C. Berry, the mate, George G. Fletcher, steward, Philip Collaman, and the three engineers, Joseph J. Illingworth, John Illingworth and Timothy Leary, and the crew generally, too much could not be said of their kindness, sympathy and generosity towards these men.

Dr. A. Chapel, Surgeon in charge at West building hospital, and whom we saw at the boat when a load of our men arrived, wrote to Mr. Wade, chairman of the committee on part of the war as follows:

"BALTIMORE, May 26, 1864.

"I am very sorry that your committee could not have seen those cases when first received. No one from these pictures (photographs) can form a true estimate of their condition then. Not one in ten was able to stand alone; some of them were so covered and eaten by vermin, that they nearly resembled cases of small pox, and so emaciated that they were *really* living skeletons, and hardly that, as the result shows, forty out of one hundred and four have died up to this date.

"If there has been anything so horrible, so fiendish, as this wholesale starvation, in the history of this satanic rebellion, I have failed to note it. Better the massacres at Lawrence, Fort Pillow and Plymouth, than to be thus starved to death by inches, through long and weary months. I wish I had possessed the power to compel all the northern sympathizers with this rebellion, to come in and look upon the work of the *chivalrous* sons of the *hospitable* and sunny south, when these skeletons were first received here. A rebel colonel, a prisoner here, who stood with sad face looking on as they were received, finally shook his head and walked away, apparently ashamed that he held any relation to men who could be guilty of such deeds."

To the individual testimony of one from Belle Island, one from Libby, with the observation of Mr. Tiffany, we give the paper drawn up by our officers at Charleston, pleading on behalf of the prisoners at Andersonville.

CONFEDERATE STATES PRISON,
CHARLESTON, S. C., August, 1864.

*To the President of the United States:*

"For some time past there has been a concentration of prisoners from all points of the Rebel territory to the State of Georgia—the *commissioned* officers being confined at *Macon* and the *enlisted men* at *Andersonville.* Recent movements of the Union troops, under General Sherman, have compelled the removal of prisoners to other points, and it is now understood that they will be removed to Savannah, Columbus and Charleston. No change of this kind holds out any prospect of relief to our poor men. Indeed, as the localities selected are far more unhealthy, there must be an increase of suffering."

"Colonel Hill, Provost Marshal General of Confederate States, at Atlanta, stated to one of the undersigned that there were thirty-five thousand prisoners at Andersonville, and by all accounts from the United States prisoners who have been confined there, the number is not overstated by him. These thirty-five thousand are confined in a field of some thirty acres, enclosed by a board fence, heavily guarded. About one-third have various kinds of indifferent shelter. The rest, without any, are exposed to the rains and storms, the cold dews of the night, and the more terrible effects of the sun, with almost tropical fierceness, upon their unprotected heads. This mass of men jostle and crowd each other up and down the limits of their enclosure by day, and at night lie upon the naked earth, with only the clothing they had when they came, few having blankets."

"Upon entering the prison every one is deliberately stripped of money and other property, and as *no clothing or blankets are ever supplied to their prisoners*, the condition of soldiers just from an active campaign can be easily imagined. Thousands are without pants or coats, and hundreds even without a pair of drawers to cover their nakedness."

To these men is issued three-fourths of a pound of bread or meal, and one-eighth of a pound of meat per day. Upon this the prisoner must live or die. The meal often unsifted and sour—the meat North would be consigned to a soap barrel. By this they are barely holding life together. To the starvation and exposure add the sickness by which, on an average, one hundred die daily."

"'Of twelve of us', said one, 'who were captured, six died and four are in the hospital. I never expect to see them again. There are but two of us left.' In 1862, at Montgomery, Alabama, under more favorable circumstances, where the prisoners were protected by sheds, one hundred and fifty to two hundred were sick from diarrhœa and chills out of seven hundred. This per cent. would give seven thousand at Andersonville."

The blood of the martyrs, it is said, was the seed of the church, but not more truly so than such men will prove the sowing afresh in the hearts of the people of this nation and the world, the seeds of liberty. Little have we felt personally so as to be able to prize the inheritance which our fathers bought for us.

We lo k on these horrors, in the cruel treatment of our men, as next to impossible—as if they had never been endured before—and indeed it is seldom that such treatment has ever been bestowed on men; particularly by those who pretend to civilization and christianity.

A young man on a flag-of-truce boat, connected with the Sanitary Commission, gave us an extract from a report which one of our paroled men had found in Richmond, which showed that in the hospitals of our men at Richmond, out of two thousand seven hundred and seventy-nine in hospitals, in January, February and March, one thousand three hundred and ninety-six had died. But laying aside all other statements or calculations, and all editorials commending cruel treatment towards our prisoners, let one single fact speak. The Richmond "Examiner" of November 10, 1864, says:

"*Since the establishment of the prison post at Andersonville, Georgia, last Spring twelve thousand of the Yankee prisoners held there have died and been buried there, and this mortality existed among a body of prisoners at no time exceeding forty thousand.*"

That is, such has been the neglect or brutality on the part of the Rebel authorities that nearly one-third of our men have died in their hands.

L. L. Key, who acted as chief of police at Andersonville on the execution, says—"When I arrived there were some 4,000 prisoners—but the number increased, till in September there were 32,000 to 35,000. In August and September the deaths were from 75 to 125 per day.

Horrible as were the horrors of the revolution, and terribly as they did suffer, there is nothing to compare in magnitude with this destruction, and the *animus* of it bears out the statement of a Captain who saw a man treated so badly that he remonstrated with the Surgeon and guard, saying, that if they did not treat them better they would kill them. To which the Surgeon replied, with an oath, "That is what we want to do."

Let us compare this with English treatment of our fathers—1776 to 1782—the men who suffered—whose lives were worn out inch by inch in the prison ships of hollow-hearted. sanctimonious, selfish England. No parallel has been seen since in this country until this imprisonment of Libby, Belle Island, Andersonville, &c.

"The story of the prisons in the city of New York, and the prison ships in the Wallabocht bay, during the war for our independence, was the darkest in the history of the Revolutionary struggle. War, at all times dreadful. here assumed its most fearful character. Occasional acts of inhumanity and cowardly brutality committed in the heat of battle when the thirst for blood is whetted by its indulgence, may be excused, as the temporary triumph of passion and vengeance over reason and humanity; but for the cold, calculating cruelty, regularly adopted, and steadily pursued towards our unfortunate countrymen, there was no excuse. The voice of civilization and humanity cried out against it, and the results proved that an insulted Providence frowned upon it with fearful indignation.

"Savage nations sometimes put their prisoners to death, but this has never been openly practiced by the civilized nations of the earth. The custom of the cultivated nations of antiquity, of selling their prisoners into slavery, met the most positive reprobation in the beginning of the feudal ages, and the system of ransom, which was then adopted, yielded, early in the seventeenth century, to the more liberal and humane policy of exchange of prisoners under *cartels.* Until that exchange took place the law of nations as well as the principles of humanity required the belligerent parties to provide proper accomodations for their prisoners and to supply them with healthy food, and in case of sickness with proper medical attendance. How England observed these rules in the case of our imprisoned countrymen the civilized nations of the world may judge.

"The battle of Brooklyn, and the capture of Fort Washington, in the Fall of 1776, put the British in possession of nearly *four thousand prisoners*, and by the arrest of citizens supposed to sympathize with the patriots they soon increased the number to *five thousand.* Our enemies were now compelled to adopt the system of parole, or to turn all the public and other large buildings in New York into prisons for their reception. Their feelings of humanity as well as their cowardly policy led them to adopt the latter course. *The churches and sugar houses and prisons were crowded with the unfortunate patriots* to such an extent, in some instances, that *there was not space for them to lie down to rest.* Among them they threw their own criminals—vile wretches gathered from the purlieus of their large cities, as if they were fit associates for men whose only crime had been love of country and liberty. But this moral pestilence did not suffice to gratify their malice; for in these crowded prisons they scattered the seeds of disease and death. The prisoners were poorly fed on worm-eaten bread and peas, and putrid beef, which not unfrequently they were compelled to eat in its raw state; and the more surely to accomplish the objects contemplated, those sick with small-pox and infectious fevers were left among them unattended, without medicines to relieve them or water to cool their parched lips. Denied the light and air of Heaven, and starved by their inhuman keepers, and broken-hearted by the supplications and groans of their distressed kindred and countrymen, they sickened and died, and were thrown like dogs into their native soil, unless it happened to be the good pleasure of Cunningham, their infamous jailor, to march them out under the cover of midnight darkness to the gallows and the grave.

"These executions were thus conducted. A guard was despatched from the Provost, about half-past twelve at night, to the Barrack-street and the neighborhood of the upper barracks, to order the people to shut their window shutters and put out their lights, forbidding them at the same time to presume to look out of their windows and doors, on pain of death; after which the unfortunate prisoners were conducted, gagged, just behind the upper barracks, and hung without ceremony, and buried by the black pioneer of the Provost. Thus about two hundred and sixty American prisoners were murdered without cause, and in violation of every law, human and divine.

"While these horrid deeds and instruments of destruction went on in the city, vessels which they had previously converted into *prison ships*, at Gravesend bay, were now removed to the Hudson and East rivers, where they were anchored for the same purposes. The soldiers taken prisoners on Long Island, and confined in these vessels, were transferred to the prisons in New York, to make room for the marine prisoners, now rapidly accumulating.

"About October 20th, 1776, the Whitby, a large transport, was removed to the Wallabocht bay, and moored opposite "Remsen's Mill." She was the first prison ship in this bay, and was crowded with prisoners when she arrived. Many prisoners from the army, and citizens arrested on suspicion were confined in her, which was not the case with the other prison ships. She was said to be the most sickly of all the hulks, and the only prison ship in the bay until 1777; and during two months in the Spring of that year, the entire beach, between the ravine and Demser's Dock, was filled with graves; and before the first day of May, the ravine itself was filled with the remains of the hundreds who died from pestilence, or were starved to death in this dreadful prison.

"May, 1777, two more ships came, and the Whitby's prisoners were transferred to them; but they were almost as sickly as the other. No exchanges took place, but death made room for the early arrivals. On Sunday afternoon, after the middle of October, 1777, one of these vessels was burned, many prisoners perishing in the flames. Another burnt in February, 1778.

"These were succeeded by the Good Hope, Scorpion, Prince of Wales, John, Falmouth, Hunter, Stromboli and Old Jersey; all of which were used in this service. In them thousands of our unfortunate countrymen suffered and died, from the inhuman treatment received from the English. So great was their suffering, that they were induced to set fire to the ships which were burned, hoping thus either to secure their liberty or hasten their death.

> "Better the greedy wave should swallow all,
> Better to meet the death conducting ball;
> Better to sleep on ocean's oozy bed,
> At once destroyed, and numbered with the dead,
> Than thus to perish in the face of day,
> Where twice ten thousand deaths one death delay."

"William Burke, from Newport, Delaware, was confined 14 months in the Old Jersey. He saw many Americans put to death by the bayonet. During the hot weather, the prisoners were admitted, one at a time, on deck through the night. When this was granted, they assembled in a crowd around the gate at the hatchway for the purpose of getting air, and to take their turn to go on deck. Often sentinels would thrust their bayonets down among them with the most wanton cruelty. Twenty-five cases were thus butchered in one night. Other witnesses speak of four, six, eight and ten victims thus murdered at times.

"On July 4th, 1782, they received the most brutal treatment because they wanted to observe that day. They were driven at the point of the bayonet below deck long before the usual hour. After the hatches were closed, they supposed they might sing a few songs for their bleeding country; but the guards directed them to stop, and went dowu among them with lanterns in one hand and cutlasses in the other, driving the crowd of defenceless victims before them, cutting and wounding all within their reach.

"In 1782, when Alexander Coffin was sent a prisoner on the Old Jersey, he found about *eleven hundred prisoners* there, many of whom, during the severity of the Winter, were without clothing to keep them warm. To remedy this evil, they were compelled to keep below, and either get into their hammocks, or walk the deck, which was almost impossible. In this way they could keep from freezing, by using great efforts, but it was not always done. We have an account of one poor fellow whose feet and legs were frozen. The toes and flesh falling from his feet while the nurse was dressing them.

"To cap the climax of infamy, Coffin says, they fed the prisoners on putrid beef and pork, and worm-eaten bread, which had been condemned on their ships of war. It was full of vermin, but they had to eat it, worms and all, or starve.

"The knowledge of these things was not confined to the petty officers and guards; their superiors knew it, and the ministers of the English Government had knowledge of them. They were not the results of circumstances nor the fruits of temporary passion. Their cruelty was a part of their policy, deliberately and remorselessly pursued.

"General Washington remonstrated in a letter to Admiral Digby, 'If the fortunes of war, sir, has thrown a number of these miserable people into your hands, I am certain your excellency's feelings for the men must induce you to proportion the ships to their accommodation and comfort, and not by crowding them together in a few ships, bring on diseases which consign them by the half-dozen to the grave.'

"Before this, on January 13th, 1777, he had written to Howe: 'I am sorry that I am under the disagreeable necessity to trouble your lordship with a letter, wholly almost on the subject of the cruel treatment which our officers and men receive in the naval department, who are unhappy enough to fall into your hands. Without descending to particulars, I call upon your lordship to say whether any treatment of your officers and men has merited so severe retaliation. I am bold to say it has not. * * * And I hope, on making the proper inquiry, you will have the matter so regulated that the unhappy persons in captivity, may not in the future have the miseries of cold, disease and famine added to their other misfortunes. Again, those who have lately been sent out give the most shocking accounts of their barbarous usage, which their miserable emaciated countenances confirm.'

"During all this time, every attempt to relieve the sufferings of the prisoners, either by their friends, or on the part of the Government, was ingeniously defeated. If money or supplies were sent, they were appropriated by their jailors. If an exchange was agreed upon, the prisoners were not sent out until they had been reduced to skeletons, by starvation and disease. Thus rendered unfit for future service, they returned, many of them only to find graves at home."—*Martyrs to the Revolution, in British Prison Ships, p. 60: New York*, 1855. *See also 2d vol. Lossing's Field Book of the Revolution, pp.* 659–661.

England has set the leaders of this rebellion an example of the way in which to treat prisoners. They have imitated them so well that the history of one, by change of dates and places, would be the history of the other. The late returns from Savannah are so many additional witnesses to the fact of the want of food, clothing and shelter.

---

## MILITARY PRISON AT POINT LOOKOUT.

On December 16, 1863, we wrote to Colonel W. Hoffman, Commissary General of Prisoners at Washington, for permission to visit and preach in the camp at Point Lookout. In a few days we received the following letter:

OFFICE OF COMMISSARY GENERAL OF PRISONERS,
WASHINGTON, D. C., December 18, 1863.

*Rev. A. B. Cross, U. S. Christian Commission, Baltimore, Md.*

*Dear Sir:*—Your letter of the 16th instant, requesting permission to visit Point Lookout for the purpose of preaching to the prisoners is received, and I beg to inform you that orders have been given to the commanding officer, to permit clergymen to address the prisoners, if they desire it, and for this purpose you need no further permission. None but relatives are allowed to visit prisoners, and only in cases of illness or other urgent cause.

Very respectfully, your obedient servant, W. HOFFMAN,
Col. 3rd Infantry, Com. Gen. of Prisoners.

On January 21st 1864, we went to Fortress Monroe with a lot of boxes of food and clothing for our men at Richmond to send by Major Mulford in the flag of truce boat. Coming up on the 22d we stopped at Point Lookout. In the morning we called on General Marsden,

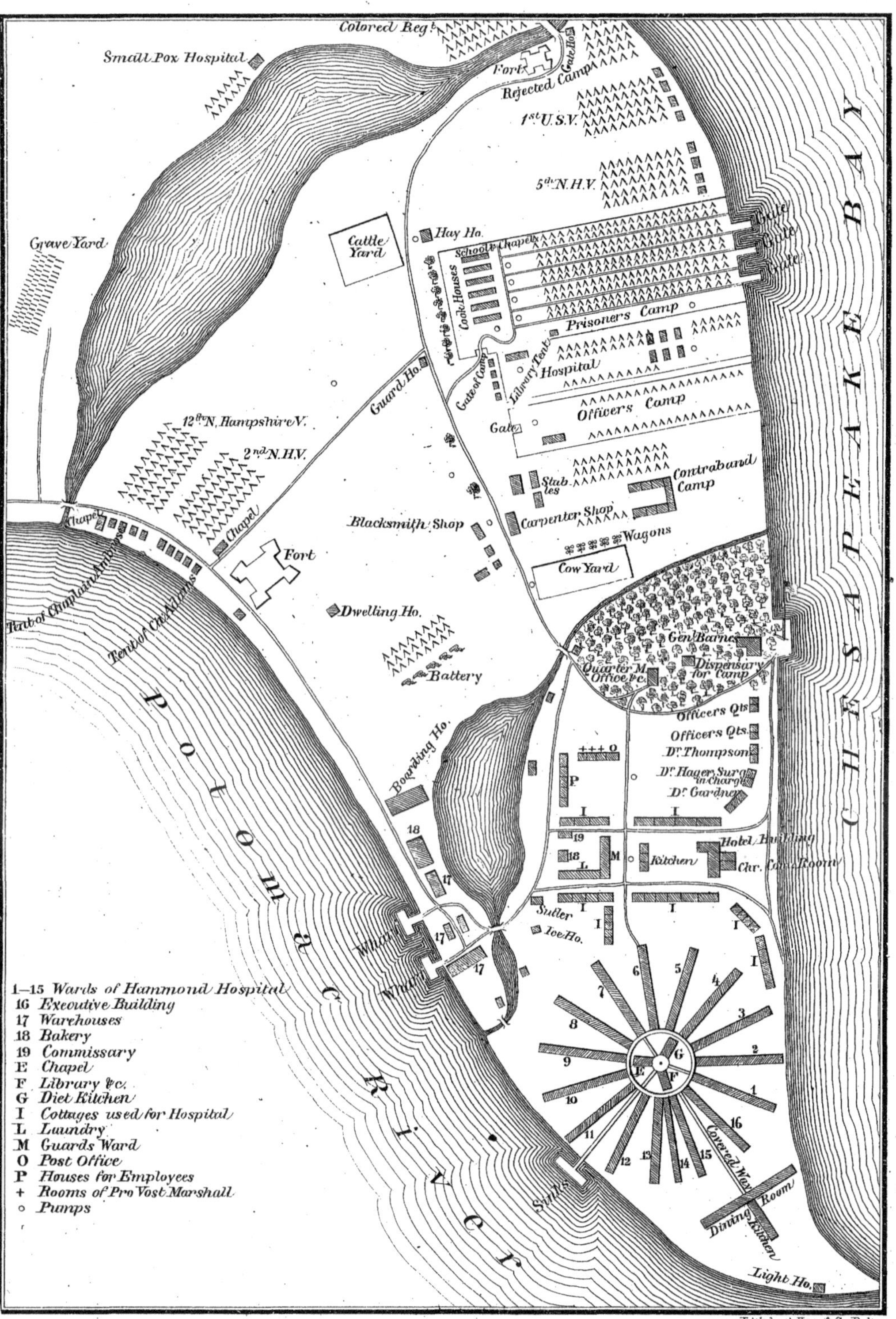


HOSPITAL & MILITARY PRISON AT POINT LOOKOUT.

By Andrew B. Cross — Baltimore.

general commanding—visited the camp, made engagement for preaching and took a general review of the whole ground, hospitals, &c. The general had sent word to the commissary in the camp, and he had tried to secure us a place for preaching on the next day, the Sabbath. We concluded on the unoccupied cook house near the gate, in case of rain or snow, which would hold about five hundred persons. Sabbath being pleasant we preferred preaching in the open air, which we did to a very large and very attentive congregation. The Rev. Mr. Ambrose, chaplain of the 12th New Hampshire, of whom we will speak again, came in. The Rev. W. W. Walker, a Methodist preacher from an adjoining county, who had been captured in a raid a short time before, was there. In the afternoon preached for the contrabands—then in the first six wards of the hospital—at night spoke in the chapel.

On Monday 25th, examined the camps of the New Hampshire regiments on guard, went into the prisoners' camp, it being dinner time, went into the house where was a table for several hundred, perhaps five hundred Every man had his provision before him of meat, soup and crackers. Remarked that it was a substantial dinner. All within reach readily assented, except an Irishman near the door who began to complain. We remarked he certainly could not complain of quantity. No. Of quality? No. After dinner we had a meeting in the cook house which the commissary had prepared on Saturday.

Mr. Ambrose suggested whether we could not get the house for meetings, which we mentioned to General Marsden and secured. It was used until they were removed to the house at the other end, where they have since held schools and meetings.

Point Lookout is a tract of land lying at the extreme south of the western shore of Maryland, bounded on the east by the Chesapeake Bay, south and south-west by the Potomac river—on the north by an inlet of water which almost makes it an island, there being not more than one hundred feet wide connecting it with the mainland, and that for one quarter of a mile deep sand. The land on the Point is level, no portion of it being above ten to fifteen feet above the level of the bay and river Beginning at a point or sand bar formed by the current of wind and tide which on each side throws up the sand, then north along the Chesapeake bay about a mile and a half to where the strip of narrow sand connects it with the main land, then an inlet from the Potomac runs out to the river on a line of about three-fourths of a mile. Here in a sort of cove the shore commences and runs gradually to a point with a slight curvature until it reaches the bay.

In going down the Potomac—and also down the bay—vessels have to *steer out* to pass Smith's Point on the south side of the Potomac, from which the probability is that it received its name—Lookout—the point from which you must *look out.*

Above the upper end of the point an arm of the bay runs in toward the Potomac, which is called *Point Look-in.* Not far above is what appears to be a point but is not, and is called *Point no Point.* At the south side of Patuxent is Cedar Point, which makes out and is really a point. From which ran the old saying among sailors—

Point Look-out and Point Look-in,
Point no Point, and Point Again.

At Point Lookout is a light house; at the upper end or the narrow passage is a gate, with guard and cannon, now a fort; on the outside of this narrows is a regiment on guard. Also south of this and outside of the Point on which are the prisoners separated by this inlet of water, is the small-pox hospital, consisting of a house, tents, &c. A short distance from the gate on the lines of the point on the bay shore, we had first what was called the *rejected camp.* Men out of the rebel camp who had applied to be admitted into our army, but were rejected on account of physical inability. Next was a regiment, the first United States volunteers, who had taken the oath and entered our service. To all these men we have often preached and furnished them while there with books, papers, &c., as far as we could. They were afterwards sent to Norfolk where they did provost duty. From a very careful observation of the men for several months, we could say nothing but in commendation of them, and of Lieutenant Colonel Dimond and Major Weymouth who were in charge of them. Next was the fifth New Hampshire—nearest to the rebel camp On the Potomac opposite the camp was the twelfth New Hampshire, running up to the inlet of water; further down on the river but adjoining was the second New Hampshire, nearer the point and between the river and road which runs to the point was a Wisconsin battery. Within these lines east of the road and along the bay was the prisoners' camp, including a tract of about forty acres; then the officers' camp—both enclosed with a plank fence about ten to twelve feet high. Nearer the point was the contraband camp, wagons, stable, carpenter shop, houses for workmen and the cow yard. Then a ditch crossing from the bay runs to a small inlet or lake which empties into the Potomac, making the point almost an island.

On the remainder of the land or the point proper is located the *Hammond Hospital*—extending from the Chesapeake shore to the Potomac, the waters of each of which reach extreme ends of the wards. Starting from a centre there are three buildings about seventy-five feet long each, and about thirty feet wide. One is a kitchen department, another a chapel, the third a library room, and for the knapsacks, &c., of the men, fronting on a covered circular platform. Between these are two or three covered ways, with plank floor elevated above the ground, extending about a hundred feet to a circular covered way with plank floor as before three to four feet above ground. Facing on this are fifteen wards of about one hundred and fifty to two hundred feet in length and about thirty feet in width, with large windows on each side, the front door of each opening on the circle. From this circle and between two of these buildings is a covered way which runs out to a large dining room connected with which is a kitchen, this building running at right angles to the passage and being entered midway on the side next the centre. Here are tables and seats for one thousand to fifteen hundred persons. To this table all those who are able or permitted by surgeons come to their meals. At the end of each of the wards next the circle is a room in which the provisions are brought from the diet kitchen, for all who are not able in that ward to go out or for whom the fare of the full diet is not permissable—from these rooms it is distributed to each patient in the ward. In all of these wards are iron bedsteads with mattrasses, sheets and blankets, extending along each side of the ward, between which is an entry or space of about ten to twelve feet. In this are several stoves by which unless in extremely severe weather, the wards are kept comfortable.

In this same circle, built as the wards, but two story in height, with rooms on each side of the entry, is what is called the Executive Building, in which is the dispensary, office of surgeon in charge, the clothes, furniture, &c., rooms of surgeons, chaplain, &c., &c.

In the centre of the whole is a well and force-pump, designed to supply water to a reservoir, on an elevation above the houses, out of which it was carried in pipes to all parts of the hospital and to the bath-room, at the pump; but the water being so strong of iron it is necessary to bring water from another pump some hundred yards from this.

Outside of the plan of the Hospital proper are rows of one-story cottages, facing the bay, and others at right angles facing on two streets, which were designed for the use of the Point as a watering place before the erection of the Hospital. Before the war Point Lookout was a fashionable resort and bathing place. About half-way along the shore is a large yellow frame building, two stories, well-built and comfortable, which was occupied as the headquarters of General Marsden, then in command—now by General Barnes. The cottages are used as hospitals, with the exception of those that have been occupied by surgeons, the officers of the department, the sisters of charity, &c. The hotel building is a hospital, excepting a few rooms occupied by the Commission.

On the roads leading from the wharves, at the Potomac, are warehouses for commissary stores, a large bakery, large supplies of wood and coal—then a sutler's house, ice-house, bakery, commissary, laundry, and guard house—a row of buildings occupied by various persons, living here, in connection with the Government employment—another row in which is the post-office, Provost Marshal, &c., various photographers, some boarding houses, &c. Lately they have erected a house, designed as a hotel or boarding house, to accommodate such persons as have business requiring them to visit the Point. North of the commander's, and running to the main road, containing six to eight, perhaps ten acres, is a pine grove which adds greatly to the relief of the level surface of the Point. A general idea of the place thus given will be more fully fixed in the mind by reference to the map which we place in this pamphlet, and by reference to which the reader will be able more intelligibly to understand the description.

There were eight to nine thousand prisoners. Of these about one thousand were in the Hammond General Hospital. Dr. Hagar is Surgeon in charge and director, and Dr. Thompson in charge of the camp. The small-pox hospital has had several changes. The general hospital and the camp had no chaplain. Beside the rebel wounded in the Hammond Hospital, many of whom were wounded at Gettysburg, there were also from one to two hundred of our own men sick and wounded. The Second New Hampshire regiment had only within a short time secured a chaplain, Rev. Mr. Adams, who had his hands full in his regiment. The contrabands had the Rev. Mr. Leonard, just appointed to see after them and reconnoitre the county in regard to negro affairs. The Rev. Mr. F. L. Ambrose was chaplain of the Twelfth New Hampshire.

He was a perfect stranger to us before we here met him; but a more kind, unassuming, brotherly minister, ready to do anything, at any hour of the night, in any kind of weather, for anybody who was in want or trouble, we have never met. He moved quietly but diligently round in his own regiment, in the hospital, in the camp, everywhere doing good. He was a most decided and firm man, ready to yield his life, as he afterwards did, for his country. At the battle of Chancellorsville scarcely a soldier in the army exposed himself more than he did, in rendering every help in his power to his regiment, and especially in attending upon and removing the wounded At Petersburg, when his regiment, in the eighteenth corps, was exposed to the most terrible fire of the enemy, he was there among them. Every day, when we would call at the eighteenth corps hospital, in the rear of his regiment, inquiring for him, we would be sure to hear he was either here this morning, or last night, or he is here now. When his regiment were in the trenches he was wont to go in among them and attend to them. As he was leaving, one day, a ball which was supposed to be a stray shot from some of the rebel works, went through his leg, between the knee and thigh. He was taken to the Chesapeake Hospital, at Fortress Monroe, where we heard he was doing well, but on going to see him we learned that his wound had commenced bleeding and that he had died from it. "Blessed are the dead who die in the Lord."

It is of this man, so loyal, so faithful, so loving to his country, that we wish to say, that he looked after the men in the camp as if they had been his own charge. Nothing that he could do for them which was right and proper would he refuse to do. Where they were in want he tried to get that want supplied, in trouble to comfort them, preaching to them the Gospel, praying with them, ministering to their dying, furnishing books, papers, tracts, &c., from every quarter that he could. We will cherish through life as one of its green spots the period which we spent with him at Point Lookout and in front of Petersburg. The knowledge of his death will make many sorry who have been in the camp and hospital, as it did many who are now there. He was a minister of the Congregationalist church. The Rev. Mr. Adams, of the Second, who was there but a short time, is now with his regiment, north of the James. The more we have seen of him the more we feel interested in him. He belongs to the Methodist church and is from New Hampshire.

We found at the Point everything that could be asked for, furnished by the Government, but were somewhat disappointed in regard to the police arrangement, in which the convenience, comfort and health of the camp and the community suffered. It was mud from the wharf to the Point, from the Point to the camp, and with some difficulty you could pass to the camp would getting into the mud. We allow for the wet weather, but there were plenty of men who would work, and there was plenty of gravel to remedy it. What was wanting was ditching, draining and graveling.

There was difficulty in getting a place to board and a room in which to sleep and to keep the books, papers, tracts, &c., which were needed for so many persons. Dr. Walton very kindly gave us the use of his office for books, &c., until we could secure one. Not having a tent and not being able to get a room, we applied to Gen. Marsden for a lot on which to set up a small shanty. To this he agreed, but could not furnish the lumber. Before building we went to see Gen. Butler, and asked him to give us the lumber. Having stated the condition of things—the number of prisoners, no chaplain, there being one nominally, who had not been in attendance for months, the number of the bad cases of the wounded, who were dying, and so many more that must die; that if we had a convenient place, we would secure what help we could from our commission, that if we had such a place we would procure Dr. Junkin for a while. Dr. J. having gone down with us before on a trip for his health and called on the General. It was at this time that the General said, and not as some one wrongfully published: "Please inform the chaplain for me, that he must resign, if he is not able to perform his service, and if he gets able to engage in his work again, and desires it, I will see that he gets another place. If he has the spirit of his master he won't want to hinder the work being done by another, which he can't do himself. In that event I will appoint Dr. Junkin there, and let the government pay the expenses instead of your commission. I won't furnish you lumber. The government has no lumber to spare; but when you go back, make out a written application to Gen. Marsden for such rooms as you need. Dr. Hagar has room in the hospital unoccupied." On returning, we made application accordingly, and received the rooms which the commission has since been occupying.

Since that the Rev. D. D. McKee has been appointed and has acted with great acceptance as Chaplain to the Hospital. The Rev. Mr. Leonard has also been appointed and acted as chaplain in the camp; lately he has gone to some other place.

The prisoners in the hospital had the liberty of the hospital grounds, which enabled those able to walk to visit any places within the limits. We wrote to a gentleman in New York, who has a heart for every good work, stating the case, and he authorized us to go to a publishing house and select out of the catalogue such books, &c., as we thought desirable, and he would give an order for them. We called on our commission also for books, papers, &c., all of which we received.

We then invited in passing any of the men who were in these wards and connected with the hospital, to come in at certain hours of every morning to take such books, papers or tracts as they desired, read and return. In each ward we secured men to collect them and furnish them to those who could not come out, and also to distribute papers and tracts among them In this way we had the fifteen wards of the circle regularly supplied; and others did the same in the buildings outside of the circle. Each of these men reported the condition of the men in their wards, enabling us daily to see the worst cases and give them such attention as was in our power.

In the camp we sought the aid of a few brethren who had charge of a tent, called the *Library Tent*, in which, and through which we furnished books, tracts, &c. for distribution in the different wards, so as to extend as far as we could the papers, tracts, hymn books, &c., making inquiry always of any who wanted testaments. The Maryland State Bible Society, through the labors of Mr. Baker, their agent, did a good work in furnishing over 13,500 testaments, with 590 copies of the bible to such as needed them, from January 1, 1864, to December, 1864.

At this time there was some difficulty in regard to furnishing to the prisoners boxes of clothing, &c., sent to them. Learning also from Mr. Shoemaker, of the Adams Express that there were boxes in his charge which he could not deliver, we went to see Mr. Stanton. He immediately said, send him a line, stating the fact, and he would issue an order for their delivery. Mr. Shoemaker wrote to Gen. Butler at same time, who also sent an order for their delivery.

The Rev. Mr. Walker, of whom we have spoken before, requested us to ask Gen. Marsden to grant him an interview, saying he had never been in the war, was exempt in his own country as a minister, would not only give his parole to take no part in the war, or if paroled, would endeavor to secure in exchange any person who would be considered an equivalent. We mentioned his case to the general, but he did not see anything that he could do. On seeing him the next time, and stating what the general had said, he was very much cast down. Trying to cheer him, we said we believe God has sent you here for some purpose, see if you can't find it out. You may find it the best field of labor you ever had, or ever will have in your life, and you may look back in eternity and praise God for this more than for any other period. There are many here who can't read. If you would only get them stirred up to learn, it would be a great thing. If you didn't teach you could get others. If you will get the scholars and teachers we will see that you get the books. Thus was started a little movement, which has grown, until more than a thousand are regularly engaged, and from simply starting to learn to read, classes have been formed in reading, writing, arithmetic, algebra, natural philosophy, the higher branches of mathematics, Latin, Greek, German, &c.

The encouragement, continuance and perfection of this work is due to Mr. Alonzo Morgan, of Sumpter, S. C., one of their engineer corps, who has devoted himself with a diligence and zeal, truly philanthropic, to aid his fellow prisoners of this school. Mr. Morgan entered upon it the 10th of March, and on the 22d of April writes as follows:

"We have had our regular exercises every day, with the exception of days of snow and heavy rains, not exceeding three in all. We have one hundred and fifty men learning to read, and nearly as many more in the writing classes. The English Grammar, Natural Philosophy, Modern and Ancient Geography and History, Geometry, Book-keeping, Algebra, Latin and Dictionary classes are all large and well attended, some of which are divided into three sections, each containing fifty or sixty pupils. But our Arithmatic class is probably the most interesting. It is divided into seven sections, commencing with numeration and extending to the most thorough instruction in the science.

One of these sections contains sixty students. The teachers have displayed fine talents in their several departments, coupled with the most laudable zeal for the cause. The following gentlemen are regularly engaged and have classes assigned them, which meet once or twice every day. These with several others, who are occasionally called in for temporary engagements form a corps of teachers of which any institution might be proud. The books, stationery, &c., which you and other friends of education have contributed have been turned to the best account.

*Teachers.*—K. J. Gwaltney, J. D. Blackwell, W. S. Arbogast, G. N. Footman,

W. A. Coates, J. Hughes, I. W. Free, P. R. Piper, J. J. White, J. N. Strout, T. Newman, A. G. Newman, E. P. Moore, D. C. Smith, H. J. Carter, M. C. Bell.

I believe we are doing all we can with the means at our disposal, but could we obtain larger supplies of books and stationery we might be able to extend the field of labor so as to include many of our comrades who are now spending the long weary days of their captivity in idleness and vice.

Returning to you, and all those kind christians, who have displayed such generosity in supplying our necessities, our sincere thanks, I subscribe myself,

With respect, yours truly,

A. MORGAN,

To Rev. A. B. CROSS. Supt. P. W. C. School."

[Since the date of this letter, the school has gone on increasing until as many as twelve hundred are daily engaged.]

March 2nd, Gen. Butler came to the Point to make arrangements in regard to paroling for exchange a number of prisoners. After preaching in the camp Mr. Walker asked if we could not see Gen. Butler in his case. We called on him in the evening; mentioned it. "I will exchange for such a man." We said we were perfectly satisfied if he could. He said he would bear it in mind. He sent for, and had an interview with him. When the flag of truce boat came up he was proposed in exchange for one of our colporteurs. The papers made out and all in readiness as we supposed, when the provost marshal said "he could not go." "Too busy to attend to it." We said, "Gen. Butler, when here was not too busy to hear it, nor too forgetful when he went to Fortress Monroe to find a man and arrange for his exchange." It was arranged in time for him to get on the boat.

Captain Little, who lost his arm at Gettysburg, through some meanness on the part of officers lately from Johnson's Island, captured only a few months before, was thrown out of the list of exchange His case was no sooner mentioned than the General asked if his name was on the list. His clerk said, no. "Put it on, and write Judge Ould, I send Captain Little, as special exchange." The bell rang, and in ten minutes the boat sailed.

That day they commenced digging ditches, hauling gravel, mending the roads, draining the ground, and a distributing of the shoes, &c. The General had upset the arrangement of the Rebel officers and directed that the oldest captured should go first. There was a sort of shout among the prisoners in the camp and many in the hospital on hearing what he had done. He had also ordered attention to the policing of the ground, &c.

Dr. Thompson, the surgeon in charge of the camp seemed grateful for the General's visit. For three months he had urged this police improvement without effect. From that visit a new face was put on the camp and the Point which has continued until this present time. The camp in general is well drained, and on the whole as comfortably fixed as is possible with so many men, and every attention is given to health, cleanliness and comfort. The Hospital department has been moved to a portion of the ground taken from the officer's camp, and in addition to the hospital tents, which are large and floored, there have been erected four barracks for hospitals, which are nice and comfortable quarters. Officers have said to us time and again, "If we were not prisoners we would like to come and stay here awhile merely for recreation and pleasure. It is this being in prison, not allowed to go beyond a certain line, that is the trouble." In the camp time and again we have heard men say the same, "If it was not for the prison we would not mind it." Others, "We would just as soon stay here until the war is over as any place."

About 11 o'clock, March 17th, the flag-of-truce boat New York, started with nine hundred and sixty-eight Rebel prisoners for exchange. As many of the wounded as could safely go were on board. On leaving the wharf, bread and meat and coffee, all of which was in abundance, were given out, and again before we arrived at Fortress Monroe.

We gathered from Captain O. H. Miller, of Georgia, the following statement:

"He was of Longstreet's corps, Hood's division, Anderson's brigade, the Fifty-ninth Georgia regiment. Colonel Brown's regiment rested on the second day at Gettysburg, in front of the railroad cut, where the first day's fight was, until about twelve o'clock. Then marched to the right, on the west side of the branch and east of the McLean House—then to the Peach orchard and Brick house. The shelling was so heavy that we had to remove on through the Peach orchard and directly across *the rocks* in Plum Run. By them our regiment was split in two, but we advanced.' I was on the right. Went acros the little branch, over the fence into the woods, among rocks, on to where it was pretty level. Here formed the regiment, fixed bayonets and charged about sixty yards to the Union forces, where they had breast-works here and there. This was their first line. We fired about three volleys, and fell back and reformed lower down. Then made a charge on the same works and got possession of them, following up in the hollow, on the right, and got possession of Little Round Top and beyond it. Then the battery of three guns turned on us and made an awful destruction of men. We turned to the left and captured the three guns. We then came into a position where a cross fire from the enemy's infantry took us. On that little knoll I was wounded, and placed in the crevice of some rocks where I lay until daylight of the 3d. Our men at early dawn carried me away. Our men held position for two or three volleys. Reinforcements arriving we had to give up and fall back to original position. The Union men charged over me and took their old position. Several Union men sat down beside me, said it was a good place to rest and keep away from bullets. Our men made another charge and drove the Union men back about sixty yards, and continued until dark. The main body withdrew, taking with them what wounded they could and burying all they could. The Texians were on my right. The wound was a compound fracture of the upper third of my right thigh. I was taken to Hood's division hospital, on John Plank's farm, where was a surgeon of the Eleventh Georgia. They carried me to a tent, but said it was no use, I would certainly die. *They ordered me to the dead-house, where I remained fifteen days.* A young man of my company got a piece of rail and with a shirt tied my leg. When they took me into Plank's house they said, I would certainly die, to give me whatever stimulants I would have. After this a surgeon from Gettysburg came, and suggested Smith's Anterior and Post-splint, which they applied with success. But in that time my leg had shortened four and a-half inches and could not be helped. On twelfth of August was taken to the Field General Hospital—third November, West's Building Hospital—fifteenth to Fort McHenry—twenty-third and twenty-fourth to Point Lookout."

We give the particulars of this case in full, because first, it is the best description of the engagement on Round Top which we have come across, all the lines of which we had seen before; in the next place, it is one case of ten thousand, where a man has been left fifteen days in the dead-house and yet lives, and shows neglect by surgeons of their own men

This from Captain Little, of Fifty-Second North Carolina:

"The fifty-second North Carolina and sixty-second Mississippi, had a skirmish with the Union cavalry June 30. July, we moved toward Gettysburg. General Pettigrew had gone on expecting a heavy force, finding the Union force larger, he sent back for fifty-second North Carolina, forty-second Mississippi and himself fell back two or three miles, having staid where we were all night. Early on morning of first, we came with the rest of Hill's corps. The whole road was filled with artillery coming where General Hill had selected his position ; we turned to the right, were the extreme regiment. Company E was the extreme right of the line to observe the motions of the enemy and report.

Generals Archer and Davis to the left, were first annoyed by cavalry and sharp-shooters, but kept position until the charge in the afternoon, when the whole line advanced to the hollow before you come to the Seminary ridge. We fell back and were relieved by Lane's brigade.

The McLean House was burned by order of Col. Marshall because of the sharp-shooters firing upon us. The men burned it very reluctantly, but it was the only way we could get them out. We had no artillery. Burnt it as we were making the advance.

The fighting was principally to the left and very heavy. The eleventh and twenty-sixth of this brigade were very heavily pressed and the forty-seventh next to the fifty-second ; Colonel Leaventhorp here. Colonel Burgwin of twenty-sixth killed in charge of this day. To the left Colonel Conally of fifty-fifth was in Davis' brigade.

The next morning where the eleventh and twenty-sixth met ours in a piece of woods there was desperate fighting. Some of the men who were in the fight said : *The men met within ten steps and fired. Some places we could distinguish the line by where the men fell, one was a Pennsylvania regiment. The ground was covered with men.* A great many of both sides. The eleventh and twenty-sixth, very large, were perfectly riddled of officers and men ; the twenty-sixth carried in above one thousand men. That evening we went back to where we had advanced from in the charge and staid until late next afternoon. Second morning Pickett's division went down to our right, took position and staid that night. We could see artillery on Round Top, and cemetery hill. Some shells from these hills hit us.

Third, our brigade put in position to the left of Pickett's division, directly behind artillery, moved about and got in place about eleven. Generals Lee, Longstreet, Hill and a number of general officers met in a shady bottom near a little branch. Lee sat on a stump, was reading a paper of some kind a long time before the action. After one gun, the whole artillery, from the whole line opened on cemetery hill, with tremendous force, from one to three and a half, when it slackened and the order was given for advance. The whole line two deep. In the advance Pettigrew's brigade of Heath's division was to the left of Pickett's, as they advanced. Pickett doubled on Pettigrew. As they got up close they were thinned out very rapidly. Going over a fence on the Emmittsburg road was shot in arm. After firing was over, and Union men came out to take prisoners one of them with one of my men helped me to a house on the Taneytown road and afterwards on account of shells, back across a marsh and rocky place where laid all night; next morning was taken in ambulance to hospital of sixth corps, where Drs. Oakley and Chamberlain gave me every attention and through that saved my life. It was at John Trostle's house. I took the names of men who I hope to see when the war is over.''

This is a republican government in which we all have some personal interest and right, and no man is worthy of his place in the country who will not feel for her honor as well as her justice—and no officers are fit for ruling in such a government who do not in some measure appreciate the words of Seneca, *sine bonitate nulla majestas*, '' without goodness there can be no such thing as majesty,''—no government can be honorable and majestic, which will do mean things. If our government should pay men to furnish vaccine matter to prevent disease and suffering, must we wink at a man who would furnish bad vaccine matter? Just on the same principle, our prison camps are to hold secure our prisoners, and our hospitals to minister to and take care of the sick and wounded.

We feel thankful that our surgeons have been able to treat with success cases of wounded and suffering men. However much may be said of neglecting wounded men, Jesus did not blame the Samaritan (Luke 10 : 34) for binding up, or pouring in oil and wine.

We ask proper treatment for our men in prison. Let us do what is *right* to those in our hands. With those whose home, friends, and associations are all south, we can bear, but not with northern men who have gone south and hold up for this rebellion. We found in this camp a man named Edey, from New York or Brooklyn, a zealous rebel, from a Texas regiment. It was in the severity of the winter when attention was needed promptly. We said to him in a company of others, go through the camp and find out any case of suffering. Let it be known that you are on the lookout for such cases, and if there be any and the provost marshal or quartermaster has not what is necessary, we will see that it is gotten. Mr. Edey never reported us one case.

One day *Mr. Morgan*, the teacher, said a man had come in two or three nights before, without a blanket—that he had come to his tent and he had to give him part of his, so that it was not comfortable to either of them. One of them was not well and was suffering from chills. He said he had gone to the keeper at the gate but he had damned him and ordered him off. He did'nt blame the keeper of the gate, because he had so many annoyances from so many continually knocking and asking for things; but said *he* could'nt stand up against such a speech as some others could. We stated the case to the Captain. He said, "it was a lie, and he didn't care a damn—that nobody had gone in without a blanket." Having the man's name and ward, we gave it to the Surgeon of the Hospital, requesting him to go and see the case, which he did immediately, and ordered the man to the Hospital. Not satisfied with this we continued our investigation until we found out the truth. It appeared that this man had come in late at night; the Captain was not there, and whoever was in charge of the gate had permitted him to go in without inquiring whether he had a blanket.

The kindness, care and regard for the condition of the men, on the part of Drs. Thompson, Walton and others, is a credit to them as surgeons. The whole camp is in small divisions, over each of which is a surgeon from among the prisoners, whose business is to see to any man who is sick and needs attention—to report his case to the Surgeon of the Hospital, who for that day is in charge of the camp, who goes and examines into his case, and if needing care orders him to the Hospital, where he is attended to regularly and promptly.

Swearing is a qualification with some men for office. To keep such a gate, without cursing occasionally, would seem like forgetting his business. Some of the prisoners, of their own accord, said that the Captain was quite clever to them and did a great many things for them. Not long after we said something to him about wanting to get a pair of pantaloons for a man. He went in and brought out a pair, of his own accord, which we took and gave the man.

About once a week there is an inspection of the camp. All the prisoners take out all their goods of every kind from their tents, and each man displays his worldly all upon the gravel street. As the Captain, or Provost Marshal rides along, and each man standing up, he sees who seems to need pantaloons, or shirt, or jacket, or shoes—orders him out of the ranks, and away he goes toward the gate—so another, and another, until you will sometimes see a small regiment of men, some for shoes, pantaloons, shirt or coat. In this way they are seen to. Of course here, like in every other department, one officer will think there is not much need for a thing that another will think important. Swearing officers would not always think giving a Bible, or preaching the Gospel to prisoners, a very important matter.

The *Officer's camp* of about ten to fifteen acres, lies parallel to the Prisoner's, with two rows of tents, and a cook-house in one corner of the camp. We do not recollect of there being over four hundred men in it at any time, unless for a night, when an exchange was being arranged.

The officers were in the wards among the wounded in the Hammond Hospital until late in March or early in April. Everything was quiet and went along very comfortably until about the middle of March. On the thirteenth of this month about three hundred and fifty rebel officers came from Johnson's Island or Elmira—among them General Jeff. Thompson and J. C. Breckinridge, son of General Breckinridge, who was in a few days exchanged, and General Thompson sent to Fort Delaware. Many of these officers were very gentlemanly and clever, behaving themselves as well as men could. Others were on the lookout for a way of escape. On their arrival the guards were doubled and greater strictness required in all who came in or went out of the lines of the hospital.

In a few days a suggestion was made to the Commander that a conspiracy was on foot, and an attempt would be made among the prisoners to escape, which led to an examination of the camp. As usual in all such investigations, innocent persons suffer. When a man's worldly estate consists of the clothes on his back, a blanket or two, a few books, Bible or Testament, a few pieces of boards put together in the best way he can for chair, or bedstead, or table, to turn all out and break up all his fixtures is a very serious item, when he does not know where or how he can replace them. It is all vain talk for men to say, prisoners have no need for such things. They are men, and have minds and affections which must work out on something. Baron Trenk brought his soul to a mouse, another eminent prisoner to a spider, and another watched daily the growing of a blade of grass that came out between the bricks and mortar of his cell. To destroy these little things, to torture and torment by depriving a prisoner of all comfort is as base and infamous as the spirit of the Church of Rome, which, in her desire to wreak vengeance upon those who leave her and protest against her, has systematized torture, and placed before the world the incarnation of satanic cruelty in her inquisition.

The prisoners at a sudden notice were ordered out of their tents. A company or two of a regiment, on guard, came in with axes, picks, spades, &c. They entered every tent of those suspected, dug up the ground in and around, threw out every thing. In the search they found one or two small box-boats prepared to float on the river or bay, and a rope-ladder with which to escape or scale the fence. In other tents nothing objectionable. Hurried out, they had left their little all of treasure which, when the house was dug up, could not be found. For a time some complained of the needless destruction.

The loafers and bummers about the hospital, who the soldiers were want to say were "nine days in the army and the rest of the time in the hospital," grumbling at everything that was done for any man unless they had a share of it, and could not see a shirt given to a naked man without being in desperate want themselves, living in the kitchen, where the best of everything passed through their hands, yet complained of hard fare, were ready to have every one of the men hung right up. Our soldiers who had gone through nearly every battle in which the army of the Potomac had been engaged, spoke very differently. Those that had been in prison at Richmond, spoke of how they would have been treated—but didn't think it was right to punish men for trying to escape. It is the duty of government to keep prisoners as securely as possible, but on the part of the prisoner, it is his right and his duty to escape just as quick as he can, and to this end we would have every one of our men at Richmond, and in other prisons, do their best to escape, and when they did we would give them the right hand and help them on their way. Indeed, we think it is a sort of honorable thing for a prisoner of war to escape.

About two hundred *officers of Morgan's men* came to the Point on Sabbath, March 20 We met them going up in front of the provost marshal's, and waited while the names were called. We noticed some of them were considerably intoxicated. As the roll was called, we were struck with the manner of one young man; answering to his name, he left an impression on us out of all the company. They were taken to the camp prepared for the officers, adjoining the main camp for prisoners. When they had gone in, an altercation occurred between this one of the officers and the one in charge of them. Several times he ordered the officer off, but he persisted in using insulting language, and possibly drew his fist in his face, &c. The lamentable result of it was, that the officer in charge shot him dead When we saw the corpse, it was the same young man. The officers at the Point generally lamented the occurrence. The man who did it was a kind man, who would do almost anything for the prisoners, and felt it severely, but supposed it was his duty. While our men lamented it, we found, on conversing with his fellow-officers, that they did not condemn the act, but attributed the conduct of the man to the fact that he had been drinking. Among these officers were many very civil, gentlemanly men of education and standing, who behaved themselves in the most unexceptionable and christian manner.

Sometime before they came, a *colored regiment* had been sent up from Fortress Monroe, to be placed among those guarding. The prisoners in the camp heard of it, and for a while the most intense anxiety was manifested. It was a new thing. The guards on the walk around noticing it, let them transgress the usual bounds, so as to look through the cracks in the fence at these passing. For a while there was a good deal of talk, and with some, threats. They were sent beyond the gate and encamped on the main land, just above where the Point connects with it, enabling them to watch and capture, as they did afterwards, those that might escape from the camp along the water.

Some of our own men, especially the Irish, among the guards of the hospital, and the substitutes of the second New Hampshire, were more excited and indignant than the prisoners. It was, however, admitted on all hands, that a Maryland regiment, we think the fourth United States, marched drilled and manœuvred as well as any they had ever seen.

In a few days, when in turn, they were put on guard, there was a little difficulty with one or two. The old saying, "Put a beggar on horse-back and he will ride to the devil," has been often seen in placing ignorant, inexperienced men in charge of companies of men, or raising men up suddenly. Some of this colored regiment, when first put on guard, hardly knew their place, or the orders they were required to carry out. Especially some young, conceited lads. A few of these at the gate, did not treat our own men, when going into the camp, with propriety. There was also complaint of the shooting by some of them when there was no necessity. These cases were promptly examined into. Among them, however, were as many well behaved, excellent guards, good soldiers, civil and trusty men, as were in either of the white regiments, and very soon, the prisoners in the camp looked upon them and acted towards them with as much respect as those of the other regiments.

Ole Johnson, *a Norwegian*, from the battery, who was sick, came to see if he could get a Norwegian testament. He had been in service over two and a half years, had learned to read English in a printing office in Madison, Wisconsin. His father and mother were dead; had five brothers and one sister in Norway. The reason he gave on finding himself at liberty to talk, for coming to our room was, to get out of the company of the men who were in the ward with him. His father was a christian, he had been trained in his principles, was trying, away from home and among strangers and wicked men, to live as a christian, and thanked us for the invitation to come when he had opportunity. We quote two of his remarks: "*When I hear a man swear, I most believe he is a liar, and won't believe him.*" "It is a fearful thing, that a man is so blind, that he will run away from his Maker."

We found *Union men* in camp, who had come there under peculiar circumstances. Two men from East Tennessee. One whose father and another his brother, had started from home in company, to get into our army in Kentucky. The father of one and brother of the other had succeeded in making their way, but these two were caught and put into the rebel army. They were captured somewhere west, had been imprisoned had applied to take the oath, had been neglected and put off. Another man was away from home in Adams county, Penn., when the army of Lee came through Waynesboro', and took him along with them. A portion of the regiment which took him were captured at Gettysburg, and he with them. His home was in Carroll county, Maryland. He was marched on down by Westminster, within eight miles of his wife and children. He had been a prisoner, until now, and carried from one place to another.

A young man from North Carolina, who had been conscripted into the service, giving us his history, said: "He would like to go north until the war was over, had applied to take the oath, was always a Union man. All his family and nearly every relation he had were old Henry Clay whigs. They had a good farm on which he had left his mother and younger children. His father was dead. His mother had always brought them all up to work and in favor of liberty. Often told them that slavery would bring on a war. That she was willing to give all she had without any pay for them. They were all opposed to slavery, and believed that it was altogether the cause of the war." That there are many who feel as we here have said, it is only necessary to refer to the fact that one whole regiment and part of another have come out and entered our service, and others have entered the navy.

Seeing Gen. Butler about other matters, and noticing the promptness with which he did what work came before him, deciding cases as it seemed to us fairly, and kindly, we brought these cases before him. They were examined into and without delay relieved.

Men in public offices have a great deal to do, but it is wonderful what men can do, if they will be good humored, civil, attentive, and industrious, with promptness and despatch. Whenever you see a public officer have time to drink a little, swear a little, get angry and treat people roughly about business which they are appointed to do; you may be sure that he will not get through his work. The man who has little or nothing to do, may get angry, be irritable, pevish, fretful, nervous, &c., but the man fully occupied ought to say as one did, "*I have got so much to do, I must keep in a good humor.*" It was wise. The faster you run the machinery the more it needs oil—he is a fool who would put sand on instead of oil, when he is in a hurry.

Let officers treat men civilly. Don't do as a general once said to us, he had abolished the word civility from his vocabulary. "I shall always be glad to see the officer of the twentieth Maine, who captured me at Round Top during the battle at Gettysburg," said a prisoner. "He behaved like a gentleman." With all the abuse of Gen. Butler by the rebel press, in the rebel camp at Point Lookout, it was a matter of pleasure among the prisoners to see him. They knew he would not compromit one hair where the interest of his government was at stake, but they felt a confidence that when a matter came before him he would attend to it, that he would not let things be done unjustly or inhumanely to them as prisoners, and that where an officer did such a thing and he learned it, he would relieve him.

We have heard some of our men speak in commendation of a rebel guard, who brought up some of his associates, with a short turn, which would not do any guard harm. "I am here to guard and keep safe these prisoners. I will not insult them—and I will not permit any man to do it, while I am on guard."

Men who are in war should remember that it will not last always. They must die. Their enemies must die, both must meet at the judgment bar of him who will there remember the kindness which gave a cup of cold water. If they both live, when the war is over, they will find that acts of humanity which they performed will do more to bind together the people of this nation, than any thing else. Out of these prisons will come men who have been there trained and disciplined by God himself.

War and imprisonment are God's school. When he permits a nation to war and fight, religion is not dead. He sends afflictions upon individuals and tries them—but on nations judgments, to punish and break down associations which have been combined in opposing his great purposes. Thus in the Scripture, Jer. 6, 8: "*Be thou instructed, O Jerusalem, lest my soul depart from thee; lest I make thee desolate, a land not inhabited.*" To the city of Nineveh he sent Jonah. Forty days and Nineveh shall be destroyed, because of her wickedness. But they repented and God turned away his anger. So Jer. 18, 7–10: "At what instant I shall speak concerning a nation and concerning a kingdom, to pluck up, and to pull down and to destroy it. If that nation against whom I have pronounced turn from their evil, I will repent of the evil that I thought to do unto them, &c."

"*I have read the New Testament through since I was in prison,*" said an officer, an educated man, who had been inclined to treat it with contempt; "*I now want to read the Bible. I never had one.*" It would surprise any man who had not been among the prisoners in our hands to see how many of them want the Scriptures and how anxiously they seek for them. Men who at home probably never opened them. Many of God's people have been in prison. Joseph, Jeremiah, John, Peter, Paul and Silas. Thence came Paul's Epistles. Christ said to his disciples "ye shall be cast into prison."

Earthly governments, ignorant and inattentive officers, may suffer individuals to pine away unjustly, or in the multitude of the cases let innocent persons suffer with the guilty, rather than trouble themselves to look into their cases, but it is not so with Christ, he will hear every call, and regard every case which presents itself before him.

A man sent to prison, in Russia, for conspiring against the life of the Emperor Nicholas, treated with scorn a minister who visited him, kicked the Bible he left, and cursed man and God for injustice, After days of solitude, loneliness and anger, he opened it on 50th Psalm, 15th v.: *Call upon me in the day of trouble and I will deliver thee, and thou shalt glorify me.* He threw away the book. After days he read again and again. God made the very despised word effectual to his salvation, and he waited in joyful hope for the day of his execution. On the day preceding, the Emperor himself came to him in his cell to let him know that he was released, and apologized for his imprisonment, having been fully satisfied of his innocence. (See Tract, *Prisoner and Emperor.*)

John Newton said, "*when I hear a knock at my study door, I hear a message from God.* Position involves responsibility. Public men who shut their doors and their ears against the petitions of individuals, should learn from the unjust judge, and remember that God has said, "*Whoso stoppeth his ear at the cry of the poor, he shall cry himself, but shall not be heard*" Prov. 21: 13.

"The Lord despiseth not his prisoners." Ps 69: 33

"Let the sighing of the prisoner come before thee." Ps. 79: 11.

"From heaven did the Lord behold, to hear the groaning of the prisoner." Ps. 102: 20.

Jesus said, "But I say unto you, love your enemies." Mat. 5: 44.

Placing our men in front of batteries, on fortifications, &c., we think fair and right to oppose with an equal number and grade on same kind of work and danger; but to withhold food and clothing and shelter from, and proper medical attention to, any prisoner or wounded man, we hope will not be entered upon the records of our nation. "*Ven-*

*geance is mine. I will repay, saith the Lord.* Therefore, if thine enemy hunger, feed him; if he thirst, give him drink; for in so doing thou shalt heap coals of fire upon his head." Rom. 12: 19, 20. Let us show our principles in contrast. God's government sets forth no such principles of retaliation. It is altogether satanic cruelty. We must have his spirit to do his acts. Success in putting down this rebellion and future prosperity is from God. Don't let us do that which will set him against us. We will do better with him on our side than with all our wise men and all our armies. 2 Kings vi: 17.

Men at Point Lookout, from Louisiana, Arkansas, Mississippi, Alabama, Texas, Missouri, Wisconsin, Illinois, Indiana Ohio, Kentucky, Tennessee Virginia, North and South Carolina, Maine, New Hampshire, Massachusetts, New York—from twenty States—colonels, captains, lieutenants, a judge, lawyers, sons of pious mothers who are dead, and they orphans, sons of widows at home, came freely to our room. We were able to give them religious reading matter, and privately to encourage, exhort and admonish as their particular case seemed to need.

From rules laid down by Secretary of War and Commissary General of Prisoners:

XII. The Commanding officer will cause requisitions to be made by his Quartermaster for such clothing as may be absolutely necessary for the prisoners; which requisition will be approved by him after a careful inquiry as to the necessity, and submitted for the approval of the Commissary General of Prisoners. * * * From the 30th of April to 1st of October, neither drawers nor socks will be allowed, except to the sick.

At Fort Delaware, in eight months, over thirty-five thousand articles were distributed among the men—shoes, stockings, shirts, drawers, woolen blankets and great coats. It is a rule not to let a man enter the camp without an overcoat or blanket. In nearly four months we were at Point Lookout, there was, as far as we could learn, but one case, and that proved by the mistake of a man letting him in late at night without knowing the rule.

XIV. The Commanding officer must give receipts for money to those to whom it belongs. These sums shall be kept in a book subject to inspection of the Commissary General at any time, or other inspecting officer, and when prisoners are transferred the amount due must be sent with him to the officer to whom they are sent, who shall receipt for it. When paroled their money will be returned to them.

Of these rules we had practical proof, and when the Rev. Mr. Walker was going away, the reason which the Provost Marshal gave for not getting him off in that boat was, that he had so many to pay he would not be able to get him in this time. He did, however, pay them, pay him, and he went down in the boat.

We have been thus particular in these matters because there is uniform complaint in regard to our men, that they not only are not furnished, or paid, but that nearly everything is taken from them and withheld when they are paroled.

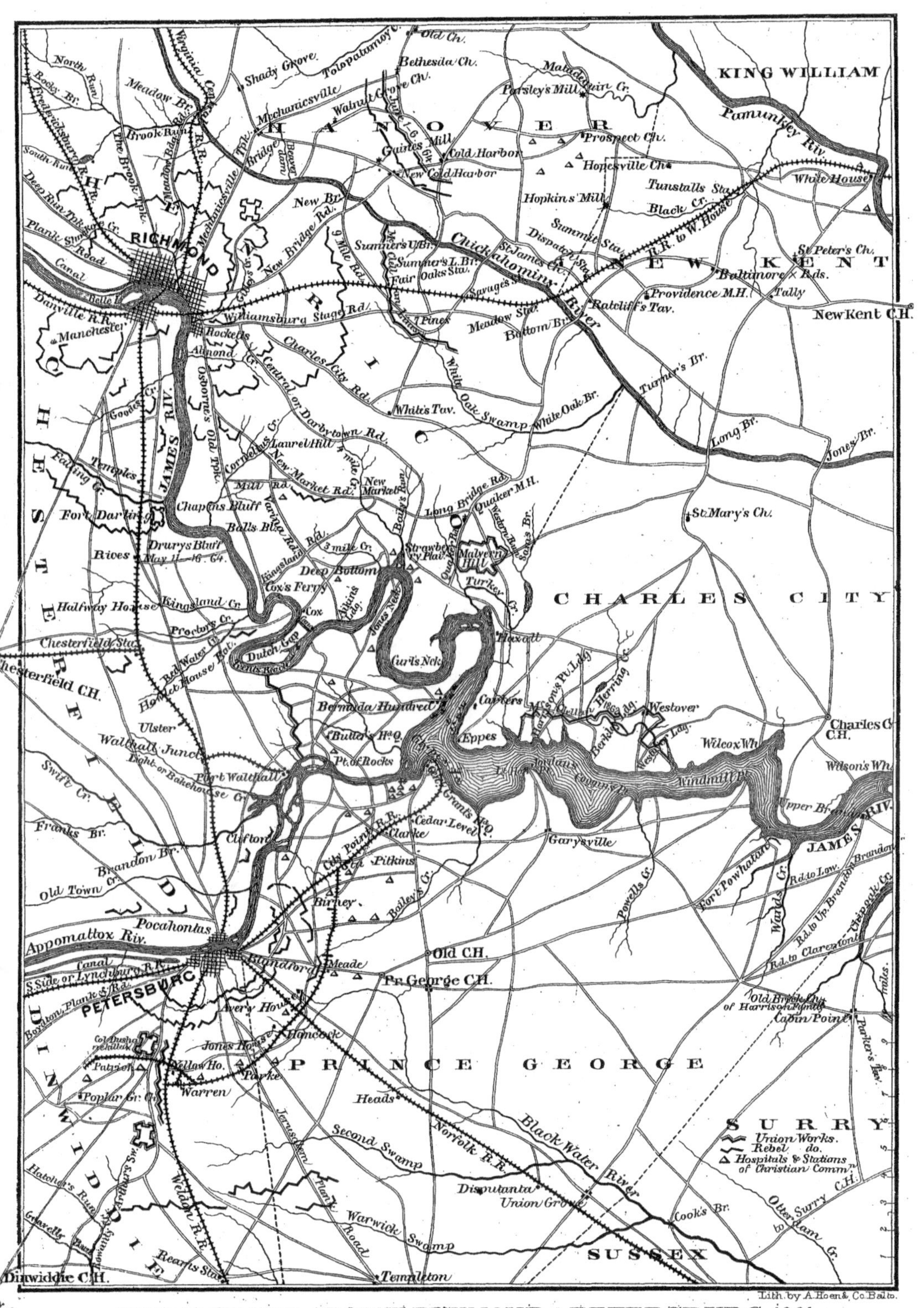


FIELD OF WAR AROUND RICHMOND & PETERSBURG 1864.

By Andrew B. Cross—Baltimore.

## ARMY OF THE POTOMAC.

As the spring of 1864 opened, the eyes of the nation were upon the two armies which had faced each other during the winter. If Grant moved—Lee must. A line of intrenchments and fortifications at every available point on the way to Richmond, or if by the James or York rivers, heavy earthworks, a second or third edition, enlarged and improved, on those against McClellan, must be encountered.

A single corps of thirty thousand men, would require about seven hundred wagons and four thousand two hundred mules The horses of officers, artillery, &c., nearly seven thousand. If good roads, each wagon will take about eighty feet, or fifty-six thousand feet, over ten miles for a train—the artillery three miles—ambulances one mile. If thirty thousand men march in single column—six miles—then cattle trains, bridge-builders and pontoons, if needed, added. So that twenty miles at least, may be laid out. Some say the supply train for the four corps was eight thousand wagons, and would reach sixty miles in length.

The second, fifth and sixth corps, under Hancock, Warren, Wright and the ninth, from Annapolis, under Burnside, are assigned to enter upon that line on which General Grant afterwards said he would fight it out. Crossing the Rapidan, then by the Wilderness, Spotsylvania Court House, the North Anna, Old Church, Bethesda, in front of Cold Harbor, for the purpose in part, of getting past Lee, and between him and Richmond. Or if the attempts along these lines fail, provision is made for the other, by sending up the tenth and eighteenth corps, under Smith and Gilmore, to Bermuda Hundred. Lee holding to advantage the line next to Richmond as far down the Chickahominy as Bottom's Bridge, with a knowledge of every hill and ravine, by-road, creek or swamp. The army of the Potomac must fight as it advances, while the enemy watches to fall upon it, unless by some skill or expedition it can succeed in getting in front of and between him and Richmond, an end which any wise and efficient commander will be on the alert to do.

Richmond was in a direct line about sixty miles from Orange Court-House where Lee's army wintered, about seventy from Culpeper Court-House where our army lay. The latter about sixty miles from Washington the former about seventy-five miles. They were about fifteen to eighteen miles apart, with the Rapidan between them.

Tuesday morning, May 3d, the order was given to move. Wilson's cavalry in the night threw a pontoon bridge over Germanna Ford, followed the next day by the fifth and sixth corps. Gregg's cavalry did the same at Ely's Ford, the second followed. The ninth remained over as a reserve to guard the supply train and protect Washington. On the evening of the 4th, the three corps encamped south of the Rapidan—and were on 5th followed by the ninth.

Thursday, May 5, our army was early in motion through the Wilderness, a tract of wild, uneven country, covered with scrub oak, low pines and thick bushes, intersected with by-roads, swamps and ravines, a surface of about twelve to fourteen miles square, with very few inhabitants. On the eastern edge is Chancellorsville, and near where Hooker, in May 1863, fought with Lee.

It was certain that Lee would with his knowledge of the country, make a quick, strong and effective assault. Our army was marching on a south-east line for the purpose of passing Lee and was necessarily extended. Lee on one side at north-east to assault, which he did after his manner, massing first on one point then another. In some of these he was successful, taking a number of prisoners. The fighting was very severe.

Friday 6th, early, the fight was renewed and continued all day. Burnside had come over the night before. There were five separate battles by the evening of this day, the last continuing into the night, in which a most desperate charge was made upon our right. Generals Seymour and Shaler were captured, their brigades scattered, and the right so pressed that the supply trains were in danger of being cut off. But by the aid of the artillery and the gathering and rallying of his forces, Sedgwick checked the enemy, and really saved the supplies to the army. General Wadsworth was killed by a bullet, which struck him in the forehead.

Saturday, 7th. The last night really closed upon a drawn battle, in which the enemy were very successful—but at early dawn this morning, a severe artillery fire was opened by our men, the fighting before was from the character of the country mostly of musketry. An advance on our part showed that Lee had fallen back, and was making south, for Spotsylvania Court House.

This battle had continued from ten minutes before twelve on Thursday noon until the morning of Saturday. It was a meeting of about two hundred thousand men, in fierce terrible and deadly conflict, and now drawn to be renewed at Spotsylvania The loss on both sides was severe. Lee took about one thousand prisoners, but did not drive any of our army back to the Rapidan, or hinder an advance.

The army of Lee had gotten the start, and secured strong fortified positions at Spotsylvania Court House before us. Our army had moved on Saturday during the darkness of the night. About daylight on Sabbath, the 8th, part of it halted in the midst of the old battle-field of Hooker and Lee, to get breakfast. In an hour or two it turned south, on the turnpike toward Spotsylvania Court House, fighting at times nearly all day.

Monday, 9th. The *Mattapony* river has four branches, *Mat, Ta, Po, Ny*. Between the *Ny* and near the *Po* is the Court House. The fortifications of Lee at this place were approached by three roads, centering in the town. On these in the form of a semicircle, he placed his army, under Longstreet, Ewell and Hill. General Meade, with the second, fifth, sixth and ninth corps, after driving him in on different points, here faced him, and advanced across the *Ny*. General Sedgwick was killed by a sharp-shooter while he was giving directions about the position of his artillery. This day there were charges and repulses, but Lee held his strong position around the Court House. The trains had come up, and the men whose rations had been exhausted were this day replenished.

Tuesday, 10th. A severe cannonade, preparatory to an attack on the whole line, was commenced. The attack was made with great force and energy. Extending over a large district of country, along the marshes of the *Ny*, in the woods and open fields, met on all sides by the shot and shell of Lee's batteries, from their strong works, yet our men entered some of these and took about 1,000 prisoners. While our loss this day was severe, Lee must have been heavily loser, when he asked for a truce on the next day, 11th, to bury the dead.

On Wednesday, 11th, General Grant sent this despatch to the Secretary of War: "We have now ended the sixth day of very hard fighting. The result has been very much in our favor. Our losses have been heavy, as well as those of the enemy. I think the loss of the enemy must be greater. We have taken over 5,000 prisoners in battle, while he has taken but few from us except stragglers. I propose to fight it out on this line, if it takes all summer."

Early Thursday, 12th, our men charged upon that portion held by General Edward Johnson, capturing him and his division. General Grant despatched: "The eighth day of battle closes, leaving between 3,000 and 4,000 prisoners in our hands, for the day's work, including two general officers and over thirty pieces of artillery. While we have lost no organization, not even a company, we have destroyed and captured one division, Johnson's—one brigade, Dobbs', and one entire regiment of the enemy."

The fight of this day was from morning until night, fourteen hours long. It could not be exceeded in resolute, determined bravery and perseverance by any preceding battle; and left us at night one mile nearer the Court House, repulsing Lee in nearly every attack. This led Lee to draw in his lines nearer his centre. The Richmond Enquirer says "that during the battle of Spotsylvania a large tree in the rear of the rebel breastworks was cut down by the concentrated force of the minnie balls. The tree fell inside of their works. After the battle one of their surgeons, Dr. Charles Magill, measured the trunk and found it twenty-two inches through and sixty-one inches in circumference. The foliage was completely trimmed from it."

We have now had most severe and terrible battles, at Wilderness and Spotsylvania for eight to ten days. The Richmond Sentinel said: "During the past two weeks the war has raged with a fury unexampled in all our previous campaigns." Our wounded from which are probably not short of twenty thousand. Lee's not less. Ours are to be attended to as far as possible, bandaged, amputated and dressed before they are removed ten to fifteen miles, to the hospital at Fredericksburg. The supply is short—some of the divisions are with scarcely anything. The medical wagons of the first division of the ninth corps, by some delay, did not reach the hospital until the fighting had ceased. Any one familiar with these movements knows the danger of wagons or men moving about in small companies, when the enemy's cavalry are waiting for the opportunity to seize and take off whatever they can. In this division the hospital was established and conducted during the first day with the con tents of the commission wagon, their tents forming the shelter for the severely wounded, while basins, sponges, scissors, lint, bandages, stimulants, beef tea, coffee, milk, crackers, &c., with the delegates as nurses, cooks, &c., rendered the only service. On Sabbath, 8th, after supplying a cavalry hospital, the team, with those from this corps, bore away for Fredericksburg. On Monday they arrived. The supplies which they had husbanded were an immediate relief, furnishing breakfast for hundreds who otherwise would have gone without anything.

A case of treachery in the mayor should not be forgotten. When the wounded from the Wilderness, who were able to walk, had come into the town ahead of the wagons and ambulances, they inquired of him for the hospital, which the government had established. He directed them as they supposed, to it, at the outer edge of the town—but where there was a number of cavalry who gobbled them up and took them prisoners to Richmond.

Those unable to walk were taken in wagons and ambulances from the Wilderness and Spotsylvania to Fredericksburg. Jarred and jolted in wagons on a rough road, is hard enough for a well man, but what must it be for men with wounds in feet, legs, thighs, arms, body, head; some with one leg, one arm, indeed every kind of wound which can be imagined among so many thousand persons; for days without food, when fed and dressed, then wagoned to Belle Plain, a landing on an arm of the Potomac, about eight to ten miles below Aquia Creek. The travel from Fredericksburg to Belle Plain was in wagons, ambulances and on foot, over a muddy, rough and dreary road. It was necessary to remove them as fast as possible, every house of every description in Fredericksburg being a hospital.

It would be a very difficult work to estimate the labors of the delegates at Wilderness, Spotsylvania, Fredericksburg and Belle Plain, who were supplied as fast as possible, and with an abundance. Bishop McIlvaine, of Ohio, says of a visit, May 23d:

"At Fredericksburg we were set down in the midst of the work. There were from 8,000 to 10,000 wounded men in the various churches, halls and other houses of the town. As some were sent away towards Washington others came in from the field. The application of the work of the commission to those poor sufferers lying in ambulances, just from the battle, and waiting to be placed under shelter, as well as to the thousands in the so-called hospitals, was just the aspect in which it would best exhibit its true character. I joined in it, messed with the delegates, saw the whole interior of how they lived and denied themselves and wrought. The morning was begun and the day was ended with devotional exercises in the open air, for the commission rooms afforded no space for about 270.

"They went out to help the surgeons, some of them surgeons themselves, to wash, to feed, to soothe, take part in the most painful operations, to minister in every wise and loving way to the sick, the maimed, the dying, to talk with them about their souls, to point them to the Lamb of God, to pray with them, under all varieties of trying and painful circumstances, to receive their last messages to dear ones at home, to comfort in all ways those dear men to whom the country is so deeply indebted, to bury them when dead.

"But I cannot expect to give an adequate idea of their work, or of their spirit in it, for all accounts to me, before I saw it, had greatly failed to make me comprehend it so as to do it any justice, greatly as I had valued it. What particularly struck me in the work was the *individuality* and *personality* of the connection between the commission agent and the wounded sufferers. There was nothing between them to make the application of aid circuitous or doubtful. It did not take the place of, or in the least interfere with, the work of the official men, the army surgeons, &c. It supplemented them. It helped them. It supplied deficiencies in special emergencies, which no government could be ready for, in all the details of such a condition of things as existed at Fredericksburg. It met the wounded on the field; it met them on their arrival at the town long before the appliances of a very overworked corps of excellent army surgeons and nurses could get to them.

"I was much struck with the high character of the men, coming from the highest social positions, reinforcements daily arriving as the time of others expired, but not reaching the necessities of the case; [on our way from Fredericksburg we met twenty or thirty on their way down, walking in the hot sun,] and then with how they *laid aside their garments and girded themselves*, and became servants to all for Christ's sake, how laboriously they wrought, and how all along, with ministrations to the body, they carried the gospel, and most of all, sought the salvation of the soldier. And how the poor sufferers welcomed them—how they appreciated their work—how they thanked them! In how many cases did I hear them say "We should have been dead by this time but for the christian commission men."

"Having seen the work, under circumstances which tested it to the uttermost, as to the sort of men it gets, the wisdom of its appliances, and the efficiency and economy of its operations, I can say, and I want to say out of my whole heart, that a work more worthy of the confidence, and affection, and co-operation of a christian public, especially of every loyal heart and hand, cannot be devised. It is wonderful to see what, from a very small beginning, it has arrived at. The sight of it is one of the most refreshing alleviations of the grief of the land, under the tribulations of this awful war, and the wicked conspiracy that originated it."

Friday, 13th. The wet weather stopped operations, except the building of fortifications and gathering of reinforcements—until Wednesday, the 18th, when the second and ninth corps were engaged, gaining two lines of Lee's intrenchments and taking some guns. On the 19th Ewell made an attempt to capture the ammunition and supply train, in which he failed, losing about twelve hundred killed and wounded and five hundred prisoners; our loss being nine hundred. Grant now stretched his line until Spotsylvania Court House lay to his right. On the 20th our men succeeded in moving south, and on Saturday, 21st, in the evening, occupied Guinney's Bowling Green, and Milford.

Both armies were marching all Saturday night. On Monday, 23rd, our forces crossed the North Anna near the central railroad, after severe opposition.

On Wednesday, 25th, at night, after burning the railroad bridge, our army was between the North and South Anna rivers. About three o'clock it was reported that the fifth corps had crossed the North Anna, but only a brigade of one division, under General Griffin, had. The whole corps were preparing to cross, and were allowed by Lee, calculating on attacking and driving them back to the river When he attacked, General Griffin maintained his position so firmly as to save the day and bring all through in safety, though Lee had opened on him with nearly one hundred cannon. Lee had also formed a new line of defence on the north side of the South Anna river, which he probably supposed General Grant would attempt to pass, as he had done at Wilderness and Spotsylvania. But he on Thursday, 26th, prepared to recross the North Anna, and in a few days had removed his army down to and across the Pamunkey, in such a position that he could communicate with White House as a base, where he had already had his supplies forwarded.

On May 5th General Butler sent a heavy force up the York river, making it probable that he was going to West Point or White House. Coming back, it was supposed he was going to Yorktown, but he returned and went up the James river to Bermuda Hundred, where he disembarked his forces, taking possession of Bermuda Hundred. Whatever was the object of the movement, one thing is certain, that Fortress Monroe was virtually removed to the junction of the James and Appomattox, and Bermuda Hundred and City Point made a position for operations which will not cease until the rebellion is overthrown. From Bermuda Hundred, on the James, Butler, with the tenth and eighteenth corps, under Smith and Gilmore, took possession of all the ground from a line above the Point of Rocks, on the Appomattox, to Trent's Reach, on the James, the line of which works will be seen on the map. He was not more than twelve miles from Petersburg, and about fifteen to seventeen from Richmond.

May 3rd, we went down to Fortress Monroe, with Mr. J. R. Miller, one of our field agents, to see where was the best place to make the base for the operations of the commission, believing it certain that the line would be the James. At the suggestion of General Butler, and with the kind attention of Captain Plato, Quartermaster at Norfolk, placed our stores in the quartermaster's warehouse for a few days.

Mr. Miller went to Yorktown. General Butler's fleet returning, he came back, and put up a tent at Fortress Monroe, where afterwards a little shanty of 12 by 32 was put up, in which has been kept part of our stores. Hundreds of our delegates, and others connected with humane purposes, some seeking their wounded children and fathers, and others the bodies of those who had fallen on the field or died in the hospital, have here been provided for.

In a few days, Mr. Miller went up and established a station at Bermuda Hundred, another about five miles west in the tenth corps, near General Gilmore's headquarters, at the eighteenth corps, (then under General Smith,) at the Point of Rocks, a third.

General Kautz, with about 3,000 cavalry from Suffolk, came up by Stony Creek, burned the railroad bridge, and came into our lines about City Point. His wounded and others who had lost their clothes, &c., in the raid, Mr. Miller saw supplied. On the 9th, General Butler announced his hopefulness of the success of Kautz to the Secretary of War. Intrenching from the Appomattox to the James; Wednesday, May 11th, he advanced out of his lines, and had a fight with the rebel forces, about 2, P. M., driving them to the outside line of their works, near Drury's Bluff; 12th and 13th they were skirmishing. On Saturday, the 14th, he drove them to their inner line. In the evening they made a sortie, and after several volleys returned. Sabbath, 15th, our sharpshooters, some within one hundred and fifty yards, kept their artillery quiet. Monday, 16th, there was a very heavy fog. The rebels taking advantage of it made a sortie, early in the morning, got around and took largely of Heckman's brigade. The engagement was very severe, and loss great on both sides. At night, our forces retired into our works. The rebels did not follow.

The wagon, under Michael Finnegan and delegates, had been on hand from the 11th to the 16th. On Sabbath (15th) they were up with our lines, and by 7 o'clock, on the 16th, were on the line of the intrenchments, where they met the wounded coming in streams They stopped the wagons and supplied coffee. tea, beef tea. crackers, milk, &c. Four to five camp kettles were boiling nearly all day. Some of the men went to Point of Rocks, others to the tenth corps hospital. There was no other provision made for any of these men until they went to the hospital, about two miles. When our delegates came to the hospital, Dr. Snow, who had it in charge, said: "I never was so rejoiced in my life. You came in the time of our greatest need." No one could have been more kind and attentive than the doctor was to our men while at the hospital. Two young men from Princeton, of the Sanitary Commission, were here rendering what aid they could, but no stores had been sent to them, nor was even a tent provided for them.

On the 9th of May, Sheridan's cavalry left near the Wilderness, crossed the Rapidan in the evening, on to Beaver Dam Station, on the Richmond and Gordonsville road, around to the right of Lee's army.—Here he tore up the railroad, destroyed three trains of cars and a large amount of stores. Turning off, made for Richmond, crossing the Chickahominy and entered the exterior defences of Richmond. Encountering the rebel cavalry, under General J. E. B. Stuart, he recrossed the Chickahominy and made for General Butler's lines.

On Saturday, (28th) at Bermuda Hundred, the troops were coming in all night and getting upon transports. On Sabbath morning we helped our wagon and horses on board a vessel, and by 10 to 12 o'clock, all was quiet and clear of troops. On Monday they were at the White House, having gone down the James and up the York river.

Lee was aiming to keep Grant from Richmond, and Grant was moving down toward his new base at White House. If Lee could cut him off, he would interfere greatly with his movements. But Lee was in danger, if he went too far in the way of cutting off supplies at White House, of opening the door for Grant into Richmond

The cavalry engagements from day to day, hindered Lee, but on the 29th, Sheridan drove him back from the west of Hanovertown toward Bethesda church. This cavalry fight one of the most severe during the war, prepared the way for our army to secure their position. Lee's lines were from Atlee's Station, on the Virginia Central railroad, on north of the Chickahominy to Shady Grove Church, about eight miles from Richmond.

On the 30th, General Warren, with the fifth corps, pressed up towards Lee's right. General Hancock, of the second corps also got into the right of the fifth. With the aid of the cavalry, on this and the 31st, the sixth and 18th coming up, our forces were enabled on the next day, June 1st, to form a line of battle, as may be seen from the map—ninth corps on west of Bethesda church, across the Mechanicsville road, fifth between that and the Walnut Grove road, eighteenth between that and the new Cold Harbor road facing Gaines' Mill, sixth across new Cold Harbor road, second across Sumner's Bridge road. Directly in front of our forces was Lee's army intrenched The battle of this day secured us Cold Harbor.

We were about the same distance from Richmond and White House. If we could move a little more to the left, and across the Chickahominy, the way would have been opened into Richmond. Wednesday night it was arranged to move on Thursday, (2d) but a severe storm hindered, and gave Lee time to complete his fortifications. On Friday, (3d) they were more strongly fortified.

The importance of this point was duly appreciated by General Grant when he commenced his work of fortifying, intrenching and advancing upon Lee, line by line, until our fortifications were within a few rods in some places of theirs—so near that men could exchange papers and hold conversation from the two armies. The position could not be carried without fearful loss of life.

Early this morning a charge, which had been ordered the preceding evening, was made, in which we suffered severely. General Tyler was wounded. Great numbers of our wounded lay on the field, though strenuous efforts were made to carry them off.

Colonel Peter B. Porter, of Niagara Falls, commanding the 8th New York heavy artillery, was killed within 5 to 6 rods of the rebel lines. Seven wounds were found upon his body. One in his neck, one between his shoulders, one on the right side, and lower part of the stomach, one on the left, and near his heart, and two in his legs. The evening before he said, "that if the charge was made he would not come out alive; but that if required, he would go into it." The last words heard from him were: "*Boys, follow me.*" We notice the following extract from his will, which was made before entering the service, which shows the man:

"Feeling to its full extent the probability that I may not return from the path of duty on which I have entered—if it please God that it be so—I can say with truth I have entered on the career of danger with no ambitious aspirations, nor with the idea that I am fitted by nature or experience to be of any important service to the Government; but in obedience to the call of duty demanding every citizen to contribute what he could in means, labor, or life to sustain the government of his country; a sacrifice made, too, the more willingly by me when I consider how singularly benefited I have been by the institutions of this land, and that up to this time all the blessings of life have been showered upon me beyond what falls usually to the lot of man."

The *White House* is on the south side of the Pamunkey river, about three-quarters of a mile below where the railroad from Richmond to West Point crosses. West Point is at the head of the York river and in the fork of the Pamunkey and Mattapony. The former is exceedingly crooked, but navigable for steamers and gunboats to the railroad bridge. For a mile or two west, and for miles south, the land is level and tillable. Its name is from an old house with brick foundation, upon which we suppose there was a comfortable and well arranged house. The walls seem to have been whitewashed. There is not now any building standing, nor when our army went there for its base, the iron of the railroad near being removed, and the ties burned by McClellan's army in 1862.

Mr. Miller with Finnegan pitched tent north of the railroad embankment and within twenty steps of the river. This became our store tent, from which our wagons for the fifth, sixth, ninth, second and eighteenth drew their supplies, and took them out in company with the Government trains to the vicinity of Cold Harbor, &c., to which ever place our tents for the corps were pitched. A few hundred yards below on the river was the barge from which we received our stores, and along the river for nearly a quarter of a mile were boats continually unloading stores, ammunition, forage and everything of every kind needed for the army. Along the shore and in procession for half a mile, coming and going, were the wagons for and with supplies. Before you get down to the White House was a little ravine through which a very small stream of water runs, over which was a bridge that at least one-half of the wagons passed coming or going. The delay at it and the damage to teams, with the swearing done by drivers, impressed upon us the importance of having *a road-master* as well as a wagon-master, whose business it should be to go along daily upon the roads where the teams travel and have logs cut out of the way, deep holes filled up, bridges repaired, and that it should be his duty to enter upon it as soon as the wagons are needed along the road. One half hours' attention at this little bridge would have saved the Government one or two mules. Near the White House foundations were the quartermaster, commissary, &c., &c., also the telegraph station. A few hundred yards below began the commission tents, and west and south-west the tents of the base hospital for the different corps. The ground of the hospital tents was as good as it could be, level, dry, covered with a heavy sod of grass which was also dry. The tents not being sufficient, men were laid upon the ground. Occasionally numbers of them were left in the ambulances and wagons until they were removed to the boats, which were daily plying to Washington and such hospitals as they were sent to. Near the hospital we had two or three large tents for goods and for delegates to eat in, and others for sleep, &c., &c. Besides the men who were in front with the field hospitals and our wagons, we had from seventy to one hundred busily occupied here at the base. Every available camp kettle was in use for coffee, tea, corn starch, farina, &c. The large supply of crackers which we had was so far used, that we had to come on the Government to get hard tack for ourselves as well as the men.

Our delegates in the front had given all the attention they could before the wounded left them, but as the ambulance, and the return wagons, which had taken out supplies, came back they brought in such numbers that it pressed everything. At the front of our tents was one continual crowd of those slightly wounded, who had walked in. They came for coffee, lemonade, crackers, farina, &c., something to eat. As soon at we had once supplied these we had to turn them over to the hospitals. Thus continued the work from day to day. Below us was the sanitary commission, busily engaged, also relief associations from different States, looking after their wounded. Our wagons and delegates who had come with the army through the whole campaign, and the one from Bermuda Hundred, were at the front with stores. There were over 2,300 wounded in the eighteenth corps. As Mr. Miller's wagon came up, Dr. Richardson, of the eighteenth, came out himself, and began to get out of the wagon, bandages, lint, &c., &c. Everything was put out at once, and the wagon sent back for more. About 15,000 were wounded.

Tuesday 7th, a truce was entered upon for the burying the dead and taking care of the wounded of both armies. White House now looked as if it was going to remain the permament base for the army. Wharves were built, the railroad laid down, &c., &c. But preparations were really making from the day of the fight near Cold Harbor of the 3d, to change to the south of Richmond, and the works carried on were really a blind.

They did not however move until Sunday night, 12th. Part of the army, the fifth and perhaps sixth corps crossed at Long Bridge and by Wilcox Landing to Windmill Point and up in front of Petersburg, the rest crossed at Jones' Bridge, passing Charles City C. H., and over the river nearly in front of Fort Powhatan, and then toward Petersburg; both on pontoons. Others crossed from Harrison's to Jordan's Point on boats

A pontoon bridge is formed by anchoring flat bottomed boats with the current of a river at such distances apart, that scantling may reach from one to the other, on which are placed thick boards, strong enough to bear heavy cannon and ammunition wagons; being equally sustained by the boats, the whole bridge may be covered with men or horses. We have noticed one regular line of the army, and again as many cavalry as could get on the bridge. In crossing, men who are on horseback are required to dismount and lead their horses. The bridge necessarily quivers under the pressure upon it, and from the fact that the ropes which anchor it are not drawn tight, and the weight on it sinks it so into the water, that they become slack. The scene of passing over the James on June 16th when the army came down, will be remembered by those who saw it with great interest. The boats, scantling, flooring, &c., are a part of army munitions, and are carried on wagons in a *pontoon train*, as regularly as anything else, when an army is passing through a country where the water is too deep to ford.

This movement was made expeditiously and without any obstacle. It was desirable to cross so low down because the enemy held Bottom's Bridge, and the further down our army went, the further it called Lee's away from Richmond to follow, making it rather hazardous for him to get so far away from the lines around Richmond with so many of his forces, and it would not have done for him to make an attack with a small part of his army.

Our army is now all on the south of the James, the headquarters of General Grant at City Point, of General Butler, about four miles to five from Bermuda Hundred, and about one mile from the Point of Rocks on the Appomattox.

About June 10th, while the forces around Cold Harbor were holding Lee in position, before they moved, we had quite an anxious time at Bermuda Hundred. on knowing that Kautz had penetrated the outer lines of the rebel works, south of Petersburg, and had to retire because support did not come to him in time. As soon as the 18th corps, from White House, by water, landed at Bermuda Hundred, Smith, on the 15th, started over the pontoon bridge at Point of Rocks, across the Appomatox, Martindale going directly along the river road, Brooks, by the City Point road, Hinks, with his colored men, came up the Jordan's Point road, Kautz, with his cavalry, went round and came up the Prince George Court House road. The batteries north east of Petersburg, with four forts, were carried. The forts were carried by the colored troops. About sixteen guns were captured, and a regiment of Wise's brigade. The second corps came up and took the south of the eighteenth. On the next day, 16th, the ninth corps came up and took position to left of second, and they captured the second line of the rebel works.

On this day a line of rifle pits were taken and some prisoners. The fifth corps came up and moved still to the left. The sixth coming, the eighteenth went back to Bermuda Hundred.

On Saturday, the 18th, our forces advanced within about one mile of

Petersburg, where they found the enemy occupying a new line of intrenchments, which after various assaults they failed to carry. But we held and have retained until the present, every line we had taken.

Sabbath 19th A flag of truce was sent in to get the dead and wounded between the lines, but refused. This Sabbath was a busy day and night for our commission, as the wounded came down by City Point to go away, our delegates supplied crackers, coffee, &c., to about three thousand men in wagons, ambulances, on stretchers, on foot and every other way.

Beauregard, who had been facing Butler's lines, came down to Petersburg, exposing the lines to our forces, which Butler was improving by taking the railroad between Richmond and Petersburg, where Lee coming down, drove him into his intrenchments.

On the 22d our forces advanced toward the Weldon road. This weakened, or opened the lines, so that Hill pressed in, producing some confusion in the corps, but was soon repulsed. Cavalry raids were made about this time by Kautz and Wilson, which, while damaging to the rebel communications, were perilous to their men.

We held the lines around Petersburg. The advance on the Weldon railroad, at Yellow House, extending breastworks, erecting forts, and the advance beyond Poplar Church, with skirmishes and pretty severe fighting at Ream's Station and at Hatcher's Run and Stony Creek.

Another series of movements have been advanced on the north side of the James. By looking at the map it will be seen that the road from our lines, at Petersburg, or from City Point, comes to the pontoon bridge at the Point of Rocks. Crossing this, there is a very good road to Jones' Landing on the James. Here a pontoon bridge had been for some time, and General Foster, with the aid of some gunboats, had kept a position open at Deep Bottom. This was but a few miles from Malvern Hill.

Thursday, July 21st. Another pontoon was stretched across to Strawberry Plains, on the other side of the creek from Deep Bottom. The nineteenth corps, which had come up from the south, had crossed over. Tuesday, 26th. The second corps, with large part of Sheridan's and Kautz's cavalry crossed over. The wagon train of the sixth corps, which was with Sheridan, also came across. On the 27th the second corps advanced across Strawberry Plains against the enemy, who was behind earthworks, capturing 4 guns taken at Drury's Bluff, May 16.

During the night of Wednesday, 27th, the second corps re-crossed, to be in readiness for the assault which was to take place after the explosion in front of Petersburg.

The mine under one of the forts, dug by men of the 48th Pennsylvania, Colonel Pleasants, most miners from Schuylkill county and coal regions, was on the 30th of July exploded, with eight tons of powder —blowing up part of a North Carolina battery with the fort.

The ninth corps, supported by the fifth and eighteenth, were to advance and storm the hill as soon as the explosion should take place, but from delays, the real cause of which we do not know, instead of effecting what was designed they were exposed to a murderous fire, by which we lost in killed, wounded and missing, five to six thousand men. General Bartlett and staff, with Colonel Wild, were captured On the 3d of August, Lee granted a truce for the burial of the dead and taking care of the wounded.

The raid into Maryland, and fight at Monocacy, are a constituent part of the operations of Lee's army and that of the Potomac. General Hunter with Crook and Sullivan had proceeded down as far as Lynchburg and was about to invest it, when Early came up and compelled him to leave Going by Gauley through Western Virginia, it left open the Shenandoah Valley. This opportunity Early embraced, and pushing up with a force of over twenty thousand men, a large body of cavalry crossed the Ohio Railroad, threatening Martinsburg. Sigel, who was there fell back, leaving Winchester, Williamsport and Harper's Ferry, &c. He held Maryland Heights.

On July 9, at the Monocacy, Gen. Wallace with far inferior force fought Early, and was compelled to fall back toward Baltimore. Though this seemed but a small fight, Rebel officers when in Frederick admit that their loss in proportion was equal if not greater than in any battle of the war. Bridges were burned by parts of his command on Northern Central Railroad, also on Philadelphia and Wilmington. General Tyler had been captured at Monocacy, and General Franklin, at Magnolia, but both succeeded in escaping.

On July 11, Early's main body came in on Seventh street road toward Washington, within six or seven miles of the city, threatening Fort Stevens. General Augur's forces drove him back. General Hunter had gotten up to Martinsburg and with Couch threatening his rear, made it necessary for him to change his course. He was pursued by General Averill, who on July 19, overtook and whipped him. At Winchester he was reinforced. After fighting him on 23d and 24th Averill fell back to Harper's Ferry. 26th Early occupied Martinsburg. Saturday 30th, General McCausland with several hundred cavalry, burned Chambersburg.

On August 8th, General Sheridan was put in command of the Middle Department, with sixth, eighth, nineteenth corps, with Crook, Averill and Kelly. By well advised and energetic moves, he in three battles at Winchester, Fisher's Hill and Cedar Creek, so completely disabled and drove back Early and Longstreet's forces, that the valley has been relieved in great measure. In pursuing his plan of weakening the military power of the enemy, beside taking a large number of prisoners, four thousand head of stock, number of horses and guns, he destroyed nearly all the grain and provender along his march—two thousand barns with wheat, hay, farming implements, &c , and over seventy mills with flour and wheat.

The battles at Winchester, 19th September, Fisher's Hill, 22d, Cedar Creek, October 19th, were all bloody and destructive, but victorious. The wounded from them could not be less than twelve to fifteen thousand. As soon as possible our delegates have been in attendance, giving every attention in their power. Our wounded, with 2,000 of the rebels, in the hospitals at Winchester, Martinsburg and Sandy Hook, bore witness to the severity of the fight.

August 12th, in the afternoon, the second corps, on board of transports, passed down the river, and after dark returned and came up to

Deep Bottom, where they landed. On the 13th, the tenth joined them and an attack was made on the enemy's works, capturing five hundred prisoners, six cannon and two mortars.

On the 16th, General Hancock moved his forces out from Strawberry Plains in such manner as to command the three principal roads, Charles city, Central and New Market. A portion of Gregg's cavalry encountered a part of General W. H. E. Lee's, under command of General J. R. Chambliss—the latter was killed. In his pocket was found a testament with this request: "If I am killed in this struggle, will some kind friend deliver this book to my wife. J. R. C., Jr.—June 8, 1864." By order of General Hancock his body was buried at the Potteries, on the New Market road near Bailey's Run. We lost, this day, Colonel Craig, who was shot through the head with a bullet. We captured four hundred prisoners, sixteen of whom were commissioned officers. Our killed, wounded and missing are supposed about one thousand. We advanced our position, and had the dead bodies of two rebel Generals, and four battle flags

18th. Our lines were from Dutch Gap to White Oak Swamp creek. While Lee was watching on this line, General Warren marched with the fifth corps to Ream's station, surprised the force guarding the Weldon railroad at that place, and took possession of the road. That evening and next day Hill tried to drive Warren out, but aided by the ninth, he repulsed him and held the road. The loss of the fifth was about five thousand.

On the 20th, the second came back in front of Petersburg to the help of fifth and ninth, who were attacked on Sunday, 21st, but succeeded in driving the enemy, and taking a large number of prisoners. At this time Colonel Dushane was killed. On the 24th (Wednesday) Lee made another fight for Ream's station, in which he suffered severely, though we lost from the second corps about two thousand prisoners, &c.

Wednesday night, September 28. The eighteenth corps, under General Ord, moved from Jones' Neck across the pontoon bridge, near Aiken's Landing, and up the Varina road; and on the morning of the 29th carried the outer works below Chapin's Farm. Fort Harrison, occupying a commanding position below Fort Darling, with heavy guns, but not well manned, became useless to the rebels. About three hundred prisoners and sixteen guns were taken. General Ord was wounded slightly, and had to leave the field. General Weitzell took his place. General Burnham was killed, and Colonel Stannard lost an arm

The tenth corps, under General Birney, moved on the Kingsland road, at the junction of this road with New Market. The New Market heights were carried. The attack on Fort Gilmor, at Laurel Hill, was unsuccessful. During this attack General Kautz's cavalry went up as far as the toll-gate, two miles from Richmond. The rebels the next day made two assaults on our lines here, but only with loss to themselves.

On the 30th, the fifth and ninth corps advanced on the Weldon road, encountering the enemy at Peeble's house, on the west of the Weldon road. They fell back to their works on the South Side railroad. There were several engagements here, in which we lost a number of prisoners.

October 7. Lee attacked Terry's division and Kautz's cavalry on the Darbytown road. The rebels made two assaults, in which they lost about one thousand men.

From the time that our army left Culpepper Court House, May 3d, it has had one continued series of desperate fights, with marchings to and fro, early and late, in rain and mud, in heat and dust. Suffering great losses in killed, wounded and prisoners, and accomplished an amount of work. in earthworks, of forts, intrenchments, rifle-pits, pass ways, bomb-proofs and embankments, with mining and ditching, which seems almost incredible. The canal through Dutch Gap has been a regular digging operation, attended all the time with great danger from the shells of the Howlett House battery. It is about three-fourths of a mile from Aiken's Landing. The width of it is about 150 feet—the length about 400. The depth in some places about 80. When completed it will shorten the channel of the river about 7 miles.

After every battle from the Wilderness, Spotsylvania, North Anna, Cold Harbor, Petersburg, Drury's Bluff, Norfolk and Weldon Roads, Deep Bottom, Strawberry Plains, Chapin's Farm, New Market, Darbytown, Charles City Road and Wilson's Landing, where Wild, with his colored troops defeated Lee's cavalry, also after raids of Kautz, Wilson and Sheridan, our delegates have been on hand with stores to supply their immediate wants, and at every hospital of the wounded, whether brigade, division, corps, base or general, they have been present to render aid as nurses, surgeons, as christian ministers and laymen, ministering to the necessities of any and all who needed aid. Beside this, they have attended to aid friends in finding their wounded and doing for them those acts of kindness, which at such times become duty, and relieve and comfort the hearts of fathers and mothers, sisters and brothers, who are at home

At the base hospital near City Point, about one mile from the landing, we had our headquarters, from which our delegates were sent to the different corps, &c. At City Point, we also had a store-house, office rooms, chapel tent, &c. Here our supplies are brought from the boats and stored for distribution. At the base hospital we had accommodation for one hundred persons at a time, and have had a large part of that number engaged a great portion of the time. In this hospital we have had from three to ten thousand persons at a time—have fed as high as three thousand in one day. We will not enter into the various times and ways, but from personal knowledge we can refer to cases where men have died neglected, and where the only attention that hundreds of them had for even a drink of water, was from delegates who met them at the boats and attended to them on the boats. Delegates have even been detailed to go up with the wounded from White House, and at the wharf at City Point the nurses begged us for supplies for wounded on their way to Washington.

Some of the severest battles were in the very hottest and driest season. Dust covered everything. As trains of wagons and ambulances, or regiments of foot or cavalry passed along the road you could scarcely distinguish whether they were white or colored men—or cavalry or wagons. Water was scarce, warm, muddy. In this condition our wounded were taken to the hospital at City Point, where the dust was as bad as any other place. The camp was covered with dust, any motion along the streets raised a cloud, which settled on the wounded in the tents, who were almost suffocated, and had scarcely water enough for drinking, and but little to bathe their wounds.

With the approbation of General Grant, the attention of General Ingalls, the good will of Mayor Chapman and the fire board of Baltimore, a steam fire engine—No. 4—was secured, which furnished water from the Appomatox, sufficient to lay the dust in the camp, cool the tents, fill tanks which General Grant had directed to be prepared, and carry the water to the commission tents at the extreme end of the camp, forcing water through 2,300 feet of hose. The supply was abundant for everything that was needed. While this experiment was being made, a man who professed to have something to do with the inspection of the army, said to us he would like to see it work, for if it succeeded he had an idea of recommending the providing engines for the army. The engineer, at our instance, followed him, and in passing his tent or one of his associates, the stream of water burst through one of the openings wetting it a little, but only for a second—but such was the difficulty growing out of it, that had it not been for the wounded, and the respect for Generals Grant and Ingalls, the whole thing would have stopped. It was an experiment over a great many difficulties, but we were indebted to the engineer, Mr. Wesley Shaw, and to James Hall and Michael Dunn, for their prompt and constant devotion, in keeping the engine, hose and everything in working order, and by their labor rendering an amount of comfort to the wounded which could not come from any other source. After its operation the government put up two small engines which have since supplied the camp with water, and have gotten two steam fire engines for the western army.

To Mr. S. M. Felton, of the Philadelphia, Wilmington and Delaware roads, we are indebted for the promptness and liberality which gave us the use of the two roads, and to officers and men of the roads, and also to individuals along the Delaware road in getting peaches, by which we were enabled to pass nearly eight hundred boxes of peaches to the men in the army around Petersburg and Richmond, and to the wounded at Winchester, Sandy Hook, &c. Also to the bay line for this and one continued series of accommodations, in passing stores and delegates from the commencement of the campaign until the present.

Continuing to make comfortable the body, might be called a small part of the work. Our delegates have sought to bring the consolation of the gospel to all who are in sorrow and trouble, who are sick, wounded or dying, point them to Christ, pray with them, write to their friends, bear messages of love, and dying farewells. They have also labored as volunteer chaplains to our soldiers in the army. Seeing that our men are furnished with the word of God, bringing to them tracts, religious papers. Throwing around them the influences and restraints of the Gospel, as at home. We believe good has been done which will appear after many days. When this war is over and the army returns home it will not be to curse, defile and pollute the communities into which they shall go. We look for the influence of the Gospel to exercise such a sanctifying power that they will go loving liberty, loving their country, loving their God, loving order and law.

We cannot number the cases of men watched over, nursed and cared for by our delegates. Many a mother's or sister's heart has been made glad on hearing of the condition of a son or brother. The son of Judson, the missionary, by the neglect and ignorance of his surgeon, reduced to the last stage of hope, was cared for by our delegates, watched over and recovered, to render service to his country. In the hospital at City Point, from Hancock's staff, entered upon his heavenly inheritance, Charles H. Dod, of Princeton, New Jersey, son of Professor Albert Dod, deceased, late of New Jersey college.

In the charge upon Petersburg, E. M. Schneider. son of the missionary, who had only returned to duty from a wound at North Anna, was shot through the body. At the hospital of the ninth corps he was carefully nursed until his death. "Don't weep," said he to his anxious friends, "write my father that I have tried to do my duty to my country and my God. Tell the boys in the regiment to stand by the dear old flag." To his brother in the navy, "stand by the flag and cling to the cross of Christ" "You will soon go home," said the surgeon. "Yes, doctor; I am going home. I am not afraid to die. I don't know how the valley will be when I get to it, but it is all right now."

Gathering up his strength, he sung before he died :

"Soon with the angels I'll be marching,
With bright laurels on my brow ;
I have for my country fallen,
Who will care for sister now ?"

In one of the assaults in front of Petersburg a young man from Connecticut, noble in body and mind, was brought into the hospital, mortally wounded by a sharpshooter. The surgeon requested Rev. Mr. Pease, one of our delegates, to inform him that he could not live more than three or four hours. He said at first—"I have not brought my mind fully to that. If it must be so, I submit." As Mr. P. closed a prayer for him, he began to pray. He first prayed that God would hear that prayer. Then in beautiful and appropriate language, he prayed for that man who shot him. He prayed that the Lord would forgive him for shooting him. He prayed that God would not take him away in his sins, but that he would give him a new heart, and fit him to come to heaven at last. Thus he spent the last three or four hours of his life, praying for those with whom he had just been engaged in deadly combat, and for beloved relations who were far away, and in sending messages to them

Along all the lines of the army, and near every hospital will be found graves and grave-yards, which contain, side by side, men from south, north, east and west—

By stranger hands their shallow graves were made ;
No stone memorial o'er their corpses laid ;
In barren sands, and far away from home, they lie,
No friend to shed a tear when passing by.

Yet known by him who said, "I am the resurrection and the life. He that believeth in me, though he were dead yet shall he live."

## GOD DEALING WITH SLAVERY.

Before the war, Henry A. Wise uttered these words: "Our fathers went to "work for the best Union they could make, and *they did give us the best Union, " and the best Government the world ever saw.* Jefferson did not make it, nor " Madison, nor his co-laborers make it. *God Almighty made it. It was the work " of inspiration. I believe that as I believe the Bible."*

We live under that Government; have been more blest than any nation or people upon the earth. We live now at the most interesting and important period in the history of this country, or of the world.

With all our privileges, civil and religious, we retained as part and parcel of our existence, an institution repugnant to the instincts of our fathers, unjust in its treatment of the rights of others, and contrary to the spirit of the Gospel of Christ—the perpetuation of which was to confirm for all time to come as right the conduct of the men who ruthlessly stole and firmly withheld from their fathers and mothers the Africans brought here as slaves.

While God bore with us, and in his providential dealing induced many to seek in such ways as were proper to turn the captivity to such account that good might come from their bondage, others sought with an avaricious desire for wealth and luxurious ease, to make permanent in the nation, and bind down for their children's children a race to be their slaves.

No matter by what agency, or in what way God's providence wrought—of this one thing, we are clearly convinced, he has opened a door by which thousands and hundreds of thousands have become free men and women. In the State of Maryland an event has taken place, the most remarkable in the whole history of the State, in which, by the vote of the people in one day, eighty thousand slaves became freemen.

This revolution, so quiet and noiseless, has scarcely attracted the attention of the people. They do not realize what God has wrought. Yet in it we see how He can carry on His work of overturning among the nations of the earth, and preparing the way for the coming of the kingdom of his Son. We also see when His time comes that no opposition will have any effect. He will work and none can hinder.

It is only four years since an effort was made in the State of Maryland and other States to turn into slavery those who had before been freed by their masters. At the very time that this class of men were striving to make slaves of freemen, they were also preparing, by organizing armies and training troops, to engage in a war against our nation, aiming to overthrow and destroy it, that they might revolutionize and build up a nation, the foundation stone of which was to be African slavery.

God, "who takes the wise in their own craftiness," "who makes the wrath of man to praise him," "who sets up one and casts down another," "by whom kings reign and princes decree justice," "who sends the stormy wind to fulfill his pleasure," permitted these very men who sought to build up this institution to engage in and inaugurate a war, which, when entered upon, must certainly prove its utter overthrow. In this event, as in the death of his own Son—"With wicked hands ye have slain the Lord of Glory,"—of which God also said, "They have done that which his counsel and foreknowledge determined before should be done."

November 29th, 1860, Rev. Dr. B. M. Palmer, of New Orleans, preached a sermon, in which he distinctly avowed, that *the South had a distinct mission, a particular trust assigned* to them, that their *fidelity in the discharge of the same was the pledge of the divine protection.* That mission and that trust was "to conserve and to perpetuate the institution of slavery as now existing." After giving his reasons for the same, he says: "This argument touches the four cardinal points of duty to ourselves, to our slaves, to the world, *and to Almighty God.* It establishes the nature and solemnity of our present trust to preserve and transmit our existing system of domestic servitude, with the right, unchanged by man, to go and rest itself wherever Providence and nature may carry it."

If Pharaoh had said, that as God in his Providence had sent Joseph down into Egypt to save the lives of Israel, it was a reason why they should remain, there would have been some plausibility in the argument. But to argue that because his ancestors had stolen from their homes children of any people, and brought them here—that as they had served them under bondage for one or two hundred years, therefore God had intrusted to them the keeping of them in bondage, and also as a duty the endeavor to carry the same principle out wherever they could have any influence; was to assume a principle which nothing less than a distinct and specific revelation from God could warrant.

God had written an entirely different history for our instruction. After four hundred years, he sent Moses, by an especial call and commission, to lead his people up out of Egypt, with all the knowledge they had acquired in Egypt, and with the spoiling of their masters and mistresses.

A wise man, a minister in the South, with God's word in his hand, should have felt every year of this life as he read that history. "If God did as marvelous a thing in the days of Pharaoh and Moses—if Pharaoh in setting himself against Israel's deliverance, was led on by the providence of God until his chariots and horsemen were overwhelmed in the Red Sea, how terribly to be apprehended is the approach of that time when God will arise to deliver these people from a bondage, which their taskmasters would make perpetual?" Year after year, the distant thunder had intimated to the people of the South that there was an unsettled atmosphere. Time and again the elements had grown into angry strife. One messenger after another they had rejected, insulted, murdered, and indeed, by state enactments, shut out these people from learning to read God's word. People South dreaded, trembled, and quaked at the signs which they saw and heard. Instead of taking counsel together to prevent the day of dreadful storm, they counselled resistance. They resolved that God has permitted them to hold this people in bondage, that His word not only permitted but even taught it as right—therefore we will not let this people go free. Maddened like Pharaoh at the signs which God had given them in the political heavens, deluded and blinded as their ministers became on the subject, losing sight of all history, of all right, human and divine, they taught that slavery was right, and God's great sacred trust, for which they must fight, "not only to maintain it where it was, but to go and root itself wherever Providence and nature may carry it."

Their leading men in Congress planned and worked. They entered into combination with those in the North who traded with them, whose political and commercial prosperity was dependent upon their aid and co-operation. Taking advantage of the position and times, they had procured arms and ammunition, trained soldiers, formed companies, gathered armies, and declared war; not against particular men or principles, but against that which pertained directly to the nation. They had already avowed their designs; their arrangements made, their officers chosen, and rebellion deep, extensive and bitter was determined upon.

Stevens, second to none in the States which united in the rebellion, in mental ability and moral worth, afterwards vice-president of the confederacy, did not then yield to the rash movements; but with a clearness and force, with a solemnity and truthfulness, which has already amounted to literal prophecy, stood up when others cowered and pointed out to the people of Georgia and the south what must necessarily take place. He set forth, beyond controversy, the fact that the south had not in truth one single thing to complain of.

"Pause, I entreat you, and consider for a moment what reason you can give "that will satisfy yourselves in calmer moments—what reasons you can give to "your fellow sufferers in the calamity that it will bring upon us—what reasons "you can give to the nations of the earth to justify it? What right has the north "assailed? What interest of the south has been assailed? What justice has "been denied? and what claim, founded in justice and right, has been withheld? "Can either of you name to-day one governmental act of wrong deliberately and "purposely done by the government of Washington, of which the south has "a right to complain? I challenge the answer."

God never leaves himself without a witness. So in the face of a war which the leaders of the south were inaugurating which was to be so terrible in its progress, he does not permit it to come on until he has fully justified his providential dealing.

"Pause, now while you can, gentlemen, and contemplate carefully and candidly these important items. Leaving out of view for the present, the countless millions of dollars you must expend in war with the north; with tens of "thousands of your sons and brothers slain in battle, and offered up as sacrifices "upon the altar of your ambition. And for what, we ask again? Is it for "the overthrow of the American government, established by our common ancestry, cemented and built up by their sweat and blood, and founded on the "broad principles of right, justice and humanity? And as such, I must declare "here, as I have often done before, and which has been repeated by the greatest and wisest statesmen and patriots in this and other lands—that it is the "best and freest government, the most equal in it rights, the most just in its "decisions, the most lenient in its measures, and the most inspiring in its principles to elevate the race of man, that the sun of heaven ever shone upon. "Now for you to attempt to overthrow such a government as this, under which "we have lived for more than three-quarters of a century—in which we have "gained our wealth, our standing as a nation, our domestic safety, while the elements of peril are around us, with peace and tranquillity, accompanied with unbounded prosperity and rights unassailed—is the height of madness, folly and "wickedness, to which I can neither lend my sanction nor my vote."

Strange as it may seem, the virulence of the storm drove even this man from the truths and principles which he uttered as with prophetic foresight. We can but hope that when the storm is over and men begin to see and think, that he will recognize his old foundations and return to aid in rebuilding what he has permitted himself for a while to abandon.

God led men of wisdom, prayer and faith, to plant colonies, and lay foundations in Africa for evangelizing it and removing the people of color from this country to the land of their fathers. He had watched over and protected them, rooting and grounding them in the confidence of the nations, and thus opening a permanent door of deliverance for the race among us when any emergency should arise to them.

We cannot see into God's ways, but by the budding of the tree we learn that the spring and summer and harvest are coming. So by these plantings of good men and by the preparing of schools and colleges and seminaries we see that God has designed some great end, which he will make manifest in his time.

To view this war, without expecting some great purpose of God to be accomplished, is to believe that God is making a great preparation for that which will end in vanity. God does not so work. If we may by signs, judge of seasons, so may we with great confidence believe that God is at work with us.

On May 4, 1607, Captain Newport, with the first English colony, landed at Point Comfort, now Fortress Monroe, and had their first interview with the natives. About five days after they landed on Jamestown Island, to which they gave the name. On the 18th the Indians threatened them. On June 15th, they had built or finished a fort. After various expeditions of adventure up the James, the Chickahominy, &c., intercourse with Indians, rescue of Smith by Pocahontas, her marriage with John Rolf, her visit to England, her baptism and death, and the death of her father Powhatan, an assembly or parliament was held at Jamestown, May, 1620; and from this commenced the government of Virginia.

A *Dutch ship* in 1620 brought over *to Virginia the first cargo of negroes.* After two hundred and forty years we have a population of 26,975,575 whites, 487,996, free negroes, 3,953,760 slaves. African slavery here, began thus early. Slavery has existed in every uncivilized nation, as the result of war, without regard to color. At the death of William the conquerer, one-tenth of the people were slaves, and more than three-fourths of them were virtually in bondage to the other fourth.

Wherever the Gospel had its influence; to steal a man was considered sinful, and until modern times, retaining possession of that stolen, was as great a sin. God seems to permit men to lose sight of rights and principles when he is about to overturn them. The Scripture speaks of blindness happening to men. Pharaoh was hardened against God's providence until God had effected his end. So in the days in which we live, what is more striking in connection with the African race, than the hardening and blinding of men? "For this purpose have I raised thee up," we may apply to Jefferson Davis. The people, and the press of the South, seem to say, "we will not let this people go." And God is in his providence taking away, not only this people, but their earrings and jewels, sons and brothers, the first-born of the South. The blindness which has fallen upon the Jews until the fulness of the Gentiles, seems to have fallen upon the South until the deliverance of these slaves. We have long entertained an idea that God would send his judgment through the countries in which slavery has been the desire of the people, and that which would save districts and States, and even families, would be that the people desired to get it removed.

Changes now are taking place with greater rapidity than in any preceding period of the world. Every sign says to us—the present is full with great events, just waiting fulfilment

The growth of our country, the place it occupies, and its power in the world, have led many to search the prophesies of Scripture, to see if they cannot find it distinctly taught. Some think they have found it in the forty-fourth and forty-fifth verses of second chapter of Daniel, as "the kingdom which shall never be destroyed," "being set up by the God of heaven, that it shall break in pieces all other kingdoms, the iron, brass, clay, silver and gold"—"That the battle of the great day will be an array of the hostile papal and monarchical powers who will combine as despotism against republicanism and human freedom"—that Napoleon, heading that despotism, will sweep away England and almost destroy us. England with her money and ships and munitions of war and merchandise is against us; France with the art and cunning and planning and combination with the South and in Mexico, have set themselves by counsel and aid against us. A few years since, they were all strong for the liberty of the negro race, yet all combine to aid in riveting his chains with us. A class of men North in the very hour of trial, combined to overthrow the government in its contest for our integrity as a nation. War was without, in arms; the attempt within of internal discord to set the house against itself, brought on a contest the like of which has seldom, if ever been on the earth, and in which no other nation could have stood forth so secure.

More than any other event, at any other time, has the last Presidential election tested the strength and stability of the government. The wars through which we have been passing tested and displayed the military power and energy of the nation. The last election, the inherent determination of the people to perpetuate to their children and future ages "the kingdom which God set up in this western wilderness." When the first Napoleon was asked, "which was the strongest and safest government?" he is said to have answered "the United States of America, because it is the government of the "people, and the government which the people want. If it was broken up to-"day, to-morrow every man in the United States would vote for the formation "of the same government." In confirmation of this, when the South renounced our Government and set up their rebellion, they adopted the same with the few modifications which we have long wanted, and which now many among us are seeking at the hands of the next Congress.

Our Government is more firm to day than it ever was. This war has given new life to us as a nation, has recast elements that were discordant. Hereafter, you will no more hear of German parties, Irish parties, Negro or Slavery parties, &c., with threats of foreign interference and opposition.

It is not certain that we are mentioned in prophecy, much as we would hope. But of *Ethiopia* we know that it is in prophecy. God has placed it in his own word of promise. The help and deliverance for it will come from him. It shall stretch out unto him the hands expressive not only of entreaty but of thanksgiving. Much as the race are ridiculed and set lightly by. For men have tried to degrade them to brutes, and then argue that they are so low and brutish that they are allied to dumb animals and not to man made in the image of God. This insult is not to man but to God. Everywhere in the South they are looking for deliverance. Will not God bring it? Will men who look upon our army as God's arm in their deliverance, fight against us? Away with such folly. To arm and train the negroes and put the musket and bayonet into their hands, is to give up the contest, and will exhibit a madness which it is almost incredible that men could come to. Men who sing as they arrive—

"Jehovah hath conquered, his people are free,"

are not going to fight hard to be slaves.

In two hundred and forty years from the little colony on Jamestown Island, a place with which more people have become familiar the past year than ever before, to the present time, we have grown to be the *American Nation*. No such help was given our fathers, and no such facilities were ever afforded any nation as are now given to the African race in this country and in the colonies on the coast of Africa.

Every movement of the advocates of slavery seems to recoil upon them, while it opens a door for the slave. Now the opening door to the African is as manifest as when Israel entered the dry land, on the bottom of the Red Sea, which had divided for them. It is in God's hand. He has led the people—led the President—led the army; at every step, opening the door. After he has accomplished his work in us as a nation, delivered us from this evil in our midst, brought us to feel our dependence upon him, he will make us as a nation thank him, and in the language of the Psalmist say,

"It was good for us that we have been afflicted."

Never before has such exertion been made to elevate any race of people as has been for the negro race in this country, within one or two years, and especially the last. One single item in connection with the Christian Commission's work in the Army of the Potomac is a request for fifteen to sixteen thousand primers and spelling books. Different bodies of people in all the States are vying with each other in their efforts. The Government has appointed a Bureau for Freedman's affairs, and are rendering every facility. The Friends, individual societies, the General Assembly of the Presbyterian church has a committee, which is actively at work establishing schools and furnishing teachers, &c., at City Point, Fortress Monroe or Hampton, Norfolk, Portsmouth, Leonardtown, in Maryland, everywhere along the lines of our armies, exertions are making. In Pennsylvania, near Oxford, Chester county, through the zeal and energy of Rev. Dr. J. M. Dickey, an institution has been established for the training up and educating of colored men for the Gospel ministry, called the Ashmun Institute. Men from it have gone as missionaries to Africa, others are preaching here. Every year is giving it favor, and now an effort is being made to endow it, so as to make it permanent and enable it to render greater facilities.

The change in public sentiment daily taking place, compels us to believe that the hand of God is in it. Before the first Bull Run fight we remarked that if our army was completely triumphant and the war soon brought to an end, the probability was, that slavery would continue for years; if we were defeated and the war protracted, it would end slavery. That defeat and the protracting of the war has prepared the people for events which have taken place. The turning attention to the able-bodied colored men, the enrolling of them, collecting them into regiments, the drilling and discipline which they must necessarily acquire, is a schooling of the very best kind, and which they will especially need before they can become a nation. It will prepare them to exert a controlling and governing influence over the lawless tribes, to systematize and lay foundations for their own nationality. It is one of the remarkable prophetic intimations of God's word, that "*Ethiopia* is stretching out her hands unto God." God led and trained Israel in Egypt, at the Red Sea, in the wilderness forty years before he brought them into Canaan, and then not those who came out of Egypt, but their children.

The slave power has in great measure, for many years, controlled national and state legislation—the press—politicians—and ministers who act upon the principles of the community in which they live. Like the mortar by which the monarchies of Europe have been builded and cemented, ignoring the rights of God and man, so this slave power by its arrogance has been considered essential to our national existence.

Dr. Owen in 1649 said, the anti-christian mortar must be shaken out of the nations to prepare them for the kingdom of God's dear Son. This slave power of selfishness, and aristocracy combined with politics and irreligion, could not come to an end without some great concussion. By this war God has shaken the political heavens. That power is gone in the State of Maryland—will soon be gone, yea—is it not gone in the nation? The New York *World* a few days since, said slavery is now dead—the party must no longer chain itself to a cast off dead carcass. Wonderful words for those allied to slavery since the days of Calhoun. Behold what God hath wrought! Who but God could have brought about such an event?

Potsherds of the earth may strive. Is. 45: 9. Kings and rulers of the earth counsel together. Ps. 2: 2. But he will laugh at them, while he breaks them with a rod of iron, and dashes them in pieces like a potter's vessel, 9 v. To his Son upon the holy hill of Zion he has given the kingdoms of this world. From the rising of the sun, even unto the going down of the same, my name shall be great among the gentiles; and in every place incense shall be offered unto my name, and a pure offering; for my name shall be great among the heathen, saith the Lord of Hosts. Malachi 1: 11.

God holds back that hidden and reserved power, which in the fullness of time he will manifest, when his Spirit is poured from on high upon the nations of the earth. The christian unity and benevolence which has operated through the Christian Commission since the beginning of this war, shows how easily he can cause his people to see eye to eye, and unite heart and hand in the advancement of the kingdom of his Son. So while he makes desolations in the earth, He also maketh wars to cease unto the ends of the earth. Ps. 46: 9.